A Reading Course in
Homeric Greek
Book II

OCEAN

OCEAN

OCEAN

OCEAN

ASIA

EGYPT

ETHIOPIA

LIBYA

THRACE

HESPERIA

GREECE

Amazons

Scythians

Phrygians

Phoenicians

CYPRUS

Smyrna

RHODES

TROY

Cicones

LESBOS

CHIOS

SAMOS

COS

CRETE

Nile River

Pygmies

LEMNOS

ATHENS

DELPHI

OLYMPUS

DODONA

MYCENAE

SPARTA

Maleia

CYTHERA

PYLOS

ITHACA

SCHERIA

LEUCAS

CALYPSO

CEPHALLENIA

ZACYNTHUS

SCYLLA

SIRENS

Cimmerians

AVERNUS
Entry to
Underworld

CIRCE

CHARYBDIS

THRINACIA

Cattle of
the Sun

AEOLUS

CYCLOPS

LAESTRYGONIA

Lotus-Eaters

R.V.S./W.N.

HOMER'S WORLD AND THE ADVENTURES OF ODYSSEUS   (See Appendix D for data)

A Reading Course in
Homeric Greek

With Photographs by the Author

Second Edition, Revised

Book II

Raymond V. Schoder, S.J., M.A., Ph.D.
Vincent C. Horrigan, S.J., M.A.

Loyola University Press
Chicago, Illinois 60657

Loyola University Press
3441 North Ashland Avenue
Chicago, Illinois 60657

Design by Jean Hollman

CONTENTS

Lesson   *Page*

OCTOPUS FOR DINNER

This storage jar, around five feet high, is decorated cleverly with an octopus, the tentacles fitting naturally wherever the artist had space to fill. Perhaps it contained pickled octopus for the palace, a special delicacy. It was found at Mycenae.

We thank the museums listed for allowing reproduction of their material. All photographs are by the author, Raymond Schoder unless otherwise indicated.

page

page

ABBREVIATIONS

acc.: accusative
act.: active
adj.: adjective
adv.: adverb
aor.: aorist
comp.: comparative
conj.: conjunction
conjg.: conjugation
cp.: compare
dat.: dative
decl.: declension
f.: feminine
fut.: future
gen.: genitive
gend.: gender
ind.: indicative
indecl.: indeclinable
inf.: infinitive
impf.: imperfect
impt.: imperative
intr.: intransitive
irreg.: irregular
m.: masculine
mid.: middle

n.: neuter
no.: number
nom.: nominative
obj.: object
opt.: optative
pass.: passive
pers.: person
pf.: perfect
pl.: plural
plpf.: pluperfect
prep.: preposition
pres.: present
pron.: pronoun
ptc.: participle
rel.: relative
sg.: singular
sub.: subject
subj.: subjunctive
supl.: superlative
tr.: transitive
vb.: verb
voc.: vocative
w.: with
#: numbered section of this book

This, the second volume in *A Reading Course in Homeric Greek,* continues the plan of the previous book. The first lesson is numbered 121, and is intended to follow immediately after the last lesson of volume one. In colleges, where both volumes may be expected to be covered in the course of a single year, no formal review period would seem to be required before taking up the new reading; in high schools, however, where the summer vacation intervenes, it is expected that three weeks (or even longer if the condition of the class demands it) be spent in *a thorough review of the grammar and vocabulary* of the first half of the course. For best results, this review should be made directly from the first-year book; some of the Readings of the first semester that had not been seen the year before might also be taken, both for the purposes of review and as relief from the monotony of class drills.

In structure the lessons are much the same as in the earlier volume. There are a hundred reading lessons, each designed to occupy one class period.* The vocabulary to be memorized is printed at the beginning of each lesson on the theory that new words are grasped most clearly and retained most permanently if they are seen first as vocables, then in the actual text, and finally reviewed briefly but frequently. No attempt, accordingly, has been made to equalize the memory burden by shifting words from one lesson to another. However, where the vocabulary load is heavy, less is demanded in the way of text. Thus, the first forty lessons, which average 6.8 new words for memory, average only 8.9 lines of Homer, while the last sixty lessons, which average only 4.1 vocables, demand on the average 15 lines of text.

In all, 1,261 lines of Homer are provided, comprising the further adventures of Odysseus and a few selections from the *Iliad.* Four to six lines are taken in each lesson in the beginning, the amount being very gradually increased until the maximum number of twenty-four is reached in the last lesson.

The vocabulary printed in smaller characters immediately beneath the text is not for memory. It consists of words that occur too infrequently to be learned but which are necessary to translate the given text. For tests, these words should be supplied the student.

The Notes are intended to point out and explain unusual forms, points of grammar, and difficult idiomatic usages, while in the Comment necessary information is given concerning the background of the story, the more literary qualities of the poems are discussed, and their perennial significance is stressed.

In a number of lessons, a brief section is devoted to explaining some additional points of grammar. The whole of second-year grammar is shown in summary form on a single page in the appendix (A).

The final section of most lessons is given to a word study. It is to be noted that all the words listed are derived from the new words seen in that particular lesson. Where the meaning or derivation is obscure, a short explanation is added.

Exercises for the lessons are printed separately and complete instructions are given for their use. For each lesson, there is a set of twenty-five questions, aimed at a close analysis of the text, practice in the use of new grammar and vocabulary, and a systematic review of previous matter. They are constructed in such a way that the answers will not require more than two or three words and can be written directly in blanks provided on the question sheet. For this material, see the Teacher's Manual.

After every ten lessons, special review lessons have been inserted. These offer a number of suggestions for review, treating the various phases of the subject matter. It is not expected that a class act on all the suggestions; the teacher should choose among them, changing or adding according to the needs and interests of the class. There is also an essay on some significant aspect of Greek culture. These essays are intended to be read and discussed in class under the guidance of the teacher. Under ordinary circumstances, it is hoped, other time can be found left from the regular assignments to spend on additional background work or reading of other Greek authors in translation.

---

*In high school use. College courses should move faster.

Attention should be called to the fact that the general vocabulary in the back of the book contains both first- and second-year words, that the numbered list of memory words is complete for the whole course, and that the summary of first-year grammar is reprinted in the appendix (A).

Finally, we wish to express again our appreciation and sincere gratitude to all those who have assisted in the preparation of this course by help with the typing, proof-reading and in working up exercises and tests.

THE PARTHENON REBORN

Nashville, Tennessee has reconstructed in exact size and basic details a replica of the most famous of ancient Greek temples. It serves as an art museum in Centennial Park. Though made of cement, not fine Pentelic marble, it gives an effective idea of the original's design and decoration.

As the story opens, we see Odysseus and his men setting sail from the dread horror of the Cyclops' island. Through his own refusal to despair and his prayerful dependence on help from the gods, Odysseus had saved most of his crew and had punished the brutal monster. As they pulled out from the island, the blinded Polyphemus had narrowly missed crushing their boat with huge rocks thrown in the direction of Odysseus' voice. In his rage and agony he had then called upon his father, Poseidon, god of the sea, to wreak vengeance for him on the Greeks.

Unfairly, to our way of thinking, but in keeping with the vague mythological notions of the ancients, Poseidon hears the prayer of his son, and determines, if he cannot altogether prevent the Greeks from reaching home, at least to make their journey as difficult and painful as possible. Pursued by the implacable hatred of such a foe, Odysseus, the prototype of the "missing" soldier, struggles on against all obstacles to win his way back to his home, his parents, his wife, and his child. Time and again it is his intense love for and loyalty to his family that sustains his courage and strengthens his will to carry on. In scarcely any other great work of literature is family unity and loyalty so vividly and touchingly portrayed.

Meanwhile, what is the situation in his Ithacan homeland? The ten long years of war had passed slowly and anxiously, with word arriving from time to time saying that Odysseus was still alive. At last the great news came that the war was over, that Troy was trampled in the dust. Soon the Greek heroes began to reach home, but Odysseus was not among them. Months lapsed into years, and friends and enemies alike gradually lost all hope of seeing him again. His mother, Anticlia, dies of grief; his father, cutting himself off from other people, lives in loneliness and sorrow. Only his faithful queen and young son refuse to abandon hope. Numerous suitors have come from all sides to urge her to marry again, but she remains firm. At length Telemachus, now grown to young manhood, sets out to find his missing father. The early part of the *Odyssey* tells the adventures of Telemachus in his unsuccessful search.

This background picture of the patient waiting of his family helps to intensify the pathos of the disappointments and strivings of Odysseus on his homeward journey with all its strange adventures and frustrations—the story which we now take up again to follow with fascination.

THE ABDUCTION OF HELEN

A sketch from a red-figured vase with particularly fine drawing. The persons are named. Paris (Alexandros) holds Helen's wrist, while Aphrodite and Pietho (goddess of persuasion) encourage her to go.

HOMER AND CALLIOPE

The 19th century French Classicist painter Jacques Louis David here depicts Homer in a trance while the Muse of Epic (whom he invokes at the start of both *Iliad* and *Odyssey*) by inspiration transfers into him her knowledge of events and people of the Heroic Age.

775. **MEMORIZE:**

Αἴολος, -ου [m]. Aeolus [ruler of the winds]

δώδεκα [indecl.] twelve

ἕξ [indecl.] six

μέγαρον, -ου [n.] large hall; [in pl.:] halls, palace

ναίω, —, νάσσα I inhabit, I dwell

νῆσος, -ου [f.] island

τεῖχος, -εος [n.] wall

χάλκεος, -ον of bronze

776. **TEXT**

The Floating Island of the Winds

340 «Αἰολίην δ' ἐς νῆσον ἀφικόμεθ'· ἔνθα δ' ἔναιεν

Αἴολος Ἱπποτάδης, φίλος ἀθανάτοισι θεοῖσιν,

πλωτῇ ἐνὶ νήσῳ· πᾶσαν δέ τέ μιν πέρι τεῖχος

χάλκεον ἄρρηκτον, λισσὴ δ' ἀναδέδρομε πέτρη.

τοῦ καὶ δώδεκα παῖδες ἐνὶ μεγάροις γεγάασιν,

345 ἓξ μὲν θυγατέρες, ἓξ δ' υἱέες ἡβώοντες·

Αἰόλιος, -η, -ον Aeolian, of Aeolus

ἀνα-τρέχω; pf. w. pres. force: *ἀνα-δέδρομα* I run up; I rise

ἄρρηκτος, -ον not to be broken, unbreakable

ἡβάω or *ἡβώω* I am in the prime of youth, vigorous

Ἱπποτάδης, -αο Hippotas' son

λισσός, -ή, -όν smooth

πλωτός, -ή, -όν floating

777. **NOTES**

342 = *περὶ πᾶσαν μίν* [*ἐστι*]. Notice again (cf. #404) that dissyllabic prepositions like *περὶ*, when placed immediately after their objects throw back their pitch mark. *μιν* refers to *νῆσος*. *τε* is frequently a difficult word to translate. Often it is to be felt rather than bluntly expressed, but its precise feeling in a given context can be assigned only on the basis of considerable experience in reading the Homeric text. As you read on in the text, therefore, do not simply bypass *τε*, but try to build up a *feeling* for it. Notice that it has two main uses: (1) as a conjunction to connect words and phrases; (2) as a particle to mark a statement as indefinite or general, and sometimes (as here) to connote a certain permanence of a given state of things.

343 Take *λισσή* as predicate: "the rocky (shore) rises up smooth."

344 *τοῦ* = from him, or simply 'his'.

778. **COMMENT**

340 Hardly more than a day and a night from the island of the Cyclops, the Greeks approach a strange and amazing island. It is the mysterious abode of Aeolus, king of the winds, situated apparently not far from, and to the south of, Sicily. In later times, and even at present, the island of Aeolus has been identified with the 'Aeolian Islands' group off the north-eastern coast of Sicily, but this location hardly fits into the Homeric description of Odysseus' route (cp. map at front of this book).

1

GOD OF THE WINDS

Aeolus and his mystic castle of the Winds is part of Homer's imaginary capturing of the mood of the world of myth.

342 $\pi\lambda\omega\tau\tilde{\eta}$: It is probable that we should take this adjective literally. To the Greeks the vague Western Mediterranean was full of just such marvels, in the same way that the Western Atlantic was to the contemporaries of Columbus and Mars is to the present generation educated with superman and superwoman comics. It has been suggested that Homer conceived the idea from the tales of mariners who may have penetrated far enough north to have seen an iceberg. The towering, sheer, shimmering sides of ice would fit in well with the smooth wall of brass and rock described by Homer, who is after all not giving a geological analysis of the island but only an imaginative glimpse of its strange qualities.

779. MASCULINE NOUNS OF THE FIRST DECLENSION

Almost all nouns of the first declension are feminine and end in -η or -a. You learned long ago how to decline them. However, a few nouns of the first declension are masculine, and it is now time to learn how to recognize and decline them also.

Masculine nouns of the first declension have nominatives in -$\eta\varsigma$, -$\bar{a}\varsigma$, or -a. The genitive ends in $\bar{a}o$, $\varepsilon\omega$, or the contracted form ω. Nouns in -$\bar{a}\varsigma$ keep $\bar{a}$ in the dat. and acc. sg.; all others have η as usual in these cases. The plural is the same as for feminine nouns.

The vocative is formed according to these rules:

        (1) Nouns in -ᾱς, have ᾱ;
        (2) Nouns in -της or -α, have α;
        (3) Other nouns in -ης, have η.

Thus: κυβερνήτης, -ᾱο steersman, pilot:

	SINGULAR	PLURAL
N.	κυβερνήτης	κυβερνήται
G.	κυβερνήτᾱο (εω, ω)	κυβερνητάων
D.	κυβερνήτῃ	κυβερνήτῃσ(ι)
A.	κυβερνήτην	κυβερνήτᾱς
V.	κυβερνῆτα	κυβερνήται

780.   **WORD STUDY**

EOLIAN HARP (a harp which gives forth music when exposed to the winds); — DODECANESE (the 'twelve islands' off the south-west coast of Asia Minor, object of many wars and international tensions); — HEX- (prefix meaning 'six-', as in *hexagon, hexameter,* etc.); PELOPONNESUS ('the island of Pelops', the southern part of the Greek peninsula connected with the rest by the narrow Isthmus of Corinth).

STRÓMBOLI

Chief of the "Aeolian Isles" north of eastern Sicily, Strómboli is still mildly volcanic. Ancient identifications of these small islands (Lípari, Vulcano, Panarea, etc.) with the story of Aeolus is attractive but does not fit the Homeric data well. (cp. Appendix D analysis of the problem).

LESSON 122

---

781. MEMORIZE:

αἰδοῖος, -η, -ον revered, honored
δαίνῡμι, δαίσω, δαῖσα I give a feast;
  [mid.:] I feast

δῶμα, -ατος [n.] house; hall
λέχος, -εος [n.] bed [pl. is often used for
  sing.]
μυρίος, -η, -ον countless, measureless

---

782. TEXT

Pleasant Living

346   οἱ δ' αἰεὶ παρὰ πατρὶ φίλῳ καὶ μητέρι κεδνῇ
      δαίνυνται, παρὰ δέ σφιν ὀνείατα μυρία κεῖται,
      κνῑσῆεν δέ τε δῶμα περιστεναχίζεται αὐλῇ
      ἤματα· νύκτας δ' αὖτε παρ' αἰδοίης ἀλόχοισιν
350   εὕδουσ' ἔν τε τάπησι καὶ ἐν τρητοῖσι λέχεσσιν.
      καὶ μὲν τῶν ἱκόμεσθα πόλιν καὶ δώματα καλά.

κεδνός, -ή, -όν trusty, faithful
κνῑσήεις, -εσσα, -εν filled with
  the savor of roasted meats
ὄνειαρ, -ατος blessing; [in pl.:]
  viands

περι-στεναχίζομαι I resound
τάπης, -ητος rug, coverlet
τρητός, -ή, -όν perforated [refer-
  ring to holes bored to admit thongs
  to support bedding]

---

783. NOTES

348 "and the house, filled with the savor of roasted meats, resounds in the courtyard" (with the
  noise of preparing the food and feasting). *αὐλῇ* limits the general expression *δῶμα*.
351 *-όμεσθα* is occasionally used for *-όμεθα,* usually for metrical reasons.

---

784. COMMENT

346-350 Notice how swiftly and effortlessly Homer gives us a picture of the idyllic life of
Aeolus and his family. We see the kindly father, and the mother ever solicitous for the contentment of her household. We see the countless dishes which without effort of their own seem to
appear before them on the table. We smell the delicious savor of meats being barbecued in the
open courtyard. We hear the crackling of the fires, the sharpening of knives, the bustling of the
cooks and waiters preparing the next banquet. We see the night come down to cover the intimate
contentment of a comfortable, married life. A splendid picture—and in sharp contrast with the
sufferings and heart-sickness of Odysseus, so many years away from home.

---

785. ACCUSATIVE OF EXTENT

The accusative case is sometimes used to denote extent of time or space, as in Latin. E.g.:

νύκτας εὕδουσι ἐν λέχεσσιν.
During (throughout) the nights they sleep in beds.

μῆνα δὲ πάντα φίλει με.
For a whole month he entertained me.

786. DATIVE PLURALS IN -σσι(ν)

In the third declension, the dative plural regularly ends in -σι or -εσσι. However, four times in this book you will meet an ending half way between these two. Instead of λεχέεσσι or λέχεσι, you will see λέχεσσι. From πούς, ποδός, you will find ποσσίν instead of ποδέσσι or ποσίν, and so on. Take a sharp look at this ending now, and it will cause you no hesitation later.

787. WORD STUDY

DOME (the vault of a house; often used in poetry to signify a whole palace or cathedral; cp. Latin *domus*); — MYRIAD (a 'countless' number of something); — TAPESTRY ('rug-like' ornamental woven goods for decorating walls).

WOMEN AT A PUBLIC FOUNTAIN
The women are getting water for their house needs from an elaborately arranged fountain house—the stream pouring out of a panther's mouth and two horsemen's steeds (perhaps Castor and Polydeuces, benevolent minor divinities). The vases in use are 3-handled hydriai.

---

788. | MEMORIZE:

ἠμέν [correlative w. ἠδέ] both
Ἴλιος, -ου [f.] Ilion, Troy
κατα-λέγω, etc. I tell in order, I relate
Κρονίων, -ίωνος Cronus' son [Zeus]
μήν, μηνός [m.] month

ὄρνυμι, ὄρσω, ὄρσα, ὄρωρα [aor. mid.
    also ὀρ(ό)μην] I incite, I raise;
    [pf. is intrans. w. pres. meaning:]
    I move, I rise
παύω, παύσω, παῦσα I stop; [mid.:]
    I cease
πομπή, -ῆς [f.] escort; safe sending-off

789. TEXT

A Propitious Start

μῆνα δὲ πάντα φίλει με καὶ ἐξερέεινεν ἕκαστα,
Ἴλιον Ἀργείων τε νέας καὶ νόστον Ἀχαιῶν·
καὶ μὲν ἐγὼ τῷ πάντα κατὰ μοῖραν κατέλεξα.
355 ἀλλ᾽ ὅτε δὴ καὶ ἐγὼν ὁδὸν ᾔτεον ἠδὲ κέλευον
πεμπέμεν, οὐδέ τι κεῖνος ἀνήνατο, τεῦχε δὲ πομπήν·
δῶκε δέ μ᾽ ἐκδείρας ἀσκὸν βοὸς ἐννεώροιο,
ἔνθα δὲ βυκτάων ἀνέμων κατέδησε κέλευθα·
κεῖνον γὰρ ταμίην ἀνέμων ποίησε Κρονίων,
360 ἠμὲν παυέμεναι ἠδ᾽ ὀρνύμεν, ὅν κ᾽ ἐθέλησιν.

ἀναίνομαι, ἀναινέομαι, ἀνηνάμην I
    refuse, I deny
Ἀργεῖοι, -ων Argives, Greeks
βυκτής, -ᾱο [adj.] roaring
ἐκ-δέρω, —, ἔκ-δειρα I flay, I skin

ἐννέωρος, -η, -ον of nine years, nine-
    year-old
ἐξ-ερεείνω I ask; I inquire about
κατα-δέω, κατα-δήσω, κατά-δησα I bind
    down; I restrain; I secure
ταμίης, -ᾱο [m.] dispenser, manager

790. NOTES

352 φίλει (impf.) = "he made me his guest."
355 ὁδόν i.e., inquired about my journey, asked leave to go, and in what direction lay Ithaca.

791. COMMENT

352 Hospitality of this sort was typical of the Greeks and the ancients in general. Unfortunately, in the fury of modern living this virtue has been very little cultivated. Not everything in our civilization is progress over the past.

355 Even amid such happy surroundings, Odysseus soon becomes restless to start off once again for home. Nothing else will satisfy him.

359 ταμίην: Notice that Aeolus in Homer is not a god or even "king" of the winds. He is simply the steward or manager. As we shall see later, various gods and goddesses had power to stir up or quell the winds. By the time of Vergil, however, Aeolus is a god and absolute master of the winds, so much so that even Juno, the queen of heaven, must ask his permission to cause a storm.

A FLUTE PLAYER
This interior of a red-figure kylix by the fine painter Douris around 480 B.C. shows use of a double flute, which became a preferred musical instrument.

792. **SPECIAL REVIEW OF VARIANT VERB ENDINGS**
Your attention was directed earlier in the course (in Lesson 53 and in the appendix of verb endings) to certain variations in the regular verb forms. It will be well to review all of them together here so that it will not be necessary to call your attention to them each time when they occur henceforward in the text.

(1) In the middle indicative, -ομεσθα may be used for -ομεθα usually for metrical reasons. E.g., λυόμεσθα may be used for λυόμεθα, ἰδόμεσθα for ἰδόμεθα, ἱκόμεσθα for ἱκόμεθα.

(2) In the middle-passive, -αται and -ατο are used for -νται and -ντο. Thus, βεβλήαται for βέβληνται, εἵατο for εἷντο, λελύαται for λέλυνται.

(3) In the active subjunctive, the older ending -ησθα may be substituted for -ης; and -ησι(ν) for -η. Thus εἴπησθα for εἴπης, βάλησθα for βάλης, πάθησθα for πάθης; ἐθέλησιν for ἐθέλη, and εἴπησιν for εἴπη.

(4) In the middle subjunctive, -ηαι sometimes contracts to η. Thus ἔλπη for ἔλπηαι and μνήση for μνήσηαι. You can always spot this contraction by noticing whether the subject is second or third person.

793. **WORD STUDY**
PAUSE;—POMP (show of magnificence, as in a grand procession: cp. #154).

794. MEMORIZE:

ἄημι I blow

ἀργύρεος, -η, -ον of silver

ἐκ-τελέω, etc. I accomplish (completely)

Ζέφυρος, -ου [m.] The West Wind

φαεινός, -ή, -όν bright, shining

795. TEXT

Safeguards

361 νηὶ δ᾽ ἐνὶ γλαφυρῇ κατέδει μέρμιθι φαεινῇ

ἀργυρέῃ, ἵνα μή τι παραπνεύσῃ ὀλίγον περ·

αὐτὰρ ἐμοὶ πνοιὴν Ζεφύρου προέηκεν ἀῆναι,

ὄφρα φέροι νῆάς τε καὶ αὐτούς· οὐδ᾽ ἄρ᾽ ἔμελλεν

365 ἐκτελέειν· αὐτῶν γὰρ ἀπωλόμεθ᾽ ἀφραδίῃσιν.

ἀφραδίη, -ης [f.] thoughtlessness, folly
κατα-δέω, κατα-δήσω, κατά-δησα
I bind down; I restrain; I secure

μέρμις, -ῑθος [f.] cord
παρα-πνέω, —, παρά-πνευσα I blow past
πνοιή, -ῆς [f.] breath, blast

796. NOTES

361 κατ-έδει: sc. ἀσκόν.

362 "that none might blow past (the fastening) even a little," and so divert the ship from the direct route home.

363 προ-έηκεν: augmented aorist of προ-ίημι. ἀῆναι: pres. act. inf. of ἄημι.

364 αὐτούς ourselves, as is clear from context.

797. COMMENT

362 ὀλίγον περ: A good storyteller like Homer would relish the vocal possibilities of this phrase.

364 οὐδ᾽ ἔμελλεν: An important literary device, called "foreshadowing." Hints of what is to come increase the interest and build up the mood proper to the event. Mystery and horror stories, for example, never fail to start off with dark and foreboding insinuations like "little did he dream of the ghastly terror that awaited him there," or "if he had been even a minute earlier he would never have begun that frightful adventure which left him an old and broken man."

798. PECULIAR PERFECT PARTICIPLES

Three verbs that you will meet in this course show a peculiarity in the declension of the perfect active participle. In addition to the regular stem formed by changing -ως to -οτ, they use also a stem which keeps the omega of the nominative, thus changing -ως to -ωτ. E.g., τεθνηώς (the perfect of θνήσκω) may be declined τεθνηότος, τεθνηότι, etc., or τεθνηῶτος, τεθνηῶτι, etc. It should be easy enough to recognize such forms when you come to them. The feminine of these participles is regular (except that θνήσκω uses the stem τεθνηκ-).

799. WORD STUDY

ZEPHYR (the West Wind; any gentle wind); — PHENOL (carbolic acid—a shiny liquid).

800. | **MEMORIZE:**

ἀγορεύω, ἀγορεύσω, ἀγόρευσα I speak
  (in assembly)
ἄργυρος, -ου [m.] silver
ἤδη [adv.] (by) now, already
κάμνω, καμέομαι, κάμον I toll; I construct; I grow weary

λεύσσω I see, I look
νωμάω, νωμήσω, νώμησα I distribute;
  I control
πούς, ποδός [m.] foot; sheet [a rope
  attached to the *foot* of the sail]

801. **TEXT**

The End in Sight

366 ἐννῆμαρ μὲν ὁμῶς πλέομεν νύκτας τε καὶ ἦμαρ,
   τῇ δεκάτῃ δ' ἤδη ἀνεφαίνετο πατρὶς ἄρουρα,
   καὶ δὴ πυρπολέοντας ἐλεύσσομεν ἐγγὺς ἐόντες·
   ἔνθ' ἐμὲ μὲν γλυκὺς ὕπνος ἐπήλυθε κεκμηῶτα,
370 αἰεὶ γὰρ πόδα νηὸς ἐνώμων, οὐδέ τῳ ἄλλῳ
   δῶχ' ἑτάρων, ἵνα θᾶσσον ἱκοίμεθα πατρίδα γαῖαν·
   οἱ δ' ἕταροι ἐπέεσσι πρὸς ἀλλήλους ἀγόρευον
   καί μ' ἔφασαν χρυσόν τε καὶ ἄργυρον οἴκαδ' ἄγεσθαι
   δῶρα παρ' Αἰόλου μεγαλήτορος Ἱπποτάδαο.

ἀνα-φαίνω, etc. I reveal; [in pass.:]
  I appear
Ἱπποτάδης, -āο Hippotas' son (Aeolus)

ὁμῶς alike, equally
πυρπολέω I tend fires

ODYSSEUS' HOMELAND
Odysseus describes his home island Ithaca as "lying low in the sea, with many inlets." Here we see
the south-east area and in the distance Atokos and Leukas islands.

9

802. **NOTES**

366 *ὁμῶς* goes with *νύκτας τε καὶ ἦμαρ*.

367 *τῇ δεκάτῃ:* understand *ἡμέρῃ* (day).

369 *κεκμηώς:* pf. act. ptc. of *κάμνω*. See #798.

374 *Αἰόλου:* must, by exception, be scanned as three longs here and in line 398.

803. **COMMENT**

367 It is reported that American soldiers, returning home hardened from battle, could not repress tears as they glimpsed the Statue of Liberty in New York harbor. What must have been Odysseus' emotions as he gazed again upon his beloved homeland which he had not seen or heard about for so many years!

368 Instead of saying how close they were to the shore, Homer gives us a concrete fact and lets us draw the conclusion for ourselves.

371 *θᾶσσον:* A word that tells much of his pathetic longing during the days and long nights of travel, — unwilling to risk losing even a single day. Only the joyous reaction to the culmination of his hopes moves him to relax his exhausted body in sleep.

373 Sadly typical of the littleness and greed of average men!

804. **DATIVE OF CAUSE**

Like the Latin ablative, the dative in Greek is used to express the *reason* or *cause*. This use is an extension of the *instrumental* sense of the dative already familiar to you. Thus: *φιλότητι ἕπονται. They follow because of friendship. οἱ τάδε ἔδωκε φιλότητι. He gave him these out of friendship. τίετο ὄλβῳ τε πλούτῳ τε καὶ υἱάσι. He was honored by reason of his happiness, his wealth, and his sons. ἡμετέρῃ ματίῃ. Because of our own folly.*

805. **WORD STUDY**

CATEGORY (a class or division of things 'spoken of according to its nature,' e.g., 'Kindliness belongs to the category of quality or virtue'), CATEGORICAL ('spoken without qualification,' as a 'categorical denial').

MYCENAEAN LION HUNT

A princely dagger-blade of bronze has been inlaid with gold, electrum, and black niello in a scene of admirable vividness and impact. The lion has turned on his attackers, who are tense with fear. The action is represented so skillfully that men and beast seem to move. There is a Homeric quality about this masterpiece: its directness, lucidity, brilliantly observed detail, vibrant life. Schliemann found this dagger, along with other treasures, in a royal tomb at Mycenae. It belonged to a real ruler in the period of history that Homer is re-creating in his poems, the Mycenaean or Heroic Age.

806. MEMORIZE:

ὤ πόποι   Oh! [a general exclamation to be trans. according to context]
φιλότης, -ητος [f.]   love, friendship

χαρίζομαι, χαριέομαι, χαρισάμην   I gratify; I give graciously

807. TEXT

Fateful Curiosity

375   ὧδε δέ τις εἴπεσκεν ἰδὼν ἐς πλησίον ἄλλον·
‘ ὦ πόποι, ὡς ὅδε πᾶσι φίλος καὶ τίμιός ἐστιν
ἀνθρώποις, ὁτεών τε πόλιν καὶ γαῖαν ἵκηται.
πολλὰ μὲν ἐκ Τροίης ἄγεται κειμήλια καλὰ
ληΐδος, ἡμεῖς δ᾿ αὖτε ὁμὴν ὁδὸν ἐκτελέσαντες
380   οἴκαδε νισσόμεθα κενεὰς σὺν χεῖρας ἔχοντες·
καὶ νῦν οἱ τάδ᾿ ἔδωκε χαριζόμενος φιλότητι
Αἴολος. ἀλλ᾿ ἄγε θᾶσσον ἰδώμεθα, ὅττι τάδ᾿ ἐστίν,
ὅσσος τις χρυσός τε καὶ ἄργυρος ἀσκῷ ἔνεστιν.’

ἔν-ειμι I am in	*νίσσομαι* I return
κειμήλιον, -ου [n.] treasure, keepsake	*ὁμός, -ή, -όν* same, equal
κενεός, -ή, -όν empty	*τίμιος, (-η), -ον* honored
ληΐς, ληΐδος [f.] booty, spoils	

808. NOTES

376   Distinguish carefully *ὡς* and *ὣς, ὧς* (with a pitch mark).
380   *σύν:* adverb — "with us."
382   *θᾶσσον:* the comparative often has the meaning *rather, quite,* hence the point here is "Hurry! Let us see . . ." *ἄγε:* "come!"
383   *ἔνεστιν:* the verb sometimes agrees with only the nearest of several subjects, though it is understood with them all.

809. COMMENT

378   Whatever booty was captured by the Greek army at Troy was piled together in the center of the camp and distributed to the soldiers according to their rank and contribution to the fighting. Odysseus, whose leadership and bravery were chiefly responsible for the successful conclusion of the siege, probably received a larger share of the spoils than did his companions. Yet we can be sure that they, too, had been awarded a fair share; more than likely, it had been gambled away or quickly spent.

381   From the conversation of the crew, rather than from direct description, Homer artfully indicates to us the winning and friendly personality of the hero.

382 Whether their motive was mere curiosity or actual larceny is not altogether clear. At least, as in the case of Pandora, the incident shows the ill effects of uncontrolled curiosity. Perhaps Odysseus is somewhat to blame for not taking his comrades into his confidence from the beginning; but on the other hand, he may have judged that if his crew knew the contents of the bag they would not have been able to resist the temptation to take just a peak at the winds inside.

810. WORD STUDY

HOMONYM (a word which sounds exactly like another word of different meaning, e.g., *read, reed*).

COMPETITION FOR ACHILLES' ARMOR
A legend, not in Homer but told by later poets, described the jealous strife of leading heroes for the prize of slain Achilles' god-made armor—won by Odysseus for his devising the Wooden Horse which at last brought Troy's fall. Douris has made that the theme of this red-figure kylix interior of the early fifth century B.C.

811. | MEMORIZE:

ἁρπάζω, ἁρπάξω, ἅρπαξα or ἅρπασα
    I snatch (up or away)
ἐγείρω, ἐγερέω, ἔγειρα, aor. mid. ἐργόμην
    I rouse, I wake
ζωός, -ή, -όν   alive, living
θύελλα, -ης [f.]   blast, storm

μερμηρίζω, μερμηρίξω, μερμήριξα   I pon-
    der (anxiously)
νῑκάω, νῑκήσω, νίκησα   I conquer, I
    prevail
ὀρούω, ὀρούσω, ὄρουσα   I rush, I dart

812.   TEXT

Sudden Calamity

ὣς ἔφασαν, βουλὴ δὲ κακὴ νίκησεν ἑταίρων·
385   ἀσκὸν μὲν λῦσαν, ἄνεμοι δ᾽ ἐκ πάντες ὄρουσαν.
τοὺς δ᾽ αἶψ᾽ ἁρπάξασα φέρεν πόντονδε θύελλα
κλαίοντας, γαίης ἄπο πατρίδος. αὐτὰρ ἐγώ γε
ἐγρόμενος κατὰ θυμὸν ἀμύμονα μερμήριξα,
ἠὲ πεσὼν ἐκ νηὸς ἀποφθίμην ἐνὶ πόντῳ,
390   ἦ ἀκέων τλαίην καὶ ἔτι ζωοῖσι μετείην.

ἀπο-φθίνω; athematic aorist ἀπο-φθίμην   μέτ-ειμι   I am among, I am with
    I perish, I die

ESCAPE OF THE WINDS
While their weary leader sleeps in the front of the ship with Ithaca finally in view, the crew, overcome by curiosity, open the mysterious bag, and the captive Winds blow them back to Aeolus, frustrating their return home.

13

813. NOTES

384 *ἑταίρων:* with *βουλή.*

389 *ἀπο-φθίμην:* Not indicative—notice the long iota! The aorist optative ending without the thematic vowel, *-ιμην* is added to the aorist stem, *ἀπο-φθι-.* The iotas contract to form *ῑ.*

814. COMMENT

385 A line typical of the swift action of the poem and of Homer's style.

385-7 Undue inquisitiveness has often proved a similar source of disaster.

389 In the black despair of frustrated longing, the terrible temptation of suicide comes upon him. Notice, however, the simple moderation and restraint with which the temptation is stated. More modern writers would never let pass such an opportunity for frenzied moaning, hair-tearing, soul-wringing, and the like.

THE GODS DEBATE THE WAR

This part of the archaic relief frieze of the Siphnian Treasury at Delphi shows gods favoring the Trojans discussing the state of the war. At the left is Ares, holding his shield, then Aphrodite, Artemis, and Apollo (turning to talk), seeking to persuade Zeus (at far right), who wants to stay neutral or at least impartial. Fine sculpture of around 525 B.C.

815. MEMORIZE:

ἤπειρος, -ου [f.]   land; mainland
καλύπτω, καλύψω, κάλυψα   I cover

κῆρυξ, -ῡκος [m.]   attendant, herald
τέκος, -εος [n.]   child

816. TEXT

Shamefaced Return

391 ἀλλ' ἔτλην καὶ ἔμεινα, καλυψάμενος δ' ἐνὶ νηὶ
κείμην. αἱ δ' ἐφέροντο κακῇ ἀνέμοιο θυέλλῃ
αὖτις ἐπ' Αἰολίην νῆσον, στενάχοντο δ' ἑταῖροι.
   ἔνθα δ' ἐπ' ἠπείρου βῆμεν καὶ ἀφυσσάμεθ' ὕδωρ,
395 αἶψα δὲ δεῖπνον ἕλοντο θοῇς παρά νηυσὶν ἑταῖροι.
αὐτὰρ ἐπεὶ σίτοιό τ' ἐπασσάμεθ' ἠδὲ ποτῆτος,
δὴ τότ' ἐγὼ κήρυκά τ' ὀπασσάμενος καὶ ἑταῖρον
βῆν εἰς Αἰόλου κλυτὰ δώματα· τὸν δὲ κίχανον
δαινύμενον παρὰ ᾗ τ' ἀλόχῳ καὶ οἷσι τέκεσσιν.

Αἰόλιος, -η, -ον Aeolian, of Aeolus   *ποτής, -ῆτος* [f.] drink

817. NOTES

391 *καλυψάμενος:* a good example of middle meaning.
392 *αἱ:* all the boats of the Greeks. Odysseus in his own ship had been leading the rest.
399 *ᾗ = ἔῃ. οἷσι = ἑοῖσι.*

818. COMMENT

391 Realizing his dreadful state of mind, we may judge this decision to be perhaps the bravest and most manly of his life.

395 One might think that Odysseus would be exercising only his right if he vented his anger on his companions and then left them to their fate. However, he seems to have said nothing and to have continued in the same relationship with them as before.

398 How embarrassed and humiliated he must have felt as he turned again to Aeolus for help!

15

LESSON 129

819. **MEMORIZE:**

ἀπο-πέμπω, etc. I send away; I send off safely	*ἐρέω* I inquire
ἄχνυμαι I grieve	*θαμβέω, —, θάμβησα* I wonder (at)
ἐνδυκέως kindly	*Ὀδυσ(σ)εύς, -ῆος* [m.] Odysseus
	οὐδός, -οῦ [m.] threshold

820. **TEXT**

Another Try

400   ἐλθόντες δ᾽ ἐς δῶμα παρὰ σταθμοῖσιν ἐπ᾽ οὐδοῦ
      ἑζόμεθ᾽· οἱ δ᾽ ἀνὰ θυμὸν ἐθάμβεον ἔκ τ᾽ ἐρέοντο·
      'πῶς ἦλθες, Ὀδυσεῦ; τίς τοι κακὸς ἔχραε δαίμων;
      ἦ μέν σ᾽ ἐνδυκέως ἀπεπέμπομεν, ὄφρ᾽ ἀφίκοιο
      πατρίδα σὴν καὶ δῶμα καὶ εἴ πού τοι φίλον ἐστίν.'
405   ὣς φάσαν, αὐτὰρ ἐγὼ μετεφώνεον ἀχνύμενος κῆρ·
      'ἄασάν μ᾽ ἕταροί τε κακοὶ πρὸς τοῖσί τε ὕπνος
      σχέτλιος. ἀλλ᾽ ἀκέσασθε, φίλοι· δύναμις γὰρ ἐν ὑμῖν.'

ἀάω, —, ἄασα I deceive, I ruin	*δύναμις, -ιος* [f.] power, ability
ἀκέομαι, —, ἀκεσάμην I heal, I provide a remedy	*μετα-φωνέω* I speak among
	χράω, —, χράον I assail, I beset [dat.]

821. **NOTES**

401   *οἱ:* Aeolus and his family.
    ἀνά: "in."
    ἐκ: they asked out (loud), in contrast to their inner wonder.
404   *εἴ που* = "wherever" (cp. the Latin *si quid* = whatever).
406   *πρὸς τοῖσι:* "besides these," "in addition to these."

822. **COMMENT**

400   Feeling too abashed to approach Aeolus directly, Odysseus takes up the position of a beggar or suppliant at the door.

406   Like a truly great man, he has little blame for others and shares their blame even when hardly deserved.

407   Notice again the forceful brevity of expression, so characteristic of Homer.

823. **WORD STUDY**

PANACEA ('all-healer,' a claimed universal remedy); — DYNAMITE (a powerful explosive); cp. other derivatives at #616.

824. MEMORIZE:

ἀλεγεινός, -ή, -όν painful, grievous
βαρύς, -εῖα, -ύ heavy; dire
δόμος, -ου [m.] house

κομίζω, κομιέω, κόμισσα I tend; I aid; I pick up
μαλακός, -ή, -όν soft, gentle
μῦθος, -ου [m.] word, speech, saying

825. TEXT

Rejected and Helpless

> ὣς ἐφάμην μαλακοῖσι καθαπτόμενος ἐπέεσσιν,
> οἱ δ' ἄνεω ἐγένοντο· πατὴρ δ' ἠμείβετο μύθῳ·
> 410 'ἔππ' ἐκ νήσου θᾶσσον, ἐλέγχιστε ζωόντων·
> οὐ γάρ μοι θέμις ἐστὶ κομιζέμεν οὐδ' ἀποπέμπειν
> ἄνδρα τόν, ὅς κε θεοῖσιν ἀπέχθηται μακάρεσσιν·
> ἔρρ', ἐπεὶ ἀθανάτοισιν ἀπεχθόμενος τόδ' ἱκάνεις.'
> ὣς εἰπὼν ἀπέπεμπε δόμων βαρέα στενάχοντα.
> 415 ἔνθεν δὲ προτέρω πλέομεν ἀκαχήμενοι ἦτορ.
> τείρετο δ' ἀνδρῶν θυμὸς ὑπ' εἰρεσίης ἀλεγεινῆς
> ἡμετέρῃ ματίῃ, ἐπεὶ οὐκέτι φαίνετο πομπή.

ἀκαχήμενος, -η, -ον grieved, grieving
ἄνεω [irreg. nom. pl.] speechless, silent
ἀπ-εχθάνομαι, —, ἀνεχθόμην I am hateful to
εἰρεσίη, -ης [f.] rowing

ἐλέγχιστος, -η, -ον vilest, most contemptible
ἔρρω I go, I wander [connotes misfortune]
καθ-άπτομαι I address, I speak
ματίη, -ης [f.] folly
προτέρω [adv.] farther, forward

826. NOTES

412 *τόν* is placed after its noun in order to introduce the relative pronoun which will explain it.

413 *τόδ' ἱκάνεις:* literally, "you come this (coming)." Although strictly a cognate accusative, *τόδε* is best translated as an adverb, "here."

417 *πομπή:* "escort"—in this case, a favoring wind; consequently they had to row.

827. COMMENT

412 The ancients were much impressed with the idea of a curse or "evil eye" that sometimes fell upon a man, ruining his life and all those who associated with him. Even today there is a surprising widespread belief in "good luck" and "bad luck" which certain people are supposed to have or to bring to others. In mythological times when the deities were so often capricious and vengeful, a prudent person like Aeolus would have to be especially careful. He wants to run no risk of angering the gods by befriending their seeming enemy.

417 ἡμετέρη: Notice that he again identifies himself with their guilt. The contrast between their former lolling ease as the wind swept them on and their present weary rowing would be all the more bitter through the realization that they had no one at all to blame except themselves.

828. WORD STUDY

MYTH, MYTHOLOGY (imaginative stories or 'sayings' about the gods or old heroes).

CARGO SHIPS

On the outside of a large wine kylix the 'Nikosthenes Painter' depicted at the end of the sixth century B.C. a vivid scene of two commercial sailing ships crossing the 'wine-dark sea'. Their graceful shapes are emphasized by the high curving sterns.

REVIEW

829. Go over again Lessons 121–130; make sure now that you have really mastered them. Here are a a few suggestions for your review:

1. *Vocabulary:* Check your mastery of the 60 new memory words.
2. *Text:* Reread the 78 lines of text, making sure you recognize all the forms.
3. *Story:* Write a 100-word summary of the Aeolus episode.
4. *Criticism:*

    a. What new points are revealed in the character of Odysseus?
    b. Do you think the psychological portrayal of the Greek sailors is sound? Why?
    c. How did the ancients look upon suicide?
    d. What can you deduce from line 361 regarding the skill of Greek metalworkers?
    e. What, in your opinion, is the most dramatic point in the story? Why?

5. *Grammar:* Explain the following:

    a. Masculine nouns of first declension, how recognized and declined.
    b. Accusative of extent.
    c Dative plural in -σσι.
    d. Variant verb endings.
    e. Peculiar perfect participles.
    f. Dative of cause.

6. *Composition:* Put into Greek:

    a. Out of friendship, Aeolus gave Odysseus a bag in which he tied the winds.
    b. They kept sailing for many days but had not yet seen the fatherland.
    c. Wondering, the children of Aeolus said that their father had sent Odysseus off safely.

830. GREEK COINS AND THEIR STORY

Like so many other things in our highly advanced civilization, the concept and use of coins for business transactions seems so wholly obvious and commonplace that we seldom consider what a remarkable and useful device coinage is. We can get a new insight into this important aspect of our daily life, and a better appreciation of its significance, by looking back into the past for the story of its origins and development. As with so many other features of our life and civilization, the search will lead us to the ancient Greeks.

Historians point out that the idea of coinage did not come easily or to many people. All primitive cultures, and indeed many which were highly developed, conducted their business on a barter-basis, a man trading a slave, for example, for ten sheep or an axehead for a cooking utensil—whatever seemed a fair exchange to both parties. A later stage of trade is by way of reference to some standard of value, such as an ox or a bronze caldron. Thus in Homer, things are generally evaluated in terms of cattle: something is worth half as much as an ox, worth four oxen, etc., without the oxen themselves being actually exchanged as barter. (It is interesting to note in this connection that the Latin word for money is *pecunia,* from *pecus;* cow, and that the

English word "fee" originates from an old root meaning cow, showing that in medieval and in early Roman times money was in the beginning a substitute for actual cattle, as simply a handier medium of exchange.)

A further advance was the use of metal pieces of uniform weight and worth as symbols of value, so that one iron cooking-spit, for instance, came to stand for a certain standardized amount of wealth, and could be exchanged for anything equal to it in value, then re-exchanged by the recipient with someone else for an altogether different object of the same worth. Bigger items could then be bought by giving four or five such metal symbols, and these came to function as true money.

COINS AS ART

These fine examples, showing Scylla, Arethusa (a nymph at Syracuse), a mythical Silen, and Zeus on his throne holding a thunderbolt indicate the interesting themes used by different cities and the high skill of the coin designers during the most splendid period of Greek culture.

With the progress of commerce and the appearance on the market of many new products of industry and importation, there was need of a further simplification and standardizing of the medium of exchange. The answer was coinage, invented about the middle of the eighth century before Christ by the Lydians, neighbors of the Greek cities along the coast of Asia Minor, and promptly taken up and developed to its full commercial role by the Greek island of Aegina off Athens.

Three things are necessary to constitute true coinage: use of some intrinsically valuable metal, use of it only in standard amounts of uniform weight (3 ounces, 12 ounces, etc.), and guarantee of its honest value by the official stamp of some responsible authority, such as a king or a city government. At first, many individuals issued coins, stamping them with their own sign of guaranteed value. But soon kings appropriated to themselves the sole right to issue coins, often making them of pure gold as token of regal splendor and wealth. By the end of the sixth century B.C., the coining of money had spread all over the Greek world, each city putting out its own coins with its own values and markings. Athenian coins were stamped with an owl, symbol of the city's patroness Athene, and with the goddess' head on the other side of the disc. The device stamped on coins of Aegina was a tortoise, of Corinth a winged horse, and so on for each city. When cities were absorbed in an empire, their coinage was suppressed and only that of the ruling city allowed, so that in time Athenian "owls" were the dominant and standard coins of the whole Aegean region.

The earliest coins were made of electrum, an alloy of gold and silver. The Lydian and Persian kings soon used only gold, whereas Greek coins were mostly of silver only (a purer form of silver, incidentally, with less alloy in it, than in American coins). Bronze was used for cheaper coins, like our penny; gold only when silver was unobtainable, which after the time of Alexander the Great was commonly the case. The unit of weight for Greek coins was the *stater*, about the equivalent in metallic content of the former American five-dollar gold piece, and amounting in comparative purchasing value to about ten dollars of our money today. The most common Greek coins were the obol (about 3¢, but many times that in purchasing value under Greek living conditions), the drachma (worth six obols), the tetradrachma ("four-drachma piece"), the mina (100 drachmas), and the talent (6000 drachmas).

It was characteristic of the Greeks, indeed inevitable, that they should strive to make the stamping on their coins as noble and beautiful as possible. The artistic style of the engraving on Greek coins closely parallels that of sculpture and painting at the same period, progressing in pace with these to a level of unparalleled beauty and sharpness of impression, so that coins of the fourth century B.C. are universally considered the most splendid examples of the art of coin stamping in either ancient or modern times. The clarity, fine details, noble designing, and exquisite workmanship of the better Greek coins make them both admired and treasured possessions of the world's museums and art collections. A large number of them have been found, no doubt because the ancients, like some moderns, buried coins in the earth for safe keeping, whence they have finally come to light, often in a condition as good as new.

Once the Greeks had perfected the art and features of coin making, all other nations have followed their principles in their own coinage. It is one more instance of the abiding influence of Greek pioneering on our own daily life.

Next time you spend a dime, you might reflect on what a remarkable invention a coin is, and on some of the long history behind it!

For six days and nights the Greeks rowed northward (apparently the winds were still blowing so strongly from the East that the light ships could make little headway against them in that direction), and came at last to the harbor of the Laestrygonians. The other ships rushed at once into the calm waters of the inner harbor and tied up there, glad to escape the rough billows of the open sea. Odysseus, with characteristic forethought, would not allow his ship to enter, but moored it to some rocks outside; he then sent two scouts with a messenger to reconnoiter. What was their horror to discover that the inhabitants of this land, too, were cannibals of gigantic stature. Though one of the scouts was lost, the other two escaped and fled with desperate speed back to their ship, pursued by the aroused savages. Surrounding the enclosed harbor, the Laestrygonians sank the escaping ships with rocks, and speared the struggling men like fish. Only the ship of Odysseus, which had not entered the harbor, escaped. Thus on that one day were destroyed utterly all the other ships and their crews.

Depressed in spirit and sorely in need of provisions, Odysseus' men had sailed on only a little way to the southwest when they came to the island of the divine sorceress, Circe. Once on shore, Odysseus divides the men into two bands, taking the command of one of them himself and giving the other to the charge of Eurylochus. They then cast lots to see which would stay by the ship and which would go to explore the land and obtain provisions. According to the lot, Eurylochus' band set out and found in the center of the island a mansion built of polished stone. They are invited by the occupant, the fair-haired sourceress, to enter, and all do so except Eurylochus who suspects a trick. Once inside they are fed drugged food and then, by a movement of the magic wand in the hand of Circe, they are *changed to swine.*

BEWARE HER SORCERY

The outside of a large wine bowl from around 600 B.C. shows Circe at work transforming some of Odysseus' companions into pathetically spiritless beasts, while the hero himself departs at the right. This is a warning against the dehumanizing effect of certain drugs on body and brain.

A SATIRIC VIEW

At the Kabeiric Sanctuary near Thebes have been found comic vases unique in Greek art for their outrageous lampooning of revered myths. Here, in a sketch of the scene on one of these fourth century B.C. cups we see Circe (identified) offering a basket to a beggarly Odysseus, while at the right, beyond the sorceress' loom, one of his incautious companions whom she had turned into a wild dog wails in misery at the sky.

CIRCE'S MAGIC

Terrified, Eurylochus rushes back to report to Odysseus, who at once girds on his armor and bids him show the way. When Eurylochus is too fearful to go, he starts off alone. Thanks to a magic herb, moly, which Hermes supplies him, Odysseus resists the magic wiles of Circe. When she attempts to wave her terrible wand over him, he draws his sword and threatens to kill her, thereby winning not only her promise to release his men but also her complete admiration and assistance. She insists on entertaining him and his men for a time, and is able through her preternatural powers to give him much good advice regarding his journey home.

But his first necessity, she tells him, is to make the awesome journey to *Hades,* there to consult the soul of Teiresias, the blind seer of Thebes, who alone can tell him his future course. Reluctantly, but encouraged by the explicit directions of Circe as well as by her supplying of the black sheep necessary for sacrifice to the nether gods, the Greeks make ready for departure to that region where only the dead belong.

831. MEMORIZE:

δάκρυον, -ου or δάκρυ, -υος [n.]   tear
δεινός, -ή, -όν   awe-inspiring, dreadful
ἐϋπλόκαμος, -ον   fair-tressed
θαλερός, -ή, -όν   blooming; vigorous; big
ἱστίον, -ου [n.]   sail [pl. often used for sg.]

κατ-έρχομαι, etc.   I come down
Κίρκη, -ης   Circe
κυανόπρωρος, -ον   dark-prowed
οὖρος, -ου [m.]   a (fair) wind

832. TEXT

A Reluctant Start

«αὐτὰρ ἐπεί ῥ᾿ ἐπὶ νῆα κατήλθομεν ἠδὲ θάλασσαν,

νῆα μὲν ἂρ πάμπρωτον ἐρύσσαμεν εἰς ἅλα δῖαν

420   ἐν δ᾿ ἱστὸν τιθέμεσθα καὶ ἱστία νηὶ μελαίνῃ,

ἐν δὲ τὰ μῆλα λαβόντες ἐβήσαμεν, ἂν δὲ καὶ αὐτοὶ

βαίνομεν ἀχνύμενοι θαλερὸν κατὰ δάκρυ χέοντες.

ἡμῖν δ᾿ αὖ κατόπισθε νεὸς κυανοπρῴροιο

ἴκμενον οὖρον ἵει πλησίστιον, ἐσθλὸν ἑταῖρον,

425   Κίρκη ἐϋπλόκαμος, δεινὴ θεὸς αὐδήεσσα.

αὐδήεις, -εσσα, -εν   using mortal speech
ἴκμενος, -η, -ον   favorable

κατόπισθε   behind, following
πάμπρωτον [adv.]   first of all
πλησίστιος, -ον   swelling the sail

833. NOTES

420   τιθέμε(σ)θα: imperfect middle first person plural of τίθημι (cp. #470).

421   ἐβήσαμεν: a first aorist, with transitive force, from βαίνω: "we caused to go, we put."
ἂν for ἀνά: with βαίνομεν in next line

834. COMMENT

418 ff. This passage exemplifies well the art of Homer in giving a sense of reality to the story by the use of concrete details. Possibly the English author most noteworthy for the same art was Daniel Defoe, whose tremendously popular *Robinson Crusoe* owes its success largely to the careful and minute attention given to details.

425 αὐδήεσσα: According to the notion current among the Greeks, there were different classes of divinity among the gods, some of whom used only divine speech, others only human speech, while some used both.

835.   THE IRREGULAR VERB ἧμαι, I SIT

This verb has no thematic vowel and is used only in the present and imperfect. Its stem is ἡς -, but the σ drops before another σ or ν. In the third person plural, η is sometimes written as ει.

Thus in the indicative:

PRESENT	IMPERFECT
ἧμαι	ἤμην
ἧσαι	ἧσο
ἧσται	ἧστο
ἤμεθα	ἤμεθα
ἧσθε	ἧσθε
ἧνται or εἴαται	ἤντο or εἴατο

YOUTHFUL RHYTHM
The painter Makron has sketched a portion of daily life in ancient Greece: a boy watching in admiration as a girl dances to the rhythm of her clappers.

836. **MEMORIZE:**

ἀγυιά, -ῆς [f.]   street, way
δύω, δύσομαι, δῡσάμην or *δῦν* I enter;
  I put (on); I sink, I set (of the sun)
ἧμαι I sit
κυβερνήτης, -αο [m.]   steersman, pilot
ὅπλον, -ου [n.]   tool; rope

τείνω, τενέω, τεῖνα, τέτακα, τέταμαι
  I stretch
Ὠκεανός, -οῦ [m.]   Ocean [a river encircling the earth, sometimes personified as a god]

837. **TEXT**

Suspense

426   *ἡμεῖς δ᾽ ὅπλα ἕκαστα πονησάμενοι κατὰ νῆα*
      ἥμεθα· τὴν δ᾽ ἄνεμός τε κυβερνήτης τ᾽ ἴθυνεν.
      τῆς δὲ πανημερίης τέταθ᾽ ἱστία ποντοπορούσης.
      δύσετό τ᾽ ἠέλιος σκιάοντό τε πᾶσαι ἀγυιαί,
430   *ἡ δ᾽ ἐς πείραθ᾽ ἵκανε βαθυρρόου Ὠκεανοῖο.*

βαθύρροος, -ον w. deep, steady
  flow
ἰθύνω I make straight, I guide

πανημέριος, -η, -ον all day long
ποντοπορέω I sail the sea
σκιάω I overshadow, I darken

838. **NOTES**

428 *ποντοπορούσης:* the stem-vowel *ε* must be considered as dropping, or irregularly contracting with *ου* to form *ου* instead of *ευ* (as it does in Attic Greek).
πανημερίης: best translated as adverb with *ποντοπορούσης.*
429 *δύσετο:* irreg., formed as if from 2 aor. *δυσόμην.*

839. **COMMENT**

429 This melodious line is formulaic, used seven times by the proud poet.

430 Homer is wise in putting the entrance to the lower world on the banks of Ocean, the world-encircling stream whose beginning no one knew and whose stretches were vast and mysterious. He is too clever a storyteller to break down the feeling of mystery by describing too exactly the location. Sometimes our own imaginations, once excited, will more easily create in us the feeling desired by the author than if he had spent pages in description. A proof of this is found in the famous *Pit and the Pendulum* of Edgar Allan Poe, — the author never tells us what is actually in the pit; he leaves that to our imagination. But who of us can say that he is not quite thoroughly convinced that it would be better to suffer all the other horrors of the dungeon rather than the one nightmare of the pit?

840. **WORD STUDY**

PANOPLY (the 'complete equipment' of some profession, e.g., 'The band turned out in full panoply').

841. MEMORIZE:

ἀήρ, ἠέρος [f.]   mist
ἀστερόεις, -εσσα, -εν   starry
δειλός, -ή, -όν   cowardly; luckless
δῆμος, -ου [m.]   realm, people
νεφέλη, -ης [f.]   cloud

ὁπ(π)ότε   when, whenever
ῥόος, -ου [m.]   stream, current
φράζω, φράσ(σ)ω, φράσ(σ)α   I point out;
   [mid.] I consider

842. TEXT

At the Ends of the Earth

431 ἔνθα δὲ Κιμμερίων ἀνδρῶν δημός τε πόλις τε,
ἠέρι καὶ νεφέλῃ κεκαλυμμένοι· οὐδέ ποτ' αὐτοὺς
ἠέλιος φαέθων καταδέρκεται ἀκτίνεσσιν,
οὔθ' ὁπότ' ἂν στείχῃσι πρὸς οὐρανὸν ἀστερόεντα,

435 οὔθ' ὅτ' ἂν ἂψ ἐπὶ γαῖαν ἀπ' οὐρανόθεν προτράπηται,
ἀλλ' ἐπὶ νὺξ ὀλοὴ τέταται δειλοῖσι βροτοῖσιν.
νῆα μὲν ἔνθ' ἐλθόντες ἐκέλσαμεν, ἐκ δὲ τὰ μῆλα
εἱλόμεθ'· αὐτοὶ δ' αὖτε παρὰ ῥόον Ὠκεανοῖο
ᾔομεν, ὄφρ' ἐς χῶρον ἀφικόμεθ', ὃν φράσε Κίρκη.

ἀκτίς, -ίνος [f.] ray
κατα-δέρκομαι I look down upon
κέλλω, —, κέλσα I bring to shore,
   I come to shore

Κιμμέριοι, -ων Cimmerian [here, an adj.]
προ-τρέπομαι, —, προ-τραπόμην I turn,
   I take my way
φαέθων, -ον bright, resplendent

843. NOTES

432 κεκαλυμμένοι: from κεκάλυμμαι, perfect passive of καλύπτω.
439 ᾔομεν: imperfect first person plural of εἶμι I go.

844. COMMENT

434-5   The daily rising and setting of the sun was a constant source of interest and puzzlement to the Greeks. Some thought that it was an altogether different sun that crossed the sky each day. Others held that it was the same sun that sneaked back to the East at night through or around Ocean. It was even suggested that the sun at night went back across the sky but that it couldn't be seen on account of the darkness! Fantastic, it is true, but characteristic of a people who invented science by wanting to know the answer to just such problems.

436 A successful storyteller must always be on the alert to pick up new and strange tales that he may hear. This tale of the Cimmerians and their land covered with perpetual night quite possibly was taken from travelers who had experienced or heard rumors of the long arctic nights. As Kipling put it:

> W'en 'Omer smote 'is blomin' lyre,
> 'E'd 'eard men sing by land and sea,
> And wot 'e thought 'e might require,
> 'E went and took, the same as me.

845. WORD STUDY

AIR; – DEMOCRACY ('rule by the people'), DEMOCRAT; — EPIDEMIC (a disease widespread and rampant, seizing 'on the whole people'); — ENDEMIC (peculiar to a particular region; native; e.g., 'Fear of the moon is endemic to aborigines of this island.'); — ACTINIC (pertaining to the chemical effect produced by radiation of the sun, etc.).

LAKE AVERNUS

In the deep crater of a former volcano water springing up from below has made a placid lake of greenish-blue tone. The crater walls are densely wooded. Vergil places here the pivotal action of the *Aeneid,* Book Six, drawing on Homeric and other ancient traditions.

846. MEMORIZE:

βόθρος, -ου [m.]   hole, pit

Εὐρύλοχος, -ου [m.]   Eurylochus [a companion of Odysseus]

νέκῡς, -υος [m.]   corpse; [pl.:]   the dead

847. TEXT

A Dread Ritual

440   ἔνθ᾽ ἱερήια μὲν Περιμήδης Εὐρύλοχός τε
      ἔσχον· ἐγὼ δ᾽ ἄορ ὀξὺ ἐρυσσάμενος παρὰ μηροῦ
      βόθρον ὄρυξ᾽, ὅσσον τε πυγούσιον ἔνθα καὶ ἔνθα
      ἀμφ᾽ αὐτῷ δὲ χοὴν χεόμην πᾶσιν νεκύεσσιν,
      πρῶτα μελικρήτῳ, μετέπειτα δὲ ἡδέϊ οἴνῳ,
445   τὸ τρίτον αὖθ᾽ ὕδατι· ἐπὶ δ᾽ ἄλφιτα λευκὰ πάλυνον.

ἄλφιτον, -ου [n]   barley; [pl.] barley-meal
ἄορ, ἄορος [n.]   sword
ἱερήιον, -ου [n.]   an animal for sacrifice
μελίκρητον, -ου   a mixture of honey and milk
μετέπειτα   afterwards, next

ὀρύσσω, ὀρύξω, ὄρυξα   I dig (up)
παλῡνω   I sprinkle, I powder
Περιμήδης, -εος   Perimedes, a companion of Odysseus
πυγούσιος, -η, -ον   a cubic in length
τρίτον [w. τό]   the third (time)
χοή, -ῆς [f.]   libation

848. NOTES

442 ἔνθα καί ἔνθα: He made the pit a cubit (18–20 inches) long and a cubit wide.

849. COMMENT

443 ff.   This strictly ordered ritual is described a number of times in the *Odyssey*. Greek religion, as a matter of fact, concerned itself almost exclusively with such ritualistic services even though, unlike most religions, it never had a genuine priesthood with exclusive ordained right to officiate in sacred functions. There were professional priests, experts in the ritual, but, as here depicted, the local leader, be he king, general, or simply head of the family, could also officially offer sacrifices. There seems to have been no definite symbolism connected with the form of the libations—which were ceremonial pouring of sacrificial liquid on the ground.

850. SPECIAL FORMS OF βοῦς, OX, COW

Besides the regular declension of βοῦς derived from the genitive βοός, three special forms occur. These forms imitate the nominative. Thus:

(1) Acc. sg. βοῦν for βόα.

(2) Acc. pl. βοῦς for βόας.

(3) Dat. pl. βουσί for βόεσσι.

ODYSSEUS AT THE EDGE OF THE UNDERWORLD
On a classic mixing bowl Odysseus is portrayed seated at the opening of Hades, pouring sacrificial blood into a trench to entice the ghost of the great prophet Tiresias to come and give the hero needed advice for his contact with the realm of the dead.

851. | MEMORIZE:

ἀγείρω, ἀγερέω, ἄγειρα [aor. mid.: ἀγερόμην] I gather together
γουνόομαι I supplicate
ἔθνος, -εος [n.] group, band, nation
ἱερεύω, ἱερεύσω, ἱέρευσα I sacrifice, I slaughter
Ἰθάκη, -ης [f.] Ithaca [the island-home of Odysseus]

κάρηνα, -ων [n. pl.] summit; heads
κατα-θνήσκω, etc. I die
κελαινεφής, -ές cloud-wrapped, dark
πυρή, -ῆς [f.] funeral-pyre, sacrificial fire
Τειρεσίης, -āο [m.] Tiresias [a blind seer of Thebes]

852. TEXT

Invoking the Dead

446 πολλὰ δὲ γουνούμην νεκύων ἀμενηνὰ κάρηνα,
ἐλθὼν εἰς Ἰθάκην στεῖραν βοῦν, ἥ τις ἀρίστη,
ῥέξειν ἐν μεγάροισι πυρήν τ’ ἐμπλησέμεν ἐσθλῶν,
Τειρεσίῃ δ’ ἀπάνευθεν ὄϊν ἱερευσέμεν οἴῳ
450 παμμέλαν’, ὃς μήλοισι μεταπρέπει ἡμετέροισιν.
τοὺς δ’ ἐπεὶ εὐχωλῇσι λιτῇσί τε, ἔθνεα νεκρῶν,
ἐλλισάμην τὰ δὲ μῆλα λαβὼν ἀπεδειροτόμησα
ἐς βόθρον, ῥέε δ’ αἷμα κελαινεφές· αἱ δ’ ἀγέροντο
ψυχαὶ ὑπὲξ ἐρέβευς νεκύων κατατεθνηώτων.

ἀμενηνός, (-ή), -όν weak, fleeting
ἀπο-δειροτομέω, ἀπο-δειροτομήσω, ἀπο-δειροτόμησα I cut the throat
ἔρεβος, -ευς [n.] darkness, realm of darkness
εὐχωλή, -ῆς [f.] prayer, vow
λιτή, -ῆς [f.] prayer

μετα-πρέπω I am preeminent among
νεκρός, -οῦ [m.] corpse, the dead
παμμέλᾱς, -αινα, -αν all-black
στεῖρα, -ης [as adj.] that has never brought forth calf
ὑπέξ forth, from

853. NOTES

447 Understand "promising."
448 ῥέξειν: to do or offer (sacrifice).
ἐσθλῶν: words of "filling" may take either genitive (= full of) or dative (= filled with)
452 (ἐλ)λισάμην: the initial consonant is sometimes doubled after the augment.
453 ἐς βόθρον, i.e., so that the blood flowed into the pit.

854. COMMENT

449 He promises to sacrifice separately to Tiresias because it was from him of course that he wished to obtain the special information he had come to seek.

453 From time immemorial fresh blood has been fancied to have a special attraction to ghosts and spirits. Why it should be so is not clear, unless perhaps blood, to the ancients the substance of life, was considered to give new vigor to the ghosts, who would thus be eager to drink it. In this case, since the blood is shed as part of the sacrifice, it may be presumed to have also a super-imposed mystical value to the souls.

ODYSSEUS AND ELPENOR'S GHOST

One of those whom Circe had changed into pigs but was forced by Odysseus to restore to human state, Elpenor in a drunken stupor fell off the roof of Circe's palace while asleep and was killed. Odysseus met his ghost in Hades and promised to give him funeral honors back on earth. This is a sketch from a fine red-figure vase.

855. SPECIAL CORRELATIVES

You have probably noticed idiomatic expressions in Latin of this type: *alius aliud dicit,* "One says one thing, another says another thing."

In Greek, ἄλλος, ἕτερος and similar words are used in the same idiom. Thus:

(1) ἕτερός ἐστι πλήρης κακῶν, ἕτερος δὲ καλῶν.
One is full of evils; the other, of good things.

(2) ἐφοίταον ἄλλοθεν ἄλλος.
They wandered, some from one direction; others, from another.

(3) ἄλλοθεν ἄλλον ἐπισταδόν.
Going up to one after the other.

(4) ἄλλοτε κακῷ κύρεται, ἄλλοτε ἐσθλῷ.
At one time he lights upon evil; at another time, on good.

856. WORD STUDY

PANEGYRIC (a laudatory speech in someone's honor, such as were commonly given in 'gatherings of all the people' to celebrate some god or hero); — ETHNOLOGY (the scientific study of races—their history, qualities, etc.), ETHNIC (pertaining to a nation or race).

857. MEMORIZE:

γέρων, -οντος [m.] old man
δέος, δέεος [n.] fear, terror
εἶμι I go, I shall go
νύμφη, -ης [f.] maiden; nymph; bride

οὐτάω, οὐτήσω, οὔτησα or οὖτα
    I wound, I pierce
τεύχεα, -ων [n. pl.] [3 decl.] arms, armor
χαλκήρης, -ες bronze-tipped

858. TEXT

Grim Company

455 νύμφαι τ᾽ ἤίθεοί τε πολύτλητοί τε γέροντες
    παρθενικαί τ᾽ ἀταλαὶ νεοπενθέα θυμὸν ἔχουσαι,
    πολλοὶ δ᾽ οὐτάμενοι χαλκήρεσιν ἐγχείῃσιν,
    ἄνδρες ἀρηίφατοι βεβροτωμένα τεύχε᾽ ἔχοντες·
    οἳ πολλοὶ περὶ βόθρον ἐφοίτων ἄλλοθεν ἄλλος
460 θεσπεσίῃ ἰαχῇ· ἐμὲ δὲ χλωρὸν δέος ᾕρει.

ἀρηίφατος, -ον slain in battle
ἀταλός, -ή, -όν young, tender
βροτόω, pf. mid. βεβρότωμαι
    I make gory or blood-stained
ἐγχείη, -ης [f.] spear, lance

ἠίθεος, -ου [m.] an unmarried youth
ἰαχή, -ῆς [f.] shriek, loud cry
νεοπενθής, -ές w. sorrow still fresh
παρθενική, -ῆς maiden, virgin
πολύτλητος, -ον having endured much

859. NOTES

455 Understand: "There were . . ."
457 οὐτάμενοι: here, with passive significance.

860. COMMENT

455 ff. Compare Vergil's imitation of this in *Aeneid* 6.306–308:

"matres atque viri, defunctaque corpora vita
magnanimum heroum, pueri innuptaeque puellae
impositique rogis iuvenes ante ora parentum.

there were mothers and husbands, and bodies,
done with life, of great-souled heroes, boys
and unwed girls, and youths placed on their
funeral pyres before the eyes of their parents."

460 The hero is not ashamed to admit that he was frightened "green" by the sight of the flitting throngs of lifeless shades and the unearthly sound they made.

33

THE GHOSTS COME TO ODYSSEUS

861. **THE IRREGULAR VERB** εἶμι, I GO, I SHALL GO

You have already memorized the participles of εἶμι: ἰών, ἰοῦσα, ἰόν. Only two other forms occur more than once in this course. Learn them now:

(1) εἶσι(ν): third singular indicative—"he/she goes, will go"

(2) ἴμεν(αι): infinitive—"to go."

862. **WORD STUDY**

NYMPH (a mythological minor goddess inhabiting a wood, spring, cave, sea, etc.).

863. MEMORIZE:

Ἀίδης, Ἀίδαο or *Ἄιδος* [m.]   Hades
   [ruler of the lower world]
δέρω, δερέω, δεῖρα   I flay
ἐπ-οτρύνω, -οτρυνέω, -ότρῦνα   I stir up
   I compel [dat. or acc.]
ἴφθῑμος, -η, -ον   mighty, doughty
κατά-κειμαι   I lie down

Περσεφόνεια, -ης   Persephone [wife of
   Hades and queen of lower world]
πρίν [adv.]   before, sooner
   [conj. + inf. or anticipatory subj.]
   before, until
σφάζω, σφάξω, σφάξα   I cut the
   throat,   I slaughter
χαλκός, -οῦ [m.]   copper, bronze

864.   TEXT

Prayer and Expectation

461   δὴ τοτ᾽ ἔπειθ᾽ ἑτάροισιν ἐποτρύνας ἐκέλευσα
   μῆλα, τὰ δὴ κατέκειτ᾽ ἐσφαγμένα νηλέι χαλκῷ,
   δείραντας κατακῆαι, ἐπεύξασθαι δὲ θεοῖσιν,
   ἰφθίμῳ τ᾽ Ἀίδη καὶ ἐπαινῇ Περσεφονείη·
465   αὐτὸς δὲ ξίφος ὀξὺ ἐρυσσάμενος παρὰ μηροῦ
   ἥμην, οὐδ᾽ εἴων νεκύων ἀμενηνὰ κάρηνα
   αἵματος ἆσσον ἴμεν, πρὶν Τειρεσίαο πυθέσθαι.

ἀμενηνός, (-ή), -όν   weak, fleeting
ἐπ-εύχομαι, etc.   I pray (to)
ἐπαινός, -ή, -όν   dread, dire

κατα-καίω, etc.   I burn, I
   consume (w. fire)

865.   NOTES

462   *ἐσφαγμένα:* perfect passive participle of *σφάζω*.
463   *δείραντας:* understand *σφέας*.
465   This formulaic line is often used.

866.   COMMENT

461   Frightened as he is, Odysseus refuses to lose his head. He encourages his men and continues with the plans.

466   Odysseus could hardly have expected to do any harm to a bodiless spirit with his sword. His action was probably more instinctive than logical (as was also Aeneas', 6.291). But perhaps he depended on the threatening gesture to help him intimidate the feeble powers of the shades pressing round him until he had time to consult the blind seer.

867. MEMORIZE:

ἀχε(ύ)ω, —, ἄκαχον I grieve
Θηβαῖος, -η, -ον Theban
κατα-λείπω, etc. I leave behind, I forsake

πρότερος, -η, -ον sooner; former
σκῆπτρον, -ου [n.] staff [usually a symbol of office]
χρύσε(ι)ος, -η, -ον of gold

868. TEXT

Singleness of Purpose

ἦλθε δ᾽ ἐπὶ ψυχὴ μητρὸς κατατεθνηκυίης,
Αὐτολύκου θυγάτηρ μεγαλήτορος Ἀντίκλεια,
470 τὴν ζωὴν κατέλειπον ἰὼν εἰς Ἴλιον ἱρήν.
τὴν μὲν ἐγὼ δάκρυσα ἰδὼν ἐλέησά τε θυμῷ·
ἀλλ᾽ οὐδ᾽ ὧς εἴων προτέρην, πυκινόν περ ἀχεύων,
αἵματος ἆσσον ἴμεν, πρὶν Τειρεσίαο πυθέσθαι.
ἦλθε δ᾽ ἐπὶ ψυχὴ Θηβαίου Τειρεσίαο
475 χρύσεον σκῆπτρον ἔχων, ἐμὲ δ᾽ ἔγνω καὶ προσέειπεν·

Ἀντίκλεια, -ης Anticlia
Αὐτόλυκος, -ου Autolycus

δακρύω, δακρύσω, δάκρυσα I weep
ἱρός = ἱερός

869. NOTES

468 ἐπί: (adv.) on, forward.

469 Ἀντίκλεια: in apposition grammatically with ψύχη, but referring to μητρός. This use is called "construction according to sense."

472 προτέρην: modifies μητέρα understood but is best translated as adverb.
πυκινόν: (adv.) "vehemently."

475 ἔχων: see note on line 469.

870. COMMENT

472 A difficult situation, in which the rule of the head over the heart, true generally of the Greeks and in the highest degree of Odysseus, is dramatically made evident.

475 When the soul departed from the body, it lost, according to ancient belief, all power of using human speech. By a special privilege and reward of the gods, Tiresias was exempted from this deprivation.

871. WORD STUDY

SCEPTRE (a royal staff).

872. MEMORIZE:

δῑογενής, -έος sprung from Zeus
δύστηνος, -ον wretched, unfortunate
Λᾱερτιάδης, -εω Laertes' son [Odysseus]
μάντις, -ιος [m.] seer

νημερτής, -ές unfailing; true; clear
πολυμήχανος, -ον resourceful
τίπτε what? why? how?
φάσγανον, -ου [n.] sword

873. TEXT

Tiresias' Greeting

476 ' *δῑογενὲς Λαερτιάδη, πολυμήχαν' Ὀδυσσεῦ,*
τίπτ' αὖτ', ὦ δύστηνε, λιπὼν φάος ἠελίοιο
ἤλυθες, ὄφρα ἴδῃ νέκυας καὶ ἀτερπέα χῶρον;
ἀλλ' ἀποχάζεο βόθρου, ἄπισχε δὲ φάσγανον ὀξύ,
480 *αἵματος ὄφρα πίω καί τοι νημερτέα εἴπω.'*
      ὣς φάτ', ἐγὼ δ' ἀναχασσάμενος ξίφος ἀργυρόηλον
κουλεῷ ἐγκατέπηξ'. ὁ δ' ἐπεὶ πίεν αἷμα κελαινόν,
καὶ τότε δή μ' ἐπέεσσι προσηύδα μάντις ἀμύμων·

ἀνα-χάζομαι, —, ἀνα-χασσάμην
  I draw back
ἀπ-ίσχω I hold off
ἀπο-χάζομαι I withdraw from
ἀργυρόηλος, -ον silver-studded

ἀτερπής, -έος joyless, painful
ἐγ-κατα-πήγνῡμι, -πήξω, -πηξα I thrust,
  down into
κελαινός, -ή, -όν dark, black
κουλεόν, -οῦ [n.] sheath, scabbard

TIRESIAS APPEARS
Accepting Odysseys' call, the famous seer comes in the tenuous condition of the dead to convey secret information and counsel.

874. NOTES

478 ἴδη: contraction of ἴδηαι.
480 αἵματος: πίνω sometimes takes a partitive genitive: "I drink of, drink some of."
483 προσηύδα: augmented and contracted (from προσ-αυδάω).

875. COMMENT

478 ἀτερπέα: To Homer's way of thinking, the underworld at its best was not a very pleasant place to live. In fact Achilles, hero of the *Iliad,* states that he would rather be the lowest slave on earth than king of the dead.

480 Once he has drunk the blood, he will have the energy and inclination to prophesy in detail Odysseus' future problems and experiences. (Recall the comment on line 453).

876. WORD STUDY

NECROMANCY (the black art pretending to foretell the future by communication with the dead).

AJAX AND HECTOR BATTLE

The master painter Douris (c. 480 B.C.) has decorated the outside of a red-figure kylix with scenes of heroic battle during the Trojan War. Here Ajax attacks the Trojan leader Hector while Athena (at far left) and Apollo look on. The figures are identified by names written above.

877. | MEMORIZE:

αἰ   if [= εἰ]

ἀργαλέος, -η, -ον   hard, painful

βόσκω, βοσκήσω, βόσκησα   I pasture, I feed

ἐννοσίγαιος, -ου   earth-shaker [epithet of Poseidon]

ἐρύκω, ἐρύξω, ἔρυξα or ἐρύκακον I check, I guard

ἴφιος, -η, -ον   fat, strong

πελάζω, πελάσω, πέλασ(σ)α   I bring near to; I go near to

φαίδιμος, -ον [never f.]   shining; glorious

χώομαι, χώσομαι, χωσάμην   I am angry (with)

878.   TEXT

A Matter of Will-Power

‘ νόστον δίζηαι μελιηδέα, φαίδιμ' Ὀδυσσεῦ·

485   τὸν δέ τοι ἀργαλέον θήσει θεός· οὐ γὰρ ὀίω

λήσειν ἐννοσίγαιον, ὅ τοι κότον ἔνθετο θυμῷ

χωόμενος, ὅτι οἱ υἱὸν φίλον ἐξαλάωσας.

ἀλλ' ἔτι μέν κε καὶ ὧς, κακά περ πάσχοντες, ἵκοισθε

αἴ κ' ἐθέλῃς σὸν θυμὸν ἐρυκακέειν καὶ ἑταίρων

490   ὁππότε κε πρῶτον πελάσῃς εὐεργέα νῆα

Θρινακίῃ νήσῳ προφυγὼν ἰοειδέα πόντον,

βοσκομένας δ' εὕρητε βόας καὶ ἴφια μῆλα

Ἠελίου, ὃς πάντ' ἐφορᾷ καὶ πάντ' ἐπακούει.

δίζημαι   I seek

ἐν-τίθημι   I put into [aor. mid. ἐν-θέμην]

ἐξ-αλαόω, —, ἐξ-αλάωσα   I blind

ἐπ-ακούω   I hear

ἐφ-οράω, etc.   I look upon

Θρινάκιος, -η, -ον   of Thrinacia [a mythical island]

ἰοειδής, -ές   violet-like, blue, dark

κότος, -ου [m.]   resentment, grudge

προ-φεύγω, etc.   I flee forth, I escape

879.   NOTES

484   δίζηαι = δίζησαι

485   ἀργαλέον: in predicate position.

486   λήσειν: σε is understood as subject accusative.

488   ἵκοισθε: "you may yet come (home)." A potential optative taking the place of a future indicative in a Vivid Future construction.

489   ἑταίρων: understand θύμους.

ἐθέλῃς: stronger than merely "wishing." Translate: "if you have the will," "if you determine."

VOTING FOR AWARD OF ACHILLES' ARMOR

The Greek captains are shown voting, under Athena's supervision, by casting ballots for Ajax or Odysseus as most worthy of being honored with the armor of slain Achilles. Odysseus won, for his stratagem of the Wooden Horse. This drove Ajax, the mightiest warrior after Achilles, to bitter jealousy leading him to suicide (the theme of Sophocles' drama *Ajax*). The same artist, Douris, handled the story differently on the vase illustrated earlier, on p. 12.

880.   COMMENT

484-5 Notice the fine contrast: "You seek a return sweet and easy; a god will make it bitter and difficult."

488 The Greeks seemed always to have a strong realization of man's free will. Much of the interference of the gods and fate in Homer is little more than mythological machinery used to externalize and dramatize the conflict of the hero with the forces of nature and his own inner psychological reactions. Here, Tiresias plainly states that Odysseus and his men have the power of winning their way home if they choose to use the power. If, later, you read the Greek tragedians, you will see there in much sharper outline the Greeks' insistence on the free will as at least a partial cause in the working out of man's destiny.

493 We are reminded of the opening lines of the poem where the cattle of the Sun were mentioned with grim foreboding.

REVIEW

881. Go over again Lessons 132–141; make sure now that you have really mastered them. Here are a few suggestions for your review:

1. *Vocabulary:* Check your mastery of the 76 new memory words.
2. *Text:* Reread the 76 lines of text, making sure you recognize all the forms.
3. *Story:*

   a. Why did the Greeks have to visit the Underworld?
   b. Where was the entrance to the Underworld?
   c. Describe the ritual of sacrifice.
   d. What special promise was made to Tiresias?
   e. What did Tiresias say of the return journey?

4. *Criticism:*

   a. How does Lesson 132 illustrate a significant point of Homer's style?
   b. Circe gave Odysseus directions for entering the Underworld. Who performed the same functions for Aeneas? for Dante?
   c. Discuss Lesson 139 from the point of view of character formation.

5. *Grammar:* Review:

   a. ἧμαι.
   b. βοῦς.
   c Special correlatives.
   d. εἶμι   I go.

6. *Composition:* Put into Greek:

   a. The sail had been stretched by the steersman going to Tiresias in Hades.
   b. Having slaughtered the cow, Laertes' son sat beside the pit until the mighty seer came down.
   c. A group of dead maidens went near to Odysseus to drink of the blood, some from one direction, others from another.

882. GREEK AS A WORLD LANGUAGE

Greece was, in many ways, a world in itself, uniting within its territorial boundaries and scattered colonies an interesting diversity of customs, outlook, occupations, and expression. Basically it was 'One World,' with a language, life-view, and civilization common to all Greeks anywhere, at least in essentials and in distinction to the characteristics of other nations around them. Still, the culture of Athens was not that of Sparta or Miletus, and life at Thurii was noticeably different from the ways and interests of the citizens of Mytilene.

So too the Greek language, though fundamentally the same throughout Greece and its colonies, manifested certain minor differences in each geographical or historical division of the nation's life. The natural result of local tradition and of contagious peculiarities of speech growing up in particular communities, largely cut off from mingling with other groups separated by barriers of sea or mountains, was the development of several distinctive dialects of the common language. This is a frequent phenomenon, and may be seen in most other nations also.

In Greece, the main dialects were three: Aeolic, Doric, and Ionic—the latter with four important subdivisions: Epic (as in Homer), New Ionic (e.g., Herodotus and Hippocrates), Attic (the great dramatists, orators, Thucydides, Plato, etc.), and Koine (later authors and the New Testament.

Aeolic is characterized by having no rough breathings, by doubling many consonants, changing vowels, and by a few special endings of verbs and nouns. For instance, Sappho, Alcaeus, or Anacreon would write ἔννεκα, ὐπά, λέγοισι, πόλλαις where Homer or Attic would have ἕνεκα, ὑπό, λέγουσι, πολλάς.

In Doric, such as that of Pindar, Theocritus, and much of the choral parts of Attic tragedy, primitive long alpha is retained instead of changing to eta as in other dialects, -τι is used for -σι and -μες for -μεν in verb endings (e.g., ἀρετά, ἔχοντι, φαμές for ἀρετή, ἔχουσι, φαμέν).

Ionic drops the digamma, changes original long alpha to eta, often resists contraction, and alters some consonants from the original form of old words when followed by certain other sounds. You are familiar with most of these features of Ionic dialect from study of Homeric usage. Attic, as a considerably later form of Ionic, differs from Homer's language mostly just in dropping many alternative endings (e.g., -οιο, -μεναι), in contracting vowels more often and sometimes a bit differently in result (εο becoming ου not ευ), by adding many new words, and by developing a more elaborate syntax.

Koine or 'common Greek' is simply a still later form of popular (in distinction to literary) Attic, with the interblending of a few words and peculiarities of other dialects. It grew up in the wake of the far-roving armies of Alexander the Great, which by 323 B.C. had brought the whole Mediterranean world, the Near East, and even western India into one vast empire, throughout which the Greek language and culture rapidly spread and became predominant. With men from all over Greece mingling together in Alexander's armies, and various foreign countries subdued by them learning to speak Greek, it was natural that the language should change and simplify somewhat and become practically uniform all over the ancient world.

When the Roman Empire had absorbed Alexander's domains and added nearly all of Europe too, Greek still remained for centuries the international language, understood from Gaul to Babylon, from North Africa to Germany. In all these nations, educated men and everyone connected with international business or commerce, and in most countries even the common people too, all spoke or understood Greek with ease. It was hardly less familiar to them than their hundred different native tongues.

That is why St. Paul, for instance, could spread the news of Christ's life, divinity, and world-changing doctrine in eighteen distinct countries scattered throughout the then known world—for in any nation or city he could reach, his fiery eloquence could be readily understood, since he spoke Greek fluently. For the same reason, the entire New Testament was written in Greek, because thus its message could be read almost anywhere. Even the Roman government used Greek, rather than Latin, in its imperial administration and decrees outside Italy. And Roman emperors like Marcus Aurelius or Julian wrote their books in Greek, not Latin, as did most other authors who wanted a worldwide audience. It was only in the third and fourth centuries after Christ that Greek gave way to Latin as the universal language of the empire and later of medieval Europe.

One of the reasons, then, why Greek is so important historically is the fact that for hundreds of years it was the common language of all the civilized nations of the West, a unifying bond of thought and culture playing a vital part in those formative influences of ancient civilization from which our own has so largely stemmed.

883. MEMORIZE:

ἀλύσκω, ἀλύξω, ἄλυξα I shun, I escape
ἀντίθεος, -η, -ον godlike
βίοτος, -ου [m.] living; possessions
ἔδνα or ἔεδνα, -ων [n. pl.] bride-price;
  dowry

μνάομαι I am mindful of; I court
πῆμα, -ατος [n.] suffering, woe
ὑπερφίαλος, -ον overbearing

884. TEXT

Life or Death

τὰς εἰ μέν κ' ἀσινέας ἐάᾳς νόστου τε μέδηαι,
495 καί κεν ἔτ' εἰς Ἰθάκην κακά περ πάσχοντες ἵκοισθε·
εἰ δέ κε σίνηαι, τότε τοι τεκμαίρομ' ὄλεθρον,
νηί τε καὶ ἐτάροις. αὐτὸς δ' εἴ πέρ κεν ἀλύξῃς,
ὀψὲ κακῶς νεῖαι, ὀλέσας ἄπο πάντας ἐταίρους,
νηὸς ἐπ' ἀλλοτρίης· δήεις δ' ἐν πήματα οἴκῳ,
500 ἄνδρας ὑπερφιάλους, οἵ τοι βίοτον κατέδουσιν.
μνώμενοι ἀντιθέην ἄλοχον καὶ ἔδνα διδόντες.

ἀλλότριος, -η, -ον another's, alien
ἀσινής, -ές unharmed
δήω [w. fut. sense] I shall find or
  come upon
κατ-έδω I eat up

μέδομαι I am mindful of
ὀψέ [adv.] late
σίνομαι I hurt, I despoil
τεκμαίρομαι I decree, I foretell

885. NOTES

494 ἐάᾳς: for ἐάῃς.
  ἀσινέας: εα form one syllable by synizesis (cp. #564.1d).
498 νεῖαι = νέεαι. νέομαι usually has future connotation.
  ὀλέσας ἄπο: (ἀπ-ολλύω) "having lost."
499 ἐν: with οἴκῳ; a quite unusual word order.
501 διδόντες: present active participle of δίδωμι.

886. COMMENT

494 ff. To Odysseus and his men listening to the prophet, this condition must have seemed absurdly simple. It was not until the time for decision actually came that they realized how hard it would be, as you will see in Lessons 172–184.

497 αὐτός: Considering the type of comrades Odysseus had and the loose control he exercised over them, one could not justly hold him responsible for their actions.

500 The welcome home intimated by Tiresias must have been far different from the one he had pictured to himself time and again during his wanderings.

43

---

887. | **MEMORIZE:**

εὐήρης, -ες   well-balanced   μνηστήρ, -ῆρος [m.]   suitor

888. **TEXT**

Revenge and Pilgrimage

ἀλλ᾽ ἦ τοι κείνων γε βίας ἀποτίσεαι ἐλθών·
αὐτὰρ ἐπὴν μνηστῆρας ἐνὶ μεγάροισι τεοῖσιν
κτείνῃς ἠὲ δόλῳ ἢ ἀμφαδὸν ὀξέι χαλκῷ,
505   ἔρχεσθαι δὴ ἔπειτα λαβὼν εὐῆρες ἐρετμόν,
εἰς ὅ κε τοὺς ἀφίκηαι, οἳ οὐκ ἴσασι θάλασσαν
ἀνέρες οὐδέ θ᾽ ἅλεσσι μεμιγμένον εἶδαρ ἔδουσιν·
οὐδ᾽ ἄρα τοί γ᾽ ἴσασι νέας φοινικοπαρῄους
οὐδ᾽ εὐήρε᾽ ἐρετμά, τά τε πτερὰ νηυσὶ πέλονται.

ἅλς, ἁλός [f.] [dat. pl. ἅλεσσι]   salt
ἀμφαδόν [adv.]   openly, without sub-
  terfuge

ἀπο-τίνω, etc.   I pay back
πτερόν, -οῦ [n.]   wing
φοινῑκοπάρῃος, -ον   red-prowed

889. **NOTES**

502 βίας: "violent deeds." The plural of an abstract noun often expresses its concrete manifestations.
505 ἔρχεσθαι: an example of the infinitive used with imperative force.
506 εἰς ὅ: "until" (same construction as ὄφρα). ἴσασι: 3 pl. of οἶδα.
507 ἀνέρες; translate with οἱ. In sense it belongs with τούς.
μεμιγμένον: from μέμιγμαι, perfect of μίσγω.

890. **COMMENT**

502 The outwitting and punishing of the suitors occupies most of the last twelve books of the *Odyssey*.

506 ff. He is to go so far inland that he comes upon people who have never seen the sea nor know of ships and oars—and consequently would not know or worship the lord of the sea, Poseidon.

891. **WORD STUDY**

PTERODACTYL ('wing-finger,' a gigantic prehistoric flying reptile with head like a bird's and bony bat-like wings).

892. MEMORIZE:

γῆρας, -αος [n.] old age
εἴρω, ἐρέω I speak, I say, I tell
ἑκατόμβη, -ης [f.] hecatomb [strictly sacrifice of 100 cattle; but usually sacrifice in general]
ἐξείης [adv., = *ἐξῆς*] in order
κάπρος, -ου [m.] boar

λιπαρός, -ή, -όν sleek; comfortable
ὄλβιος, -η, -ον happy, prosperous
πήγνυμι, πήξω, πῆξα I fix, I make fast
σῆμα, -ατος [n.] sign; mound
σῦς, συός [m./f.] pig, swine
τοῖος, -η, -ον such
ὦμος, -ου [m.] shoulder

893. TEXT

Reconciliation and a Happy Ending

510 σῆμα δέ τοι ἐρέω μάλ' ἀριφραδές, οὐδέ σε λήσει.
ὁππότε κεν δή τοι συμβλήμενος ἄλλος ὁδίτης
φήῃ ἀθηρηλοιγὸν ἔχειν ἀνὰ φαιδίμῳ ὤμῳ,
καὶ τότε δὴ γαίῃ πήξας εὐῆρες ἐρετμόν,
ῥέξας ἱερὰ καλὰ Ποσειδάωνι ἄνακτι,

515 ἀρνειὸν ταῦρόν τε συῶν τ' ἐπιβήτορα κάπρον,
οἴκαδ' ἀποστείχειν ἔρδειν θ' ἱερὰς ἑκατόμβας
ἀθανάτοισι θεοῖσι, τοὶ οὐρανὸν εὐρὺν ἔχουσιν,
πᾶσι μάλ' ἐξείης. θάνατος δέ τοι ἐξ ἁλὸς αὐτῷ
ἀβληχρὸς μάλα τοῖος ἐλεύσεται, ὅς κέ σε πέφνῃ

520 γήραι ὕπο λιπαρῷ ἀρημένον, ἀμφὶ δὲ λαοὶ
ὄλβιοι ἔσσονται. τὰ δέ τοι νημερτέα εἴρω.'

ἀβληχρός, -ή, -όν feeble, gentle
ἀθηρηλοιγός, -οῦ [m.] winnowing-fan
ἀπο-στείχω, etc. I go away
ἀρημένος, -η, -ον worn out, hurt
ἀριφραδής, -ές clear, manifest
ἐπιβήτωρ, -ορος [m.] (the) male

συμ-βάλλω, -βλήσω, -βλήμην I set together; [mid.] I fall in with
ὁδίτης, -αο [m.] traveller, passer-by
πέφνον [2 aor. only] I killed
ταῦρος, -ου [m.] bull

894. NOTES

512 *φήῃ:* present subjunctive third singular of *φημί.*
ἔχειν: understand *σε* as subject accusative.
514 *ῥέξας: ῥέζω* and *ἔρδω* when used in reference to worship usually mean "I sacrifice."
516 Further infinitives used as imperatives.
519 *μάλα τοῖος:* lit.: "quite such," i.e., "ever so (gentle)," an expression usually accompanied by some appropriate gesture.
521 Distinguish: *εἴρομαι, εἰρήσομαι, ἐρόμην* I ask
   ἐρέω I ask
   εἴρω, ἐρέω I speak, I say

895. COMMENT

512 Odysseus is to carry an oar over his shoulder as he travels. Certain proof that he has reached the people intended will be given when those who meet him no longer recognize the oar he carries but think it must be a winnowing-fan (a sort of flail for separating the grains of wheat from the chaff).

514 There, in a land where no worship had ever been offered to Poseidon, Odysseus is to perform solemn sacrifice in his honor, thus appeasing him for the supposed wrong done his son, Polyphemus, and obtaining relief from his merciless persecution.

518 ἐξ ἁλὸς: It is not clear what kind of death is meant by a "death from the sea," or whether Homer means to say that death will come upon him "away from the sea." In any event, the following words make it clear that he will die in peace and comfort, honored and served by happy subjects. Even as his sufferings are certain, so also is the future happiness which will be the reward of his manliness and piety.

896. WORD STUDY

SEMAPHORE ('a sign-bearer,' a means of signalling by putting flags, lights, mechanical arms in certain agreed-on positions); SEMANTICS (the science of the origin and history of words as 'signs' of ideas); — SYMBOL (a mark, object, or drawing standing for or representing something by being traditionally 'set together' with it in meaning, e.g., a skull-and-crossbones signifying death), SYMBOLIC, SYMBOLISM.

ODYSSEUS' PALACE

This plan, based on all evidence in the poem and archaeological finds, shows the living quarters at the top and the adjunct buildings, all surrounded by a wall of brushwood to make a secure complex. The main room (A) is the Mégaron, with a central raised fireplace/hearth (γ)—above which the roof was open to the sky to let air in and smoke out. Corner pillars (δ) supported a roof over the rest of the megaron, which had sleeping rooms on a second level. Auxiliary storerooms, workshops, offices are on either side. Around the central courtyard (αὐλή: B) are pens for the farm animals; in the middle is an altar (η). See visualization of megaron in the illustration on p. 119.

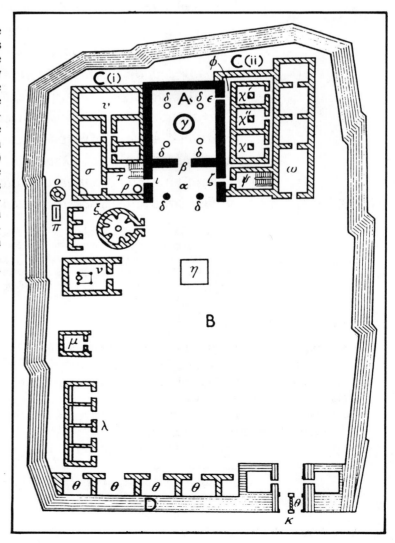

897. MEMORIZE:

ἀτρεκέως   truly, exactly

898. TEXT

The Heart Speaks

ὣς ἔφατ’, αὐτὰρ ἐγώ μιν ἀμειβόμενος προσέειπον·
‘ Τειρεσίη, τὰ μὲν ἄρ που ἐπέκλωσαν θεοί αὐτοί·
ἀλλ’ ἄγε μοι τόδε εἰπὲ καὶ ἀτρεκέως κατάλεξον.
525 μητρὸς τήνδ’ ὁράω ψυχὴν κατατεθνηκυίης·
ἡ δ’ ἀκέουσ’ ἧσται σχεδὸν αἵματος, οὐδ’ ἑὸν υἱὸν
ἔτλη ἐσάντα ἰδεῖν οὐδὲ προτιμυθήσασθαι·
εἰπέ, ἄναξ, πῶς κέν με ἀναγνοίη τὸν ἐόντα;’

ἀνα-γιγνώσκω, etc. I recognize	ἐπι-κλώθω, -κλώσω, -κλωσα I spin,
ε(ἰ)σάντα [adv.) in the face, face	I assign as one’s lot
to face	προτι-μῡθέομαι, —, -μῡθησάμην
	I speak (to)

THE THREE FATES
The three Fates were thought to determine the length and events of each human life, partly under the control of Zeus, partly forcing him to carry out their will. In this sketch from a Roman relief now in Germany are depicted Clotho (at left) who spins the thread of life, Láchesis deciding on the thread's length, and at the right Átropos ('The Immovable') cutting it off—which brings death. She is here represented drawing the person's lot.

899. NOTES

525 τήνδε: "here."
528 ἀναγνοίη: optative of expectation.
   τόν: predicate: "how she can recognize me as being that man who I am (her son)."

900. COMMENT

523 που: Odysseus is not one to waste time and energy in useless self-pity. He resigns himself to what must be and turns his mind to the present situation.

ἐπέκλωσαν: Man's destiny was often conceived of as a thread which was spun for him by the gods or Fate. From this notion grew the expanded mythological fancy of the three Fates: Clotho (from κλώθω I spin) who spins the thread of life; Lachesis (from λάχον aorist of λαγχάνω I am assigned by lot) who measures the thread of life; and Atropos (from ἀ-τρέπω, not-to-be-turned-aside) who cuts the thread of life.

αὐτοί: The implication seems to be that they did it entirely of their own will without consulting Odysseus.

524 Not having drunk the blood, Anticlia does not have the power to speak to or even to recognize her son; yet, perhaps through some dim consciousness of familiarity, she has lingered near him.

---

901. MEMORIZE:

ἔ(ι)σω [adv.] within	ὀλοφῦρομαι, ὀλοφῦρέομαι, ὀλοφῦράμην
ἔμπεδος, -ον firm, unchanged	I lament, I commiserate
θέσφατος, -ον divinely decreed; a divine decree	ὀπίσ(σ)ω [adv.] behind; back; hereafter

---

902. TEXT

Formula for Communication

ὣς ἐφάμην, ὁ δέ μ᾽ αὐτίκ᾽ ἀμειβόμενος προσέειπεν·

530   ᾽ ῥηίδιόν τοι ἔπος ἐρέω καὶ ἐπὶ φρεσὶ θήσω.

ὅν τινα μέν κεν ἐᾷς νεκύων κατατεθνηώτων

αἵματος ἆσσον ἴμεν, ὁ δέ τοι νημερτὲς ἐνίψει·

ᾧ δέ κ᾽ ἐπιφθονέῃς, ὁ δέ τοι πάλιν εἶσιν ὀπίσσω.᾽

ὣς φαμένη ψυχὴ μὲν ἔβη δόμον Ἄιδος εἴσω

535   Τειρεσίαο ἄνακτος, ἐπεὶ κατὰ θέσφατ᾽ ἔλεξεν·

αὐτὰρ ἐγὼν αὐτοῦ μένον ἔμπεδον, ὄφρ᾽ ἐπὶ μήτηρ

ἤλυθε καὶ πίεν αἷμα κελαινεφές. αὐτίκα δ᾽ ἔγνω,

καί μ᾽ ὀλοφυρομένη ἔπεα πτερόεντα προσηύδα·

ἐπι-φθονέω   I begrude, I refuse [dat.]

---

903. NOTES

530   ἔπος: a simple "rule."
531   ἐᾷς: contracted from ἐάῃς.
534   φαμένη: present middle participle of φημί.
535   κατὰ: with ἔλεξεν.
537   ἔγνω: understand ἐμέ.

---

904. COMMENT

530   The simple rule for communicating with the dead was to allow them to drink the blood, apparently because it revived their life-powers enough to speak.

---

905. WORD STUDY

ESOTERIC (secret, confidential, confined to a select 'inner circle').

906. | MEMORIZE:

ἐνθάδε [adv.]   here, hither
πεζός, -ή, -όν   on foot; by land

περάω, περήσω, πέρησα   I cross, I pass
   through
τέκνον-ου [n.]   child

907. TEXT

A Mother's Solicitude

> ‛ τέκνον ἐμόν, πῶς ἦλθες ὑπὸ ζόφον ἠερόεντα
> 540 ζωὸς ἐών; χαλεπὸν δὲ τάδε ζωοῖσιν ὁρᾶσθαι.
> μέσσῳ γὰρ μεγάλοι ποταμοὶ καὶ δεινὰ ῥέεθρα,
> Ὠκεανὸς μὲν πρῶτα, τὸν οὔ πως ἔστι περῆσαι
> πεζὸν ἐόντ', ἢν μή τις ἔχῃ εὐεργέα νῆα.
> ἦ νῦν δὴ Τροίηθεν ἀλώμενος ἐνθάδ' ἱκάνεις
> 545 νηί τε καὶ ἑτάροισι πολὺν χρόνον; οὐδέ πω ἦλθες
> εἰς Ἰθάκην, οὐδ' εἶδες ἐνὶ μεγάροισι γυναῖκα; ’

ἠερόεις, -εσσα, -εν hazy, dark   ῥέεθρον, -ου [n.] stream
ζόφος, -ου [m.] gloom, darkness

908. NOTES

540 χαλεπόν: understand ἐστί.

542 ἔστι: "it is possible." (Notice that the pitch mark moves back to the first syllable when the word has this meaning.) It takes an accusative with infinitive here.

545 ἑτάροισι: an ordinary instrumental dative. The companions are perhaps considered merely as rowers.

χρόνον: with ἀλώμενος.

909. COMMENT

539 πῶς ἦλθες: Not so much a real question as an exclamation.

542 πρῶτα: This word would lead us to expect something about the other rivers and streams that follow, but nothing does. Anticlia is so excited at seeing her son again that she starts talking at full speed, hardly realizing what she is saying.

543 πεζὸν ἐόντ': A bit of extreme naïveté, indicative of his mother's state of mind.

544 She can hardly believe that he should still be wandering on his way home and has not yet reached his wife. Strength of family affection is prominent throughout this whole episode, lines 524–608.

910. FUTURE PARTICIPLE TO EXPRESS PURPOSE

The future participle may be used to express purpose or desire. Thus:

(1) ἤγαγέν με εἰς Ἀίδαο Τειρεσίῃ χρησόμενον.
It brought me to Hades *in order to consult Tiresias.*

(2) εἵματα ἄγομαι ἐς ποταμὸν πλυνέουσα.
I bring the clothes to the river *in order to wash* them.

APOLLO AND ARTEMIS
On this mid-fifth century B.C. lekythos (flask for olive oil) the artist known as the 'Villa Giulia Painter' (because of one of his works in that museum) has represented Apollo with lyre and libation bowl and his twin sister Artemis accompanied by a deer faun. A notable example of Classic style: neat, clear, dignified, making optimum use of space.

911. MEMORIZE:

ἀγανός, -ή, -όν   gentle
Ἄρτεμις, -ιδος [f.]   Artemis [twin sister of Apollo]
βέλος, -εος [n.]   missile, arrow
ἐπ-οίχομαι   I go towards or round, I assail; I work (at)
ἕπομαι, ἕψομαι, ἑσπόμην   I follow (with)
ἰοχέαιρα, -ης   shooter of arrows

κατά-πεφνον [2 aor. only]   I slew
κήρ, κηρός [f.]   fate, death
νύ   now [a weak temporal or inferential particle]
ὀϊζύς, -ύος [f.]   sorrow, distress
Τρῶες, -ων [m. pl.]   Trojans
χρε(ι)ώ, -όος [f.]   need, necessity

912. TEXT

Explanations

ὣς ἔφατ', αὐτὰρ ἐγώ μιν ἀμειβόμενος προσέειπον·
' μῆτερ ἐμή, χρειώ με κατήγαγεν εἰς Ἀΐδαο
ψυχῇ χρησόμενον Θηβαίου Τειρεσίαο·
550   οὐ γάρ πω σχεδὸν ἦλθον Ἀχαιΐδος, οὐδέ πω ἁμῆς
γῆς ἐπέβην, ἀλλ' αἰὲν ἔχων ἀλάλημαι ὀϊζύν,
ἐξ οὗ τὰ πρώτισθ' ἑπόμην Ἀγαμέμνονι δίῳ
Ἴλιον εἰς ἐΰπωλον, ἵνα Τρώεσσι μαχοίμην.
ἀλλ' ἄγε μοι τόδε εἰπὲ καὶ ἀτρεκέως κατάλεξον·
555   τίς νύ σε κὴρ ἐδάμασσε τανηλεγέος θανάτοιο;
ἦ δολιχὴ νοῦσος, ἦ Ἄρτεμις ἰοχέαιρα
οἷς ἀγανοῖς βελέεσσιν ἐποιχομένη κατέπεφνεν;

αἰέν = αἰεί
ἁμός, -ή, -όν   our
Ἀχαιΐς, -ίδος [f.]   Achaean (land)
γῆ, γῆς [f.]   earth, land
δολιχός, -ή, -όν   long
ἐΰπωλος, -ον   abounding in fine foals

κατ-άγω, etc.   I bring down
πρώτιστα [w. τά] [adv.]   first
τανηλεγής, -ές   bringing long woe
χράομαι, χρήσομαι   I consult (an oracle) [w. dat.]

913. NOTES

548   Ἀΐδαο: δόμον is understood (cp. the English usage, e.g., "Services will be held at St. Paul's.")

552   ἐξ οὗ: "from the time when"

555   κὴρ θανάτοιο: "fate of death," i.e., the particular kind of death fated for each person.

continued on next page

THE SLAYING OF THE NIOBIDS

A sketch from a famous large vase in the Louvre, dating to around 465 B.C., showing Apollo shooting the sons of Niobe while Artemis slays the daughters. This was how death was attributed when due to natural causes, not violence. The ancient Greeks saw divinities active in all events of human life and death.

914. COMMENT

547 An instance of Homer's masterly technique in allowing his characters to speak for themselves. It is from their own self-expression that we come really to know other people.

550 ἀμῆς: He delicately refers to it as still "our" land, as though his mother were yet alive.

556 To the goddess Artemis and her gentle arrows was attributed the sudden, peaceful death of women; that of men, to Apollo.

555-7 Lines of striking melodic beauty and poetic charm.

915. | MEMORIZE:

γέρας, -αος [n.]   prize (of honor); estate
πότν(ι)α, -ης [f.]   queen; [as adj.] revered
φθίνω, φθίσω, φθῖσα I waste away, I
    pass away

φυλάσσω, φυλάξω, φύλαξα   I guard; I
    observe

916. TEXT

News From Home

> εἰπέ δέ μοι πατρός τε καί υἱέος, ὅν κατέλειπον,
> ἢ ἔτι πὰρ κείνοισιν ἐμὸν γέρας, ἦέ τις ἤδη
> 560 ἀνδρῶν ἄλλος ἔχει, ἐμὲ δ᾽ οὐκέτι φασὶ νέεσθαι.
> εἰπὲ δέ μοι μνηστῆς ἀλόχου βουλήν τε νόον τε,
> ἠὲ μένει παρὰ παιδὶ καὶ ἔμπεδα πάντα φυλάσσει,
> ἦ ἤδη μιν ἔγημεν Ἀχαιῶν ὅς τις ἄριστος. ᾽
>   ὣς ἐφάμην, ἡ δ᾽ αὐτίκ᾽ ἀμείβετο πότνια μήτηρ·
> 565 ᾽ καὶ λίην κείνη γε μένει τετληότι θυμῷ
> σοῖσιν ἐνὶ μεγάροισιν· ὀϊζυραὶ δέ οἱ αἰεὶ
> φθίνουσιν νύκτες τε καὶ ἤματα δάκρυ χεούσῃ.

μνηστή, -ῆς [adj.] wooed, wedded   *ὀϊζυρός, -ή, -όν* wretched, miserable

917. NOTES

558 *πατρός:* sometimes the genitive follows *εἶπον* with the sense "tell of."
559 *πὰρ κείνοισιν:* understand *ἐστί:* "is still in their hands."
560 *φασί:* present indicative third plural of *φημί.* The subject is indefinite.
563 *μιν:* his wife. The subject of *ἔγημεν* is the clause introduced by *ὅς τις.*
565 *τετληότι:* perfect participle of *τλάω.*

918. COMMENT

559 *γέρας:* His property, and the hereditary dignity and honor of a king.
560 If Odysseus were dead, his son Telemachus should by rights become king; but since he was yet a minor, Odysseus fears that one of the powerful nobles had seized power and had expelled Telemachus and Laertes, the father of Odysseus, from any share in the wealth or rights of the kingly family.

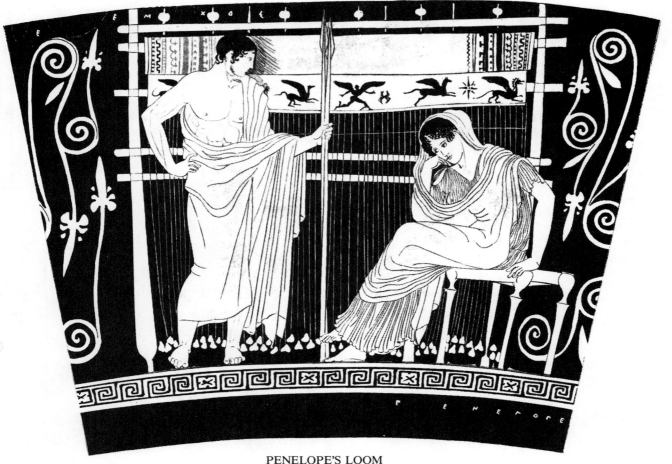

PENELOPE'S LOOM

A fine high-Classical treatment (here sketched from a vase found at Chiusi) of Penelope's ruse of weaving a shroud for Odysseus' old father Laertes, which she insists with the Suitors for her hand she must finish before deciding on whom to marry, since Odysseus is presumed dead. But at night she undid what she wove by day, to prolong the excuse. She is seen seated dejectedly at her loom, while young Telemachus urges his mother to make up her mind. Extremely fine and detailed drawing for the difficult technique of vase painting.

563   The obvious way for a noble to have himself proclaimed king would be to marry the widow-queen; it would take no little strength of will for her to resist long their arguments and importunities and even threats, as Odysseus is presumed dead.

It is not hard to sympathize with this soldier's wife. During her household tasks of the day the thought of her beloved husband fighting, perhaps suffering and dying, far away from all his loved ones, would often bring sudden tears to her eyes. The sight, too, of her baby growing up without the love and care of a father, and her husband's inability to share with her in their son's joyous delight in the strange and wonderful world of childhood must indeed have caused her many a heartache. And at night, when apart from the distractions of the daytime and alone with her sorrow, her longing for her beloved's return must have been intensified, and even her sleep must have been disturbed by fitful dreams about him.

919. MEMORIZE:

ἀγρός, -οῦ [m.]   field, country [opp. to city]

αὐτόθι [adv.]   right here, right there

δαίς, δαιτός [f.]   feast, portion

εἷμα, -ατος [n.]   garment; [pl.] clothes

ἔκηλος, -ον   at rest, undisturbed

ἔννῦμι, ἕσ(σ)ω, ἕσ(σ)α   I clothe, I put on; [pass.:]   I wear

εὐνή, -ῆς [f.]   bed; anchor-stone

ἶσος, (ἐ)ἴση, ἶσον   equal, fair; trim

καλέω, καλέω, κάλεσ(σ)α   I call; I invite

σῑγαλόεις, -εσσα, -εν   shining

τέμενος, -εος [n.]   land marked off [for a god or as private property]

χλαῖνα, -ης [f.]   cloak

χρώς, χροός [m.]   skin, body, person

920. TEXT

Of Son and Father

σὸν δ᾽ οὔ πώ τις ἔχει καλὸν γέρας, ἀλλὰ ἔκηλος

Τηλέμαχος τεμένεα νέμεται καὶ δαῖτας ἐίσας

570 δαίνυται, ἃς ἐπέοικε δικασπόλον ἄνδρ᾽ ἀλεγύνειν·

πάντες γὰρ καλέουσι. πατὴρ δὲ σὸς αὐτόθι μίμνει

ἀγρῷ, οὐδὲ πόλινδε κατέρχεται. οὐδέ οἱ εὐναὶ

δέμνια καὶ χλαῖναι καὶ ῥήγεα σιγαλόεντα,

ἀλλ᾽ ὅ γε χεῖμα μὲν εὕδει, ὅθι δμῶες ἐνὶ οἴκῳ,

575 ἐν κόνι ἄγχι πυρός, κακὰ δὲ χροῒ εἵματα εἷται·

ἀλεγύνω   I partake of [w. acc.]

δέμνια, -ων [nt. pl.]   couch

δικασπόλος, -ον   busied about judgments, administering justice

ἐπ-έοικε   it is fitting

κόνις, -ιος [f.] [dat. κόνι]   dust, earth

ῥῆγος, -εος [n.]   rug, coverlet

Τηλέμαχος, -ου   Telemachus [son of Odysseus and Penelope]

χεῖμα, -ατος [n.]   winter, cold

921. NOTES

569 τεμένεα: εα is scanned as one syllable by synizesis.

572 εὐναί: predicate—"nor does he have for bedding a couch, etc."

575 εἷται: perfect passive of ἔννῦμι with, as often, present sense.

922. COMMENT

569-571 Telemachus is undisturbed in his possession of the gardens and farms set aside as crown-lands. At the banquet table he sits in a place of honor and receives the deference becoming to one who is or will soon be the king and therefore the dispenser of justice to his people. Nor is there a single important feast to which he, because of his rank, is not invited. Telemachus, it seems, is a worthy son of a noble father, and maintains his position despite the ambitious princes.

571-575 Laertes, the father of Odysseus, was a man whose whole life became wrapped up in that of his hero son. When his son fails to return, the world and all its struggles and interests become flat and stale to his taste. Social life becomes abhorrent; he loses all concern about his comfort and his appearance; he hardly lives, but just exists.

923. GNOMIC AORIST

The aorist indicative regularly expresses a single past act. By an extension of this use, peculiar to the Greeks, the aorist was used in certain contexts to express a single concrete fact from which the reader or hearer was expected to infer that what happened thus once was typical of what always or frequently happens in such circumstances. Hence, the aorist indicative (besides the present) came to be used to express general truths, maxims, or proverbs. When thus used, it is called the *gnomic* aorist (from γνώμη: "proverb").

(1) *νοῦσος μάλιστα μελέων ἐξείλετο θυμόν.*
Disease most frequently *takes* the life from our limbs.

(2) *ὣς τις κατέκτανε βοῦν ἐπὶ φάτνῃ.*
Just as a man *kills* an ox at the manger.

(3) *ὅς κε θεοῖς ἐπιπείθηται, μάλα τ' ἔκλυον αὐτοῦ.*
Whoever obeys the gods, him they especially *hear*.

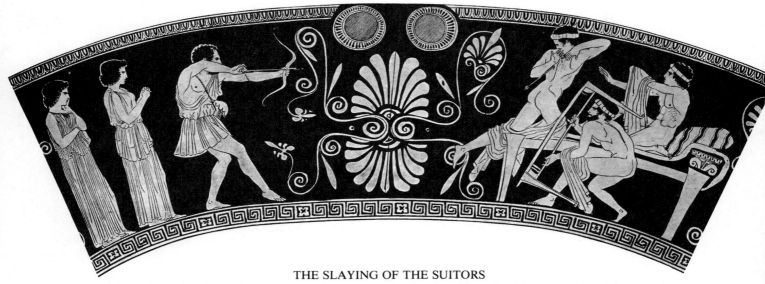

THE SLAYING OF THE SUITORS

This sketch 'unfolds' the whole scene around a Classical skyphos found in an Etruscan tomb at Tarquinia, now in Berlin. Odysseus shoots down the dissolute Suitors, while two handmaidens of the palace look on in fright. The story is graphically told in the closing books of the *Odyssey*.

924. **MEMORIZE:**

ἀλωή, -ῆς [f.] threshing-floor; garden
ἐφ-έπω, ἐφ-έψω, ἐπί-σπον I meet;
   I drive; I pursue
κλίνω, κλινέω, κλῖνα I lean; [mid.:] I lie
μάλιστα [supl. of *μάλα*] especially
πάντη [adv.] on all sides, everywhere

πένθος, -εος [n.] sorrow, grief
πότμος, -ου [m.] fate, death
στυγερός, -ή, -όν hateful, gloomy
τέθηλα or *τέθαλα* [pf. w. pres. meaning[
   I flourish
φύλλον, -ου [n.] leaf

925. **TEXT**

Parental Love

576   *αὐτὰρ ἐπήν ἔλθησι θέρος τεθαλυῖά τ᾽ ὀπώρη,*
      πάντη οἱ κατὰ γουνὸν ἀλωῆς οἰνοπέδοιο
      φύλλων κεκλιμένων χθαμαλαὶ βεβλήαται εὐναί.
      ἔνθ᾽ ὅ γε κεῖτ᾽ ἀχέων, μέγα δὲ φρεσὶ πένθος ἀέξει
580   *σὸν νόστον ποθέων, χαλεπὸν δ᾽ ἐπὶ γῆρας ἱκάνει.*
      οὕτω γὰρ καὶ ἐγὼν ὀλόμην καὶ πότμον ἐπέσπον·
      οὔτ᾽ ἐμέ γ᾽ ἐν μεγάροισιν ἐύσκοπος ἰοχέαιρα
      οἷς ἀγανοῖς βελέεσσιν ἐποιχομένη κατέπεφνεν
      οὔτε τις οὖν μοι νοῦσος ἐπήλυθεν, ἥ τε μάλιστα
585   *τηκεδόνι στυγερῇ μελέων ἐξείλετο θυμόν·*
      ἀλλά με σός τε πόθος σά τε μήδεα, φαίδιμ᾽ Ὀδυσσεῦ,
      σή τ᾽ ἀγανοφροσύνη μελιηδέα θυμὸν ἀπηύρα.᾽

ἀγανοφροσύνη, -ης [f.] mildness
ἀπ-αυράω I take away
γουνός, -οῦ [m.] swell, knoll
ἐξ-αιρέω, etc. I take from
ἐύσκοπος, -ον sharp-sighted,
  aiming well·
θέρος, -εος [n.] (early) summer
μῆδος, -εος [n.] plan, counsel

οἰνόπεδος, -ον vine-bearing
ὀπώρη, -ης [f.] late summer, harvest
  time
πόθος, -ου [m.] longing, mourning
τηκεδών, -όνος [f.] a wasting or pin-
  ing away
χθαμαλός, -ή, -όν on the ground, low

GIRLS ON A SEE-SAW
A pleasant glimpse of an age-old sport, on a fragment of a red-figured vase by the 'Leningrad Painter,' around 455 B.C.

926. NOTES

577 *πάντῃ:* with *κεκλιμένων.*

578 *κεκλιμένων:* from *κέκλιμαι,* perfect of *κλίνω.*
βεβλήαται: perfect passive third person plural of *βάλλω* w. present sense.
Take *χθαμαλαί* as predicate—"are laid on the ground."

579 *μέγα:* predicate after *ἀέξω,* I make grow."

580 *ἐπί:* adverbial "besides."

581 *οὕτω = οὕτως.*

586 *με:* double accusative with a verb of depriving.
σός: represents an objective genitive. *μήδεα* and *ἀγανοφροσύνη* follow in thought after *πόθος:* "longing for you and (for) your counsels, etc."

587 *ἀπ-ηύρα:* augmented and contracted.

927. COMMENT

582 *ἰοχέαιρα:* Artemis (cf. comment on line 556).

582–584 Having Anticlia answer her son's question in detail is not just a device to fill up space. The repetition enforces the ideas previously introduced, makes certain that the hearer will be perfectly clear on the peculiar reason for her death, and without question is a good way of keeping the interest and attention of an audience, especially if composed of simple and unsophisticated people, as were most of Homer's original hearers.

586–587 Notice the pathetic repetition and emphatic position of "your." The beauty and strength of family relations in Homeric times, as portrayed in these and the preceding lines, is remarkable.

928. WORD STUDY

CLINIC (a ward where patients 'lie' awaiting medical care); — CHLOROPHYL (the chemical substance in plants which makes their 'leaves green').

58

REVIEW

929. Go over again Lessons 143–152; make sure now that you have really mastered them. Here are a few suggestions for your review:

1. *Vocabulary:* Check your mastery of the 70 new memory words.
2. *Text:* Reread the 94 lines of text, making sure you recognize all the forms.
3. *Story:*

   a. Upon the fulfillment of what condition will the Greeks be able to return home?
   b. What was the nature and purpose of the pilgrimage Odysseus will have to make?
   c. How was Odysseus to end his life?
   d. Describe the family of Odysseus and their feelings for one another.

4. *Criticism:*

   a. Compare Homer's picture of family devotion with what you know of typical American families.
   b. Do you think that Homer weakens story-interest by prophesying the future? Do contemporary writers of stories depend much upon surprise endings? What are the advantages of each method?

5. *Grammar:* Explain:

   a. Fut. ptc. of purpose.
   b. Gnomic Aor.

6. *Composition:* Put into Greek:

   a. Necessity led him to Hades, to know (ptc.) the divine decrees.
   b. Whoever tries to escape all sufferings always finds even more sorrow. (Do not use present.
   c. The mother of Odysseus thought that gentle death was sent by Artemis, the shooter of arrows.

930. GREEK SPORTS

One thing, at least, that we have no difficulty in understanding about the Greeks is their love of athletics. Their literature, their philosophy, their language itself may take long study before we can properly master and appreciate them. But a love of sports needs no explanation to modern minds. The enjoyment of games is one more bond of union between us and the ancient Greeks.

This could not be said of other ancient people. There is no evidence (indeed there are signs to the contrary) that the Egyptians or Assyrians, for instance, ever had any interest in sports as such. Nowhere else in the world of antiquity do we find the spirit of athletic competition for the sake of pleasure and achievement. It is written all over Greek civilization. Yet it practically died out with the decline of Greece. Only in modern times has any equivalent interest in sports prevailed.

This is remarkable testimony to the vigor and perennial youthfulness of the Greek view of life. In their zest for living, the Greeks invented play. While the whole ancient world around them went its somber, fear-ridden, drudging way, the Greeks took time out from their energetic pursuits in politics and business to enjoy various games of single or group athletics. When Greek civilization first bursts into history, this love of play is already evident. The *Iliad,* our earliest literary picture of Greek life, has an elaborate description (in Book 23) of the games staged for the army by Achilles in honor of Patroclus at his funeral: chariot-racing, boxing, wrestling, foot-racing, a sham battle in armor, discus-throwing, archery, hurling the spear.

As Greek cities grew in size and complexity, athletics became organized on a broader scale, in great civic competitions and national meets usually every year. These events were so important an item of Greek life that a sacred truce was always established when they were imminent, to insure safe conduct in the midst of any wars going on for those traveling to the national games. Each city-state vied to have its own outstanding athletes, to uphold its honor at the games and win it fame by capturing the choicest prizes. A winner of the great Olympic games, or of the scarcely less prominent Isthmian, Pythian, or Nemean meets, was looked upon as a national hero and won the greatest respect and reputation. Even victorious generals of the army would yield in deference to a star athlete crowned in the All-Greek competitions.

Interestingly enough, some of the most splendid of Greek poetry is concerned with athletic triumphs and takes its origin in exultant congratulation of the winner in some popular sports event. Pindar is the most famous of these poets of the games, and many of his Pythian or Olympian Odes in honor of national champions are among the very loftiest productions of any litera-

OLYMPIA

An air view of the national Greek shrine to Zeus which became especially associated with athletic contests in the god's honor, every four years since the original celebration in 776 B.C. The Stadium is at the right, the great temples of Hera and of Zeus below Kronion hill, the Kladeos river at upper left, the Leonidaion (square with circle in center) at bottom left; it was a hotel for honored guests and visiting officials.

OLYMPIA RESTORED

This accurate reconstruction of the buildings of Olympia shows how full the sanctuary of Zeus (the Altis) was of fine monuments. The great Temple of Zeus dominates the whole area; at the top left is the smaller and older Temple of Hera. The round building to its left is the Philippeion, put up by the family of Alexander the Great. Above center is the semi-circular Exedra with a fountain of cool drinking water piped in from the hills. To the right of that is a line of temple-like 'Treasuries' of different cities, displaying trophies and other memorials of achievement. Down the right side runs the tile-roofed Echo Colonnade.

ture. This is possible because to the Greeks beauty and grace of body were almost as precious as nobility of soul, and indeed were looked upon as exterior indications of it. Athletic prowess, then, was a symbol and proof of singular strength, harmony, and vigor of character. As such, it won the utmost admiration of the Greeks and supplied their poets and sculptors with much of their noblest material.

The supreme athletic event was always the 'Pentathlon' or five-fold competition at the national games. This consisted in a 200-yard dash, followed by the broad jump, then throwing the discus, hurling the javelin, and finally a wrestling match. Whoever came out the best all-around performer won the glory of being champion of all Greece and was rewarded with substantial monetary prizes and the highest civic honors.

Other sports common in Greece were boxing, relay races, boat regattas, and various forms of ball games. Young children played very much as today, with spinning tops, swings, seesaws, rolling-hoops, marbles, balls, and kites; among their games were hide-and-seek, duck-on-a-rock, blind man's buff, tug-of-war. Everywhere, sport was popular; it added to the fun of life, trained in character and self-control, and promoted that physical fitness and graceful harmony of body which was a Greek passion.

Not only our revival of the Olympic Games, but modern sport in general has much in common with the Greek spirit of play, one of their finest contributions to Western culture. The very name "athletics" is Greek in origin (from ἆθλον: prize-contest). Where we fall behind the Greeks in this field is our less elevated concept of the significance of athletics in the larger view of education and character. Where is the modern Pindar?

931. **MEMORIZE:**

ἀγαυός, -ή, -όν admirable, noble

ἀμφότερος, -η, -ον both

ἄχος, -εος [n.] grief, pain

γόος, -ου [m.] groan, lamentation

ἐφ-ορμάω, ἐφ-ορμήσω, ἐφ-όρμησα I urge on; [mid. and pass.:] I rush forward, I am eager to

μέμαα [pf. w. pres. meaning] I am eager

ὀδύρομαι, ὀδύρέομαι, ὀδῡράμην I bewail I lament

ὄνειρος, -ου [m.] dream

ὀτρύνω, ὀτρυνέω, ὄτρῡνα I urge on; I send

πέτομαι, πτήσομαι, πτάμην I fly

τέρπω, τέρψω, τέρψα or *(τε)ταρπόμην* I comfort, I cheer; [mid.:] I take my fill of

φωνέω, φωνήσω, φώνησα I lift up my voice, I utter

932. **TEXT**

Frustrated Love

> ὣς ἔφατ', αὐτὰρ ἐγώ γ' ἔθελον φρεσὶ μερμηρίξας
> μητρὸς ἐμῆς ψυχὴν ἑλέειν κατατεθνηκυίης.
>
> 590 τρὶς μὲν ἐφωρμήθην, ἑλέειν τέ με θυμὸς ἀνώγει,
> τρὶς δέ μοι ἐκ χειρῶν σκιῇ εἴκελον ἢ καὶ ὀνείρῳ
> ἔπτατ'. ἐμοὶ δ' ἄχος ὀξὺ γενέσκετο κηρόθι μᾶλλον,
> καὶ μιν φωνήσας ἔπεα πτερόεντα προσηύδων·
> ' μῆτερ ἐμή, τί νύ μ' οὐ μίμνεις ἑλέειν μεμαῶτα,
>
> 595 ὄφρα καί εἰν Ἀίδαο φίλας περὶ χεῖρε βαλόντε
> ἀμφοτέρω κρυεροῖο τεταρπώμεσθα γόοιο;
> ἦ τί μοι εἴδωλον τόδ' ἀγαυὴ Περσεφόνεια
> ὤτρυν', ὄφρ' ἔτι μᾶλλον ὀδυρόμενος στεναχίζω;'

εἴδωλον, -ου [n.] shape, phantom
εἴκελος, -η, -ον like to
κρυερός, -ή, -όν chilling, numbing

μᾶλλον [comp. of *μάλα*] more, rather
σκιή, -ῆς [f.] shadow
στεναχίζω I groan, I lament

933. **NOTES**

590 *ἐφωρμήθην:* aorist passive of *ἐφ-ορμάω*.

591 *εἴκελον:* adverbial.

592 *κηρόθι:* -*θι* is a special case-ending added in the same way as -*θεν* and -*φι*. It expresses place where. (cp. *αὐτόθι*)

595 *φίλας:* with *χεῖρε*. Take *περί* as an adverb: "about (each other)."

934. COMMENT

589 Touched to the heart by his mother's love and sad plight, Odysseus impulsively tries to embrace her, only to find, alas, that his yearning arms clasped on nothingness.

594 ff. Sick at heart and with only the vaguest notions of the spirit world, he cannot understand why his mother slips so from his grasp, unless, indeed, she be a mere phantom sent by the infernal powers to torment him yet more.

595 Ἀΐδαο: To us, Hades denotes a place, but not so to the Greeks. Hades was always thought of by them as a person, the god of the other world. No doubt the later idea is due to the abbreviated expression "to Hades' (house)."

935. οὗτος, αὗτη, τοῦτο: "THIS":

(1) Declension:

οὗτος	αὗτη	τοῦτο
τούτου, οιο	ταύτης	τούτου, οιο
τούτῳ	ταύτῃ	τούτῳ
τοῦτον	ταύτην	τοῦτο
οὗτοι	αὗται	ταῦτα
τούτων	ταυτάων	τούτων
τούτοισ(ι)	ταύτῃσ(ι)	τούτοισ(ι)
τούτους	ταύτας	ταῦτα

N.B. You will have no difficulty with this pronoun if you remember three things:

1. The endings are *regular* (like κεῖνος, -η, -ο)

2. The rough breathing takes the place of τ in the same forms as in ὁ, ἡ, το.

3. The stem diphthong has *o* whenever the ending has an o-sound; it has *a* whenever the ending has an a-sound (*a, η*).

(2) Use:

ὅδε and οὗτος both mean "this." Sometimes they are used without much distinction. In general, however, there are two differences:

1. ὅδε refers more to the first person; οὗτος, more to the second person. ἥδε χείρ = *this hand* (of mine). οὗτος ἀνήρ = *this man* (you are interested in).

2. ὅδε refers more to the future; οὗτος more to the past. τόδε λέξω = *I shall say this* (something to follow). ταῦτα εἶπε = *he said this* (which has just been reported).

936. WORD STUDY

ONEIROMANCY (the supposed art of foretelling the future by analysis of dreams); — SQUIRREL (by mispronunciation of σκίουρος: 'shadow-tail').

937. MEMORIZE:

αἰθόμενος, -η, - ον   burning, blazing

ἠΰτε as

ἴς, ἰνός [f.]   sinew; strength

μετόπισθε(ν) [adv.]   behind, later, afterward

οὗτος, αὕτη, τοῦτο   this

938. TEXT

The Mystery of Death

ὣς ἐφάμην, ἡ δ᾽ αὐτίκ᾽ ἀμείβετο πότνια μήτηρ·

600 ' ὤ μοι, τέκνον ἐμόν, περὶ πάντων κάμμορε φωτῶν,

οὔ τί σε Περσεφόνεια Διὸς θυγάτηρ ἀπαφίσκει,

ἀλλ᾽ αὕτη δίκη ἐστὶ βροτῶν, ὅτε τίς κε θάνῃσιν·

οὐ γὰρ ἔτι σάρκας τε καὶ ὀστέα ἶνες ἔχουσιν,

ἀλλὰ τὰ μέν τε πυρὸς κρατερὸν μένος αἰθομένοιο

605 δαμνᾷ, ἐπεί κε πρῶτα λίπῃ λεύκ᾽ ὀστέα θυμός,

ψυχὴ δ᾽ ἠΰτ᾽ ὄνειρος ἀποπταμένη πεπότηται.

ἀλλὰ φάοσδε τάχιστα λιλαίεο· ταῦτα δὲ πάντα

ἴσθ᾽, ἵνα καὶ μετόπισθε τεῇ εἴπῃσθα γυναικί. '

ἀπαφίσκω I trick, I beguile
ἀπο-πέτομαι, etc. I fly away
δαμνάω I overcome; I consume

κάμμορος, -ον fate-ridden, wretched
ποτάομαι pf. w. pres. force: πεπότημαι
I fly, I flit about

939. NOTES

600 ὤ μοι: an exclamation like the English "Ah me!" or "Oh my!"

603 ἔχουσιν: i.e., hold together.

605 θυμός . . . ψυχή: Homer does not distinguish exactly between these terms, but in general θυμός refers to physical manifestations of life (e.g., courage, anger, madness, desire, devising, etc.), while ψυχή has reference to the principle of life. In this passage, θυμός probably means the vitality or life of the body which ceases at death; and ψυχή the immortal spirit which leaves behind the dead body.

607 λιλαίεο: "long for," i.e., "make your way with all speed."

608 ἴσθ᾽: "keep in mind."

940. COMMENT

602 ff. The world beyond the grave is a fascinating thought. Great literary men like Homer, Vergil, and Dante have described imaginary journeys to the otherworld in considerable detail. The revelations of Christianity treat many aspects of life after death. Yet, united with and immersed in materiality as we are, it is still hard for us to realize or imagine a world of spirits. We should hardly by surprised, then, that the ancient Greeks struggled with the idea with varying success. Homer's description of the soul flying out of the body consumed on the funeral pyre is

not too bad, though his concept of the afterlife is scarcely adequate. In general, he seemed to conceive of the soul as existing forever with its own individuality, but with a life not as full or free as when it was in the body. It still retained the shape of the body to which it had been united, and, at least sometimes, some of the body's materiality, being affected, for example by hunger and thirst.

608 His experience and sights in the world of the dead will natuirally be a prime subject of conversation with Penelope, once they are reunited.

* * * *

With these final words, Anticlia fades back into the gloom. Other shades then rush forward to drink of the blood. Watching them in wonder, Odysseus recognizes many of them, as Homer goes on to relate in the following lessons.

LORDS OF THE UNDERWORLD
A terracotta plaque from the Greek colony Locri in southern Italy, showing Pluto, god of the world of the dead, enthroned with his queen Persephone. Pluto, whose name means 'the rich one' because eventually all fall into his hands, was brother of Zeus (god of the sky) and Poseidon (lord of the seas). An example of moulded clay baked to hardness, from 5th century B.C.

941. τοιοῦτος, τοιαύτη, τοιοῦτον: "SUCH":

This pronoun is a combination of τοι and οὗτος. τοι is kept unchanged while οὗτος is declined as usual, but with the omission of the initial τ and the addition of ν in the nominative and accusative neuter singular. E.g., fem. dat. pl. = τοιαύτῃσ(ι); neut. acc. pl. = τοιαῦτα.

942. WORD STUDY

ETHER (the upper air in ancient thought, conceived of as 'burning' with the sun's heat; in philosophy and science, a hypothetical all-pervading medium throughout the universe, carrying the wave-vibrations of light, heat, electricity, radio, etc.; a volatile liquid which burns furiously), ETHEREAL (like the upper air: light, airy, heavenly).

943.

MEMORIZE:

ἀνάσσω, ἀνάξω, ἄναξα   I am lord of, I reign

ἄφαρ [adv.]   straightway, at once

ἐξ-εναρίζω, -εναρίξω, -ενάριξα   I strip (off); I kill

Θήβη, -ης [also pl.] [f.]   Thebes

944.   TEXT

The Tragedy of Oedipus

μητέρα τ' Οἰδιπόδαο ἴδον, καλὴν Ἐπικάστην,

610   ἣ μέγα ἔργον ἔρεξεν ἀιδρείῃσι νόοιο

γημαμένη ᾧ υἷι· ὁ δ' ὃν πατέρ' ἐξεναρίξας

γῆμεν· ἄφαρ δ' ἀνάπυστα θεοὶ θέσαν ἀνθρώποισιν.

ἀλλ' ὁ μὲν ἐν Θήβῃ πολυηράτῳ ἄλγεα πάσχων

Καδμείων ἤνασσε θεῶν ὀλοὰς διὰ βουλάς·

615   ἡ δ' ἔβη εἰς Ἀΐδαο πυλάρταο κρατεροῖο,

ἁψαμένη βρόχον αἰπὺν ἀφ' ὑψηλοῖο μελάθρου,

ᾧ ἄχεϊ σχομένη· τῷ δ' ἄλγεα κάλλιπ' ὀπίσσω

πολλὰ μάλ', ὅσσα τε μητρὸς ἐρινύες ἐκτελέουσιν.

ἀϊδρείη, -ης [f.] ignorance	καλ-λείπω = κατα-λείπω
ἀνά-πυστος, -ον known, revealed	μέλαθρον, -ου [n.] roof-beam
βρόχος, -ου [m] noose, halter	Οἰδιπόδης, -āο [m.] Oedipus
Ἐπικάστη, -ης Epicaste	πολυήρατος, -ον lovely, charming
Ἐρῑνύς, -ύος [m.] Erinys, Fury	πυλάρτης, -āο [m.] gate-keeper
Καδμεῖοι, -ων [m.] Cadmeans, Thebans	

945.   NOTES

610   *μέγα:* "great" in the sense of "monstrous."

ἀιδρείῃσι: the plural of abstract nouns is often used (where the English has the singular) to refer to the occasions or manifestations of the abstract idea, or to make it concrete. (Cp. line 502.)

611   *υἷι:* irregular dative singular.

612   *ἀνάπυστα:* i.e., the circumstances of the marriage.

616   *αἰπύν:* predicate, with its original meaning "on high."

617   *σχομένη:* with passive rather than with middle force.

946.   COMMENT

609   This incident is important because of the use made of the story it tells by the great tragedians in some of their best known plays, especially the *Oedipus Rex* of Sophocles. The story as developed by subsequent writers told how Laius, King of Thebes, was warned by an oracle that his son would ruin him. Despite the warning, he begot a son, but cast him out to perish. This child, Oedipus, saved by shepherds and grown to manhood without any suspicion of his origin, unwittingly killed his father in a fight resulting from an incident on the road. Proceeding thence

OEDIPUS AND THE SPHINX
A vase found in south Italy illustrates the famous myth of the monster near Thebes with body of a lion, head of a woman, eagle's wings, serpent's tail who challenged passersby to tell what creature having a single voice moves in the morning on four legs, on two at noon, and three in the evening. She killed all who could not answer the riddle. Oedipus thought it out: MAN, who crawls on all fours as an infant, walks on two legs as adult, adds a staff in old age. The Sphinx then committed suicide, and Oedipus the savior of Thebes was acclaimed the king.

to Thebes, he cleverly rid the city of a destructive monster, the Sphinx, and as his reward was given the widowed queen Epicaste or Jocasta as his wife. The queen, of course, was actually his mother, and when at last the dreadful incest was revealed through the shepherds, she could not endure the disgrace and remorse, and hanged herself. Oedipus, terribly shocked by the revelation and still more by the tragedy of his mother-wife, stabs out his eyes and is driven into exile. Notice, however, that the account of Homer makes no mention of his blindness in exile. Again, Homer implies that the incestuous marriage was discovered almost at once, but later writers speak of four children, whose lives as well are dogged by the avenging curse that has settled on their family. The Classical Tragedians creatively enlarged on the old myths.

618 Since Oedipus was the cause, even though unwillingly so, of his mother's death, it was thought that the avenging spirits which safeguarded maternal reverence would harass his mind and conscience for the rest of his days, even to the length of madness.

---

947. | MEMORIZE:

δηλέομαι, δηλήσομαι, δηλησάμην I harm   πῶυ, πώεος [n.] flock
κατα-κτείνω, etc. I slay, I kill   χέρσος, -ου [f.] dry land, land

948. TEXT

Agamemnon Tells His Fate

' Ἀτρεΐδη κύδιστε, ἄναξ ἀνδρῶν Ἀγάμεμνον,

620   τίς νύ σε κὴρ ἐδάμασσε τανηλεγέος θανάτοιο;

ἦε σέ γ' ἐν νήεσσι Ποσειδάων ἐδάμασσεν

ὄρσας ἀργαλέων ἀνέμων ἀμέγαρτον ἀυτμήν;

ἦέ σ' ἀνάρσιοι ἄνδρες ἐδηλήσαντ' ἐπὶ χέρσου

βοῦς περιταμνόμενον ἠδ' οἰῶν πώεα καλά,

625   ἠὲ περὶ πτόλιος μαχεούμενον ἠδὲ γυναικῶν;'

ὣ ἐφάμην, ὁ δέ μ' αὐτίκ' ἀμειβόμενος προσέειπεν·

' διογενὲς Λαερτιάδη, πολυμήχαν' Ὀδυσσεῦ,

οὔτ' ἐμέ γ' ἐν νήεσσι Ποσειδάων ἐδάμασσεν

ὄρσας ἀργαλέων ἀνέμων ἀμέγαρτον ἀυτμήν,

630   οὔτε μ' ἀνάρσιοι ἄνδρες ἐδηλήσαντ' ἐπὶ χέρσου,

ἀλλά μοι Αἴγισθος τεύξας θάνατόν τε μόρον τε

ἔκτα σὺν οὐλομένῃ ἀλόχῳ, οἰκόνδε καλέσσας,

δειπνίσσας, ὣς τίς τε κατέκτανε βοῦν ἐπὶ φάτνῃ.

Αἴγισθος, -ου Aegisthus (a Greek prince)
ἀμέγαρτος, -ον miserable; dire, dreadful
ἀνάρσιος, -ον unfriendly, hostile
Ἀτρεΐδης, -āο [m.] Atreus' son
δειπνίζω, —, δείπνισσα I entertain at dinner

κύδιστος, -η, -ον most glorious
μόρος, -ου [m.] fate, lot
οὐλόμενος, -η, -ον destructive, cursed
περι-τάμνω I surround (to drive away)
τανηλεγής, -ές bringing long woe
φάτνη, -ης [f.] crib, manger

949. NOTES

620 cf. line 555.

624 οἰῶν: the breathing mark is moved by poetic license.

625 μαχεούμενον: o is lengthened for the sake of the meter.

632 ἔκτᾰ: irregular athematic aorist third singular of κτείνω.

633 κατέκτανε: a gnomic aorist.

ROYAL PORTRAIT

Another of the several fascinating death masks in thin gold plate pressed onto a clay or wooden likeness of some great king at Mycenae and buried with him as a perpetual memorial. It was found by Schliemann in 1876 in the Grave Circle at Mycenae. The differences from the mask shown on page 182 of Book I confirm the reliable individuality of these noble portraits.

950.   COMMENT

619   The next figure to appear out of the gloom and to drink of the blood is the noble Agamemnon, "king of men," commander-in-chief at Troy. Odysseus is astounded to see him, for he had assumed that Agamemnon and his party had reached home safely.

622   A notable example of alliteration, for special effect.

623   There were no supply trains in those days to pour a steady stream of food and munitions to an expeditionary army. Instead, the army itself sent out regular foraging columns throughout the whole surrounding countryside and they simply took what they wanted even at the cost of human slaughter. Then, too, hardened and brutalized as soldiers inevitably become, they would at times storm and sack a city merely for personal plunder and the savage pleasure to be gained at the expense of its unfortunate women.

627   A formulaic line often used.

631   During the long absence of Agamemnon, Clytemnestra, his wife, lonely and brooding over the wrong done to her by her husband in sacrificing her daughter, Iphigeneia, to obtain fair winds for sailing to Troy, allowed her affections to be won by a certain Aegisthus. When word is brought that Agamemnon is coming home, they plot to receive him with great pomp and show of love, to welcome him as a returning hero at a great banquet, and then, when he is least suspecting, to cut down both him and his retinue. The whole story is dramatized with skill and remarkable force in the *Agamemnon* of Aeschylus, one of the greatest of all tragic dramas.

633   "Like an ox at the manger" emphasizes the disgrace and treachery of the blow.

951. | MEMORIZE:

ἀφνειός, (-ή), -όν wealthy [sometimes w. dat. or gen.]

γάμος, -ου [m.] marriage; marriage feast

οἰκτρός, -ή, -όν [alternative supl.: *οἴκτιστος*] pitiful, miserable

τράπεζα, - ης [f.] table

ὑσμίνη, -ης [f.] battle, conflict

φόνος, -ου [m.] death, slaughter

952. TEXT

Blood!

> ὣς θάνον οἰκτίστῳ θανάτῳ· περὶ δ' ἄλλοι ἑταῖροι
> 635 νωλεμέως κτείνοντο σύες ὣς ἀργιόδοντες,
> οἵ ῥά τ' ἐν ἀφνειοῦ ἀνδρὸς μέγα δυναμένοιο
> ἢ γάμῳ ἢ ἐράνῳ ἢ εἰλαπίνῃ τεθαλυίῃ.
> ἤδη μὲν πολέων φόνῳ ἀνδρῶν ἀντεβόλησας,
> μουνὰξ κτεινομένων καὶ ἐνὶ κρατερῇ ὑσμίνῃ·
> 640 ἀλλά κε κεῖνα μάλιστα ἰδὼν ὀλοφύραο θυμῷ,
> ὡς ἀμφὶ κρητῆρα τραπέζας τε πληθούσας
> κείμεθ' ἐνὶ μεγάρῳ, δάπεδον δ' ἅπαν αἵματι θῦεν.

ἀντι-βολέω, — ἀντι-βόλησα I take part in, I am present at

ἀργιόδους, -οντος white-tusked

δάπεδον, -ου [n.] pavement, floor, ground

εἰλαπίνη, -ης [f.] banquet

ἔρανος, -ου [m.] feast

θύω I run, I flow

μουνάξ singly, alone

νωλεμέως without pause, without flinching

πλήθω I am filled, I am full

953. NOTES

635 *ὣς:* translate before *σύες.*

636 *οἵ:* the verb is carried down from the preceding line.

ἐν: understand *δόμῳ.*

640 *μάλιστα:* with *ὀλοφύραο.*

ὀλοφύραο: contrary-to-fact in past time. The supposition is implied in *ἰδών.*

641 *ὡς:* "*how* we lay . . .''; explains *κεῖνα*

954. COMMENT

634-642 The vividness and terse vigor of this whole passage are noteworthy.

635-636 By use of an effective simile, Homer intensifies our feeling of the magnitude and ruthlessness of the slaughter. Notice that he speaks of a *very* rich man, — therefore one who would have large herds of swine and would think nothing of killing hundreds, if need be. He speaks, too, of a great feast, perhaps the wedding feast of his daughter, for which the lord would spare no expense or effort.

640 The point seems well taken. Killing in the heat and excitement of open battle would not arouse the same horror as cold-blooded, premeditated murder.

955. GENITIVE OF COMPARISON

In Latin, adjectives and adverbs of the comparative degree may take either the ablative of comparison or *quam* plus the nominative or accusative. E.g., Vergil might say:

Nihil est mutabilius femina, *or* quam femina (est).
Nothing is more changeable than a woman.

In Greek, the genitive is used in the same way. Thus Homer could say:

Οὐδέν ἐστι αἰνότερον ὑσμίνης, or *ἢ ὑσμίνη (ἐστίν)*
Nothing is more dreadful than a battle.

956. WORD STUDY

TRAPEZOID, TRAPEZIUM (geometrical plane quadrilaterals looking something like a 'small table'); TRAPEZE (a swinging bar for exercise, forming, along with its ropes and support, a table-shaped area).

ACHILLES QUARRELS WITH AGAMEMNON

This mosaic from Pompeii visualized the opening of the *Iliad*—how Achilles, furious over many insults to his honor and other injustices threatens to run his sword through Agamemnon the Commander in Chief of the Greeks at Troy, but is held back by Athena, who represents divine influence on conscience and emotions.

LESSON 159

957. | MEMORIZE:

ἀεικής, -ές unseemly, shameful
αἰνός, -ή, -όν dreadful, terrible
ἀκούω, ἀκούσομαι, ἄκουσα I hear
   [sometimes w. gen.]
ἔξοχα [adv.] chiefly, above the rest
ἐρείδω, ἐρείσω, ἔρεισα I rest; I lean;
   I press

κουρίδιος, -η, -ον wedded
ὄψ, ὀπός [f.] voice
πόσις, -ιος [m.] husband
προτί or *ποτί* = *πρός*
Πρίαμος, -ου Priam [king of Troy]
στόμα, -ατος [n] mouth
τοιοῦτος, τοιαύτη, τοιοῦτον such

958. TEXT

The Disgrace of Womanhood

οἰκτροτάτην δ᾽ ἤκουσα ὄπα Πριάμοιο θυγατρὸς
Κασσάνδρης, τὴν κτεῖνε Κλυταιμνήστρη δολόμητις
645 ἀμφ᾽ ἐμοί, αὐτὰρ ἐγὼ ποτὶ γαίῃ χεῖρας ἀείρων
βάλλον ἀποθνήσκων περὶ φασγάνῳ· ἡ δὲ κυνῶπις
νοσφίσατ᾽, οὐδέ μοι ἔτλη ἰόντι περ εἰς Ἀίδαο
χερσὶ κατ᾽ ὀφθαλμοὺς ἑλέειν σύν τε στόμ᾽ ἐρεῖσαι.
ὣς οὐκ αἰνότερον καὶ κύντερον ἄλλο γυναικός
650 ἤ τις δὴ τοιαῦτα μετὰ φρεσὶν ἔργα βάληται·
οἷον δὴ καὶ κείνη ἐμήσατο ἔργον ἀεικὲς
κουριδίῳ τεύξασα φόνον πόσι᾽· ἦ τοι ἔφην γε
ἀσπάσιος παίδεσσιν ἰδὲ δμώεσσιν ἐμοῖσιν
οἴκαδ᾽ ἐλεύσεσθαι· ἡ δ᾽ ἔξοχα λυγρὰ ἰδυῖα
655 οἷ τε κατ᾽ αἶσχος ἔχευε καὶ ἐσσομένῃσιν ὀπίσσω
θηλυτέρῃσι γυναιξί, καὶ ἥ κ᾽ εὐεργὸς ἔῃσιν.᾽

αἶσχος, -εος [n.] shame, dishonor
ἀπο-θνήσκω, etc. I die
ἀσπάσιος, -η, -ον welcome, delightful
δολόμητις, -ιος wily
ἐνεργός, -όν well-doer, upright
θηλυτέρη, -ης [adj.] female
Κασσάνδρη, -ης Cassandra

Κλυταιμνήστρη, -ης Clytemnestra
  [wife of Agamemnon]
κύντερος, -η, -ον more shameless
  (more dog-like)
κυνῶπις, -ιδος shameless (dog-eyed)
νοσφίζομαι, —, νοσφισάμην I turn
  away (from)

959. NOTES

643 *οἰκτροτάτην:* with predicate idea. "The most pitiful thing I heard was the voice . . ."

645-6 ". . . but raising my hands (in supplication) I dropped them as I lay dying on the ground with the sword through me."

648 *κατ':* w. *ἐλέειν* = "to close."

    σύν: adv., "to press together."

649 *οὐκ:* understand *ἐστίν.*

650 *βάληται:* i.e., "considers." (cp. Latin "jacto").

651 *οἷον δὴ καί:* "such as the shameless deed (for example) which . . ."

653 *ἀσπάσιος:* if the subject of the infinitive is the same as that of the main verb, it and its modifiers are kept in the nominative case in Greek.

654 *ἰδυῖα:* shortened from *εἰδυῖα.*

655 *κατ';* with *ἔχευε,* which it merely strengthens.

    ἐσσομένῃσιν: future participle of *εἰμί.*

656 *ἔῃσιν:* an older form of *ᾗ.* The understood antecedent of *ἥ* is *κείνη.*

960. COMMENT

644 Men are supposed to be particularly obtuse and conceited in the way they take for granted the loving devotion, loyalty, and self-sacrifice of their wives. However that may be, we cannot help but marvel at the self-assurance with which Agamemnon openly brings home with him his concubine, Cassandra. A woman of the strong type of Clytemnestra was not likely to fall upon her neck in welcome with anything less than a knife.

649 "The female of the species is more deadly than the male," Kipling put it, and even the gentle Vergil has a god declare, "A woman is always a fickle and an inconsistent creature" (*Varium et mutabile semper femina:* 4.569). To what lengths a woman will go in jealousy and betrayed love is nowhere perhaps better expressed than in the *Medea* of Euripides, to which, in fact, the Dido episode in Vergil is thought to be much in debt.

656 Even a good woman, Agamemnon says, will always feel shame to be of the same sex as his "doglike" wife.

961. WORD STUDY

CALLIOPE (a 'fair-voiced' musical instrument operated by steam and a keyboard); — ASPASIA (a woman's name).

962. MEMORIZE:

γλυκερός, -ή, -όν sweet	*μήν* [a stronger form of *μέν*] truly, indeed
μενεαίνω, —, μενέηνα I desire eagerly;	*νέφος, -εος* [n.] cloud
I rage	*σκιόεις, -εσσα, -εν* shadowy

963. TEXT

Tantalizing

καὶ μὴν Τάνταλον εἰσεῖδον κρατέρ᾽ ἄλγε᾽ ἔχοντα
ἑσταότ᾽ ἐν λίμνῃ· ἡ δὲ προσέπλαζε γενείῳ·
στεῦτο δὲ διψάων, πιέειν δ᾽ οὐκ εἶχεν ἑλέσθαι·
660 ὁσσάκι γὰρ κύψει᾽ ὁ γέρων πιέειν μενεαίνων,
τοσσάχ᾽ ὕδωρ ἀπολέσκετ᾽ ἀναβροχέν, ἀμφὶ δὲ ποσσὶν
γαῖα μέλαινα φάνεσκε, καταζήνασκε δὲ δαίμων.
δένδρεα δ᾽ ὑψιπέτηλα κατὰ κρῆθεν χέε καρπόν,
ὄγχναι καὶ ῥοιαὶ καὶ μηλέαι ἀγλαόκαρποι
665 συκέαι τε γλυκεραὶ καὶ ἐλαῖαι τηλεθάουσαι·
τῶν ὁπότ᾽ ἰθύσει᾽ ὁ γέρων ἐπὶ χερσὶ μάσασθαι,
τὰς δ᾽ ἄνεμος ῥίπτασκε ποτὶ νέφεα σκιόεντα

ἀγλαόκαρπος, -ον of splendid fruit, luxuriant	*μαίομαι, —, μασάμην* (w. *ἐπὶ*) I lay hold of
ἀνα-βρόχω, aor. pass. *ἀνα-βρόχην* I swallow down	*μηλέη, -ης* [f.] apple tree
γένειον, -ου [n.] chin	*ὄγχνη, -ης* [f.] pear-tree
διψάω I thirst	*ὁσσάκι* [adv.] as often as
ἐλαίη, -ης [f.] olive-tree	*προσ-πλάζω* I beat on
ἰθύω, —, ἴθυσα I am eager, I strive	*ῥοιή, -ῆς* [f.] pomegranate
κατ-αζαίνω, —, κατ-άζηνα I make dry	*στεῦμαι* I press forward
κρῆθεν from above on the head	*συκέη, -ης* [f.] fig-tree
κύπτω, —, κύψα I stoop, I bend over	*Τάνταλος, -ου* Tantalus
λίμνη, -ης [f.] lake, water	*τηλεθάω* I flourish
	τοσσάκι [adv.] so often
	ὑψιπέτηλος, -ον with lofty foliage

964. NOTES

658 *ἑσταότ᾽:* perfect active participle of *ἵσταμαι;* two syllables, by synezesis.
659 *εἶχεν: ἔχω* with the infinitive sometimes means "I have the ability, I can."
665 *συκέαι: εαι* is scanned as one syllable by synezesis.

965. COMMENT

657 Looking through the gloomy portals of Hades, Odysseus makes out several notorious sinners who have been condemned to a special punishment for their crimes. The first is Tantalus. He is said to have revealed the secrets of the gods and to have stolen nectar and ambrosia from

TANTALUS

their table. Cicero says that he was punished for his intemperance and assumptions of grandeur ("ob scelera animique impotentiam et superbiloquentiam," *Tusc.* 4.16.35).

658 The agony of frustration engendered by the water actually lapping against his chin and almost touching his parched and thirst-blackened lips, and by the juicy, tree-ripe fruit blown by the wind almost into his mouth is a vivid picture of the origin of our word "tantalize."

666 Though knowing from previous attempts repeated over and over again that he will not be able to grasp the elusive fruit, he cannot restrain himself from trying again, and then once more, with more quickness or with more craft, only to see the branches tossed lightly up out of his reach as effectively as if they were the clouds themselves.

966. WORD STUDY

MELON (a fruit like a large 'apple'); — SYCAMORE (a tree of the fig-mulberry variety), SYCO-PHANT ('one who reveals the figs,' an informant; a flatterer—the origin of both meanings is now lost); — TANTALIZE (to torment by arousing hopes, then dashing them).

---

967. MEMORIZE:

κάρη, καρή(α)τος or *κρᾱ́(α)τος*
[n.] head
κονίη, -ης [f.] dust
κυλίνδω I roll

λᾶας, λᾶος [acc. *λᾶαν*; m.] stone
λόφος, -ου [m.] crest, summit
ὠθέω, ὤσω, ὦσα I push

---

968. TEXT

Eternal Frustration

> καὶ μὴν Σίσυφον εἰσεῖδον κρατέρ' ἄλγε' ἔχοντα
> λᾶαν βαστάζοντα πελώριον ἀμφοτέρῃσιν.
> 670 ἦ τοι ὁ μὲν σκηριπτόμενος χερσίν τε ποσίν τε
> λᾶαν ἄνω ὤθεσκε ποτὶ λόφον· ἀλλ' ὅτε μέλλοι
> ἄκρον ὑπερβαλέειν, τότ' ἀποστρέψασκε κραταιίς·
> αὖτις ἔπειτα πέδονδε κυλίνδετο λᾶας ἀναιδής.
> αὐτὰρ ὅ γ' ἂψ ὤσασκε τιταινόμενος, κατὰ δ' ἱδρὼς
> 675 ἔρρεεν ἐκ μελέων, κονίη δ' ἐκ κρατὸς ὀρώρει.

ἀναιδής, -ές shameless, pitiless
ἄνω [adv.] up, upwards
ἀπο-στρέφω, —, ἀπό-στρεψα
  I turn back
βαστάζω I lift, I bear
ἱδρώς, -ῶτος [m.] sweat

κραταιίς [nom. only] [f.] mighty force
πέδον, -ου [n.] earth, (lower) ground
Σίσυφος, -ου Sisyphus
σκηρίπτομαι I brace myself
τιταίνω I stretch, [mid.] I strive
ὑπερ-βάλλω, etc. I throw over

---

969. NOTES

669 *ἀμφοτέρῃσιν:* understand *χερσίν.*
675 *κρατός:* genitive of *κάρη.*

---

970. COMMENT

970 Sisyphus, the next victim of divine justice seen by Odysseus, was conceived as the type of the cunning man. He is said (by Theognis, an early lyric poet) to have devised an escape from Hades, but was brought back and given the punishment described here.

673 *ἀναιδής:* A bold adjective, attributing to the stone a personal malicious satisfaction in rolling back down. Still, such personification is a common phenomenon. Golfers have been known to break a club into small bits in punishment for missing an important shot, and gamblers not infrequently plead with the ivory cubes to "come seven!".

Note this line as an instance of how the meter can reflect and enhance the sense. If you read it aloud several times, you can almost hear the rock tumbling and bouncing down the slope and coming to a jolting stop. Successful poets and songwriters must develop a strong sense for the sound and rhythm of words. The tone-quality of a poem is to be felt, and is difficult to analyze without seeming to exaggerate. To appreciate it, try to listen to the music of the lines, as well as to their sense, when reading poetry. Compare, for example, these two lines from Vergil:

and
monstrum horrendum informe ingens cui lumen ademptum
quadrupedante putrem sonitu quatit ungula campum.

If you have read them aloud, you will not be surprised to learn that the first describes the blinded Cyclops lumbering down the mountain, and that the second pictures a colt prancing across a plain. Or again, the special "sound-effects" in this line from Poe's *Raven* are not merely accidental:

And the silken, sad, uncertain rustling of each purple curtain.

674 The eagerness and persistence with which Sisyphus continued to work are probably to be explained on the ground of some belief or even certainty on his part that, if he ever pushed the rock over the brink of the hill, he would be allowed to effect a second, permanent escape.

971. WORD STUDY

CYLINDER (a hollow 'roller-like' vessel); — APOSTROPHE (a comma-like symbol indicating omission of a letter, possessive case, etc.; a figure of speech in which one 'turns aside' to address an absent person as though present).

SISYPHUS

972. | MEMORIZE:

δεσμός, -οῦ [m.]   bond
θεά, -ᾶς [f.]   goddess
λειμών, -ῶνος [m.]   meadow
μετ-αυδάω   I speak among

μῡθέομαι, μῡθήσομαι, μῡθησάμην   I relate, I say
πιέζω, πιέσ(σ)ω, πίεσα   I press; I oppress
Σειϝήν, -ῆνος [f.]   Siren

As the myriad shades of the dead began to crowd around them, Odysseus and his men became anxious and afraid that some evil might befall them. Accordingly they hurried on to their ship and, with a fair wind, soon came back to the island of Circe. After only a day's rest, they set off again with abundant provisions supplied by the goddess and with detailed instructions regarding their journey. Shortly after the start, Odysseus calls together his crew.

973.   TEXT

"Forewarned Is Forearmed"

676   δὴ τότ᾽ ἐγὼν ἑτάροισι μετηύδων ἀχνύμενος κῆρ·
' ὦ φίλοι, οὐ γὰρ χρὴ ἕνα ἴδμεναι οὐδὲ δύ᾽ οἴους
θέσφαθ᾽, ἄ μοι Κίρκη μυθήσατο, δῖα θεάων·
ἀλλ᾽ ἐρέω μὲν ἐγών, ἵνα εἰδότες ἤ κε θάνωμεν
680   ἤ κεν ἀλευάμενοι θάνατον καὶ κῆρα φύγοιμεν.
Σειρήνων μὲν πρῶτον ἀνώγει θεσπεσιάων
φθόγγον ἀλεύασθαι καὶ λειμῶν᾽ ἀνθεμόεντα.
οἶον ἔμ᾽ ἠνώγει ὄπ᾽ ἀκουέμεν· ἀλλά με δεσμῷ
δήσατ᾽ ἐν ἀργαλέῳ, ὄφρ᾽ ἔμπεδον αὐτόθι μίμνω,
685   ὀρθὸν ἐν ἱστοπέδῃ, ἐκ δ᾽ αὐτοῦ πείρατ᾽ ἀνάψαι.
εἰ δέ κε λίσσωμαι ὑμέας λῦσαί τε κελεύω,
ὑμεῖς δὲ πλεόνεσσι τότ᾽ ἐν δεσμοῖσι πιέζειν.'

ἀν-άπτω, etc.   I fasten
ἀνθεμόεις, -εντος   flowery
ἱστοπέδη, -ης [f.]   mast-step
πεῖραρ, -ατος [n.]   rope

974.   NOTES

677   χρή: "it is (not) befitting."
680   φύγοιμεν: a shift to the optative to show the less probability of escaping.
687   πλεόνεσσι: for πλειόνεσσι.

975. COMMENT

679 There would be a certain satisfaction in knowing the danger they must face, and, if they must die, in knowing at least the cause of their death.

681 The Sirens were two beautiful, honey-voiced sea-maidens who lived on an island past which the ship's journey lay. They were accustomed, with their far-reaching, intriguing song, to lure unfortunate mariners to their death on the island.

683 Circe permitted Odysseus himself to hear the Sirens, possibly to convince him of the truth of her warning to shun them, to safeguard him against unforeseen trouble from another quarter, and to satisfy his natural curiosity.

686 Realistically, Odysseus distrusts his strength of will to resist the powerful appeal of the Sirens.

687 Perhaps to hold our attention and curiosity, Homer does not here say how Odysseus alone is to hear the Sirens' song, while his companions do not.

976. WORD STUDY

SIREN (a shrill moaning whistle); a seductive temptress.

A SHOEMAKER'S SHOP
An interesting scene: a lady (with big feet!) is being measured for custom built shoes while her worried husband tries to supervise the work. Instruments of the trade are also represented.

977. MEMORIZE:

ἀν-ίστημι, etc.   I stand up

ἀπήμων, -ον   safe; propitious

ἐπ-είγω   I drive on; [mid.:]   I hasten

κοιμάω, κοιμήσω, κοίμησα   I put to sleep; I calm

κῦμα, -ατος [n.]   wave

πιφαύσκω   I make known

τόφρα   so long, meanwhile

978. TEXT

A Dangerous Calm

ἦ τοι ἐγὼ τὰ ἕκαστα λέγων ἑτάροισι πίφαυσκον·

τόφρα δὲ καρπαλίμως ἐξίκετο νηῦς εὐεργὴς

690   Σειρήνων ἐς νῆσον ἔπειγε γὰρ οὖρος ἀπήμων.

αὐτίκ᾽ ἔπειτ᾽ ἄνεμος μὲν ἐπαύσατο, ἡ δὲ γαλήνη

ἔπλετο νηνεμίη, κοίμησε δὲ κύματα δαίμων.

ἀνστάντες δ᾽ ἕταροι νεὸς ἱστία μηρύσαντο

καὶ τὰ μὲν ἐν νηὶ γλαφυρῇ θέσαν, οἱ δ᾽ ἐπ᾽ ἐρετμὰ

695   ἑζόμενοι λεύκαινον ὕδωρ ξεστῇς ἐλάτῃσιν.

γαλήνη, -ης [f.]   a calm

ἐλάτη, -ης [f.]   pine (tree); pine oar

ἐξ-ικνέομαι, etc.   I arrive (at), I come

λευκαίνω   I make white

μηρύομαι, —, μηρῡσάμην   I furl, fold

νηνεμίη, -ης   windless

ξεστός, -ή, -όν   hewn, polished

979. NOTES

694   τά: the sail.

980. COMMENT

691   It would seem that the sudden stopping of the wind was somehow caused by the enchanted island of the Sirens. On a calm sea with absolutely no wind, their voices would be heard clearly; and since the sailors must row past, the sea-maidens would have longer time to work their spell on them.

981. WORD STUDY

COMA (a deep sleep).

THE SIRENS' ISLES

In ancient times these two small islands in the Tyrrhenian Sea south of Capri were identified with the location of the mythical Sirens. They are known as I Galli. This is a telescopic view from along the famous Amalfi Drive.

REVIEW

982. Go over again Lessons 154–163; make sure now that you have really mastered them. Here are a few suggestions for your review:

1. *Vocabulary:* Check your mastery of the 68 new memory words.
2. *Text:* Reread the 108 lines of text, making sure you recognize all the forms.
3. *Story:*

    a. Tell briefly the story of Oedipus.
    b. What was the fate of Agamemnon?
    c. What were the punishments of Tantalus and Sisyphus?
    d. Who were the Sirens? Who warned Odysseus against them?

4. *Criticism:*

    a. How does Homer describe death and the afterlife? Where do you think he is right? Where wrong? Why would Odysseus seem surprised at what he finds out about the nature of the world beyond?
    b. Do you think it is characteristic of the Greeks that the punishments here described have a definite psychological emphasis? Give your reasons.
    c. Is Agamemnon fair in his condemnation of womanhood?

5. *Grammar:* Review

    a. οὗτος.
    b. τοιοῦτος.
    c Gen. of comparison.

6. *Composition:* Put into Greek

    a. Who said that there is nothing more shameful and dreadful than such a (τοιοῦτος) woman?
    b. When he had said this, he stood up and made known everything to his eager men.
    c. Meanwhile, the ship, urged on by the winds, hastened to the great island of these Sirens.

983. GREEK PAINTING

As might be expected, few actual Greek paintings have survived the destructive forces of time, weather, and war down to our own days, except the decorations on ancient vases—which have been preserved in large numbers. Ordinary paintings on wood, canvas, walls of buildings have largely perished with the impermanent surfaces into which they were worked. Some highly interesting wall-frescoes from early Crete, Thera, Tiryns, etc. are still extant, however, and show a striking liveliness of conception and fine taste in beautiful color-contrasts. There are also a few portraits of individuals by Greek artists which have been found in almost perfect condition in Egypt; and many of the extant mosaics of Pompeii or Herculaneum are in themselves but marble copies of famous Greek paintings. Most of our information in the matter, however, is had from the descriptions of ancient writers on Greek art, particularly Pliny, Lucian, and Pausanias.

It is known that the first great painter of Greece was Polygnotus, who in the early fifth century B.C. won fame for his simple, dignified, lifelike rendering of scenes from history or mythology. Toward the end of the same century, Apollodorus introduced effective shading, while the great masters Zeuxis and Parrhasius worked out the technique of highlighting, beautiful tones,

A MYSTIC INITIATION

The climactic scene in a series of episodes representing a woman's initiation into the Dionysiac Mysteries religious ceremony, still on the wall of the Villa of Mysteries at Pompeii where some great Greek artist painted it around 50 B.C. for a wealthy home. The initiate, at the center, is being tested by flagellation at the hands of a winged spirit and in the scene at the right dancing in ecstasy on completion of the privileged rite. The standing woman holding a long rod has a face of remarkable refined beauty superior to practically anything surviving from ancient art.

and a remarkable realism—in fact, it is said that the birds pecked at some grapes which Zeuxis had drawn, so natural did they seem. The supreme painter of antiquity, though, was Apelles, who lived in the fourth century B.C. and was famous for the exceptional charm of his work, due to the fusion of high technical skill, beautiful arrangement of material, fine color shading, and the bright play of his artistic imagination. One of his most celebrated works was a splendid portrait of Alexander the Great. Later painters were less gifted, but they advanced the principle of perspective and natural background to a high level of perfection; they preferred still-life scenes and landscapes to the more vigorous interests of the older masters in human or mythological themes.

A similar progressive development can be traced in the Greek art of vase painting. Early examples of decorated pottery in Greece, from the ninth and eighth centuries before Christ, usually have geometrical patterns of triangles, circles, angular lines, or rather clumsy representations of men and animals. In the seventh century, there is noticeable a strong orientalizing influence, due to contact with Phoenician merchant traders, leading to depiction of mythological animals such as griffins or winged bulls, and to a crowding of little rosettes, dots, or other ornaments into every vacant space of the surface. These figures were commonly painted in black on a red background, but later yellow, white, green, and other colors were also added, to give beautiful polychrome effects.

By the sixth century, however, the true Greek spirit asserted itself in a shift to human themes, taken from mythology or actual daily life, and a steady development of ever more beautiful and elevated decoration technique. There is naturally a marked similarity with contemporary styles of sculpture, the "archaic" and "transitional" periods. The figures are stiff, angular, with long beards and sharp noses, more symbolic caricatures than serious attempts at realistic portraiture. They are arranged in groups of unified action, so that there is always a discernible story or plot or clear reference to some particular episode of poetry or myth. There is usually also some geometric ornamentation as border or background or filler of empty spaces. As the drawing at this period is uniformly black on the natural red surface of the baked clay, these are known as "black-figure" vases. Not a few, especially toward the end of this phase, are strikingly beautiful and show admirable draughtsmanship. Exekias is the most famous of vase painters of this period. (See the example of his work in our other volume, p. 163.)

The peak of ancient vase painting was reached in the next stage, lasting throughout the fifth century and half of the fourth. The greatest masters of the art were Duris, Euphronius, Pistoxenus, and Brygos, many of whose original works are still extant as precious exhibits in the world's museums. This was the period of "red-figure" vases, since about 530 B.C. there was a sudden and universal change-over of technique, whereby the background was painted on in black or pure white, leaving the design in the soft reddish glow of the unpainted clay, as being closer to the natural color of the body. The workmanship parallels that of sculpture in its "classical" period, and shares with it the emphasis on noble conception, serene, idealized human warmth, great simplicity and restraint, delicate drapery of the garments, and fine precision of outline with splendid mastery of details and a refined anatomical naturalness. There is little if any filling in of open spaces, no crowding on of unnecessary ornamentation. Lettered speech is often printed near the heads of the principal figure, and many of the vases are signed with their maker's name, in justifiable pride of accomplishment. Besides their great beauty, these vases also teach us much about the features and conditions of Greek life, and are an admirable supplement to a study of ancient literature.

Vase painting in the Hellenistic period, after 325 B.C., continued to possess fine detail and execution, but became more lavish and modernistic. At this stage, the figures were often moulded in raised relief before being painted, to seem more real. Classical Greece has bequeathed the world a rich, indeed unparalleled, heritage of beauty. Of those treasures of Greek culture still open for our enjoyment and profit, these magnificent vases are deservedly among the most admired.

DEIFIED HERCULES
When in the late sixth century B.C. Greek painters developed a new technique of painting the background black while leaving figures in red much improved subtlety of detail was possible and the over-all effect more free and life-like. Here we see Hercules admitted among the gods of Olympus in reward for his good deeds to men and his divine parentage (Zeus for father). He is on a banquet couch, holding an elegant wine cup (kantharos) while Athena in her helmet welcomes him to the divine abode.

A HEAVENLY CHARIOT

A splendid example of late-sixth-century black-figure vase decoration. It shows Leto, mother of Apollo and Artemis, mounting a chariot, probably for a visit to earth. Apollo stands by with his lyre. Details are scratched through the black glaze down to the natural red clay, with some over-paint in red and for ivory and femine flesh, white.

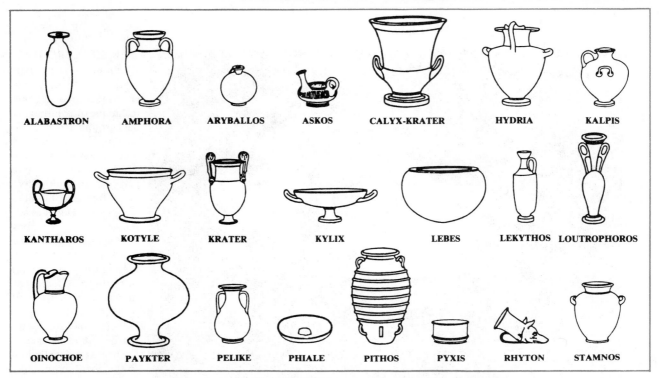

ALABASTRON   AMPHORA   ARYBALLOS   ASKOS   CALYX-KRATER   HYDRIA   KALPIS

KANTHAROS   KOTYLE   KRATER   KYLIX   LEBES   LEKYTHOS   LOUTROPHOROS

OINOCHOE   PAYKTER   PELIKE   PHIALE   PITHOS   PYXIS   RHYTON   STAMNOS

SHAPES OF GREEK VASES

984. MEMORIZE:

ἀλείφω, ἀλείψω, ἄλειψα I anoint, I daub
ἀοιδή, -ῆς [f.] song
αὐγή, -ῆς [f.] light; ray
ἰαίνω, —, ἴηνα I warm, I melt, I cheer

κηρός, -οῦ [m.] wax
ὁμοῦ together, at the same time
οὖας, -ατος [dat. pl. also ὦσι] [n.] ear
ῥίμφα [adv.] swiftly
στιβαρός, -ή, -όν stout, strong

985. TEXT

Extreme Measures

696 αὐτὰρ ἐγὼ κηροῖο μέγαν τροχὸν ὀξέι χαλκῷ
τυτθὰ διατμήξας χερσὶ στιβαρῇσι πίεζον·
αἶψα δ᾽ ἰαίνετο κηρός, ἐπεὶ κέλετο μεγάλη ἲς
Ἠελίου τ᾽ αὐγὴ Ὑπεριονίδαο ἄνακτος·
700 ἐξείης δ᾽ ἑτάροισιν ἐπ᾽ οὔατα πᾶσιν ἄλειψα.
οἱ δ᾽ ἐν νηί μ᾽ ἔδησαν ὁμοῦ χεῖράς τε πόδας τε
ὀρθὸν ἐν ἱστοπέδῃ, ἐκ δ᾽ αὐτοῦ πείρατ᾽ ἀνῆπτον·
αὐτοὶ δ᾽ ἑζόμενοι πολιὴν ἅλα τύπτον ἐρετμοῖς.
ἀλλ᾽ ὅτε τόσσον ἀπῆμεν, ὅσον τε γέγωνε βοήσας,
705 ῥίμφα διώκοντες, τὰς δ᾽ οὐ λάθεν ὠκύαλος νηῦς
ἐγγύθεν ὀρνυμένη, λιγυρὴν δ᾽ ἔντυνον ἀοιδήν·

ἀν-άπτω, etc. I fasten
δια-τμήγω, —, διά-τμηξα I cut up, I separate
ἐντΰνω I prepare; I strike up
ἱστοπέδη, -ης [f.] mast-step
λιγυρός, -ή, -όν clear-toned

πεῖραρ, -ατος [n.] rope
τροχός, -οῦ [m.] wheel; round mass
τυτθός, (-ή), -όν small
Ὑπερῑονίδης, -αο = Ὑπερΐων
ὠκύαλος, -ον swift on the sea, swift sailing

986. NOTES

697 τυτθά: (adv.) "into small pieces."
704 τόσσον: so great a distance. γέγωνε: recall note on line 333 (#769).
705 διώκοντες: here with causative sense (understand νῆα) = driving along the ship.

ODYSSEUS AND THE SIRENS

This mosaic from a Roman site in north Africa is indication of how widely the Homeric story was known and admired.

987. COMMENT

697 The pressure exerted by his hands, along with the hot rays of the sun, would easily cause the wax to grow soft.

700 Not until now does the poet explicitly say Odysseus prepared the wax. It is not, of course, necessary for him to belabor the point that thus the crewmen will not be able to listen to the voices of the Sirens.

705 Any hopes Odysseus may have entertained that his ship would be able to slip by without attracting the attention of the deadly Sirens are soon dashed. The Sirens are on the alert and begin their enchanting tunes. He can only hope now that his strategy will work out as planned.

988. WORD STUDY

KEROSENE (an inflammable oil chemically related to wax).

989. MEMORIZE:

δεῦρο [adv.]   hither

κῦδος, -εος [n.]   honor, glory

μογέω, —, μόγησα   I toil, I suffer

990. TEXT

Song of the Sirens

' δεῦρ' ἄγ' ἰών, πολύαιν' Ὀδυσεῦ, μέγα κῦδος Ἀχαιῶν,

νῆα κατάστησον, ἵνα νωιτέρην ὄπ' ἀκούσῃς.

οὐ γάρ πώ τις τῇδε παρήλασε νηὶ μελαίῃ,

710   πρίν γ' ἡμέων μελίγηρυν ἀπὸ στομάτων ὄπ' ἀκοῦσαι,

ἀλλ' ὅ γε τερψάμενος νεῖται καὶ πλείονα εἰδώς·

ἴδμεν γάρ τοι πάνθ', ὅσ' ἐνὶ Τροίῃ εὑρείῃ

Ἀργεῖοι Τρῶές τε θεῶν ἰότητι μόγησαν,

ἴδμεν δ', ὅσσα γένηται ἐπὶ χθονὶ πουλυβοτείρῃ.'

715   ὣς φάσαν ἱεῖσαι ὄπα κάλλιμον· αὐτὰρ ἐμὸν κῆρ

ἤθελ' ἀκουέμεναι, λῦσαί τ' ἐκέλευον ἑταίρους

ὀφρύσι νευστάζων· οἱ δὲ προπεσόντες ἔρεσσον.

Ἀργεῖοι, -ων Argives, Greeks	νωΐτερος, -η, -ον our [of two only]
ἐρέσσω I row	παρ-ελαύνω, etc. I drive past, I sail
ἰότης, -ητος [f.] will, decree	past
καθ-ίστημι, etc. I stop, I station	πολύαινος, -ον much praised, glorious
κάλλιμος, -ον fair	πουλυβότειρα, -ης [adj.] feeding
μελίγηρυς, -υος [adj.] sweet-voiced	many, fruitful
νευστάζω I nod, I motion	προ-πίπτω, etc. bend forward

991. NOTES

707   ἄγ' = ἄγε: imperative of ἄγω used interjectionally: "Come!"

715   ἱεῖσαι: from ἱείς, ἱεῖσα, ἱέν, present active participle of ἵημι.

992. COMMENT

707 ff. The Sirens' song is craftily composed to appeal to the noble and intellectual Greek leader. The chief attraction they offer him is knowledge—new and exciting reports about the famous war in which he himself took part and about the heroes he had once known so well; secret, preternatural information to answer the constant questionings about the world of men and nature, always so full of wonders and mysteries. St. Paul, twelve centuries later, could still characterize the Greeks as "always desirous of hearing something new."

716 It seems a little strange to see Odysseus yearning to make a fool of himself while his companions, whom he usually has to cajole and restrain from ruining themselves, are now the checking and saving force. Nevertheless, the situation is really to the credit of Odysseus, since the restraining influence of his men was possible only through his healthy mistrust of his own powers of will.

PASSING THE SIRENS' ISLE

A famous vase (red-figured stamnos) showing Odysseus tied to the mast as his men row past the seductive Sirens, as Circe had warned. The artist is a bit free with details, however: three Sirens are shown, but Homer always speaks of them in the dual, therefore two. There may have been alternative versions of the story besides in Homer, which have influenced the artist here.

714 The song of the Sirens has been much admired. Cicero, for instance, greatly esteemed it and has thus translated it into Latin (*De Fin.* 5.18):

> O decus Argolicum, quin puppim flectis, Ulixe,
> Auribus ut nostros possis adgnoscere cantus?
> Nam nemo haec unquam est transvectus caerula cursu,
> Quin prius adstiterit vocum dulcedine captus;
> Post variis avido satiatus pectore musis
> Doctior ad patrias lapsus pervenerit oras.
> Nos grave certamen belli clademque tenemus,
> Graecia quam Troiae divino numine vexit;
> Omniaque e latis rerum vestigia terris.

The picture of one of the greatest of the Romans sitting some two thousand years ago and wrinkling his forehead as he works out a translation of this same passage that we are now translating should impress us with a sense of the continuity of our culture.

993. WORD STUDY

KUDOS (glory, fame, renown).

994. TEXT

Safety! — And New Peril

> αὐτίκα δ᾽ ἀνστάντες Περιμήδης Εὐρύλοχός τε
> πλείοσί μ᾽ ἐν δεσμοῖσι δέον μᾶλλόν τε πίεζον.
> 720 αὐτὰρ ἐπεὶ δὴ τάς γε παρήλασαν, οὐδ᾽ ἔτ᾽ ἔπειτα
> φθογγῆς Σειρήνων ἠκούομεν οὐδέ τ᾽ ἀοιδῆς,
> αἶψ᾽ ἀπὸ κηρὸν ἕλοντο ἐμοὶ ἐρίηρες ἑταῖροι,
> ὅν σφιν ἐπ᾽ ὠσὶν ἄλειψ᾽, ἐμέ τ᾽ ἐκ δεσμῶν ἀνέλυσαν.
> ἀλλ᾽ ὅτε δὴ τὴν νῆσον ἐλείπομεν, αὐτίκ᾽ ἔπειτα
> 725 καπνὸν καὶ μέγα κῦμα ἴδον καὶ δοῦπον ἄκουσα.
> τῶν δ᾽ ἄρα δεισάντων ἐκ χειρῶν ἔπτατ᾽ ἐρετμά,
> βόμβησαν δ᾽ ἄρα πάντα κατὰ ῥόον· ἔσχετο δ᾽ αὐτοῦ
> νηῦς, ἐπεὶ οὐκέτ᾽ ἐρετμὰ προήκεα χερσὶν ἔπειγον.
> αὐτὰρ ἐγὼ διὰ νηὸς ἰὼν ὤτρυνον ἑταίρους
> 730 μειλιχίοις ἐπέεσσι παρασταδὸν ἄνδρα ἕκαστον·

ἀνα-λῡ́ω, etc. I loose
βομβέω, —, βόμβησα I hum; I splash
δοῦπος, -ου [m.] thudding, roaring
καπνός, -οῦ [m.] smoke, vapor, mist
μᾶλλον [adv.] more, rather
παρασταδόν [adv.] standing beside, stepping up beside

παρ-ελαύνω, etc. I drive past, I row past
Περιμήδης, -αο Perimedes
προήκης, -ες sharpened, tapering
φθογγή, -ῆς [f.] = φθόγγος, -ου voice

995. NOTES

723 *ὠσίν:* apparently a contraction from *οὐατσίν.*
727 *κατὰ ῥόον:* "down into the water."

996. COMMENT

719 Faithful to his previous instructions, two of his companions get up and tie him still more securely despite his struggles to free himself and his efforts to order them to release him.

721 *ἠκούομεν:* He means, of course, when we were no longer *able* to hear them. The crew waited until they were so far past the island that there would be no possibility of the Sirens' voices carrying so far.

723 Once the actual temptation is removed, Odysseus recovers his normal self-discipline, and can be released without fear of his wishing to return to the island.

723 They are approaching now the north end of the perilous strait between Sicily and Italy. Already they can see the vapor and spray rising above the rocks and the rough water of the narrow channel, and can hear the booming of the pounding surf. With their small vessel confronted by the tremendous power of the sea, a feeling of helplessness comes over them.

729 Like a good captain, Odysseus must re-awaken in them their courage.

997. WORD STUDY

ANALYSIS (a breaking-up or 'loosening' of some complex object or problem into its component parts), ANALYTICAL.

998. | MEMORIZE:

(ἐ)έργω, ἔρξω, ἔρξα I keep off; I shut up
εἰλ(έ)ω, —, (ἔ)ελσα I confine; I check; [pass.:] I throng; I crouch
ἐκτός [adv.] outside, away from
ἐπι-τέλλω, —, ἐπί-τειλα I enjoin; I give orders to

κεῖσε [adv.] thither
μιμνήσκω, μνήσω, μνῆσα I remind; [mid.:] I remember [with gen.]
σκόπελος, -ου [m.] crag

999. TEXT

Odysseus, the Leader

731 ' ὦ φίλοι, οὐ γάρ πώ τι κακῶν ἀδαήμονές εἰμεν·
οὐ μέν δὴ τόδε μεῖζον ἔπι κακόν, ἢ ὅτε Κύκλωψ
εἴλει ἐνὶ σπῆι γλαφυρῷ κρατερῆφι βίηφιν·
ἀλλὰ καὶ ἔνθεν ἐμῇ ἀρετῇ, βουλῇ τε νοῷ τε,

735 ἐκφύγομεν, καί που τῶνδε μνήσεσθαι ὀίω.
νῦν δ᾽ ἄγεθ᾽, ὡς ἄν ἐγὼ εἴπω, πειθώμεθα πάντες.
ὑμεῖς μὲν κώπησιν ἁλὸς ῥηγμῖνα βαθεῖαν
τύπτετε κληΐδεσσιν ἐφήμενοι, αἴ κέ ποθι Ζεὺς
δώῃ τόνδε γ᾽ ὄλεθρον ὑπεκφυγέειν καὶ ἀλύξαι·

740 σοὶ δέ, κυβερνῆθ᾽, ὧδ᾽ ἐπιτέλλομαι· ἀλλ᾽ ἐνὶ θυμῷ
βάλλευ, ἐπεὶ νηὸς γλαφυρῆς οἰήια νωμᾷς.
τούτου μὲν καπνοῦ καὶ κύματος ἐκτὸς ἔεργε
νῆα, σὺ δὲ σκοπέλου ἐπιμαίεο, μή σε λάθησιν
κεῖσ᾽ ἐξορμήσασα καὶ ἐς κακὸν ἄμμε βάλησθα.'

ἀδαήμων, -ονος inexperienced, ignorant of
ἐκ-φεύγω, etc. I escape
ἐξ-ορμάω, etc. I rush forth
ἔφ-ημαι I sit at
καπνός, -οῦ [m.] smoke, vapor, mist

κώπη, -ης [f.] hilt (of sword), handle of an oar, oar
οἰήϊον, -ου [n.] rudder [pl. sometimes used for sg.]
ποθί ever, somehow
ῥηγμίς, -ῖνος [f.] surf; surging sea
ὑπ-εκ-φεύγω I flee out from under, I escape

1000. NOTES

732 *ἔπι:* a shortened form of *ἔπ-εστι* meaning "there is" or simply "is." (Notice the position of the pitch-mark.)

733 *εἴλει:* understand *ἡμέας.*

735 *μνήσεσθαι:* understand "we" as subject.

738 *δώῃ:* understand *ἡμῖν:* "grant us." The conditional clause has the idea, "with the hope that, etc."

743 *ἐπιμαίεο:* "keep the ship close to the crag lest it (the ship) etc."

1001. COMMENT

734 Odysseus is not boasting. He reminds them of his former exploit only in order to arouse them to action, if not in reliance on their own strength, then on the sagacity and invention of their leader.

735 A memorable line. They can remember, he tells them, the narrow escapes they have had before; these troubles, too, they will live to look back on and talk abut. Vergil brings out this thought even more clearly in his imitation of the passage (*Aen.* 1.198–203):

> O socii (neque enim ignari sumus ante malorum),
> O passi graviora, dabit deus his quoque finem.
> Vos et Scyllaeam rabiem penitusque sonantes
> accestis scopulos, vos et Cyclopia saxa
> experti: revocate animos, maestumque timorem
> mittite; forsan et haec olim meminisse iuvabit.

739 Notice, in this and many other places in the poem, how frequently the thought of the gods was in the minds of the Greeks, and how much they took for granted their dependence on the divine will and providence.

742 The situation is this. The narrow strait causes tricky currents which form a gigantic whirlpool near the Sicilian shore. On the opposite side, great, dangerous, knife-sharp crags jut threateningly into the water. Odysseus lays a grave command on his pilot to keep the ship as close as he safely can to the rocks, and to be constantly on the alert lest the ship veering suddenly too far out into the channel be gripped by the outer swirling waters of the monstrous vortex and be whirled to destruction.

ZEUS AND HERA
This decorative panel (metope) from the fine Temple "E" at Selinus in Sicily (early 5th century B.C.) presents the King of the Gods seated and his wife Hera standing before him. He is holding her arm as a sign of husbandly benevolence at the moment.

1002. WORD STUDY

ECTODERM (in biology, the 'outside skin' or wall of tissue of a cell or organism).

LESSON 169

1003. MEMORIZE:

θωρήσσω, —, θώρηξα   I arm
ἴκρια, -ων [n. pl.]   deck
ὄσσε [n. dual]   eyes

παπταίνω, —, πάπτηνα   I look
   about sharply (for)
Σκύλλη, -ης [f.]   Scylla
ὦκα   quickly, swiftly

1004. TEXT

Between Scylla —

745   ὣς ἐφάμην, οἱ δ᾽ ὦκα ἐμοῖς ἐπέεσσι πίθοντο.
         Σκύλλην δ᾽ οὐκέτ᾽ ἐμυθεόμην, ἄπρηκτον ἀνίην,
         μή πώς μοι δείσαντες ἀπολλήξειαν ἑταῖροι
         εἰρεσίης, ἐντὸς δὲ πυκάζοιεν σφέας αὐτούς.
         καὶ τότε δὴ Κίρκης μὲν ἐφημοσύνης ἀλεγεινῆς
750   λανθανόμην, ἐπεὶ οὔ τί μ᾽ ἀνώγει θωρήσσεσθαι·
         αὐτὰρ ἐγὼ καταδὺς κλυτὰ τεύχεα καὶ δύο δοῦρε
         μάκρ᾽ ἐν χερσὶν ἑλὼν εἰς ἴκρια νηὸς ἔβαινον
         πρῴρης· ἔνθεν γάρ μιν ἐδέγμην πρῶτα φανεῖσθαι
         Σκύλλην πετραίην, ἥ μοι φέρε πῆμ᾽ ἑτάροισιν.
755   οὐδέ πῃ ἀθρῆσαι δυνάμην, ἔκαμον δέ μοι ὄσσε
         πάντῃ παπταίνοντι πρὸς ἠεροειδέα πέτρην.

ἀθρέω, —, ἄθρησα   I see, I behold
ἀνίη -ης [f.]   grief, trouble, vexation
ἀπο-λλήγω, ἀπο-λλήξα   I cease from
ἄπρηκτος, -ον   unconquerable, un-
   avoidable
εἰρεσίη, -ης [f.]   rowing
ἐντός [adv.]   within, inside

ἐφημοσύνη, -ης [f.]   command
ἠεροειδής, -ές   hazy, misty
κατα-δύω, etc.   I sink; I put on
πετραῖος, -η, -ον   of the rock
πῃ   in any way, anywhere
πρῴρη, -ης [f.]   prow
πυκάζω   I hide, I cover

1005. NOTES

734 *οὐκέτ᾽:* "I didn't go on to mention Scylla," i.e., he added no details to the vague reference
    to σκοπέλου.
748 *ἐντός:* within the hold of the ship.
750 *οὐ:* Greek and Latin sometimes put the negative with the main verb although it really nega-
    tives the subordinate verb.
753 *ἐδέγμην:* an athematic aorist of δέχομαι with the sense "I expect."
755 *ἀθρῆσαι:* the understood object is μιν.

1006.   COMMENT

745   A good example of the necessity of responsible leadership and the good that it can accomplish.

746   Scylla was a fearsome monster dwelling in a cave amid the destructive rocks of the strait, and in fact was probably a personification of those rocks which had caused the death of so many sailors attempting to sail through. Circe had told him that the misshapen creature was hidden up to her middle in the cave, but that her multiple, exceedingly long necks, each surmounted by an awful head, were constantly stretched out to snatch up fishes, dolphins, or any larger creature that was unfortunate enough to come within her reach. No wonder Odysseus thought it better not to mention her in any more detail to his already jittery comrades!

749-750   Circe had warned him that it was hopeless to attempt any defence against the dread evil except flight, that it would be wiser to reconcile himself to losing a few men than, while trying to fight back, to double the number of victims by giving her a chance for a second onslaught. However, the warrior's heart of Odysseus would not permit him to stand passively by while his men were being attacked.

754   By getting a little ahead of his narrative Homer "foreshadows" the sickening end of his story.

SCYLLA'S ROCK

On the Italian side of the narrow strait between the mainland and Sicily north of Messina is this jutting crag which since ancient times has been considered the location of Scylla, neatly fitting Homer's story.

1007. | MEMORIZE:

ἑτέρωθι   on the other side   κυκάω, κυκήσω, κύκησα   I stir (up)
κοῖλος, -η, -ον   hollow   I confuse
κῡάνεος, -η, -ον   dark (blue)

CHARYBDIS
The swirling waters of the most famous of all whirlpools, in a modern interpretation.

1008. TEXT

— And Charybdis

ἡμεῖς μὲν στεινωπὸν ἀνεπλέομεν γοάοντες·
ἔνθεν μὲν Σκύλλη, ἑτέρωθι δὲ δῖα Χάρυβδις
δεινὸν ἀνερροίβδησε θαλάσσης ἁλμυρὸν ὕδωρ.
760 ἦ τοι ὅτ᾽ ἐξεμέσειε, λέβης ὣς ἐν πυρὶ πολλῷ
πᾶσ᾽ ἀναμορμύρεσκε κυκωμένη, ὑψόσε δ᾽ ἄχνη
ἄκροισι σκοπέλοισιν ἐπ᾽ ἀμφοτέροισιν ἔπιπτεν·
ἀλλ᾽ ὅτ᾽ ἀναβρόξειε θαλάσσης ἁλμυρὸν ὕδωρ,
πᾶσ᾽ ἔντοσθε φάνεσκε κυκωμένη, ἀμφὶ δὲ πέτρη
765 δεινὸν ἐβεβρύχει, ὑπένερθε δὲ γαῖα φάνεσκε
ψάμμῳ κυανέη· τοὺς δὲ χλωρὸν δέος ᾕρει.
ἡμεῖς μὲν πρὸς τὴν ἴδομεν δείσαντες ὄλεθρον·
τόφρα δέ μοι Σκύλλη κοίλης ἐκ νηὸς ἑταίρους
ἐξ ἕλεθ᾽, οἳ χερσίν τε βίηφί τε φέρτατοι ἦσαν.

ἁλμυρος, -η, -ον briny, salty
ἀνα-βρόχω, —, ἀνά-βροξα I
   swallow up, I gulp down
ἀνα-μορμύρω I foam up
ἀνα-πλέω I sail up
ἀνα-ρροιβδέω, —, ἀνα-ρροίβδησα
   I swallow [down]
ἄχνη, -ης [f.] foam, froth

βρῡχάομαι, pf. w. pres. sense:
   βέβρῡχα I roar
ἐξ-εμέω, —, ἐξ-έμεσα I vomit forth
λέβης, -ητος [m.] basin, kettle
στεινωπός, -οῦ [m.] strait (of the sea)
ὑπένερθε below, beneath
φέρτατος, -η, -ον best, bravest
Χάρυβδις, -ιος [f.] Charybdis
ψάμμος, -ου [f.] sand

1009. NOTES

758 ἔνθεν: understand ἦν.
760 ὥς: take before λέβης.

1010. COMMENT

758 Charybdis was the name given to the whirlpool on the other side of the strait. To be caught between Scylla and Charybdis has become proverbial for a choice between alternatives, each of which will lead to ruin.

760 The whirlpool apparently had also some geyser-like effects, for from time to time the water which was swallowed down was boiled up again by built-up pressures in the interior. The simile of a furiously-boiling pot with clouds of steam rising above it pictures well the surging, foam-covered vortex with spray being shot so high that it falls on the rocks on both sides of the channel.

763 When the process is reversed, the whirling waters roar so loudly that the surrounding rocks catch and echo the sound, and the centrifugal force becomes so great that the waters part to show the very bottom of the strait.

768 With all eyes fixed in terror on frightful Charybdis, they are caught completely unawares by the sudden, stealthy thrust of Scylla—and so is Homer's audience.

1011. WORD STUDY

CYANIDE (a poisonous chemical which turns dark blue in water); — EMETIC (a medicine to provoke vomiting).

LESSON 171

1012. MEMORIZE:

ἀσπαίρω I gasp   κλαζω, κλάγξω, κλάγξα I shriek

δηιοτής, -ῆτος [f.] strife   ὕπερθεν (from) above

ἰχθύς, -ύος [m.] fish

1013. TEXT

Unspeakable Horror

770   σκεψάμενος δ᾽ ἐς νῆα θοὴν ἅμα καὶ μεθ᾽ ἑταίρους

ἤδη τῶν ἐνόησα πόδας καὶ χεῖρας ὕπερθεν

ὑψόσ᾽ ἀειρομένων· ἐμὲ δὲ φθέγγοντο καλεῦντες

ἐξονομακλήδην, τότε γ᾽ ὕστατον, ἀχνύμενοι κῆρ.

ὡς δ᾽ ὅτ᾽ ἐπὶ προβόλῳ ἁλιεὺς περιμήκεϊ ῥάβδῳ

775   ἰχθύσι τοῖς ὀλίγοισι δόλον κατὰ εἴδατα βάλλων

ἐς πόντον προΐησι βοὸς κέρας ἀγραύλοιο,

ἀσπαίροντα δ᾽ ἔπειτα λαβὼν ἔρριψε θύραζε,

ὣς οἵ γ᾽ ἀσπαίροντες ἀείροντο προτὶ πέτρας·

αὐτοῦ δ᾽ εἰνὶ θύρῃσι κατήσθιε κεκλήγοντας,

780   χεῖρας ἐμοὶ ὀρέγοντας ἐν αἰνῇ δηιοτῆτι·

οἴκτιστον δὴ κεῖνο ἐμοῖς ἴδον ὀφθαλμοῖσιν

πάντων, ὅσσ᾽ ἐμόγησα πόρους ἁλὸς ἐξερεείνων.

ἄγραυλος, -ον field-dwelling	ὀρέγω I extend
ἁλιεύς, -ῆος [m.] fisherman	περιμήκης, -ες lofty, long
ἐξ-ερεείνω I question, I explore	πόρος, -ου [m.] way, passage
ἐξοναμακλήδην [adv.] by name	πρόβολος, -ου [m.] projecting point
κατ-εσθίω, etc. I devour	ῥάβδος, -ου [m.] wand, rod
κέρας, -αος [n.] horn; [here] a hook made of horn	σκέπτομαι, —, σκεψάμην I look
	φθέγγομαι I utter a sound, I shout

1014. NOTES

770   *μεθ᾽:* "for my comrades."

773   *ὕστατον:* (adv.) "for the last time."

774   *ὡς:* "just as," introduces the simile, whereas *ὣς* in line 778 applies it.

775   *δόλον:* predicate—"as bait."

     κατά: with *βάλλων.*

776   *προ-ίησι:* present active third singular of *προ-ίημι.*

777   *ἀσπαίροντα:* predicate after *ἰχθύν,* the understood object of *ἔρριψε.*

     ἔρριψε: gnomic aorist.

     θύραζε: from the literal meaning "to the door," this word came to mean "out" from anything.

779   *κεκλήγοντας:* a peculiar perfect active participle of *κλάζω* with present ending and meaning.

781   *οἴκτιστον:* with predicate force.

SCYLLA AND CHARYBDIS
This graphic visualization of the grim story brings out its horrifying impact and the deadly dilemma facing Odysseus, who chose the loss of several brave companions rather than the whole ship and crew in the violent whirlpool.

1015. COMMENT

770 Odysseus had taken his position on the prow platform expecting the attack from that quarter. But now, as he glances back into the ship to assure himself that his comrades are still safe, he is just in time to see the legs and arms of some of his men dangling from the jaws of the monster.

773 ὕστατον: A fine touch of pathos, suggesting well the bitterness and heartsickness of Odysseus.

774-778 Homeric similes are noteworthy for the way in which they build up a complete picture, including many details which are not in themselves necessary for the particular point of comparison. Here, the precise analogy is between the agonized gasping of the fish as they are hauled up by the fisherman and the agonized gasping of the Greek sailors being drawn up inexorably to Scylla's cave.

781 Such a sight must, indeed, have haunted him for the rest of his days.

1016. WORD STUDY

RHINOCEROS ('nose-horn'); — PORE (a 'passage' in the skin); — SCEPTIC (one who 'looks' critically at everything, a doubter).

1017. TEXT

The Cattle of the Sun

αὐτὰρ ἐπεὶ πέτρας φύγομεν δεινήν τε Χάρυβδιν

Σκύλλην τ᾽, αὐτίκ᾽ ἔπειτα θεοῦ ἐς ἀμύμονα νῆσον

785 ἱκόμεθ᾽ ἔνθα δ᾽ ἔσαν καλαὶ βόες εὐρυμέτωποι,

πολλὰ δὲ ἴφια μῆλ᾽ Ὑπερίονος Ἠελίοιο.

δὴ τότ᾽ ἐγὼν ἔτι πόντῳ ἐὼν ἐν νηὶ μελαίνῃ

μυκηθμοῦ τ᾽ ἤκουσα βοῶν αὐλιζομενάων

οἰῶν τε βληχήν· καί μοι ἔπος ἔμπεσε θυμῷ

790 μάντιος ἀλαοῦ, Θηβαίου Τειρεσίαο,

Κίρκης τ᾽ Αἰαίης, οἵ μοι μάλα πόλλ᾽ ἐπέτελλον

νῆσον ἀλεύασθαι τερψιμβρότου Ἠελίοιο.

δὴ τότ᾽ ἐγὼν ἑτάροισι μετηύδων ἀχνύμενος κῆρ·

Αἰαίη, -ης of Aea [island of Circe]
ἀλαός, -ή, -όν blind, sightless
αὐλίζομαι I am shut up in the farm-
   yard
βληχή, -ῆς [f.] bleating
ἐμ-πίπτω, etc. I fall into, I come into

εὐρυμέτωπος, -ον with broad forehead
μυκηθμός, -οῦ [m.] lowing (of cattle)
τερψίμβροτος, -ον delighter of mortals
Χάρυβδις, -ιος [f.] Charybdis

1018. NOTES

789 *οἰῶν:* the breathing-mark is moved by poetic license.

791 *πόλλ᾽:* (adv.) = "seriously," "with much emphasis."

1019. COMMENT

784 Odysseus had no intentions of visiting this island, and in fact if he had known its exact location he would have done everything in his power to avoid it. But even had he known, the absence of all navigating instruments, the vicissitudes of winds and tide, and the malevolence of his archenemy, Poseidon, might well have frustrated all his efforts.

785 After hearing the cattle of the sun referred to several times previously with foreboding, Homer's audience might well experience a tingle of anticipation now that they actually have been reached.

793 With his heart sinking at the sight of the island so potent in evil for him and his men, Odysseus calls together the crew for a meeting, to warn them.

1020. MEMORIZE:

αὕτως [adv.] in the same way; just
γυῖον, -ου [n.] limb
κάματος, -ου [m.] toil, weariness

κλύω, —, (κέ)κλυον [athematic in aor.
impt.] I hear (sound of), I attend to
σιδήρεος, -η, -ον of iron

1021. TEXT

A Mutinous Mood

' κέκλυτέ μευ μύθων κακά περ πάσχοντες ἑταῖροι,
795 ὄφρ' ὑμῖν εἴπω μαντήια Τειρεσίαο
Κίρκης τ' Αἰαίης, οἵ μοι μάλα πόλλ' ἐπέτελλον
νῆσον ἀλεύασθαι τερψιμβρότου Ἠελίοιο·
ἔνθα γὰρ αἰνότατον κακὸν ἔμμεναι ἄμμιν ἔφασκον·
ἀλλὰ παρὲξ τὴν νῆσον ἐλαύνετε νῆα μέλαιναν. '
800   ὣ ἐφάμην, τοῖσιν δὲ κατεκλάσθη φίλον ἦτορ.
αὐτίκα δ' Εὐρύλοχος στυγερῷ μ' ἡμείβετο μύθῳ·
' σχέτλιός εἰς, Ὀδυσεῦ· πέρι τοι μένος, οὐδέ τι γυῖα
κάμνεις· ἦ ῥά νυ σοί γε σιδήρεα πάντα τέτυκται,
ὅς ῥ' ἑτάρους καμάτῳ ἀδηκότας ἠδὲ καὶ ὕπνῳ
805 οὐκ ἐάᾳς γαίης ἐπιβήμεναι, ἔνθα κεν αὖτε
νήσῳ ἐν ἀμφιρύτῃ λαρὸν τετυκοίμεθα δόρπον,
ἀλλ' αὕτως διὰ νύκτα θοὴν ἀλάλησθαι ἄνωγας
νήσου ἀποπλαγχθέντας ἐν ἠεροειδέι πόντῳ.

ἀδέω, pf: ἄδηκα I am sated with
Αἰαίη, -ης of Aea [island of Circe]
ἀμφίρυτος, -η, -ον flowed-about, sea-
girt
ἀπο-πλάζω, aor. pass.: ἀπο-πλάγχθην
I drive off from, I cause to wander
ἠεροειδής, -ές hazy, misty

κατα-κλάω; [aor. pass.] -κλάσθην I
break down, I crush
λαρός, -ή, -όν sweet, delicious
μαντήιον, -ου [n.] oracle, prophecy
παρέξ outside (of), past
τερψίμβροτος, -ον delighter of mortals

1022. NOTES

798 ἔφασκον: iterative of φημί.
802 πέρι: a shortened form of πέρ-εστι, "is excelling." (Notice the position of the pitch-mark.)
803 σοὶ πάντα: "everything about you," "your whole person."
804 ὕπνῳ: i.e., sleepiness, lack of sleep.
805 ἐάᾳς = ἐάεις.
ἐπιβήμεναι: a less frequent form of ἐπιβῆναι, modelled on the pres. inf.
ἔνθα: here with force of a relative.
806 τετυκοίμεθα: a second aorist of τεύχω.

1023.   COMMENT

794 ff.   Odysseus comes rapidly to the point and gives them a direct command to sail on past the island, hoping thus to avoid argument that can lead to only one decision.

800 ff.   As he feared, the prospect of sailing on through the night without warm food or sleep brings out loud groans from the men. Still, they might have obeyed anyway had not Eurylochus, with whom Odysseus had had trouble before, dared to face him as their spokesman.

802-8   A fine roundabout tribute to Odysseus' manly strength and moral stamina.

1024.   WORD STUDY

ICONOCLAST (one who 'breaks the icons,' i.e., the sacred images of the saints, as certain heretics have done in defiance of Catholic doctrine on veneration of the saints; loosely, anyone who assails traditional beliefs in religion, politics, or culture).

A READING FROM HOMER

The artist Alma-Tadema has caught the intense absorption of the listeners as the poem is read aloud, transporting all into another world of bright light and ardent enthusiasms.

1025. MEMORIZE:

ἀέκητι [adv.]   against the will of

αἰνέω, αἰνήσω, αἴνησα   I praise; I consent

Νότος, -ου [m.]   Notus [South Wind]

1026. TEXT

Success of the Mutiny

ἐκ νυκτῶν δ᾽ ἄνεμοι χαλεποί, δηλήματα νηῶν,

810 γίγνονται· πῇ κέν τις ὑπεκφύγοι αἰπὺν ὄλεθρον,

ἤν πως ἐξαπίνης ἔλθῃ ἀνέμοιο θύελλα,

ἢ Νότου ἢ Ζεφύροιο δυσαέος, οἵ τε μάλιστα

νῆα διαρραίουσι θεῶν ἀέκητι ἀνάκτων;

ἀλλ᾽ ἦ τοι νῦν μὲν πειθώμεθα νυκτὶ μελαίνῃ

815 δόρπον θ᾽ ὁπλισόμεσθα θοῇ παρὰ νηὶ μένοντες,

ἠῶθεν δ᾽ ἀναβάντες ἐνήσομεν εὐρέι πόντῳ. ᾽

ὣς ἔφατ᾽ Εὐρύλοχος, ἐπὶ δ᾽ ᾔνεον ἄλλοι ἑταῖροι.

καὶ τότε δὴ γίγνωσκον ὅ δὴ κακὰ μήδετο δαίμων,

καί μιν φωνήσας ἔπεα πτερόεντα προσηύδων·

δήλημα, -ατος [n.]   destruction

δια-ρραίω   I tear in pieces

δυσᾱής, -ές   harsh-blowing, stormy

ἐν-ίημι, etc.   I put in; I launch, I put to sea

ἐξαπίνης [adv.]   suddenly

ἠῶθεν [adv.]   in the morning

πῇ   in what way, whither?

ὑπ-εκ-φεύγω, etc.   I flee out from under, I escape

1027. NOTES

809 ἐκ νυκτῶν: "after nightfall."

815 ὁπλισόμεθα: Homer uses a few first aorist subjunctive forms without lengthening the thematic vowel.

816 ἐνήσομεν: as in comparable English expressions, νῆα is understood.

818 ὅ = the adverbial accusative of ὅς, ἥ, ὅ used as a conjunction = ὅτι. (cp. Latin *quod*).

1028. COMMENT

810 Eurylochus argues that in the utter darkness of the night they will be unable to handle the ship in the sudden squalls, which (he claims) come especially during the night.

817 With the psychology of a mob which is rarely critical enough to see beyond the immediate present, the other sailors shout vigorously their approval.

818 Odysseus knows at once that he is beaten, and sees in the stubbornness of the crew the baneful influence of some god, probably Poseidon.

REVIEW

1029. Go over again Lessons 165–174; make sure now that you have really mastered them. Here are a few suggestions for your review:

1. *Vocabulary:* Check your mastery of the 42 new memory words.
2. *Text:* Reread the 124 lines of text, making sure you recognize all the forms.
3. *Story:*

    a. How did Odysseus plan to resist the Sirens' spell?
    b. What was the chief temptation offered by the Sirens?
    c. Describe Scylla and Charybdis.
    d. How does Homer describe the seizure of his men by Scylla?
    e. Enumerate the arguments of Eurylochus for stopping at the island.

4. *Criticism:*

    a. Try your hand at translating into English verse the song of the Sirens. You need not use the hexameter; you might fit the words to the tune of a popular song.
    b. Compare the speech of Odysseus to his men (Lesson 168) with the similar speech of Aeneas (*Aeneid* 1.198–207).
    c. How would *you* have refuted the argument of Eurylochos?

5. *Composition:* Put into Greek:

    a. If Odysseus had not daubed wax in their ears, they would have heard the song of the Sirens and swiftly suffered evil.
    b. He told them to remember how they were confined in the Cyclops' cave.
    c. Because of their great weariness, the men wished to land upon the island of the Sungod, even against the will of Odysseus.

1030. ARISTOTLE AND IMMORTALITY

We often do not realize what a tremendous advance Christianity has made in our thinking on certain vital points, beyond what merely natural wisdom could teach us. We take too many things for granted, without appreciating how little light other people, even of the greatest intelligence, possess regarding them. A clear instance is the doctrine of the immortality of the human soul, certainly one of the most basic and insistent problems of life, and one which everyone must face.

There have been few, if any, thinkers in human history of greater brilliance and profundity than Aristotle, "the teacher of those who know," as Dante calls him. Living in the fourth century before Christ, for twenty years a student in Plato's school of philosophical research (the Academy), for nine years private tutor of Alexander the Great, then founder of a scientific and philosophical school of his own, the Lyceum at Athens, Aristotle employed his staggering mental energies and great originality of thought in working out a deep and detailed analysis of practically all fields of human speculation.

ARISTOTLE ADMIRING HOMER
Aristotle, the greatest mind of antiquity, refers to Homer 169 times throughout his various works on literature, poetic theory, philosophy, and science, always with highest respect and approval, often citing him as a conclusive source of truth in disputed problems of geography, history, astronomy, biology, zoology, etc. Rembrandt has masterfully expressed his attitude in this famous painting.

Many of his works have been lost in the tumult of wars and history, and most of those which survive are but digests of his class lectures. But they fill thousands of pages even so, and range over almost the whole field of knowledge. Aristotle's books on logic, metaphysics, the philosophy of science, ethics, theory of government, literary criticism, art of writing and speaking, psychology, astronomy, biology, and other branches of philosophy and science are works of amazing profundity and acumen. They are still the starting point—and in some cases practically the final solution also—of modern studies in those areas. Even where thought in a particular field has progressed far beyond Aristotle's analysis, experts in those subjects acknowledge with a kind of awe Aristotle's remarkable brilliance and insight in his pioneer work in so many branches of knowledge and the great advance these made under the impact of his genius. His influence on subsequent scientific and philosophical thinking has been, and still remains, profound and highly stimulating. His writings are prominent on practically all the various lists of the world's greatest books.

Yet when faced with the problem of man's ultimate destiny, this great thinker admits his ignorance, confusion, and uncertainty. Despite his awareness of Plato's ardent conviction of the personal immortality of the soul—a doctrine which Plato was sure of but could not quite prove or clarify to his own or others' satisfaction—Aristotle could not see how immortality was possible, however much he would have *liked* to hold it.

His difficulties were three: (1) since, according to his philosophy, the soul is the 'form' or 'actualizing principle' of the body, making it a body, how can it exist apart from that body, to give which existence and actuality is the soul's primary and natural purpose? (2) since all thought seems to depend on an accompanying phantasm or mental image, the production of which is possible only by the joint activity of both soul and body, the soul apart from the body would be cut off from all phantasms and so unable to think—which is essential to its life as soul; (3) there seems, he thought, to be an immortal and imperishable *part* of the soul, the mind as such, but this does not enter into emotions or memory, which belong to lower parts of the soul operating in conjunction with bodily organs; hence, even if this higher part of the soul lives on after the dissolution of the body, it could not exercise any love, desire, joy, recollection of its past, or even be conscious of its identity or individual personality—and such an existence could hardly be called survival of the same human person who lived in this world, that is, personal immortality in the only sense that matters to us.

In fact, he goes so far as to say, in logical pursuance of these principles, that "death is the most terrifying thing of all, for it is the *end,* and, as it seems, there is no longer any such thing as either good or evil for one who has once died" (*Ethics* 1115a 26–7). A dreadful and somber prospect, indeed, and one which takes the very bottom out of life, leaving man without hope for the future and inevitably embittered at being frustrated of his soul's natural, unquenchable longings for a constant continuation of life and happiness.

It was only great Christian thinkers like St. Augustine and St. Thomas Aquinas who, in the light of Christ's teaching on immortality and the future life, finally found the solution to Aristotle's philosophical difficulties on the nature of the soul, thereby explaining both its function when in the body and its capacity for unending existence beyond the grave. They did this on Aristotle's own principles, thus making the fact of personal immortality not merely a matter of religious faith but also a conclusion susceptible of logical proof and rational demonstration.

Human reason has its triumphs. But of itself alone it is inadequate to answer many of the deepest and most important of life's problems. This, Aristotle, himself one of human reason's noblest glories, would be among the first to admit.

1031. MEMORIZE:

βρώμη, -ης or βρῶσις, -ιος [f.]   food
ἐδητύς, -ύος [f.]   eating; food
ἔρος, -ου [m.]   love, desire
λιμήν, -ένος [m.]   harbor
ὄμνῡμι, ὀμέομαι, ὄμοσ(σ)α   I swear

ὅρκος, -ου [m.]   oath
πόσις, -ιος [f.]   drink
τελευτάω, τελευτήσω, τελεύτησα
   I bring to pass, I finish

ODYSSEUS DISCOVERED

This Roman terracotta relief illustrates Homer's account of how his old nurse Eurykleia recognized Odysseus when bathing his feet, by the scar from a wound suffered in his youth during a wild boar hunt.

1032.   TEXT

The Die Is Cast

820   ' Εὐρύλοχ᾽, ἦ μάλα δή με βιάζετε μοῦνον ἐόντα.
ἀλλ᾽ ἄγε νῦν μοι πάντες ὀμόσσατε καρτερὸν ὅρκον·
εἴ κέ τιν᾽ ἠὲ βοῶν ἀγέλην ἢ πῶυ μέγ᾽ οἰῶν
εὕρωμεν, μή πού τιν᾽ ἀτασθαλίῃσι κακῇσιν
ἢ βοῦν ἠέ τι μῆλον ἀποκτάμεν· ἀλλὰ ἔκηλοι
825   ἐσθίετε βρώμην, τὴν ἀθανάτη πόρε Κίρκη. '
ὣς ἐφάμην, οἱ δ᾽ αὐτίκ᾽ ἀπώμνυον, ὡς ἐκέλευον.
αὐτὰρ ἐπεί ῥ᾽ ὄμοσάν τε τελεύτησάν τε τὸν ὅρκον,
στήσαμεν ἐν λιμένι γλαφυρῷ ἐυεργέα νῆα
ἄγχ᾽ ὕδατος γλυκεροῖο, καὶ ἐξαπέβησαν ἑταῖροι
830   νηός, ἔπειτα δὲ δόρπον ἐπισταμένως τετύκοντο.
αὐτὰρ ἐπεὶ πόσιος καὶ ἐδητύος ἐξ ἔρον ἔντο,
μνησάμενοι δὴ ἔπειτα φίλους ἔκλαιον ἑταίρους,
οὓς ἔφαγε Σκύλλη γλαφυρῆς ἐκ νηὸς ἑλοῦσα·
κλαιόντεσσι δὲ τοῖσιν ἐπήλυθε νήδυμος ὕπνος.

ἀγέλη, -ης [f.] herd	ἐξ-απο-βαίνω, etc. I come out of,
ἀπο-κτείνω, etc. I slay	I disembark
ἀπ-ομνύω I swear (not to do)	επισταμένως [adv.] skillfully, w.
ἀτασθαλίαι, -ᾶων [f. pl.] folly,	expert knowledge
recklessness	καρτερός = κρατερός
	νήδυμος, -ον sweet, refreshing

1033.   NOTES

820   βιάζετε: plural, because he speaks to them all through their spokesman Eurylochus.
μοῦνον: he was forced to yield because he was alone in his opinion.

824   ἀποκτάμεν: an athematic aorist active infinitive of ἀπο-κτείνω.

830   τετύκοντο: from τέτυκον, a special aorist of τεύχω, used only when referring to food.

831   ἐξ ἔντο: second aorist middle of ἐξ-ίημι I put off, I rid myself of.

1034.   COMMENT

821   Hoping still to save them from themselves, he makes them swear solemnly to leave the
cattle alone.

832   Now, in the quiet of the evening, they have leisure to realize the tragic loss of their comrades, whose absence at the meal is only too painfully realized.

1035.   WORD STUDY

EPISTEMOLOGY (the philosophical 'science of knowledge,' i.e., of the mind's ability to attain
the truth).

1036. | MEMORIZE:

ἀγορή, -ῆς [f.]   assembly

λαῖλαψ, -απος [f.]   tempest

νεφεληγερέτα, -āο   cloud-gatherer
(epithet of Zeus)

χορός, -οῦ [m.]   dance, dancing-place

MASTERPIECE FROM THE PARTHENON

At the north corner of the eastern pediment of the Parthenon the horses of the Moon goddess Selene were shown sinking exhausted toward the horizon after pulling her chariot all night across the sky. This magnificent head exhibits the superb skill and sensitivity of the great sculptors of the Classical age.

1037. TEXT

A New Warning

835 ἦμος δὲ τρίχα νυκτὸς ἔην, μετὰ δ' ἄστρα βεβήκει,
ὦρσεν ἔπι ζαῆν ἄνεμον νεφεληγερέτα Ζεὺς
λαίλαπι θεσπεσίῃ, σὺν δὲ νεφέεσσι κάλυψε
γαῖαν ὁμοῦ καὶ πόντον· ὀρώρει δ' οὐρανόθεν νύξ.
ἦμος δ' ἠριγένεια φάνη ῥοδοδάκτυλος Ἠώς,
840 νῆα μὲν ὡρμίσαμεν κοῖλον σπέος εἰσερύσαντες·
ἔνθα δὲ νυμφάων ἦσαν χοροὶ ἠδὲ θόωκοι·
καὶ τότ' ἐγὼν ἀγορὴν θέμενος μετὰ μῦθον ἔειπον·
' ὦ φίλοι, ἐν γὰρ νηὶ θοῇ βρῶσίς τε πόσις τε
ἔστιν, τῶν δὲ βοῶν ἀπεχώμεθα, μή τι πάθωμεν·
845 δεινοῦ γὰρ θεοῦ αἴδε βόες καὶ ἴφια μῆλα,
Ἠελίου, ὃς πάντ' ἐφορᾷ καί πάντ' ἐπακούει.

ἄστρον, -ου [n.] star, constellation	ζάῆς, -ές fiercely-blowing
εἰσ-ερύω, etc. I draw in	θόωκος, -ου [m.] seat, abode
ἐπ-ακούω, etc. I hear	ὁρμίζω, —, ὅρμισα I moor, I make fast
ἐφ-οράω I look upon	τρίχα [adv.] in the third (part)

1038. NOTES

835 μετά: (adv.) had passed "over" the meridian, i.e., near morning.
836 ζαῆν: irregular for ζαέα.
837 σύν: adverb.
842 θέμενος: second aorist participle of τίθημι.

1039. COMMENT

835 The third part of the night would be just before dawn. The Romans divided the night into four watches, but the Greeks, at least of this period, had only three divisions.

838 To the Greeks, Night rose to the zenith and fell to the horizon in the same way as the sun or stars. Night rushing from the heavens would mean that it is leaving the sky and that day is about to break. For the picture, cp. Vergil's statement (*Aen.* 2.251): "*vertitur interea caelum et ruit Oceano nox*," which shows Night speeding from the horizon up toward the zenith — at just the opposite stage of the process to that here described by Homer.

840 Expecting to set sail early the next morning, they had merely moored the ship to the shore upon their landing.

841 A large cave with ready access to the sea easily suggests to the Greeks that it must be a sacred spot of the nymphs.

843 Odysseus is taking no chances on his comrades' forgetting their oath.

1040. WORD STUDY

CHORUS, CHORAL; — ASTRONOMY.

1041. MEMORIZE:

ἀράομαι, ἀρήσομαι, ἀρησάμην I
pray (to)
Ὄλυμπος, -ου [m.] Olympus

ὄρνις, ὄρνῑθος [m., f] bird
σκέπας, -αος [n.] shelter

1042. TEXT

The Crisis

> ὣς ἐφάμην, τοῖσιν δ᾽ ἐπεπείθετο θυμὸς ἀγήνωρ.
> μῆνα δὲ πάντ᾽ ἄλληκτος ἄη Νότος, οὐδέ τις ἄλλος
> γίγνετ᾽ ἔπειτ᾽ ἀνέμων εἰ μὴ Εὖρός τε Νότος τε.
> 850 οἱ δ᾽ ἧος μὲν σῖτον ἔχον καὶ οἶνον ἐρυθρόν,
> τόφρα βοῶν ἀπέχοντο λιλαιόμενοι βιότοιο.
> ἀλλ᾽ ὅτε δὴ νηὸς ἐξέφθιτο ἤια πάντα,
> καὶ δὴ ἄγρην ἐφέπεσκον ἀλητεύοντες ἀνάγκῃ,
> ἰχθύας ὄρνιθάς τε, φίλας ὅτι χεῖρας ἵκοιτο,
> 855 γναμπτοῖς ἀγκίστροισιν, ἔτειρε δὲ γαστέρα λιμός·
> δὴ τότ᾽ ἐγὼν ἀνὰ νῆσον ἀπέστιχον, ὄφρα θεοῖσιν
> εὐξαίμην, εἴ τίς μοι ὁδὸν φήνειε νέεσθαι.
> ἀλλ᾽ ὅτε δὴ διὰ νήσου ἰὼν ἤλυξα ἑταίρους,
> χεῖρας νιψάμενος, ὅθ᾽ ἐπὶ σκέπας ἦν ἀνέμοιο,
> 860 ἠρώμην πάντεσσι θεοῖς, οἳ Ὄλυμπον ἔχουσιν·
> οἱ δ᾽ ἄρα μοι γλυκὺν ὕπνον ἐπὶ βλεφάροισιν ἔχευαν.

ἄγκιστρον, -ου [n.] hook
ἄγρη, -ης [f.] chase, hunt
ἀλητεύω I wander
ἄλληκτος, -ον unceasing
ἀπο-στείχω, etc. I go away
γναμπτός, -ή, -όν bent, supple
ἐκ-φθίνω; pf. pass.: ἐξ-έφθιμαι I use up

ἐπι-πείθομαι I yield, I obey
ἐρυθρός, -ή, -όν ruddy, red
Εὖρος, -ου [m.] Eurus [East wind]
ἤια, -ων [n. pl.] provisions
λῑμός, -οῦ [m.] hunger
νίζω, νίψω, νίψα I wash

1043. NOTES

848 ἄη: imperfect third singular of ἄημι, I blow.

851 βιότοιο: "longing for, or desirous of, living." They were afraid of being punished by death.

853 ἐφέπεσκον: iterative of ἐφ-έπω. Translate: "they pursued the chase, (hunting) fish with barbed hooks, and birds. . . ."

854 ὅτι: from ὅς τις.

858 ἤλυξα: aor. of ἀλύσκω.

859 ἐπί: (adv.) "at hand," "near by."

1044. COMMENT

   851 Odysseus' appeal to the motive of fear had apparently impressed his comrades.

   853 Prevented from sailing for a full month by stormy and adverse winds, they soon exhaust their supplies and are forced to fish and hunt for food, but with little success. The pangs of hunger begin to make themselves felt. The situation is growing desperate. And all the time, grazing before their famished eyes, are the fat, goodly cattle of the Sun.

   856 Realizing the dangers inherent in the situation, Odysseus characteristically turns to prayer. Afterwards, sleep overcomes him.

1045. WORD STUDY

OLYMPIAN (pertaining to the major deities, who were thought to dwell on Mt. Olympus in northern Greece; loosely, of the greatest geniuses, e.g., '. . . among the Olympians of literature'); ORNITHOLOGY (the science of the characteristics and classifications of birds).

SINGLE COMBAT FOR HELEN

This is the other side of the fine kylix decorated with scenes of the Trojan War by the great artist Douris seen on page 38. There it was Ajax vs. Hector. Here it is Paris (also called Alexandros) battling with Menelaus for possession of Helen (who is at the far left), while Artemis (at right) looks on. Homer tells this episode at the beginning of Book Three of the *Iliad*.

1046. MEMORIZE:

χολόω, (κε)χολώσω, χόλωσα   I anger, [mid.]   I am angry [dat. of person; gen. of cause]

1047. TEXT

Temptation!

Εὐρύλοχος δ' ἑτάροισι κακῆς ἐξάρχετο βουλῆς·
' κέκλυτέ μευ μύθων κακά περ πάσχοντες ἑταῖροι.
πάντες μὲν στυγεροὶ θάνατοι δειλοῖσι βροτοῖσιν,
865   λιμῷ δ' οἴκτιστον θανέειν καὶ πότμον ἐπισπεῖν.
ἀλλ' ἄγετ', Ἠελίοιο βοῶν ἐλάσαντες ἀρίστας
ῥέξομεν ἀθανάτοισι, τοὶ οὐρανὸν εὐρὺν ἔχουσιν.
εἰ δέ κεν εἰς Ἰθάκην ἀφικοίμεθα, πατρίδα γαῖαν,
αἶψά κεν Ἠελίῳ Ὑπερίονι πίονα νηὸν
870   τεύξομεν, ἐν δέ κε θεῖμεν ἀγάλματα πολλὰ καὶ ἐσθλά.
εἰ δὲ χολωσάμενός τι βοῶν ὀρθοκραιράων
νῆ' ἐθέλῃ ὀλέσαι, ἐπὶ δ' ἔσπωνται θεοὶ ἄλλοι,
βούλομ' ἅπαξ πρὸς κῦμα χανὼν ἀπὸ θυμὸν ὀλέσσαι,
ἢ δηθὰ στρεύγεσθαι ἐὼν ἐν νήσῳ ἐρήμῃ. '

ἄγαλμα, -ατος [n.] delight, splendid gift
ἅπαξ [adv.] once, once for all
δηθά [adv.] long, for a long time
ἐξ-άρχω I make beginning of
ἐρῆμος, -η, -ον deserted, desolate

λῖμος, -οῦ [m.] hunger
ὀρθόκραιρος, -η, -ον straight-horned
στρεύγομαι I waste away
χαίνω, —, χάνον I yawn, I open the mouth

1048. NOTES

864   στυγεροί: in predicative position; understand εἰσί.
865   οἴκτιστον: predicate with ἐστί understood.
867   ῥέξομεν: an aorist subjunctive with the thematic vowel not lengthened—"let us sacrifice."
872   ἐπί: (adv.) if they follow "along," i.e., agree.

1049. COMMENT

862   Again, it is the unpleasant Eurylochus who acts as spokesman.

863   A clever speech, and psychologically appealing. He can hardly expect the sacrifice of the cattle, stolen from one of their number, to please the Immortals, but they can at least try it and promise even more pleasing sacrifices upon their safe return. Such promises probably will have doubtful value on lips stained with sacrilegious meat; but if the gods do punish them, at least they will die with less lingering pains.

SACRIFICE TO APOLLO

This illustrates the ritual of sacrifice: roasting part of the victim over a fire on an altar, offering wine and cakes, and pouring a libation to the god.

1050. CRASIS

Generally speaking, the Greeks seemed to have disliked two vowel sounds coming together in adjoining syllables. You have already seen several methods they devised to prevent it. If the two vowels came together within a word, they frequently *contracted* them to one vowel sound, or sometimes simply pronounced them as one vowel (*synizesis*). If the succession occurred between two words, they placed a special consonant (*ν-moveable*) at the end of the first word, or they dropped the final vowel of the first word (*elision*). If, however, the first word could not be elided, or take the *ν-movable*, another method, called *crasis* might be tried.

Crasis (κρᾶσις "mingling") is the contraction of a vowel or diphthong at the end of a word with a vowel or diphthong beginning the following word. In order to indicate the contraction, a special mark called *corōnis* (κορωνίς "hook"), identical with a smooth breathing, is written over the resulting syllable. Thus: τὰ ἄλλα "those other things," may be written τἆλλα. πρὸ ἔφαινον, "they showed forth," may be written προὔφαινον, etc.

1051. MEMORIZE:

ἐύσσελμος, -ον   w. fine rowing-benches
εὐχετάομαι   I declare myself, I exult;
   I pray (to)
κνίση, -ης [f.]   fat; savor
ὀβελός, -οῦ [m.]   spit

πείρω, —, πεῖρα   I pierce, I stick, I pass
   through
σπένδω, σπείσω, σπεῖσα   I pour a libation
τῆλε   far (away)

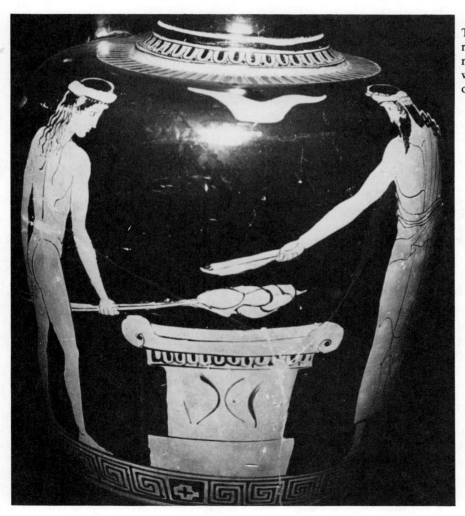

SACRIFICE AT AN ALTAR
The artist has depicted a sacrificial rite in its simplest and essential elements: roasting meat over an altar while a libation of wine is poured over the offering.

1052.   TEXT

A Fateful Meal

875   ὣς ἔφατ᾽ Εὐρύλοχος, ἐπὶ δ᾽ ᾔνεον ἄλλοι ἑταῖροι.
         αὐτίκα δ᾽ Ἠελίοιο βοῶν ἐλάσαντες ἀρίστας
         ἐγγύθεν, οὐ γὰρ τῆλε νεὸς κυανοπρῴροιο
         βοσκέσκονθ᾽ ἕλικες καλαὶ βόες εὐρυμέτωποι,
         τὰς δὲ περίστησάν τε καὶ εὐχετάοντο θεοῖσιν,
880   φύλλα δρεψάμενοι τέρενα δρυὸς ὑψικόμοιο·
         οὐ γὰρ ἔχον κρῖ λευκὸν ἐυσσέλμου ἐπὶ νηός.
         αὐτὰρ ἐπεί ῥ᾽ εὔξαντο καὶ ἔσφαξαν καὶ ἔδειραν,
         μηρούς τ᾽ ἐξέταμον κατά τε κνίσῃ ἐκάλυψαν
         δίπτυχα ποιήσαντες, ἐπ᾽ αὐτῶν δ᾽ ὠμοθέτησαν.
885   οὐδ᾽ εἶχον μέθυ λεῖψαι ἐπ᾽ αἰθομένοις ἱεροῖσιν,
         ἀλλ᾽ ὕδατι σπένδοντες ἐπώπτων ἔγκατα πάντα.
         αὐτὰρ ἐπεὶ κατὰ μῆρα κάη καὶ σπλάγχνα πάσαντο,
         μίστυλλόν τ᾽ ἄρα τἆλλα καὶ ἀμφ᾽ ὀβελοῖσιν ἔπειραν.

δίπτυξ, -υχος double	λείβω, —, λεῖψα I pour (a libation)
δρέπω, —, δρέψα I break off, I pluck	μέθυ [indecl. n.] wine
δρῦς, δρυός [f.] oak (tree)	μηρ(ί)α, -ων [n. pl.] thigh-bones
ἔγκατα, -ων [n. pl.] entrails, vitals	μιστύλλω I cut into small pieces
ἐκ-τάμνω, —, ἐκ-ταμον I cut (out)	περι-ίστημι, etc. I stand around
ἕλιξ, -ικος [adv.] sleek	σπλάγχνα, -ων [n. pl.] vitals
ἐπ-οπτάω I roast	τέρην, -ενος [adj.] soft, tender
εὐρυμέτωπος, -ον with broad fore-head	ὑψίκομος, -ον with lofty foliage
κρῖ [indecl. n.] barley	ὠμο-θετέω, —, ὠμο-θέτην I place pieces of raw flesh (upon)

1053.   NOTES

883   κατά: (adv.) "throughout," "all over."
884   δίπτυχα: understand κνίσην.
885   ἱεροῖσιν: (substantive) "the offerings."
887   κάη: aorist passive of καίω.
      κατά: adverbial
      πάσαντο: with the accusative instead of the usual genitive.
888   τἆλλα: cp. #1050.

1054.   COMMENT

875   Again the Greek sailors uncritically accept whatever Eurylochus offers.
880 ff.   They proceed through all the ritualistic movements, substituting crushed leaves for the sacred barley and water for the prescribed red wine, hoping that the gods will be satisfied, since this is the best they can do under the circumstances.

1055. MEMORIZE:

ἄγγελος, -ου [m.] messenger
ἀμφιέλισσα, -ης easily-directed
    [epithet of ships]

ἄτη, -ης [f.] infatuation; ruin
θίς, θῖνος [f.] beach
κίω, —, κίον I go

1056. TEXT

A Bitter Discovery

καὶ τότε μοι βλεφάρων ἐξέσσυτο νήδυμος ὕπνος,
890 βῆν δ᾽ ἰέναι ἐπὶ νῆα θοὴν καὶ θῖνα θαλάσσης.
ἀλλ᾽ ὅτε δὴ σχεδὸν ἦα κιὼν νεὸς ἀμφιελίσσης,
καὶ τότε με κνίσης ἀμφήλυθεν θερμὸς ἀϋτμή.
οἰμώξας δὲ θεοῖσι μέγ᾽ ἀθανάτοισι γεγώνευν·
‘ Ζεῦ πάτερ ἠδ᾽ ἄλλοι μάκαρες θεοὶ αἰὲν ἐόντες,
895 ἦ με μάλ᾽ εἰς ἄτην κοιμήσατε νηλέι ὕπνῳ,
οἱ δ᾽ ἔταροι μέγα ἔργον ἐμητίσαντο μένοντες.᾽
ὠκέα δ᾽ Ἡελίῳ Ὑπερίονι ἄγγελος ἦλθεν
Λαμπετίη τανύπεπλος, ὅ οἱ βόας ἔκταμεν ἡμεῖς.
αὐτίκα δ᾽ ἀθανάτοισι μετηύδα χωόμενος κῆρ·

αἰέν = αἰεί
ἀμφ-έρχομαι, etc. I come around
θερμός, (-ή), -όν hot
Λαμπετίη, -ης Lampetia [a nymph]

μητίομαι, —, μητῑσάμην I devise, I
    contrive
νήδυμος, -ον sweet, refreshing
τανύπεπλος, -ον with trailing robes

1057. NOTES

889 ἐξέσσυτο: from ἐκ-σεύω.
890 ἰέναι: infinitive of εἶμι, I go. (Explanatory infinitive)
    βῆν: translate "I set out to go." (cp. the English: "I am going to go.")
893 μέγ᾽: adverb with γεγώνευν.
896 μέγα: "great" in sense of "monstrous."
897 ἄγγελος: predicate—"as a messenger, saying . . ."
898 ὅ = ὅτι (cf. line 818)
    ἔκταμεν: an athematic aorist of κτείνω.

1058. COMMENT

892 What must have been the feelings of Odysseus when he smelled the pleasant savour of roasting beef and realized that, despite all his pleas and their promises, his men had committed the sin that would bring certain and speedy death to them all! No wonder he is constrained to reproach the gods for the sleep that kept him away at the critical time.

897 ff. Notice the swiftness of the action. No sooner was the deed performed than the message was taken to the Sun. As soon as he heard the report, he at once addressed the assembly of the gods.

115

1059. MEMORIZE:

κεάζω, κεάσω, κέασ(σ)α I shatter   οἶνοψ, -οπος wine-dark

κεραυνός, -οῦ [m.] thunderbolt   φαείνω I give light

1060. TEXT

The Doom Is Sealed

900   'Ζεῦ πάτερ ἠδ' ἄλλοι μάκαρες θεοὶ αἰὲν ἐόντες,

     τῖσαι δὴ ἑτάρους Λαερτιάδεω Ὀδυσῆος,

     οἵ μευ βοῦς ἔκτειναν ὑπέρβιον, ᾗσιν ἐγώ γε

     χαίρεσκον μὲν ἰὼν εἰς οὐρανὸν ἀστερόεντα,

     ἠδ' ὁπότ' ἂψ ἐπὶ γαῖαν ἀπ' οὐρανόθεν προτραποίμην.

905   εἰ δέ μοι οὐ τίσουσι βοῶν ἐπιεικέ' ἀμοιβήν,

     δύσομαι εἰς Ἀίδαο καὶ ἐν νεκύεσσι φαείνω.'

     τὸν δ' ἀπαμειβόμενος προσέφη νεφεληγερέτα Ζεύς·

     ' Ἠέλι', ἦ τοι μὲν σὺ μετ' ἀθανάτοισι φάεινε

     καὶ θνητοῖσι βροτοῖσιν ἐπὶ ζείδωρον ἄρουραν·

910   τῶν δέ κ' ἐγὼ τάχα νῆα θοήν ἀργῆτι κεραυνῷ

     τυτθὰ βαλὼν κεάσαιμι μέσῳ ἐνὶ οἴνοπι πόντῳ.'

αἰέν = αἰεί	ζείδωρος, -ον fruitful
ἀμοιβή, -ῆς [f.] exchange, requital	προ-τρέπω, —, πρό-τραπον I turn
ἀπ-αμείβομαι, etc. I answer	προσ-έφη I spoke to, I addressed
ἀργής, -ῆτος [adj.] white gleaming	τυτθός, (-ή), -όν small, little
ἐπι-εικής, -ές fitting, suitable	ὑπέρβιον [adv.] wantonly

1061. NOTES

902   ᾗσιν: "in which."

906   φαείνω: the first person of the subjunctive sometimes expresses resolution or insistence (what the imperative expresses for the second person).

911   τυτθά: (adv.) "into bits."

     κεάσαιμι: the potential optative, which ranges in meaning from mere possibility to future fact. Perhaps the meaning here is, "and I expect that I shall shatter, etc."

1062. COMMENT

900 ff.   Homer is not above poking a little sly humor at the gods even on such an occasion as this. The speech is serious enough, but the sulking threat to go down and shine among the dead must have been sung with a smile on the poet's lips.

902   Note that Helios exempts Odysseus himself from guilt and penalty.

908 ff.   The father of the gods soothes the petulant sun-god, and promises personal attention to the matter.

CHARIOT OF THE SUN

The 'Lydos Painter' here presents the sun-god Helios riding back to the East at night to be ready to rise again at dawn next morning and traverse the sky while looking down on all activities of men on earth. The chariot is drawn by winged horses, and the fish below symbolize a journey over the sea.

1063. MEMORIZE:

νεικέω, νεικέσω, νείκεσ(σ)α   I quarrel with; I rebuke

1064. TEXT

An Ominous Calm

αὐτὰρ ἐπεί ῥ’ ἐπὶ νῆα κατήλυθον ἠδὲ θάλασσαν,
νείκεον ἄλλοθεν ἄλλον ἐπισταδόν, οὐδέ τι μῆχος
εὑρέμεναι δυνάμεσθα, βόες δ’ ἀποτέθνασαν ἤδη.
915   τοῖσιν δ’ αὐτίκ’ ἔπειτα θεοὶ τέραα προῦφαινον·
εἷρπον μὲν ῥινοί, κρέα δ’ ἀμφ’ ὀβελοῖσι μεμύκει,
ὀπταλέα τε καὶ ὠμά, βοῶν δ’ ὣς γίγνετο φωνή.

ἑξῆμαρ μὲν ἔπειτα ἐμοὶ ἐρίηρες ἑταῖροι
δαίνυντ’ Ἠελίοιο βοῶν ἐλάσαντες ἀρίστας·
920   ἀλλ’ ὅτε δὴ ἕβδομον ἦμαρ ἐπὶ Ζεὺς θῆκε Κρονίων,
καὶ τότ’ ἔπειτ’ ἄνεμος μὲν ἐπαύσατο λαίλαπι θύων,
ἡμεῖς δ’ αἶψ’ ἀναβάντες ἐνήκαμεν εὐρέι πόντῳ,
ἱστὸν στησάμενοι ἀνά θ’ ἱστία λεύκ’ ἐρύσαντες

ἀπο-θνήσκω, shortened plpf. 3 pl.:
  ἀπο-τέθνασαν   I die
ἕβδομος, -η, -ον   seventh
ἐν-ίημι, etc.   I put in; I launch
ἑξῆμαρ   for six days
ἐπισταδόν [adv.]   coming up to
ἕρπω   I creep
θύω   I run, I rush

μῆχος, -εος [n.]   remedy, relief
μυχάομαι; plpf. as impf.: μεμύκεα
  I low [of cattle]
ὀπταλέος, -η, -ον   roasted
προ-φαίνω, etc.   I show forth
ῥινός, -οῦ [m.]   hide, skin
τέρας, -αος [n.]   sign, portent
ὠμός, -η, -ον   raw, uncooked

NESTOR'S PALACE AT PYLOS
Excavations by Prof. Carl Blegen and associates since 1939 have revealed extensive remains of a Mycenaean Age palace in the western Peloponnesus that are readily identified with Homer's references to the home of old Nestor "at sandy Pylos." This view over the storerooms at the back of the complex shows the square central Megaron, with raised circular hearth, then the vestibule and outer courtyard, with other rooms at the right.

NESTOR'S MEGARON

A reliable reconstruction, from all evidence and descriptions, of the main room of the palace at Pylos—the open roof over the circular hearth, with glimpse of upper rooms, the Cretan-style pillars holding up the ceiling over the rest of the Megaron, polished gypsum floors, brightly painted walls and ceiling. By the expert archaeological artist Piet de Jong.

1065. NOTES

917 ὥς: take before βοῶν.

920 δὴ ἕβδομον: δη and εβ form one syllable by synizesis.

ἐπὶ θῆκε: "put . . . beside," "added" to the other six.

922 ἐνήκαμεν: understand νῆα.

1066. COMMENT

913 In his anger and disappointment, Odysseus vigorously dresses down his men, but he soon realizes the uselessness of it all. The harm has been done and is irreparable.

915 Upheavals in the moral order are often thought of as causing a kind of sympathetic vibration in the physical order. In Shakespeare's *Julius Caesar,* for example, marvelous portents of nature were observed on the night before the fatal stabbing. So here, the laws of nature are upset; the hides begin to creep about and the slices of meat on the spits give forth a sound as of mooing.

918 Their sin is not committed in a moment of weakness and repented of immediately afterwards; the unholy feasting continues through six days.

1067, WORD STUDY

HEBDOMADAL (relating to seven, especially to seven days: weekly).

1068. MEMORIZE:

ἄμυδις   at the same time, together
ἀπο-αίνυμαι   I take away
ἐλίσσω, —, (ἐλ)έλιξα   I whirl, I turn
θέω   I run

κατα-χέω, -χεύσω, -χεῦα or -χύμην   I pour down; [mid.]   I fall down
κεφαλή, -ῆς [f.]   head
πλήσσω, πλήξω, πλῆξα   I smite
ῥήγνῡμι, ῥήξω, ῥῆξα   I smash, I break

1069. TEXT

Paid in Full

ἀλλ᾽ ὅτε δὴ τὴν νῆσον ἐλείπομεν, οὐδέ τις ἄλλη
925   φαίνετο γαιάων, ἀλλ᾽ οὐρανὸς ἠδὲ θάλασσα,
δὴ τότε κυανέην νεφέλην ἔστησε Κρονίων
νηὸς ὕπερ γλαφυρῆς, ἤχλυσε δὲ πόντος ὑπ᾽ αὐτῆς.
ἡ δ᾽ ἔθει οὐ μάλα πολλὸν ἐπὶ χρόνον· αἶψα γὰρ ἦλθε
κεκληγὼς Ζέφυρος μεγάλη σὺν λαίλαπι θύων,
930   ἱστοῦ δὲ προτόνους ἔρρηξ᾽ ἀνέμοιο θύελλα
ἀμφοτέρους· ἱστὸς δ᾽ ὀπίσω πέσεν, ὅπλα τε πάντα
εἰς ἄντλον κατέχυνθ᾽. ὁ δ᾽ ἄρα πρυμνῇ ἐνὶ νηὶ
πλῆξε κυβερνήτεω κεφαλήν, σὺν δ᾽ ὀστέ᾽ ἄραξε
πάντ᾽ ἄμυδις κεφαλῆς· ὁ δ᾽ ἄρ᾽ ἀρνευτῆρι ἐοικὼς
935   κάππεσ᾽ ἀπ᾽ ἰκριόφιν, λίπε δ᾽ ὀστέα θυμὸς ἀγήνωρ.
Ζεὺς δ᾽ ἄμυδις βρόντησε καὶ ἔμβαλε νηὶ κεραυνόν·
ἡ δ᾽ ἐλελίχθη πᾶσα Διὸς πληγεῖσα κεραυνῷ,
ἐν δὲ θεείου πλῆτο, πέσον δ᾽ ἐκ νηὸς ἑταῖροι.
οἱ δὲ κορώνῃσιν ἴκελοι περὶ νῆα μέλαιναν
940   κύμασιν ἐμφορέοντο, θεὸς δ᾽ ἀποαίνυτο νόστον.

ἄντλος, -ου [m.]   bilge, hold [the bottom of a ship inside]
ἀράσσω, —, ἄραξα   I hammer, I crush
ἀρνευτήρ, -ῆρος [m.]   diver
ἀχλύω, —, ἄχλῡσα   I grow dark
βροντάω, —, βρόντησα   I thunder
ἐμ-βάλλω, etc.   I throw in, I cast upon

ἐμ-φορέω   I bear among
θέειον, -ου [n.]   sulphur
θύω   I run, I rush
ἴκελος, -η, -ον   like, resembling
καπ-πίπτω, etc.   I fall down
κορώναι, -άων [f. pl.]   sea gulls
πρότονος, -ου [m.]   fore-stay [of a ship]
πρυμνός, -ή, -όν   hindemost, end-most

1070. NOTES

928   ἐπί: "for."
929   κεκληγώς: perfect participle of κλάζω with present force.
932   ὁ: the mast.
933   σύν: adverbial.

935 ἰκριόφιν: formed according to rule from what would be the singular of ἴκρια.
937 ἐλελίχθη: aorist passive of ἑλίσσω.
    πληγεῖσα: aorist passive of πλήσσω.
938 ἐν . . . πλῆτο: irregular aorist passive of ἐμ-πίπλημι, I fill full of.

1071. COMMENT

928 The avenging anger of Zeus was not long deferred. Hardly had they passed out of sight of land, when it burst upon them with all the fury of enraged nature.

930 In a Greek ship, the strain on the mast was divided among three ropes. The two forestays led forward and were fastened to either side of the bow; one backstay stretched to the stern. Consequently, if the two forestays snapped simultaneously, the mast would fall back almost directly on the stern. As it fell it would naturally cause all the rigging and tackle to tumble down also into the hold.

933 We can almost hear the sickening crunch with which the heavy wood fell on the pilot's skull and knocked him overboard headfirst like a diver.

938 When strong charges of electricity pass through the air, they form a pungently-smelling gas which we now know as ozone. This is what Homer is referring to as a sulphurous smell.

939 The men are thrown from their shattered ship and for a time their heads can be seen bobbing up and down on the dark waves, much in the way that sea-gulls ride the waves as they rest on the water. Then one by one they disappear into the black depths, and finally Odysseus can make out only the empty sea. His men have paid the full penalty. The dire prophecy in their regard at the very start of the poem (lines 6–9) has been fulfilled.

1072. WORD STUDY

AUTOCEPHALOUS (independent, self-governing, 'its own head'); — HEMORRHAGE (a 'breaking forth of blood'); — BRONTOSAURUS ('thundering lizard,' a huge prehistoric reptile like a dinosaur).

A DIVER
This remarkable fine painting on the side of a tomb at Paestum, a Greek colony in central Italy, dating to the fifth century B.C., shows a boy diving gracefully from a platform, presumably in sport. It is background to the reference to diving in the text here.

1073. MEMORIZE:

Καλυψώ, -όος [f.]   Calypso [a nymph]   *Ὠγυγίη, -ης* [f.]   Ogygia [a mythical
στῆθος, -εος [n.]   breast, chest   island

1074. TEXT

Calypso Falls in Love

941   Ὠγυγίη τις νῆσος ἀπόπροθεν εἰν ἁλὶ κεῖται·
     ἔνθα μὲν Ἄτλαντος θυγάτηρ δολόεσσα Καλυψὼ
     ναίει ἐυπλόκαμος, δεινὴ θεός· οὐδέ τις αὐτῇ
     μίσγεται οὔτε θεῶν οὔτε θνητῶν ἀνθρώπων·

945   ἀλλ᾽ ἐμὲ τὸν δύστηνον ἐφέστιον ἤγαγε δαίμων
     οἶον, ἐπεί μοι νῆα θοὴν ἀργῆτι κεραυνῷ
     Ζεὺς ἔλσας ἐκέασσε μέσῳ ἐνὶ οἴνοπι πόντῳ.
     ἔνθ᾽ ἄλλοι μὲν πάντες ἀπέφθιθεν ἐσθλοὶ ἑταῖροι,
     αὐτὰρ ἐγὼ τρόπιν ἀγκὰς ἑλὼν νεὸς ἀμφιελίσσης

950   ἐννῆμαρ φερόμην· δεκάτῃ δέ με νυκτὶ μελαίνῃ
     νῆσον ἐς Ὠγυγίην πέλασαν θεοί, ἔνθα Καλυψὼ
     ναίει ἐυπλόκαμος, δεινὴ θεός, ἥ με λαβοῦσα
     ἐνδυκέως ἐφίλει τε καὶ ἔτρεφεν ἠδὲ ἔφασκε
     θήσειν ἀθάνατον καὶ ἀγήραον ἤματα πάντα·

955   ἀλλ᾽ ἐμὸν οὔ ποτε θυμὸν ἐνὶ στήθεσσιν ἔπειθεν.

ἀγήραος, -ον free from old age
ἀγκάς [adv.] in the arms
ἀπο-φθίνω; [irreg. aor. 3 pl. *ἀπο-φθιθεν*] I perish
ἀργής, -ῆτος [adj.] white, bright

Ἄτλας, -αντος [m.] Atlas [a Titan, condemned for revolt to hold up the earth on his shoulders]
δολόεις, -εσσα, -εν crafty, sly
ἐφέστιος, -ον at home, to (one's) home
τρόπις, -ιος [f.] keel

1075. NOTES

943   *θεός:* frequently used for the feminine.
947   *ἔλσας:* from *εἰλ(έ)ω*.
951   *ἔνθα:* here, with force of relative.
953   *ἐφίλει:* "befriended," "entertained."
      ἔφασκε: iterative of *φημί*.
954   *θήσειν:* "cause me to be," "make me."

1076. COMMENT

941   We can picture Odysseus taking a long breath, as it were, after the intensity of the last scene, and starting his story off again from a slightly different point of view.

LAOCOON

A priest of Apollo at Troy, who tried to prevent admission of the Wooden Horse within the walls and who had offended the gods in serious ways, is shown being attacked, along with his two sons, by avenging serpents. The sculpture was likely made in Rhodes around 150 B.C. and illustrates the sensationalism and violence often characterizing art of the Hellenistic period after Alexander the Great.

946 *οἶον:* The striking position of the word emphasizes the fact that now Odysseus must go on—*alone.*

950 Clinging desperately to bits of wreckage, Odysseus is swept by wind and wave back to the narrow strait, and narrowly escapes being swallowed up by Charybdis (as Homer describes elsewhere). Still at the mercy of the elements, he is tossed about for nine days until at length he drifts to the island of Calypso.

953 More dead than alive through exhaustion and lack of nourishment, he is treated kindly by the nymph and nursed back to health—and finds himself confronted with a problem more subtly difficult than any he had hitherto encountered. Calypso had fallen in love with him! It speaks eloquently of the manly physique and noble personality of the Greek hero that this goddess, always previously scorning the company of mortals and immortals alike, should lose her heart so completely to him that she promises him deathlessness and eternal youth if only he will reciprocate her love. How appealing a prospect to one just returned from the dim, dreary realm of the dead!

955 A simple line without rhetoric or dramatics, and yet, in the circumstances, packed with meaning. Odysseus lives for an ideal—to return to his homeland and family—and refuses to be turned aside.

1077. WORD STUDY

ATLAS (a book of maps, holding the world); ATLANTIC (the ocean near Atlas, whose position was near Gibraltar).

123

REVIEW

1078. Go over again Lessons 176–185; make sure now that you have really mastered them. Here are a few suggestions for your review:

1. *Vocabulary:* Check your mastery of the 45 new memory words.
2. *Text:* Reread the 136 lines of text, making sure you recognize all the forms.
3. *Story:*

    a. How did Odysseus try to safeguard his men from the danger on the island?
    b. Why did the Greeks draw up their boat on the morning following their arrival instead of at once?
    c. What was the situation after a month on the island?
    d. How did the Sun-god regard the eating of his cattle?
    e. Describe the final doom of the crew.

4. *Criticism:*

    a. Was Odysseus in any way blameworthy for the fate that overtook his comrades? Prove your answer by references to the text.
    b. How would you have answered the argument of Eurylochus (in Lesson 179)?
    c. Granting the mythological suppositions of the story, what would you judge to be the kind and degree of the sailors' moral guilt?

5. *Grammar:* Explain the principles of crasis.

6. *Composition:* Put into Greek:

    a. The cloud-gatherer Zeus told the Sun-god that the ship of Odysseus would be shattered by his whirling thunderbolt.
    b. He was angry at his men because of the oath which they swore but forgot.
    c. For them, the desire of food and drink became greater than their desire of life.

ATHENA THE WRITER
This red-figured amphora is given a single figure without distracting background. Athena, patroness of the arts, is shown writing on a tablet, absorbed in thought and for a moment putting aside her martial role.

SCHOOL SCENE

On this kylix by Douris we see lessons being given in music and reading. At the far right the boy's guardian ('pedagogue') waits, with interest in the teacher's material himself.

1079. ATHENIAN EDUCATION

"Given the right education," Plato wrote, "man is the most peaceful and god-like of living beings; but if he lacks adequate good training, he is the most savage beast on earth." (*Laws* 766a).

The wisdom of this remark, founded on man's vast capacities for good and for evil because of his free will and creative intellect, agrees with the general attitude of the Greeks toward education. For them, it means not merely the accumulation of facts and practical skills, but essentially a process of balanced self-realization, an unfolding of all those specifically human powers which make man man.

Education's goal, especially at Athens, was to prepare for the *right enjoyment of leisure* on the highest human plane and the *right use of one's talents* for one's own and the common good. It was primarily education for the good life, the life of reason and virtue; its fruit was that well-being of character and personality which may be trusted to flow over into well-doing in the conduct of private life and public services. The proof of good education was, according to Plato and Aristotle, "the developed habit of consistently and almost instinctively taking pleasure or offense in the right things." This implies a trained sensitivity to beauty, good taste, refinement of standards, and sound moral principles dominating one's every reaction and activity. From this would flow happiness, a higher enjoyment of life, and that nobility of character which makes a citizen both a credit and an asset to the state.

The emphasis in Athenian education was on reason and moral training rather than on mere intellect, though this too was amply cultivated. Technical or vocational skills were learned at home, on the apprentice system. The school concerned itself essentially with imparting that liberal education which opens the mind to an appreciation of universal truths and human problems in the large. How fruitful this system was can be judged from the unrivalled fertility of little Greece in producing world-shaping giants of thought and culture.

Schools at Athens were private institutions, not state-controlled. The child began his schooling at about six, being escorted to class by a trusted old slave called the "pedagogue" (cp. #179), whose duty it was to carry little Aristocles' books and see that he got into no mischief. For six or eight years, the child would study reading, writing, and arithmetic, and learn to play the lyre or the flute. Not having any written textbooks, he would be taught to memorize large sections of Homer, Hesiod, and Aesop, which would then be explained and commented on by the teacher and serve as a springboard for filling out the whole picture of life, history, learning and national ideals. So well was the memory trained that these passages of literature would often remain in the mind for life, a constant source of renewed enjoyment and instruction. In fact, it was not rare for a Greek to be able to recite the whole of Homer from memory (over 28,000 lines!). Naturally enough, it was on Homer that the entire Greek educational system was based. His outlook permeated all Greek thinking.

For the poor, this elementary education, lasting to about the age of twelve or fourteen, was generally all that could be afforded; but it was a good basis for intelligent living, and satisfied the majority. Sons of wealthier parents would, however, proceed to secondary education for several more years, up to the two-year period of military service at eighteen. Music and gymnastics, geometry, geography, drawing, advanced studies of literature and rhetoric, and discussions of political and ethical principles were the main subjects of study in this (so to speak) high school and college period of a young Athenian's education.

Advanced studies in mathematics, philosophy, science, statecraft would then be available for the talented upper levels of young intellectuals. For the others, general adult education was obtainable from the lectures of traveling professors, such as the sophists Gorgias, Protagoras, Hippias, Prodicus, and others, who specialized in teaching (for a set fee) a gentleman's knowledge of practically everything, but especially the pragmatic techniques making for success, such as How to win friends and influence people, or How to talk your way out of any lawsuit, or How to make everyone else seem ignorant by comparison. Like most popular education even today, these lecture courses were often superficial and showy rather than searching studies of truth in itself; aimed more at producing practical material results than at a sincere pursuit of knowledge for its own sake, whether pleasant or 'useful' or not. As such, they were vigorously denounced by the brilliant philosophers Plato and Aristotle, who were the real intellectual leaders of Greece and the greatest of ancient teachers.

Merely to live in classical Athens was a liberal education. In the midst of all that eager ferment of thought and originality characteristic of Greek culture at its best, mingling with so many men of genius and their works of art or literature, surrounded on all sides by glorious works of beauty, the citizen of Athens must have been constantly uplifted by noble ideas and stimulated to vigorous mental activity. "Athens," Pericles could justly boast, "is the school of Greece." Even more truly was it the school of every Athenian, fulfilling, as no other city ever had, Plato's ideal of an environment which is itself an education to nobility: "Let our youth dwell in a land of health, surrounded by fair sights and sounds and drinking in good from everything about them. Let beauty, the radiance of noble works, flow into their eyes and ears like a health-giving breeze from a purer region, and insensibly draw their souls from earliest years toward a likeness and sympathy with the beauty of reason" (*Republic,* Book 3).

There is much that we today can learn from the Greeks about the nature, aims, and process of education. Not least by bringing our minds into vital contact with their literature and art, until something of their contagious love of beauty, nobility, and humanism works its way into our own souls. If that is not education, what is?

1080. | MEMORIZE:

ἀγγελίη, -ης [f.]   message; news   ἀτρύγετος, -ον   barren

ἄμβροτος, -ον [f.]   fragrant; immortal   σχεδίη, -ης [f.]   raft

THE LINCOLN MEMORIAL

In tribute to a great man and noble leader, the country has erected one of its most beautiful buildings—going to ancient Greece for the artistic principles and inspiration.

1081. TEXT

Loyalty and Release

956 ἀλλ᾽ ἐγὼ ἂμ πέτρῃσι καὶ ἠιόνεσσι καθῖζον,
πόντον ἐπ᾽ ἀτρύγετον δερκόμενος, ἄλγεσι φθινων,
νόστον ὀδυρόμενος θ᾽ ἱμειρόμενός τε ἰδέσθαι
ἂψ ἄλοχον, τῆς τ᾽ αἰὲν ἐέλδομαι ἤματα πάντα.

960 ἔνθα μὲν ἑπτάετες μένον ἔμπεδον, εἵματα δ᾽ αἰεὶ
δάκρυσι δεύεσκον, τά μοι ἄμβροτα δῶκε Καλυψώ·
ἀλλ᾽ ὅτε δὴ ὀγδόατόν μοι ἐπιπλόμενον ἔτος ἦλθεν,
καὶ τότε δή μ᾽ ἐκέλευσεν ἐποτρύνουσα νέεσθαι
Ζηνὸς ὑπ᾽ ἀγγελίης, ἢ καὶ νόος ἐτράπετ᾽ αὐτῆς.

965 πέμπε δ᾽ ἐπὶ σχεδίης πολυδέσμου, πολλὰ δ᾽ ἔδωκεν,
σῖτον καὶ μέθυ ἡδύ, καὶ ἄμβροτα εἵματα ἕσσεν·
οὖρον δὲ προέηκεν ἀπήμονά τε λιαρόν τε.

δέρκομαι I look, I behold	ἠιών, -όνος [f.] [in pl.:] seashore,
δεύω I moisten	strand
ἐέλδομαι I am desirous of	ἱμείρω I desire, I long
ἐπι-πέλομαι, ect. I come on or round;	λιαρός, -ή, -όν warm
[ptc.:] revolving	μέθυ [n. indecl.] wine
ἑπτάετες [adv.] for seven years	ὀγδόατος, -η, -ον eighth
ἔτος, -εος [n.] year	πολύδεσμος, -ον having many
	bonds, sturdy

1082. NOTES

962 δὴ ὀγδόατον: δη and ογ are scanned as one syllable by synezesis.

964 ἐτράπετ᾽: a second aorist of τρέπω with passive meaning.

966 ἕσσεν: understand μέ.

1083. COMMENT

956 An impasse is reached. Odysseus will not give in to Calypso, and she in turn will not allow him to leave the island. So, day after day, he sits idly by the sea, eating his heart out with loneliness and longing for home and the company of his beloved wife, Penelope.

959 A picture, surely, of admirable conjugal love and devotion.

960 Seven years! Time, which is the acid test of every good resolution, had tried Odysseus and found him true gold.

963 Suddenly, there is a change. In the eighth year, Calypso unexpectedly tells him he is free to go, with her blessing and her assistance. Homer tells us elsewhere that Zeus, finally having mercy on the undeserved plight of the hero, sent Hermes to order the nymph to release him. However, it would seem from her generous acquiescence, that her own selfish love had finally been conquered by her admiration for Odysseus' noble devotion to his wife, whatever his failings may have been.

1084. WORD STUDY

ETESIAN (yearly, in annual cycles, e.g., the etesian winds of the Mediterranean regions).

1085. | MEMORIZE:

ἀδινός, -ή, -όν thick-thronging; vehement
Ἀλκίνοος, -ου Alcinoüs [king of Phaeacians]
γηθέω, γηθήσω, γήθησα I rejoice (at)

ἐνοσίχθων, -ονος earth-shaker
νήχω, νήξομαι, νηξάμην I swim
ὀρίνω, —, ὄρῑνα I agitate
Φαίηκες, -ων Phaeacians

1086. TEXT

Poseidon Strikes Again

ἑπτὰ δὲ καὶ δέκα μὲν πλέον ἤματα ποντοπορεύων,
ὀκτωκαιδεκάτῃ δ᾽ ἐφάνη ὄρεα σκιόεντα
970 γαίης Ἀλκινόου, γήθησε δέ μοι φίλον ἦτορ
δυσμόρῳ· ἦ γὰρ ἔμελλον ἔτι ξυνέσεσθαι ὀιζυῖ
πολλῇ, τήν μοι ἐπῶρσε Ποσειδάων ἐνοσίχθων,
ὅς μοι ἐφορμήσας ἀνέμους κατέδησε κελεύθου,
ὤρινεν δὲ θάλασσαν ἀθέσφατον, οὐδέ τι κῦμα
975 εἴα ἐπὶ σχεδίης ἀδινὰ στενάχοντα φέρεσθαι.
τὴν μὲν ἔπειτα θύελλα διεσκέδασ᾽· αὐτὰρ ἐγώ γε
νηχόμενος μέγα λαῖτμα διέτμαγον, ὄφρα με γαίῃ
Φαιήκων ἐπέλασσε φέρων ἄνεμός τε καὶ ὕδωρ.

ἀθέσφατος, -ον portentous, terrible, endless
δια-σκίδνημι, —, δια-σκέδασα I scatter, I shatter
δια-τμήγω, —, διά-τμαγον I cut in two, I cut through
δύσμορος, -ον doomed to an evil fate, ill-starred

ἐπ-όρνῡμι, etc. I rouse (upon)
κατα-δέω, etc. I bind, I hinder from
ξύν-ειμι; fut. inf.: ξυν-έσεσθαι I am (joined) with
ὀκτω-και-δέκατος, -η, -ον eighteenth
ποντοπορεύω I sail the sea

1087. NOTES

975 εἴα: from ἐάω. Take κῦμα as subject, and understand ἐμέ.

1088. COMMENT

968 For seventeen uneventful, wearying days he sails slowly but successfully eastward, and on the eighteenth is rejoiced to sight an unknown island. Land again!

971 ξυνέσεσθαι: This word is frequently used in the sense of being with one as a traveling companion, and in that sense fits in well with the gloomy presentiment of Odysseus.

976 Mercilessly, Poseidon scatters the raft and hurls him into the waves. Not yet, though, will Odysseus give up; he starts swimming stoutly across the gulf, trying to take advantage of the direction of the wind and waves.

ODYSSEUS AND HIS RAFT
The weary hero struggles to keep afloat in the fierce storm which Poseidon has raised against him.

1089. MEMORIZE:

ἀμβρόσιος, -η, -ον   fragrant
ἀπείρων, -ον   boundless

(ἐ)είδομαι, —, (ἐ)εισάμην   I appear, I seem (like to)

1090. TEXT

A Long Swim and a Long Sleep

ἔνθα κέ μ᾿ ἐκβαίνοντα βιήσατο κῦμ᾿ ἐπὶ χέρσου,
980 πέτρης πρὸς μεγάλῃσι βαλὸν καὶ ἀτερπέι χώρῳ·
ἀλλ᾿ ἀναχασσάμενος νῆχον πάλιν, ἧος ἐπῆλθον
ἐς ποταμόν, τῇ δή μοι ἐείσατο χῶρος ἄριστος,
λεῖος πετράων, καὶ ἐπὶ σκέπας ἦν ἀνέμοιο.
ἐκ δ᾿ ἔπεσον θυμηγερέων, ἐπὶ δ᾿ ἀμβροσίη νὺξ
985 ἤλυθ᾿. ἐγὼ δ᾿ ἀπάνευθε διιπετέος ποταμοῖο
ἐκβὰς ἐν θάμνοισι κατέδραθον, ἀμφὶ δὲ φύλλα
ἠφυσάμην· ὕπνον δὲ θεὸς κατ᾿ ἀπείρονα χεῦεν.
ἔνθα μὲν ἐν φύλλοισι φίλον τετιημένος ἦτορ
εὗδον παννύχιος καὶ ἐπ᾿ ἠῶ καὶ μέσον ἦμαρ.
990 δείλετό τ᾿ ἠέλιος καί με γλυκὺς ὕπνος ἀνῆκεν.

ἀνα-χάζομαι, —, ἀνα-χασσάμην I draw back
ἀν-ίημι, etc. I loose; I leave
ἀτερπής, -ές joyless, painful
βιάομαι, βιήσομαι, βιησάμην I force
δείλομαι I draw towards evening
διιπετής, -έος [adj.] rain-fed
ἐκ-βαίνω, etc. I go out, I go forth

θάμνος, -ου [m.] bush, shrub
θυμηγερέων, -ον making a fight for life, rallying
κατα-δαρθάνω, —, κατά-δραθον I fall asleep
λεῖος, -η, -ον smooth, free from
παννύχιος, -η, -ον all night long
τετίημαι I grieve

1091. NOTES

979 κέ: makes the indicative contrary-to-fact.
983 ἐπί: (adv.) "at hand."
984 Transl.: "Coming out of the water I fell down, gasping for breath . . ."

1092. COMMENT

980 Caught by the breakers, he is very nearly dashed against a section of jagged rocks, and only with difficulty does he manage to swim back and seek a better spot.

984 Fortunately, he was just able to make the bank before the sudden darkness of the Mediterranean fell upon him. A few minutes later it might have been impossible for him to get to shore without serious injury.

985 διιπετέος: Fed by rain from the sky, which was often identified with Zeus.

989 After his seventeen days and nights on the raft and his struggle in the water, a long sleep was physically imperative.

1093. WORD STUDY
   AMBROSIAL (fragrant, heavenly — of foods or scents).

WHERE TO LAND
This rocky inlet along the coast of Corfu suggests to many the rough conditions where Odysseus was first driven landward by the surging sea. He was able nevertheless to swim to a more hospitable beach and come safely ashore.

1094. MEMORIZE:

ἀπήνη, -ης [f.] wagon
ἀραρίσκω, ἄρσομαι, ἄρσα or ἄραρον I
  fit together; I am fitted with

ἡμίονος, -ου [f.] mule
μέλω, μελήσω, μέλησα I am a care to
τρεῖς, τρία three

We now for a time leave Odysseus sleeping quietly in the thicket, while the scene is shifted to the palace of Alcinous, king of the Phaeacians, to whose land Odysseus has just come. Up to this point in our story, Homer has allowed Odysseus to give his own account of his adventures; but now the poet takes over and speaks in his own person.

As the curtain rises, we see a young and strikingly beautiful girl, Nausicaa, princess of the Phaeacians, speaking to her father:

1095. TEXT

Enter the Princess

991 «πάππα φίλ᾽, οὐκ ἂν δή μοι ἐφοπλίσσειας ἀπήνην
    ὑψηλὴν ἐύκυκλον, ἵνα κλυτὰ εἴματ᾽ ἄγωμαι
    ἐς ποταμὸν πλυνέουσα, τά μοι ῥερυπωμένα κεῖται;
    καὶ δὲ σοὶ αὐτῷ ἔοικε μετὰ πρώτοισιν ἐόντα
995 βουλὰς βουλεύειν καθαρὰ χροῒ εἴματ᾽ ἔχοντα.
    πέντε δέ τοι φίλοι υἶες ἐνὶ μεγάροις γεγάασιν,
    οἱ δύ᾽ ὀπυίοντες, τρεῖς δ᾽ ἠίθεοι θαλέθοντες·
    οἱ δ᾽ αἰεὶ ἐθέλουσι νεόπλυτα εἴματ᾽ ἔχοντες
    ἐς χορὸν ἔρχεσθαι· τὰ δ᾽ ἐμῇ φρενὶ πάντα μέμηλεν.»
1000   ὣς ἔφατ᾽· αἴδετο γὰρ θαλερὸν γάμον ἐξονομῆναι
    πατρὶ φίλῳ. ὁ δὲ πάντα νόει καὶ ἀμείβετο μύθῳ·
    «οὔτε τοι ἡμιόνων φθονέω, τέκος, οὔτε τευ ἄλλου.
    ἔρχευ, ἀτάρ τοι δμῶες ἐφοπλίσσουσιν ἀπήνην
    ὑψηλὴν ἐύκυκλον, ὑπερτερίῃ ἀραρυῖαν.»

αἴδομαι [= αἰδέομαι] I feel embar-
  rassment, I blush
ἐξ-ονομαίνω, —, ἐξ-ονόμηνα I (utter
  the) name, I mention aloud
ἐύκυκλος, -ον well-wheeled
ἐφ-οπλίζω, -οπλίσσω, -όπλισσα
  I prepare
ἠίθεος, -ον an unmarried youth
θαλέθω I flourish, I am in the
  prime of life
καθαρός, -ή, -όν clean, spotless

νεόπλυτος, -ον newly-washed
ὀπυίω I wed, I am married
πάππα "father," "daddy"
πέντε five
πλύνω, πλυνέω, πλῦνα I wash
ῥυπάω; pf. mid.: ῥερύπωμαι I am
  dirty, I become soiled
ὑπερτερίη, -ης [f.] receptacle, box
  (fixed on a wagon)
φθονέω I am begrudging of

133

ODYSSEUS MEETS NAUSICAA
The painter Aison has decorated the lid of a pyxis (powder jar) with a scene explicitly illustrating Homer's story of the reluctant Odysseus appealing to Nausicaa, who remains calm while her girl companions run away.

1096. NOTES

994 ἐόντα: instead of agreeing with σοί, it apparently agrees with σέ understood as subject accusative of βουλεύειν.

999 μέμηλεν: perfect of μέλω with present force.

1000 θαλερόν: marriage in the bloom of youth, "her maidenly marriage."

1004 ἀραρυῖαν: perfect participle of ἀραρίσκω.

1097. COMMENT

991 This delightful little speech, composed, we must not allow ourselves to forget, almost three thousand years ago, ought to impress us with the truth of the worn-out saying that times change but people do not. Would you say that the general approach of the Phaeacian princess is a great deal different from that of the American girl asking her father for the loan of his convertible for an errand, the nature of which she is somewhat reluctant for her father to inquire into?

999 It was not thought extraordinary for a Homeric king or princess to work with the servants in performing the tasks of household or farm. To Nausicaa, the only daughter in a large family, it would naturally fall to help her mother with such chores as the laundry.

1000 The real reason she wishes to do the washing herself is to get ready her clothes and finery for her wedding, which she considers herself now old enough to expect to take place soon.

1001 Her father, like most fathers of all ages, understands his child better than the child imagines.

134

1098. MEMORIZE:

ἐδωδή, -ῆς [f.]   food
ἔλαιον, -ου [n.]   olive oil
ἐσθής, -ῆτος [f.]   clothing
ἐύξεστος, (-η), -ον   well-polished

ζεύγνῡμι, ζεύξω, ζεῦξα   I yoke
ἡνία, -ων [m. pl.]   reins
θάλαμος, -ου [m.]   bed-room, store-room
κούρη, -ης [f.]   girl, daughter

1099. TEXT

A Picnic-Lunch

1005
ὣς εἰπὼν δμώεσσιν ἐκέκλετο, τοὶ δὲ πίθοντο.
οἱ μὲν ἄρ᾽ ἐκτὸς ἄμαξαν ἐύτροχον ἡμιονείην
ὥπλεον, ἡμιόνους θ᾽ ὕπαγον ζεῦξάν θ᾽ ὑπ᾽ ἀπήνῃ.
κούρη δ᾽ ἐκ θαλάμοιο φέρεν ἐσθῆτα φαεινήν.
καὶ τὴν μὲν κατέθηκεν ἐυξέστῳ ἐπ᾽ ἀπήνῃ,

1010
μήτηρ δ᾽ ἐν κίστῃ ἐτίθει μενοεικέ᾽ ἐδωδὴν
παντοίην, ἐν δ᾽ ὄψα τίθει, ἐν δ᾽ οἶνον ἔχευεν
ἀσκῷ ἐν αἰγείῳ· κούρη δ᾽ ἐπεβήσατ᾽ ἀπήνης.
δῶκεν δὲ χρυσέῃ ἐν ληκύθῳ ὑγρὸν ἔλαιον,
ἧος χυτλώσαιτο σὺν ἀμφιπόλοισι γυναιξίν.

1015
ἣ δ᾽ ἔλαβεν μάστιγα καὶ ἡνία σιγαλόεντα,
ἡμίονοι δὲ πέτοντο, φέρον δ᾽ ἐσθῆτα καὶ αὐτήν,
οὐκ οἴην, ἅμα τῇ γε καὶ ἀμφίπολοι κίον ἄλλαι.

αἴγειος, -η, -ον   of a goat; of goatskin
ἐύτροχος, -ον   having good wheels
ἡμιόνειος, -η, -ον   drawn by mules
κίστη, -ης [f.]   box, chest
λήκυθος, -ου [f.]   oil-flask
μάστιξ, -ῑγος [f.]   whip

μενοεικής, -ές   heart-satisfying, pleasing
ὁπλέω   I get ready, I prepare
ὄψον, -ου [n.] [in pl.]   cooked meats,
   relish
ὑπ-άγω, etc.   I lead under (the yoke)
χυτλόω, χυτλώσω, χύτλωσα   I anoint

1100. NOTES

1007 ὑπ᾽: they harnessed them under the yoke of the wagon.
1012 ἐπεβήσατ᾽: a first aorist of βαίνω, unusual in the intransitive sense here.
1013 χρυσέῃ: synizesis.
1014 ἧος: with a purpose idea. (Cp. the Irish: "Come here till I whack you!")
1017 ἄλλαι: i.e., "also," "besides."

135

1101. COMMENT

1010 Her mother bringing out the picnic lunch, not forgetting the relish, adds the last homey touch to the scene.

1013 Olive oil was used extensively in Greece as a sort of soap, and as a tonic and protection of the skin.

1015 It would seem that the wagon used was so small that it could not conveniently accommodate more than the clothes and the princess. Her attendants probably walked along beside or behind it.

1102. WORD STUDY

ZEUGMA (a figure of speech in which one verb or adjective is joined or 'yoked' to two nouns, to one of which it has a related but not quite normal applicability, e.g., 'They *ate* the rich food and sparkling wine'); — CHEST (a box; the lung-box of the body).

FEMININE ELEGANCE

Terracotta statuettes, usually six to ten inches in height, became a popular household ornament in Classical Greece. They usually represent people in some aspect of daily life and dress. Many are finely moulded; most had soft coloration that survives poorly. This example, from Tanagra near Thebes, represents a lady with flowing garments, hand fan, and fancy hat.

1103. MEMORIZE:

ἔρις, -ιδος [f.]   strife; rivalry
καθαίρω, καθαρέω, κάθηρα   I cleanse
λοέω, λοέσσω, λόεσ(σ)α [frequently
   contracts to λούω, etc.]   I wash

περικαλλής, -ές   very beautiful
σεύω, —, (σ)σεῦσα or (σ)σύμην   I set in
   motion, I drive; [mid.]   I rush
χρίω, χρίσομαι, χρῖσα   I anoint

1104. TEXT

All Work—

αἱ δ' ὅτε δὴ ποταμοῖο ῥόον περικαλλέ' ἵκοντο,
ἔνθ' ἦ τοι πλυνοὶ ἦσαν ἐπηετανοί, πολὺ δ' ὕδωρ
1020 καλὸν ὑπεκπρόρεεν μάλα περ ῥυπάοντα καθῆραι,
ἔνθ' αἵ γ' ἡμιόνους μὲν ὑπεκπροέλυσαν ἀπήνης.
καὶ τὰς μὲν σεῦαν ποταμὸν πάρα δινήεντα
τρώγειν ἄγρωστιν μελιηδέα· ταὶ δ' ἀπ' ἀπήνης
εἵματα χερσὶν ἕλοντο καὶ ἐσφόρεον μέλαν ὕδωρ,
1025 στεῖβον δ' ἐν βόθροισι θοῶς ἔριδα προφέρουσαι.
αὐτὰρ ἐπεὶ πλῦνάν τε κάθηράν τε ῥύπα πάντα,
ἐξείης πέτασαν παρὰ θῖν' ἁλός, ἧχι μάλιστα
λάιγγας ποτὶ χέρσον ἀποπλύνεσκε θάλασσα.
αἱ δὲ λοεσσάμεναι καὶ χρισάμεναι λίπ' ἐλαίῳ
1030 δεῖπνον ἔπειθ' εἵλοντο παρ' ὄχθῃσιν ποταμοῖο,
εἵματα δ' ἠελίοιο μένον τερσήμεναι αὐγῇ.

ἄγρωστις, -ιος [f.]   clover, grass
ἀπο-πλύνω   I wash away from myself, I wash up
δῑνήεις, -εσσα, -εν   eddying, swirling
ἐπηετανός, -όν   never-failing, ever-
   flowing
ἐσ-φορέω   I bring in
ἧχι   where
λᾶιγξ, λάιγγος [f.]   pebble
λίπα [adv.]   richly, plenteously
ὄχθη, -ης [f.]   bank, shore
πλῡ́νω, πλυνέω, πλῦνα   I wash

πλυνός, -οῦ [m.]   place for washing,
   washing-trough
προ-φέρω, etc.   I display
ῥύπα, -ων [n. pl.]   defilement, dirt
ῥυπάω   I am dirty, I am soiled
στείβω   I trample, I tread on
τερσαίνω [pres. inf. τερσήμεναι]   I dry
τρώγω   I nibble, I crop
ὑπ-εκ-προ-λύω, etc.   I loose from
   under and out, I release
ὑπ-εκ-προ-ρέω   I flow up and out from
   beneath

1105. NOTES

1020 *ῥυπάοντα:* understand εἵματα.
1024 *μέλαν:* "dark," even though clear (καλόν), because of its depth.
   ὕδωρ: place to which (#18 d,2).
1026 *ῥύπα:* i.e., ἐξ εἱμάτων.
1031 *μένον:* αἱ is still the subject.

HERMONES BEACH
This would be the placid and safe landfall Odysseus sought, further along the coast of Corfu—which is plausibly considered the basis of Homer's Phaeacia. It has the outlet of a stream and the sandy beach which the story of the meeting with Nausicaa describes.

1106. COMMENT

1019 Apparently regular basins had been hollowed out alongside the river and lined with stone. At either end, openings would be made so that the water of the river could be channeled to flow through them in a steady stream.

1025 They trample the clothes with their feet to loosen the dirt, gaily vying with one another to see who can tread most vigorously and most quickly, making a sort of game out of the work.

1030 The picture of the girls having their picnic lunch on the grassy bank of the river is another proof of the marvelous way that Homer seems to make his characters thoroughly human. In few pieces of world literature will you find people so charmingly natural and true to life as in Homer.

1107. WORD STUDY

ERISTIC (disputatious, prone to controversy); — CHRISM (a consecrated oil used for ritual anointing in the Sacrament of Confirmation).

1108. MEMORIZE:

γλαυκῶπις, -ιδος flashing-eyed [epithet of Athene]
δμωή, -ῆς [f.] handmaid
ἔλαφος, -ου [f.] deer
ἡγέομαι, ἡγήσομαι, ἡγησάμην I lead, I guide

κρήδεμνον, -ου [n.] veil
λευκώλενος, -ον white-armed
Ναυσικάā, -ας Nausicaa
πτύσσω, πτύξω, πτύξα I fold
ῥεῖα [adv.] easily, at ease

1109. TEXT

— and Some Play

αὐτὰρ ἐπεὶ σίτου τάρφθεν δμωαί τε καὶ αὐτή,
σφαίρῃ ταὶ δ᾽ ἄρ᾽ ἔπαιζον ἀπὸ κρήδεμνα βαλοῦσαι·
τῇσι δὲ Ναυσικάα λευκώλενος ἤρχετο μολπῆς.
1035 οἴη δ᾽ Ἄρτεμις εἶσι κατ᾽ οὔρεα ἰοχέαιρα,
ἢ κατὰ Τηΰγετον περιμήκετον ἢ Ἐρύμανθον,
τερπομένη κάπροισι καὶ ὠκείης ἐλάφοισιν·
τῇ δέ θ᾽ ἅμα νύμφαι, κοῦραι Διὸς αἰγιόχοιο,
ἀγρονόμοι παίζουσι, γέγηθε δέ τε φρένα Λητώ·
1040 πασάων δ᾽ ὑπὲρ ἥ γε κάρη ἔχει ἠδὲ μέτωπα,
ῥεῖά τ᾽ ἀριγνώτη πέλεται, καλαὶ δέ τε πᾶσαι·
ὣς ἥ γ᾽ ἀμφιπόλοισι μετέπρεπε παρθένος ἀδμής.
   ἀλλ᾽ ὅτε δὴ ἄρ᾽ ἔμελλε πάλιν οἰκόνδε νέεσθαι
ζεύξασ᾽ ἡμιόνους πτύξασά τε εἵματα καλά,
1045 ἔνθ᾽ αὖτ᾽ ἄλλ᾽ ἐνόησε θεά, γλαυκῶπις Ἀθήνη,
ὡς Ὀδυσεὺς ἔγροιτο ἴδοι τ᾽ ἐυώπιδα κούρην,
ἥ οἱ Φαιήκων ἀνδρῶν πόλιν ἡγήσαιτο.

ἀγρόνομος, -ον haunting the fields
ἀδμής, -ῆτος [adj.] unwedded
ἀρίγνωτος, -η, -ον known, recognizable
ἄρχω, ἄρξω, ἄρξα I make beginning of, I lead off
Ἐρύμανθος, -ου [m.] Erymanthus [a mountain in Achaea]
ἐυῶπις, -ιδος [adj.] fair, beautiful
Λητώ, -όος [f.] Leto [mother of Apollo and Artemis
μετα-πρέπω I am preeminent among

μέτωπον, -ου [n.] forehead
μολπή, -ῆς [f.] play; singing
οὖρος, -εος [n.] mountain
παίζω I play, I sport
παρθένος, -ου [f.] maiden, virgin
περιμήκετος, -η, -ον of great height, lofty
σφαῖρα, -ης [f.] ball
Τηΰγετος, -ου [m.] Taÿgetus [a mountain above Sparta]

139

1110.   NOTES

1032   *τάρφθεν:* aorist passive third plural indicative (with irregular ending) of *τέρπω.*

1033   *ἀπό:* adverbial, with *βαλοῦσαι.*

1035   *οἵη:* transl.: "just as." *εἶσι:* cp. #861.

1037   *τερπομένη:* "taking delight in."

1038   *τῇ:* with *ἅμα.*

1039   *γέγηθε:* perfect, with present force, of *γηθέω.*

1040   *ὑπέρ:* adverbial.

1041   *πᾶσαι:* understand *εἰσίν.* Notice that an independent clause is used instead of a concessive clause ("although").

1045   *ἐνόησε:* "thought other things," "planned otherwise."

1046   *ὡς:* "namely, how. . . ."

1047   *οἱ:* ("who might be guide) for him."

1111.   COMMENT

1033   The game is thought to have been played by tossing a ball unexpectedly to one of the players after "faking" it towards someone else, possibly to the accompaniment of some sort of chant or song. Whichever player or team missed the ball least often probably would be considered the winner.

1035 ff.   To give us an idea of how striking Nausicaa looked among her maidens as they sported about in the game, Homer compares her to Artemis, goddess of the hills and forests, who runs lightly with the nymphs playing round her and outshines them all in her stateliness and beauty.

1044   When the princess was beginning to think of folding the clothes and harnessing up to go home, Athene interferes to bring help to Odysseus, her faithful worshiper.

1112.   WORD STUDY

HEGEMONY (leadership, priority of power, as 'An aim of the Communist Party is to establish Russian hegemony throughout the world'); — EXEGESIS (a 'leading out' of the meaning of some scriptural or other text by explaining its background and significance); — ARCHCONSPIRATOR (the chief or 'leading' conspirator), ARCHENEMY, ARCHBISHOP; ARCHITECT (*τέκτων,* builder, hence 'chief-builder, master-builder who plans and directs the whole), ARCHITECTURE; — ANARCHY ('lack of leadership,' confusion due to absence of or revolt against central authority).

1113. **MEMORIZE:**

ἀϋτή, -ῆς [f.] shout

ἀΰω, αὐσω, ἄϋσα I shout

ὁρμαίνω, —, ὅρμηνα I ponder

1114. **TEXT**

An Eventful Encounter

> *σφαῖραν ἔπειτ᾽ ἔρριψε μετ᾽ ἀμφίπολον βασίλεια·*
> *ἀμφιπόλου μὲν ἅμαρτε, βαθείῃ δ᾽ ἔμβαλε δίνῃ·*
> 1050 *αἱ δ᾽ ἐπὶ μακρὸν ἄϋσαν· ὁ δ᾽ ἔγρετο δῖος Ὀδυσσεύς,*
> *ἑζόμενος δ᾽ ὥρμαινε κατὰ φρένα καὶ κατὰ θυμόν·*
> *"ὤ μοι ἐγώ, τέων αὖτε βροτῶν ἐς γαῖαν ἱκάνω;*
> *ἦ ῥ᾽ οἵ γ᾽ ὑβρισταί τε καὶ ἄγριοι οὐδὲ δίκαιοι,*
> *ἦε φιλόξεινοι καί σφιν νόος ἐστὶ θεουδής;*
> 1055 *ὥς τέ με κουράων ἀμφήλυθε θῆλυς ἀϋτή,*
> *νυμφάων, αἳ ἔχουσ᾽ ὀρέων αἰπεινὰ κάρηνα*
> *καὶ πηγὰς ποταμῶν καὶ πίσεα ποιήεντα.*
> *ἦ νύ που ἀνθρώπων εἰμὶ σχεδὸν αὐδηέντων;*
> *ἀλλ᾽ ἄγ᾽ ἐγὼν αὐτὸς πειρήσομαι ἠδὲ ἴδωμαι."*
> 1060 *ὣς εἰπὼν θάμνων ὑπεδύσετο δῖος Ὀδυσσεύς,*
> *ἐκ πυκινῆς δ᾽ ὕλης πτόρθον κλάσε χειρὶ παχείῃ*
> *φύλλων, ὡς ῥύσαιτο περὶ χροῒ μήδεα φωτός.*

αἰπεινός, -ή, -όν high, lofty
ἀμφ-έρχομαι, etc. I come around, I surround
αὐδήεις, -εσσα, -εν using (mortal) speech
βασίλεια, -ης [f.] queen, princess
δίνη, -ης [f.] whirlpool, eddy
ἐμ-βάλλω, etc. I throw in
θάμνος, -ου [m.] bush
θεουδής, -ές god-fearing
κλάω, —, κλάσα I break
μῆδος, -εος [n.] [always pl.] nakedness

πηγή, -ῆς [f.] spring
πῖσος, -εος [n.] water-meadow
ποιήεις, -εσσα, -εν grassy
πτόρθος, -ου [m.] branch
ῥύομαι, —, ῥῦσάμην I protect, I hide
σφαῖρα, -ης [f.] ball
ὑβριστής, -άο wanton, violent
ὑπο-δύομαι, —, ὑπο-δῦσόμην I come forth from
φιλό-ξεινος, -ον well-disposed to strangers, hospitable

1115. **NOTES**

1048 *μετ᾽:* "towards" or "at."

1049 *ἅμαρτε:* the subject of this and *ἔμβαλε* is still *βασίλεια.*

1050 *ἐπὶ μακρόν:* "over a great (distance)," i.e., "loudly."

1051 *ἑζόμενος:* here, of course, "sitting up."

NAUSICAA'S HANDMAIDENS

1052 ἱς μοι ἐγώ: an exclamation, representing some such idea as "alas for me! Woe is me!"
τέων: synizesis.
ἱκάνω: We would expect a perfect; but the present result is emphasized at the expense of the action required to produce it.

1053 οἵ: understand εἰσί.

1055 ὥς: "as of girls."
θῆλυς: i.e., "shrill."

1059 ἴδωμαι: not a mere future fact as πειρήσομαι, but an exhortation to do something.

1062 περὶ χροΐ: "so that it (being tied) around his person. . . ."

1116. COMMENT

1050 After the careful build-up, the action itself takes place in a flash—they scream; he awakes; his rescue is under way.

1052 As a point of Homer's art, notice that he allows his characters not only to develop the action themselves but also to dramatize their very thoughts by thinking aloud.

1052-9. Remember that Odysseus had heard no human voice nor seen any mortal for over eight years.

1056 The Greeks were remarkable for their view of nature. They were never satisfied merely with *things,* however wonderful or beautiful. They had always to find in things a *life* akin to their own, a life with personality. Hence, the mountains and springs and meadows, all had, to the imaginative Greeks, their own personal spirits. Idolatry, which dominated the whole ancient world and had to be stamped out so vigorously even among the Jews, seems never to have occurred to the Greeks.

1062 With a natural and unaffected modesty, Odysseus feels it unbecoming to investigate the voices without some sort of covering.

1117. WORD STUDY

SPHERE (a ball or globe), ATMOSPHERE (ἀτμός, vapor; hence, the 'ball of air' surrounding the earth).

1118. MEMORIZE:

ἀλκή, -ῆς [dat. sg. ἀλκί. f.] defence; prowess
ἄλμη, -ης [f.] brine, briny crust
ἄντα [n. gen.] before, opposite
δαίω I light up; [pass.] I blaze

δείκνῡμι, δείξω, δεῖξα I show
λέων, -οντος [m.] lion
σμερδαλέος, -η, -ον frightful, terrible

1119. TEXT

Odysseus Comes Forth

βῆ δ᾽ ἴμεν ὥς τε λέων ὀρεσίτροφος ἀλκὶ πεποιθώς,
ὅς τ᾽ εἶσ ὑόμενος καὶ ἀήμενος, ἐν δέ οἱ ὄσσε
1065 δαίεται· αὐτὰρ ὁ βουσὶ μετέρχεται ἢ ὀίεσσιν
ἠὲ μετ᾽ ἀγροτέρας ἐλάφους· κέλεται δέ ἑ γαστὴρ
μήλων πειρήσοντα καὶ ἐς πυκινὸν δόμον ἐλθεῖν·
ὣς Ὀδυσεὺς κούρῃσιν ἐυπλοκάμοισιν ἔμελλεν
μίξεσθαι γυμνός περ ἐών· χρειὼ γὰρ ἵκανε.
1070 σμερδαλέος δ᾽ αὐτῇσι φάνη κεκακωμένος ἅλμῃ,
τρέσσαν δ᾽ ἄλλυδις ἄλλη ἐπ᾽ ἠιόνας προὐχούσας.
οἴη δ᾽ Ἀκλκινόου θυγάτηρ μένε· τῇ γὰρ Ἀθήνη
θάρσος ἐνὶ φρεσὶ θῆκε καὶ ἐκ δέος εἵλετο γυίων.
στῆ δ᾽ ἄντα σχομένη· ὁ δὲ μερμήριξεν Ὀδυσσεύς,
1075 ἢ γούνων λίσσοιτο λαβὼν ἐυώπιδα κούρην,
ἦ αὔτως ἐπέεσσιν ἀποσταδὰ μειλιχίοισιν
λίσσοιτ᾽, εἰ δείξειε πόλιν καὶ εἵματα δοίη.

ἀγρότερος, -η, -ον wild
ἄλλυδις (ἄλλη): some one way, others another way
ἀποσταδά standing aloof, at a distance
γυμνός, -ή, -όν naked, uncovered
ἐυῶπις, -ιδος fair, beautiful
ἠιών, -όνος [f.] [in pl.] seashore, strand

θάρσος, -εος [n.] courage, daring
κακόω: pf. mid.: κεκάκωμαι I outrage, I befoul
μετ-έρχομαι, etc. I mingle with
ὀρεσίτροφος, -ον mountain-bred
προ-έχω, etc. I project, I jut out
τρέω, —, τρέσσα I flee (in fright)
ὕω I rain; [pass.:] I am rained upon

1120. NOTES

1063 πεποιθώς: perfect participle of πείθω (with present sense) meaning here "I trust in."
1064 ἀήμενος: passive participle of ἄημι. (cp. ὑόμενος)
ἐν: adverbial—"within," i.e., with the inner fire of savage hunger and excitement.
1067 καί: "even."
πυκινὸν δόμον: the carefully-closed fold.
1069 ἵκανε: understand μίν.
1074 στῆ ἄντα: "she stood facing him."
σχομένη: i.e., from flight.
1075 γούνων: partitive genitive after λαμβάνω when it means 'I take hold of.'

THE ENCOUNTER

1121.   COMMENT

1063 ff.   The Homeric simile is imaginative rather than intellectual; it presents a complete picture rather than merely the scientifically analyzed point of similarity. The main point of comparison here is the necessity that drove both the lion and the Greek to do something rather desperate. A secondary point is the consternation that would seize the unsuspecting sheep, on the one hand, and, on the other, the unsuspecting girls.

1070   This line is thought to have been made especially harsh in sound, to match the idea expressed in it. That is part of poetic skill.

1072   It is not surprising that the girls should have been frightened by the sight he presented; yet the young princess refuses to flee and holds her ground, facing him. The poet explains this as the inspiration of Athene, but such an explanation is really nothing more than the mythological externalization of psychology. Nausicaa was a girl of high character and spirit. Besides, any girl who had grown up with five brothers would inevitably have a more masculine and fearless attitude toward men.

1075   This custom, for one begging a favor to clasp the knees of his expected benefactor as a sign of humble supplication, was the universal practice of the Greeks and would not in itself surprise Nausicaa. What Odysseus feared was that the maiden would be frightened and run away if he approached too near with his present savage appearance, or might misinterpret his action and become angered.

1077   Odysseus could hardly fail to notice the clothes laid out conspicuously to dry.

1122.   WORD STUDY

GYMNASIUM, GYMNASTICS (because the ancients took their exercise lightly clad).

1123. MEMORIZE:

εἶδος, -εος [n.] appearance, face
ναιετάω I dwell, I inhabit; I am situated; I exist

τοιόσδε, -ήδε, -όνδε such (as this, as that)

1124. TEXT

Odysseus, the Orator

ὡς ἄρα οἱ φρονέοντι δοάσσατο κέρδιον εἶναι,
λίσσεσθαι ἐπέεσσιν ἀποσταδὰ μειλιχίοισιν,
1080 μή οἱ γοῦνα λαβόντι χολώσαιτο φρένα κούρη.
αὐτίκα μειλίχιον καὶ κερδαλέον φάτο μῦθον·
"γουνοῦμαί σε, ἄνασσα· θεός νύ τις, ἦ βροτός ἐσσι;
εἰ μέν τις θεός ἐσσι, τοὶ οὐρανὸν εὐρὺν ἔχουσιν,
Ἀρτέμιδί σε ἐγώ γε, Διὸς κούρη μεγάλοιο,
1085 εἶδός τε μέγεθός τε φυήν τ᾽ ἄγχιστα ἐΐσκω·
εἰ δέ τίς ἐσσι βροτῶν, οἳ ἐπὶ χθονὶ ναιετάουσι,
τρὶς μάκαρες μὲν σοί γε πατὴρ καὶ πότνια μήτηρ,
τρὶς μάκαρες δέ κασίγνητοι· μάλα πού σφισι θυμὸς
αἰὲν ἐυφροσύνῃσιν ἰαίνεται εἵνεκα σεῖο,
1090 λευσσόντων τοιόνδε θάλος χορὸν εἰσοιχνεῦσαν.
κεῖνος δ᾽ αὖ πέρι κῆρι μακάρτατος ἔξοχον ἄλλων,
ὅς κέ σ᾽ ἐέδνοισι βρίσας οἰκόνδ᾽ ἀγάγηται.

ἄγχιστα = supl. of ἄγχι	εἰσ-οιχνέω I come in, I enter
αἰέν = αἰεί	ἔξοχον = ἔξοχα
ἄνασσα, -ης [f.] queen, protectress	ἐυφροσύνη, -ης [f.] gladness,
ἀποσταδά standing aloof, at a distance	merriment
βρίθω, —, βρῖσα I weigh down, I	θάλος, -εος [n.] young shoot;
prevail	youthful person
δοάσσατο [defective verb] it seemed,	κερδαλέος, -η, -ον cunning, clever
it appeared	μέγεθος, -εος [n.] stature
ἐΐσκω I liken to	φυή, ῆς [f.] form

1125. NOTES

    1083   τοί: its antecedent is a θεῶν implied in θεός.

    1087   μάκαρες: εἰσί is understood.

    1089   ἐυφροσύνῃσιν: another example of the plural of abstract nouns used to refer to repeated occasions or actions.

    1090   λευσσόντων: agreeing in sense with the preceding dative of possession;

        εἰσοιχνεῦσαν: agrees with the natural gender of θάλος (in this case a girl).

        τοιόνδε: for declension, see #1149.

    1091   πέρι: (adv.) "exceedingly."

        μακάρτατος: compared as adjectives in -ης and -υς.

    1092   σ': object of ἀγάγηται.

1126. COMMENT

    1078   Even here Odysseus' agile mind works furiously to decide the better way of winning his point. If anything is characteristic of Odysseus it is the remarkable way he thinks about each problem and plans each step.

    1082   This speech might well be studied as a model of psychological approach. Notice that he addresses her at once as "queen," and wonders if she is goddess or mortal—a question that was not likely to be displeasing to a young girl, and especially to one who knew that she was beautiful.

    1085   εἶδος would refer to the face, μέγεθος to her stature, and φυήν to her body.

    1087   Compare the similar sentiments of Aeneas to Dido on their first meeting (*Aen.* 1.605–6):

> *Quae te tam laeta tulerunt*
> *saecula? Qui tanti talem genuere parentes?*

    1091   A poet in the *Anthology* is still more enthusiastic:

> εὐδαίμων ὁ βλέπων σε· τρισόλβιος ὅστις ἀκούει·
> ἡμίθεος δ' ὁ φιλῶν· ἀθάνατος δ' ὁ γαμῶν.

(The first line is read as a regular hexameter; the second is scanned thus:

$$-\smile\smile\,|-\smile\smile\,|-\,\|-\smile\smile\,|-\smile\smile\,|-\,\|$$) .

    1092   Large presents were expected to be given to the father of the sought-for bride. The keen competition suggested here would, of course, be a great compliment to the beauty and accomplishments of the girl.

THE HERA TEMPLE AT PAESTUM

The Greek colony Poseidonia in west central Italy had a row of fine temples, most of them in honor of Hera, queen of the gods. The finest, and best preserved, is this one, commonly mis-named for Poseidon, god of the sea. It was built around 460 B.C., half a generation before the Parthenon. Here the strong beauty of the Doric style is evident, with its mathematically precise proportions and relationships of part to part. Its rhythmic order and lucid intellectual pattern stir awe and admiration in the beholder.

REVIEW

1127.   Go over again Lessons 187–196; make sure now that you have really mastered them. Here are a few suggestions for your review:

1. *Vocabulary:* Check your mastery of the 54 new memory words.
2. *Text:* Reread the 137 lines of text, making sure you recognize all the forms.
3. *Story:*

    a.   How did Odysseus react to the proposal of Calypso?
    b.   How did he finally get on Phaeacian soil?
    c.   Describe the royal family of the Phaeacians.
    d.   Describe the technique used by Nausicaa and her handmaids in washing the clothes.
    e.   Describe the meeting of Nausicaa and Odysseus.

4. *Criticism:*

    a.   What new revelations of the character of Odysseus can you find in these ten lessons?
    b.   Do you think Homer succeeds in making Nausicaa a very appealing person? Explain your answer.
    c.   Would you say that the meeting of Odysseus and Nausicaa is brought about naturally, in a plausible manner? Explain.

5. *Composition:* Put into Greek:

    a.   It is said that Alcinous, king of the Phaeacians, was immortal in appearance.
    b.   In order to persuade her father, the girl said that washing clothes for him and his sons was her care.
    c.   Who would not yoke the mules to (= under) the wagon for the very beautiful daughter of the king!

1128.   THE SPIRIT OF GREEK ARCHITECTURE

Architecture's purpose is to build a dwelling which is both suited to its specific function and pleasing to look at; that is, to provide a shelter for man which befits his humanity, supplying his body protection and his soul beauty.

The Greek contribution to the progress of architecture is what might be expected: it combines beauty with practicality, simplicity with splendor. So noble a formula for architectural design did the Greeks work out that it has been the admiration of all the world, receiving on all sides the highest proof of esteem: imitation. It will be both interesting and important to learn some details about this branch of Greek art, with which every educated person is supposed to be at least basically familiar.

The earliest Greek buildings which still survive well enough preserved to reveal their design and features are the huge "Cyclopēan" stone walls and chambers of Mycenae and Tiryns, built with massive stone blocks carefully fitted together into rectangular, triangular, and circular patterns (see pictures, p. 205 and vol. 1, p. 321). Buildings in the subsequent period were of of wood and have perished. Toward the sixth century B.C., however, Greece was prosperous enough again to build in stone, and rapidly evolved complete architectural styles of its own.

THE THOLOS AT DELPHI

Most Greek buildings were rectangular, but a few round ones introduced a pleasing variety of style. This 'Tholos' in the great religious center at Delphi was considered by the ancients as one of the most beautiful structures anywhere, and Theodoros of Phocaea wrote a book describing it and its design-principles based on mathematical/musical proportions. Three circular platforms of fine marble supported a circle of twenty Doric columns, inside which was a cylindrical wall encircled by ten Corinthian pillars. The floor was of black limestone except a central ring of white, giving a luxurious effect.

The Doric 'order' of building design developed first, an early example being the great temple of Hera at Olympia, c. 640 B.C., and the most famous the Parthenon, two centuries later. The simple, rugged Doric style was economical to construct, but had a strong manly dignity which made for striking beauty. It is characterized by sturdy pillars rising directly from the floor without ornamental base, to a height about 5½ times their bottom diameter. The columns taper gently toward the top and are cut with wide shallow flutings. Above the column rests a simple capital made up of a beveled moulding and a square block. Atop the capital is a great stone beam (the 'architrave') running the whole length or width of the building, surmounted by an ornamental frieze of sculptured figures alternating with raised plates or 'triglyphs' carrying two deep vertical grooves and connecting with the cornice above. The triangular space ('tympanum') under the slant of the roof was filled with sculpted figures in a unified group. For examples, see illustrations on p. xiv, 127 and 147.

The Ionic style, which came into vogue in the sixth century B.C., was more delicate and highly wrought. Its pillars were thinner and taller, averaging nine times their diameter in height, and rested on an ornamental base of rounded mouldings. Fluting of the columns was narrow and deep. At the top was a scroll-like volute supporting an architrave made in three horizontal overhanging steps. Sculpture on the frieze was continuous, not broken up by interjected triglyphs. See the diagram on p. 151 and the picture of the Temple of Winged Victory, p. 149

VICTORY'S TEMPLE
At the southwest corner of the Acropolis of Athens stands the little temple of Wingless Victory (so she cannot fly away elsewhere). It is a gem of the Ionic style. Some of the sculptured frieze above the pillars is still in place. This view is from the Propylaea, entrance framework to the Parthenon and other buildings on the Acropolis.

More elaborate yet, the Corinthian order is distinguished by its inverted-bell-shaped capital adorned with a double row of gracefully curling acanthus leaves. Its pillar, base, and frieze are similar to those of the Ionian style, but more elegant. This was the most popular style of architecture with the Romans, and is the most widely copied in modern buildings. See the splendid example below.

Greek architectural features have a simple directness and harmonious refinement which give them great charm. Their delicacy, strength, and restraint are quite characteristic of the whole Greek spirit in art. The ancient world was filled with their grandeur. To them, much modern architecture goes back for inspiration and example. The ancient Greeks have contributed much to the beauty of our own cities today.

THE OLYMPIEION

The remains of the largest temple in Greece, SW of the Acropolis. It is a fine example of Corinthian style. There were two rows of columns (65 ft. high) all around, but three across the shorter ends. The platform is 354 ft. x 135. Begun in 515 B.C., the work was several times interrupted and taken up again, until the Roman Emperor Hadrian had it completed in A.D. 132, 700 years after it was started. The great size gives it special majesty, the careful workmanship a finished beauty. It was dedicated to Olympian Zeus, king of gods.

GREEK ARCHITECTURAL ORDERS

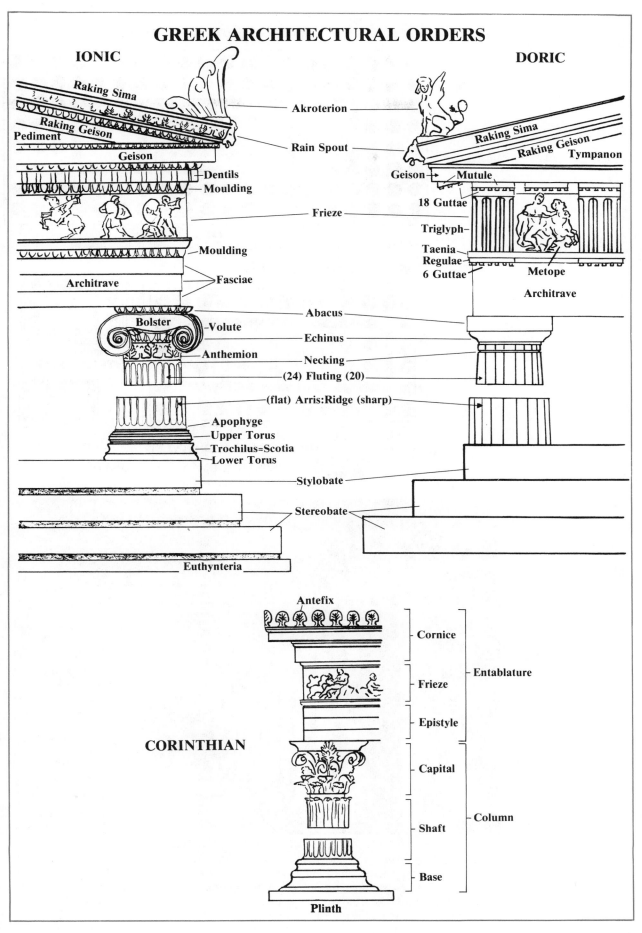

IONIC

DORIC

Raking Sima

Akroterion

Raking Geison

Rain Spout

Pediment

Raking Sima

Geison

Raking Geison

Tympanon

Dentils

Geison

Mutule

Moulding

18 Guttae

Frieze

Triglyph

Moulding

Taenia

Regulae

Architrave

Fasciae

6 Guttae

Metope

Architrave

Abacus

Bolster

Volute

Echinus

Anthemion

Necking

(24) Fluting (20)

(flat) Arris:Ridge (sharp)

Apophyge

Upper Torus

Trochilus=Scotia

Lower Torus

Stylobate

Stereobate

Euthynteria

Antefix

Cornice

Frieze

Entablature

Epistyle

CORINTHIAN

Capital

Shaft

Column

Base

Plinth

151

Plan of Greek Temples

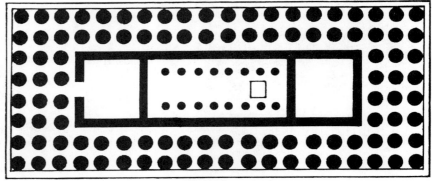

**Dipteral
(OCTASTYLE)**

Parts of Greek Temple

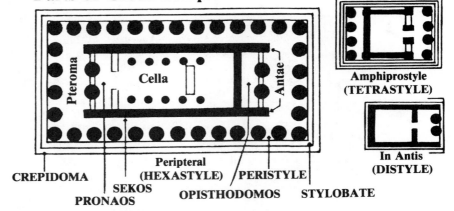

CREPIDOMA

SEKOS

PRONAOS

**Peripteral
(HEXASTYLE)** / PERISTYLE

OPISTHODOMOS

STYLOBATE

**Amphiprostyle
(TETRASTYLE)**

**In Antis
(DISTYLE)**

A GREAT PUBLIC BUILDING RESTORED

This is the lower corridor of the Stoa of Attalus in the Agora at Athens, rebuilt from 1956 on exactly as it was in ancient times and incorporating whatever remained of the original structure. Not only an impressive frame for one side of the Agora, the Stoa also served public needs, providing a pleasant refuge from hot sun or rain, and at the back a series of shops. The outer columns are Doric in style, the inner row unfluted Ionic.

1129. MEMORIZE:

δήν [adv.] long

κῆδος, -εος [n.] care, woe

νέος, -η, -ον young, fresh, new

πάροιθε(ν) before

1130. TEXT

"How to Make Friends—

οὐ γάρ πω τοιόνδε ἴδον βροτὸν ὀφθαλμοῖσιν,
οὔτ᾽ ἄνδρ᾽ οὔτε γυναῖκα· σέβας μ᾽ ἔχει εἰσοράοντα.

1095 Δήλῳ δή ποτε τοῖον Ἀπόλλωνος παρὰ βωμῷ
φοίνικος νέον ἔρνος ἀνερχόμενον ἐνόησα·
ἦλθον γὰρ καὶ κεῖσε, πολὺς δέ μοι ἕσπετο λαός,
τὴν ὁδόν, ᾗ δὴ μέλλεν ἐμοὶ κακὰ κήδε᾽ ἔσεσθαι.
ὣς δ᾽ αὔτως καὶ κεῖνο ἰδὼν ἐτεθήπεα θυμῷ

1100 δήν, ἐπεὶ οὔ πω τοῖον ἀνήλυθεν ἐκ δόρυ γαίης,
ὡς σέ, γύναι, ἄγαμαί τε τέθηπά τε, δείδια δ᾽ αἰνῶς
γούνων ἅψασθαι· χαλεπὸν δέ με πένθος ἱκάνει.
χθιζὸς ἐεικοστῷ φύγον ἤματι οἴνοπα πόντον·
τόφρα δέ μ᾽ αἰεὶ κῦμα φόρει κραιπναί τε θύελλαι

1105 νήσου ἀπ᾽ Ὠγυγίης. νῦν δ᾽ ἐνθάδε κάββαλε δαίμων,
ὄφρ᾽ ἔτι που καὶ τῇδε πάθω κακόν· οὐ γὰρ ὀΐω
παύσεσθ᾽, ἀλλ᾽ ἔτι πολλὰ θεοὶ τελέουσι πάροιθεν.

ἄγαμαι I admire
ἀν-έρχομαι, etc. I come up
βωμός, -οῦ [m.] altar; pedestal
Δῆλος, -ου [m.] Delos [an island east of Greece]
ἐεικοστός, -ή, -όν twentieth
ἔρνος, -εος [n.] young tree, sapling
καβ-βάλλω, etc. I cast (down or ashore)

κραιπνός, -ή, -όν swift
σέβας [indecl. n.] awe, wonder
τέθηπα [pf. with pres. sense] I am amazed, I am stunned
φοῖνιξ, -ῑκος [f.] palm-tree
φορέω I bear, I carry [implies repeated or habitual action]
χθιζός, -ή, -όν of yesterday, yesterday

continued on next page

1131. NOTES

1098 &ὁδόν:* Cognate accusative with ἦλθον.

&ἔσεσθαι:* future infinitive of εἰμί.

1099 &ὡς δ' αὔτως . . . ὡς:* the comparison is in reversed order: "just so did I admire it . . . as I admire you."

1100 &δόρυ:* here refers to the trunk of the young tree.

1103 &χθιζός:* another example of an adjective of time being used instead of the adverb.

1104 &φόρει:* often the verb agrees with the nearer subject only, though it goes in sense with both.

1107 &παύσεσθ':* understand κακόν as subject accusative.

&πολλά:* κακά is implied.

&πάροιθεν:* i.e., before the evils stop.

APOLLO AND ARTEMIS ON DELOS

This black-figure amphora of about 520 B.C. shows Apollo and Artemis next to the famous palm-tree at the site of their birth.

DELOS: SANCTUARY RUINS

Next to Delphi the most important religious center in ancient Greece, Delos was devastated by Mithradates in 88 B.C. and later suffered further destruction of its many monuments, mostly in marble. The whole Sanctuary area, sacred to Apollo and Artemis, is here seen from the highest point on the island, Mt. Kynthos.

1132.   COMMENT

1095 Delos was especially noted for worship of Apollo; it was considered the birthplace of the twin-gods, Apollo and Artemis.

1096 Moderns are not so likely to speak of trees in order to bring out human qualities as were people living much closer than we to nature. Hebrew poetry, for example, frequently compares persons to the "cedars of Libanus." David's daughter Tamar = 'palm tree'.

1097 A seemingly casual remark, but designed to impress on the girl that she was not dealing with an ordinary tramp or lost sailor; indeed, it hints that this is a man of importance who once had many followers.

1106 Nothing could be more expected to arouse her sympathy and inspire her spontaneous aid.

1133.   WORD STUDY

SEBASTIAN ('wonderful, awe-inspiring, august'); SEVASTOPOL ('august city,' a large Russian city in the Crimea).

1134. | MEMORIZE:

ἀντίος, -η, -ον   opposite; towards; in reply   ἐλεαίρω   I pity
δυσμενής, -ές   hostile   ἔμπης [adv.]   nevertheless

1135.   TEXT

— and Influence People"

ἀλλά, ἄνασσ', ἐλέαιρε· σὲ γὰρ κακὰ πολλὰ μογήσας
ἐς πρώτην ἱκόμην, τῶν δ' ἄλλων οὔ τινα οἶδα
1110   ἀνθρώπων, οἳ τήνδε πόλιν καὶ γαῖαν ἔχουσιν.
ἄστυ δέ μοι δεῖξον, δὸς δὲ ῥάκος ἀμφιβαλέσθαι,
εἴ τί που εἴλυμα σπείρων ἔχες ἐνθάδ' ἰοῦσα.
σοὶ δὲ θεοὶ τόσα δοῖεν, ὅσα φρεσὶ σῇσι μενοινᾷς,
ἄνδρα τε καὶ οἶκον, καὶ ὁμοφροσύνην ὀπάσειαν
1115   ἐσθλήν· οὐ μὲν γὰρ τοῦ γε κρεῖσσον καὶ ἄρειον,
ἢ ὅθ' ὁμοφρονέοντε νοήμασιν οἶκον ἔχωσιν
ἀνὴρ ἠδὲ γυνή· πόλλ' ἄλγεα δυσμενέεσσι,
χάρματα δ' εὐμενέτῃσι, μάλιστα δέ τ' ἔκλυον αὐτοί. "
τὸν δ' αὖ Ναυσικάα λευκώλενος ἀντίον ηὔδα
1120   "ξεῖν', ἐπεὶ οὔτε κακῷ οὔτ' ἄφρονι φωτὶ ἔοικας—
Ζεὺς δ' αὐτὸς νέμει ὄλβον Ὀλύμπιος ἀνθρώποισιν,
ἐσθλοῖς ἠδὲ κακοῖσιν, ὅπως ἐθέλῃσιν, ἑκάστῳ·
καί που σοὶ τάδ' ἔδωκε, σὲ δὲ χρὴ τετλάμεν ἔμπης·

ἀμφι-βάλλω, etc.   I throw around
ἄνασσα, -ης [f.]   queen, protectress
αὐδάω   I speak, I address (3 sg. impf.:
    ηὔδα)
ἄφρων, -ονος   foolish; simpleton
εἴλυμα, -ατος [n.]   wrapper
εὐμενέτης, -ᾱο   well-wisher
κρείσσων, -ον   stronger, mightier
μενοινάω   I wish, I purpose
νόημα, -ατος [n.]   thought, plan

ὁμοφρονέω   I am of like mind, I
    sympathize
ὁμοφροσύνη, -ης [f.]   oneness of
    mind, concord
Ὀλύμπιος, -ον   Olympian, dwelling
    on Olympus
ὅπως   as, however
ῥάκος, -εος [n.]   rag
σπεῖρον, -ου [n. pl.]   clothes
χάρμα, -ατος [n.]   joy, cause of joy

1136.   NOTES

1108   σέ: is moved from its normal position as object of ἐς to show strong emphasis.

1110   τήνδε: he has not yet seen the city but he knows from the presence of the girls that it must
be quite near.

1110   πόλιν . . . ἄστυ: no particular difference in meaning here. Ordinarily, ἄστυ indicates a
group of dwelling-places, while πόλις emphasizes the corporate or political unity of the
group.

1111 *ἀμφιβαλέσθαι:* the middle removes the need of expressing *ἐμέ.*

1112 *εἴ τι:* "whatever" (Cp. Lat. "si quid").

εἴλυμα σπείρων: the coarser cloth in which the clothes were wrapped when carrying them.

1115 *οὐ:* i.e., *οὐδέν ἐστι.*

1116 *ἦ ὅθ':* an explanation of the genitive of comparison, *τοῦ* = "than that, I mean than when . . ."

1117 *ἄλγεα:* in loose apposition to the whole thought of the preceding.

1118 *ἔκλυον:* a gnomic aorist. They hear it (i.e., realize it) most of all in their own hearts and need neither the envy of enemies nor the congratulations of friends to tell them of their happiness.

1120 *ἐπεί:* the main clause is sufficiently expressed by her attitude. "Since it is not your fault, I will help you."

1123 *τετλάμεν:* perfect infinitive of *τλάω.*

1137. COMMENT

1108 Having won her good will by his respect, courtesy, and nicely-phrased compliments, having intrigued her woman's curiosity by his vague mention of his own royalty, and finally having aroused her feminine instinct of sympathy with the recital of his woes past and to come, he now makes a direct appeal to her for *action,* the essential fruit of real oratory.

1111 He now makes his general appeal for help completely specific; but yet keeps his requests quite modest and reasonable.

1113 The final touch is added to a perfect speech by showing her the reward she can expect to receive in return for her action. He shrewdly selects the very desire that is at the moment uppermost in her mind and which would naturally appeal most to a girl of her age.

1115 He expresses in words, as he has already expressed by his own deeds, his beautiful and idealistic picture of the natural dignity and joys of high-minded married life.

1121 This speech of Odysseus convinces Nausicaa that he is neither evil nor foolish. His miserable condition, therefore, must not be his fault but the arbitrary dispensation of Zeus. Therefore, she implies, he is most worthy of her help.

1138. TEXT

The Princess Takes Over

νῦν δ᾽, ἐπεὶ ἡμετέρην τε πόλιν καὶ γαῖαν ἱκάνεις,

1125 οὔτ᾽ οὖν ἐσθῆτος δευήσεαι οὔτε τευ ἄλλου,

ὧν ἐπέοιχ᾽ ἱκέτην ταλαπείριον ἀντιάσαντα.

ἄστυ δέ τοι δείξω, ἐρέω δέ τοι οὔνομα λαῶν.

Φαίηκες μὲν τήνδε πόλιν καὶ γαῖαν ἔχουσιν,

εἰμὶ δ᾽ ἐγώ θυγάτηρ μεγαλήτορος Ἀλκινόοιο,

1130 τοῦ δ᾽ ἐκ Φαιήκων ἔχεται κάρτος τε βίη τε."

ἦ ῥα καὶ ἀμφιπόλοισιν ἐυπλοκάμοισι κέλευσεν·

"στῆτέ μοι, ἀμφίπολοι· πόσε φεύγετε φῶτα ἰδοῦσαι;

ἦ μή πού τινα δυσμενέων φάσθ᾽ ἔμμεναι ἀνδρῶν;

οὐκ ἔσθ᾽ οὗτος ἀνὴρ διερὸς βροτός, οὐδὲ γένηται,

1135 ὅς κεν Φαιήκων ἀνδρῶν ἐς γαῖαν ἵκηται

δηιοτῆτα φέρων· μάλα γὰρ φίλοι ἀθανάτοισιν.

οἰκέομεν δ᾽ ἀπάνευθε πολυκλύστῳ ἐνὶ πόντῳ,

ἔσχατοι, οὐδέ τις ἄμμι βροτῶν ἐπιμίσγεται ἄλλος

ἀντιάω, —, ἀντίασα I meet	ἱκέτης, -αο [m.] suppliant
δεύω, δευήσομαι I have need of, I lack	κάρτος = κράτος
διερός, -ή, -όν living, nimble	πολύκλυστος, -ον much-surging
ἐπ-έοικε it is fitting	πόσε whither?
ἐπι-μίσγομαι, etc. I mingle with, I come to	ταλαπείριος, -η, -ον sorely-tried, much-suffering
ἔσχατος, -ον extreme, most remote	

1139. NOTES

1126 ὧν: plural in agreement with the sense of τευ ἄλλου. It is genitive because μὴ δεύεσθαι must be understood, on the strength of οὐ δευήσεαι in the preceding line.
ἀντιάσαντα: understand τινα as object.

1130 τοῦ ἐκ ἔχεται; (lit.: "from whom holds itself") = "on whom depends."

1132 μοι: "I beg you," "please"—Sometimes called the 'ethical dative,' showing the speaker's special interest in what is said.

1133 ἦ μή φάσθ᾽ [μιν]: "you don't think, do you, that he . . . ?"

1134 Transl.: "That man does not exist as a living mortal, nor will such a one be born . . ."
γένηται: is practically equivalent to the future, and therefore has οὐ instead of μή.

1136 φίλοι: understand εἰμέν.

1138 ἄμμι = ἡμῖν.

1140.   COMMENT

1124   A second reason for aiding him, Nausicaa believes, is that he has come to her land as a suppliant, and, of course, to the Greek mind suppliants had a special sacredness, as dear to "Zeus Guardian of guests," (cp. lines 130–131).

1138   The western and northern parts of the Mediterranean were still very much unexplored by the Greeks of this time. In their small and fragile sailing boats they tended to stick very close to their own coasts. No one in living memory had ever come to the Phaeacians' island home.

WARRIOR ATHENA

The goddess holds a spear in her left hand, her crested helmet in her right. For breastplate she wears the dread Aegis with its snaky border and at its center the head of the Gorgon Medusa, meant to strike terror into all who see it. A splendid red-figure masterpiece of vase decoration.

1141. MEMORIZE:

δηρόν [adv.] long   χιτών, -ῶνος [m.]   tunic
φᾶρος, -εος [n.]   mantle

1142. TEXT

A Welcome Bath

ἀλλ' ὅδε τις δύστηνος ἀλώμενος ἐνθάδ' ἱκάνει,
1140   τὸν νῦν χρὴ κομέειν· πρὸς γὰρ Διός εἰσιν ἅπαντες
ξεῖνοί τε πτωχοί τε, δόσις δ' ὀλίγη τε φίλη τε.
ἀλλὰ δότ', ἀμφίπολοι, ξείνῳ βρῶσίν τε πόσιν τε,
λούσατέ τ' ἐν ποταμῷ, ὅθ' ἐπὶ σκέπας ἔστ' ἀνέμοιο."
ὣς ἔφαθ', αἱ δ' ἔσταν τε καὶ ἀλλήλῃσι κέλευσαν,
1145   κὰδ δ' ἄρ' Ὀδυσσῆ' εἷσαν ἐπὶ σκέπας, ὡς ἐκέλευσε
Ναυσικάα θυγάτηρ μεγαλήτορος Ἀλκινόοιο·
πὰρ δ' ἄρα οἱ φᾶρός τε χιτῶνά τε εἵματ' ἔθηκαν,
δῶκαν δὲ χρυσέῃ ἐν ληκύθῳ ὑγρὸν ἔλαιον,
ἤνωγον δ' ἄρα μιν λοῦσθαι ποταμοῖο ῥοῇσιν.
1150   δή ῥα τότ' ἀμφιπόλοισι μετηύδα δῖος Ὀδυσσεύς·
"ἀμφίπολοι, στῆθ' οὕτω ἀπόπροθεν, ὄφρ' ἐγὼ αὐτὸς
ἅλμην ὤκ' ὤμων ἀπολούσομαι, ἀμφὶ δ' ἐλαίῳ
χρίσομαι· ἦ γὰρ δηρὸν ἀπὸ χροός ἐστιν ἀλοιφή.
ἄντην δ' οὐκ ἄν ἐγώ γε λοέσσομαι· αἰδέομαι γὰρ
1155   γυμνοῦσθαι κούρῃσιν ἐυπλοκάμοισι μετελθών."

ἀλοιφή, -ῆς [f.]   ointment
ἄντην [adv.]   openly, in one's presence
ἀπο-λούω, etc.   I wash off
γυμνόω   I make naked, I strip
δόσις, -ιος [f.]   gift, loan

κομέω   I tend, I care for
λήκυθος, -ου [f.]   oil-flask
μετ-έρχομαι, etc.   I mingle with
πτωχός, -οῦ [m.]   beggar
ῥοή, -ῆς [f.]   stream

1143. NOTES

1139 τις, etc.: "some unfortunate wanderer."
1140 τὸν: relative.
1141 δόσις, etc.: a proverbial expression—"Even a little gift is welcome."
1143 ἐπί: (adv.) "at hand."
1144 ἔσταν: shortened from ἔστησαν.
1145 εἷσαν: aorist of ἕζομαι with irregular augment.
1149 λοῦσθαι: apparently an unusual shortened form of λούεσθαι.
1147 πάρ = παρά.
      εἵματ': predicative, "for clothes."
1151 οὕτω = οὕτως. Probably accompanied by a pointing gesture.
1154 ἄν: gives the future a less positive force—"I would not."

A SHOWER

Panther head spouts provide a stream of cool water for showering after exertion. Appropriate theme for this black-figure hydria (water jar) of late sixth century B.C.

1144. COMMENT

1140 Nausicaa reassures her frightened handmaids by reminding them of the sacred laws of hospitality and by suggesting that they have nothing to fear from a suppliant sent by Zeus. She then sets them to work with generosity befitting a princess.

1147 Odysseus had asked only for the rough cloth in which the clothes had been wrapped, but he is given a complete set of fine clothes.

1151 The Greek hero apparently had a sense of decency and modesty considerably more developed than that of his contemporaries. There is evidence that the men of the time were frequently assisted by female servants in their bathing. Although we have every reason to believe that this was a dignified and perfectly proper performance, yet Odysseus was thoughtful enough to perceive its unwisdom here.

161

1145. MEMORIZE:

κάλλος, -εος [n.] beauty   χαρίεις, -εσσα, -εν graceful, pleasing
κόμη, -ης [f.] hair

1146. TEXT

A Marvel to Behold

ὣς ἔφαθ᾽, αἱ δ᾽ ἀπάνευθεν ἴσαν, εἶπον δ᾽ ἄρα κούρῃ.
αὐτὰρ ὁ ἐκ ποταμοῦ χρόα νίζετο δῖος Ὀδυσσεὺς
ἅλμην, ἥ οἱ νῶτα καὶ εὐρέας ἄμπεχεν ὤμους,
ἐκ κεφαλῆς δ᾽ ἔσμηχεν ἁλὸς χνόον ἀτρυγέτοιο.

1160 αὐτὰρ ἐπεὶ δὴ πάντα λοέσσατο καὶ λίπ᾽ ἄλειψεν,
ἀμφὶ δὲ εἵματα ἕσσαθ᾽, ἅ οἱ πόρε παρθένος ἀδμής,
τὸν μὲν Ἀθηναίη θῆκεν Διὸς ἐκγεγαυῖα
μείζονά τ᾽ εἰσιδέειν καὶ πάσσονα, κὰδ δὲ κάρητος
οὔλας ἧκε κόμας, ὑακινθίνῳ ἄνθει ὁμοίας.

1165 ὡς δ᾽ ὅτε τις χρυσὸν περιχεύεται ἀργύρῳ ἀνὴρ
ἴδρις, ὃν Ἥφαιστος δέδαεν καὶ Παλλὰς Ἀθήνη
τέχνην παντοίην, χαρίεντα δὲ ἔργα τελείει,
ὣς ἄρα τῷ κατέχευε χάριν κεφαλῇ τε καὶ ὤμοις.
ἕζετ᾽ ἔπειτ᾽ ἀπάνευθε κιὼν ἐπὶ θῖνα θαλάσσης,

1170 κάλλεϊ καὶ χάρισι στίλβων. θηεῖτο δὲ κούρη.

ἀδμής, -ῆτος [adj.] unwedded
ἀμπ-έχω I surround, I cover
Ἀθηναίη = Ἀθήνη
ἄνθος, -εος [n.] flower
δάω, —, δέδαα I get to know; I teach
ἐκ-γίγνομαι, etc. I am born from
Ἥφαιστος, -ου Hephaestus [god of fire and metal-work]
θηέομαι I look (w. wonder)
ἴδρις, -ιος skilled, skilful
λίπα [adv.] richly, plenteously
νίζω I wash

οὖλος, -η, -ον wooly, curly
Παλλάς, -άδος Pallas (Spear-wielder)
παρθένος, -ου [f.] maiden, virgin
πάσσων = comp. of παχύς
περι-χέω, etc. I pour about, I overlay
σμήχω I wipe off
στίλβω I am bright, I am resplendent
τελείω = τελέω
τέχνη, -ης [f.] skill, art
ὑακίνθινος, -η, -ον of the hyacinth
χνόος, -ου [m.] salty crust

INLAID SILVER CUP

A precious drinking cup made of silver with patterns and animal heads inlaid in gold and black niello. From a Mycenaean tomb on Cyprus of 14th century B.C.

1147. NOTES

1156 *ἴσαν:* imperfect indicative 3rd plural of *εἶμι* "I go."

1157 *ἐκ ποταμοῦ:* an abbreviated construction—"with water from the river."
      νίζετο: with double accusative.

1158 *νῶτα:* the plural is sometimes used for the singular when a thing may be considered as having parts.

1161 *ἔσσαθ':* from *ἕννῡμι.*

1162 *θῆκεν:* "caused to be" = "made."

1165 *τις:* with *ἀνήρ.*
      περιχεύεται = περι-χεύηται. The thematic vowel is occasionally left unlengthened in the aorist subjunctive.

1166 *δέδαεν:* verbs of teaching in Greek and Latin ordinarily take two accusatives.

1148.   COMMENT

1156 The report of Odysseus' action brought back by the servants must have impressed Nausicaa even more with the man's character.

1163 Again Homer attributes to the action of the gods what is really no more than a subjective change in the attitude of the princess. The attraction she has begun to feel towards Odysseus is tremendously intensified when she beholds him now in a more ordinary condition. Her youthful imagination begins to exaggerate the breadth of his shoulders, the beauty and curliness of his hair. As he sits down near the sea, his whole person seems to her to be glowing with vigor and manliness. Such an experience might be admitted by others who have fallen in love.

1165 To illustrate how attractive the person of Odysseus seemed to her, Homer pictures one of the most beautiful objects familiar to his audience. A silver bowl richly edged with gold by a master craftsman, such as Homer here describes, was actually excavated by Schliemann in Greece. Virgil imitates the passage (*Aen.* 1.589–593):

> namque ipsa decoram
> caesariem nato genetrix lumenque iuventae
> purpureum et laetos oculis afflarat honores:
> quale manus addunt ebori decus, aut ubi flavo
> argentum Pariusve lapis circumdatur auro.

1149.   *τοιόσδε, τοιήδε, τοιόνδε:* "SUCH (AS THIS, AS THAT)"

τοι- and *-δε* are not declined; *-οσ-, -η-, -ον-* are declined according to the regular endings of the first and second declensions. E.g.,

fem. dat. sg. = *τοιῆδε;* neut. acc. pl. = *τοιάδε.*

1150.   WORD STUDY

COMET (a heavenly body which trails long streamers of tiny particles illuminated by reflected sunlight, seeming like flowing locks of 'hair'); — TECHNICAL (pertaining to skills or crafts), TECHNICIAN (a skilled mechanic), TECHNIQUE (skill or art in doing something); — HYACINTH.

1151.
> **MEMORIZE:**
>
> ἀνδάνω, ἀδήσω, ἄδον   I am pleasing (to)   πολύτλας [only nom.]   much-enduring

1152.   TEXT

Love at Second Sight

1171   δὴ ῥα τότ᾽ ἀμφιπόλοισιν ἐυπλοκάμοισι μετηύδα·
"κλῦτέ μευ, ἀμφίπολοι λευκώλενοι, ὄφρα τι εἴπω.
οὐ πάντων ἀέκητι θεῶν, οἳ Ὄλυμπον ἔχουσιν,
Φαιήκεσσ᾽ ὅδ᾽ ἀνὴρ ἐπιμίσγεται ἀντιθέοισιν·
1175   πρόσθεν μὲν γὰρ δή μοι ἀεικέλιος δέατ᾽ εἶναι,
νῦν δὲ θεοῖσιν ἔοικε, τοὶ οὐρανὸν εὐρὺν ἔχουσιν.
αἲ γὰρ ἐμοὶ τοιόσδε πόσις κεκλημένος εἴη
ἐνθάδε ναιετάων, καί οἱ ἅδοι αὐτόθι μίμνειν.
ἀλλὰ δότ᾽, ἀμφίπολοι, ξείνῳ βρῶσίν τε πόσιν τε."
1180   ὣς ἔφαθ᾽, αἱ δ᾽ ἄρα τῆς μάλα μὲν κλύον ἠδὲ πίθοντο,
πὰρ δ᾽ ἄρ᾽ Ὀδυσσῆι ἔθεσαν βρῶσίν τε πόσιν τε.
ἦ τοι ὁ πῖνε καὶ ἦσθε πολύτλας δῖος Ὀδυσσεὺς
ἁρπαλέως· δηρὸν γὰρ ἐδητύος ἦεν ἄπαστος.

ἀεικέλιος, -η, -ον unseemly, wretched
  shabby
ἄπαστος, -ον not partaking of
ἁρπαλέως heartily, voraciously
	δέατο [impf. of defective verb] he
	  seemed, he appeared
	ἐπι-μίσγομαι, etc. I mingle with

1153.   NOTES

1173   οὐ: with ἀέκητι.
1177   αἲ γάρ: introduces a wish (#106, a).
       κεκλημένος εἴη: a periphrasis (circumlocution), i.e., the use of more words than are necessary to express an idea. Transl.: "might be called," or simply, "might be."
1180   μάλα: "very willingly."
1181   πὰρ = παρά.

1154.   COMMENT

1172 With the typical psychology of a lover, she cannot believe that it can be merely chance that has brought this object of her affections to her shores. From all time, the gods must have been planning to bring about their meeting.

1177 This wish has been thought over-bold for a maiden, but under the circumstances it is not. She speaks with the charming frankness and directness that seem characteristic of her; and, of course, the remark could not have been heard by Odysseus, but was meant only for her confidential friends of the same sex and age, with whom she probably shared many such confidences.

1179 With refined politeness, despite the ravenous hunger caused by three strenuous days without eating, Odysseus does not ask for food but remains sitting quietly by the sea until, by Nausicaa's kind thoughtfulness, the servants bring him a share of their picnic lunch.

A HELMET MAKER

A young craftman is putting finishing touches on a bronze helmet. Some of his tools hang on the wall. The interior of a red-figured kylix, c. 500 B.C.

1155. MEMORIZE:

ἀλεείνω I avoid, I shun
δαΐφρων, -ον sagacious
ἡγεμονεύω, -σω, -σα I lead (the way)

ὀνομάζω, ὀνομάσω, ὀνόμασα I name, I call (by name)

1156. TEXT

The Plan of March

αὐτὰρ Ναυσικάα λευκώλενος ἄλλ᾽ ἐνόησεν.

1185 εἵματ᾽ ἄρα πτύξασα τίθει καλῆς ἐπ᾽ ἀπήνης,
ζεῦξεν δ᾽ ἡμιόνους κρατερώνυχας, ἂν δ᾽ ἔβη αὐτή,
ὤτρυνεν δ᾽ Ὀδυσῆα, ἔπος τ᾽ ἔφατ᾽ ἔκ τ᾽ ὀνόμαζεν·
"ὄρσεο δὴ νῦν, ξεῖνε, πόλινδ᾽ ἴμεν, ὄφρα σε πέμψω
πατρὸς ἐμοῦ πρὸς δῶμα δαΐφρονος, ἔνθα σέ φημι
1190 πάντων Φαιήκων εἰδησέμεν ὅσσοι ἄριστοι.
ἀλλὰ μάλ᾽ ὧδ᾽ ἔρδειν, δοκέεις δέ μοι οὐκ ἀπινύσσειν.
ὄφρ᾽ ἂν μέν κ᾽ ἀγροὺς ἴομεν καὶ ἔργ᾽ ἀνθρώπων,
τόφρα σὺν ἀμφιπόλοισι μεθ᾽ ἡμιόνους καὶ ἄμαξαν
καρπαλίμως ἔρχεσθαι· ἐγὼ δ᾽ ὁδὸν ἡγεμονεύσω.
1195 αὐτὰρ ἐπὴν πόλιος ἐπιβήομεν, ἧχι πολῖται—
τῶν ἀλεείνω φῆμιν ἀδευκέα, μή τις ὀπίσσω
μωμεύῃ· μάλα δ᾽ εἰσὶν ὑπερφίαλοι κατὰ δῆμον·

ἀδευκής, -ές harsh, unkind	*μωμεύω* I blame, I reproach
ἀπινύσσω I lack understanding, I am foolish	*πολίτης, -αο* [m.] man of the city, citizen
ἧχι where	*φῆμις, -ιος* [f.] speech, talk
κρατερῶνυξ, -υχος solid-hoofed	

1157. NOTES

1186 *ἂν = ἀνά.*

1188 *ὄρσεο:* imperative of a rare "mixed" aorist with first aorist stem and second aorist endings.

1190 *εἰδησέμεν:* used as future infinitive of *οἶδα.*
ὅσσοι: understand *εἰσί.*

1192 *ἴομεν:* subjunctive of *εἶμι* with unlengthened thematic vowel. Understand "along" or "through."
ἔργ᾽: "the worked (fields)" = "the farms."

1195 *ἐπιβήομεν = ἐπι-βήωμεν.*

1197 *μωμεύῃ:* understand *ἐμέ.*

1158.   COMMENT

1191   Since he is a man of understanding, he will not be offended by her apparent inhospitality. She will lead the way in the small wagon until they reach the edge of the city, but she does not dare to parade through the city with him.

1195   When she mentions the townsfolk, she impulsively breaks off her thought to tell him what she thinks of them.

1159.   WORD STUDY

COSMOPOLITE ('citizen of the world,' one at home everywhere from his broad experience and knowledge; a person free from local prejudice and narrow interests).

NAUSICAA LEADS THE WAY

Odysseus follows Nausicaa's wagon as they enter the Phaeacian capital with the princess leading the way to her father's palace.

1160. MEMORIZE:

νεμεσ(σ)άω, νεμεσ(σ)ήσω, νεμέσ(σ)ησα
I am indignant (with)

πλάζω, πλάγξω, πλάγξα, —, —, πλάγχθην
I beat; [pass.:] I wander

1161. TEXT

Human Nature

καί νύ τις ὧδ᾽ εἴπῃσι κακώτερος ἀντιβολήσας·
'τίς δ᾽ ὅδε Ναυσικάᾳ ἕπεται καλός τε μέγας τε
1200 ξεῖνος; ποῦ δέ μιν εὗρε; πόσις νύ οἱ ἔσσεται αὐτῇ.
ἦ τινά που πλαγχθέντα κομίσσατο ἧς ἀπὸ νηὸς
ἀνδρῶν τηλεδαπῶν, ἐπεὶ οὔ τινες ἐγγύθεν εἰσίν·
ἦ τίς οἱ εὐξαμένη πολυάρητος θεὸς ἦλθεν
οὐρανόθεν καταβάς, ἕξει δέ μιν ἤματα πάντα.
1205 βέλτερον, εἰ καὐτή περ ἐποιχομένη πόσιν εὗρεν
ἄλλοθεν· ἦ γὰρ τούσδε γ᾽ ἀτιμάζει κατὰ δῆμον
Φαίηκας, τοί μιν μνῶνται πολέες τε καὶ ἐσθλοί.'
ὣς ἐρέουσιν, ἐμοὶ δέ κ᾽ ὀνείδεα ταῦτα γένοιτο.
καὶ δ᾽ ἄλλῃ νεμεσῶ, ἥ τις τοιαῦτά γε ῥέζοι,
1210 ἥ τ᾽ ἀέκητι φίλων, πατρὸς καὶ μητρὸς ἐόντων,
ἀνδράσι μίσγηται, πρίν γ᾽ ἀμφάδιον γάμον ἐλθεῖν.

ἀμφάδιος, -η, -ον open, public
ἀντι-βολέω, —, ἀντι-βόλησα I meet
ἀτιμάζω I slight, I disdain
βέλτερος, -ον better

ὄνειδος, -εος [n.] shame, reproach
πολυάρητος, -ον much prayed for
τηλεδαπός, -ή, -όν lying far off, from
    a far country

1162. NOTES

1198 ἀντιβολήσας: understand ἡμέας.
1200 οἱ αὐτῇ: "for her very own."
1201 ἧς = ἕης.
1204 ἕξει: θεός is still subject. In such contexts, ἔχω has the technical meaning of "have as wife."
1205 βέλτερον: understand πού ἐστιν. καὐτή: crasis (cp. #1050).
1210 ἐόντων: "being alive."

169

1163.   COMMENT

1199   The less pleasant side of human nature showed itself in ancient as well as in modern times by such catty remarks and bitter gossiping.

1203   In his opening words Odysseus had said that Nausicaa looked like a goddess. Now the princess artfully returns the compliment by saying that the townspeople might mistake him for a god.

1205   Nausicaa would be accused of "husband-hunting" and of arranging the marriage herself, instead of, as was proper, allowing her parents to do so.

1207   A coy intimation, perhaps, to Odysseus that she is not unfamiliar with men's attentions?

1210   She means that a girl whose parents are dead and who has received little home-training might be pardoned for her ignorance of proprieties. But for one like herself, there would be no excuse. In Homeric times, it would seem that a girl had considerable freedom in choosing her spouse; nevertheless, even as today, the family could bring no little influence to bear on her decision, and secrecy was severely frowned upon.

THE SETTING FOR ALCINOUS' PALACE

Many of the descriptions in Homer of Phaeacia correspond closely with places in Corfu island (ancient Kerkyra), and the poet may have based his stories on knowledge of the island. Here, seen from above, Palaiokastritsa is a strong contender for being the site of Alcinous' palace—on the hilly point at the right. Nearby are the three harbors that Nausicaa mentions.

1164.   WORD STUDY

NEMESIS (the 'indignation' of the gods at a mortal's undeserved or extreme good fortune, leading to divine retribution by way of fall from success; hence, retributive justice, a misfortune balancing off great former prosperity).

1165. MEMORIZE:

τυγχάνω, τεύξομαι, τύχον   I happen (upon); I obtain [gen.]

1166.   TEXT

Plan of Action

ξεῖνε, σὺ δ᾽ ὦκ᾽ ἐμέθεν ξυνίει ἔπος, ὄφρα τάχιστα
πομπῆς καὶ νόστοιο τύχῃς παρὰ πατρὸς ἐμοῖο.
δήεις ἀγλαὸν ἄλσος Ἀθήνης ἄγχι κελεύθου

1215   αἰγείρων· ἐν δὲ κρήνη νάει, ἀμφὶ δὲ λειμών·
ἔνθα δὲ πατρὸς ἐμοῦ τέμενος τεθαλυῖά τ᾽ ἀλωή,
τόσσον ἀπὸ πτόλιος, ὅσσον τε γέγωνε βοήσας.
ἔνθα καθεζόμενος μεῖναι χρόνον, εἰς ὅ κεν ἡμεῖς
ἄστυδε ἔλθωμεν καὶ ἱκώμεθα δώματα πατρός.

1220   αὐτὰρ ἐπὴν ἡμέας ἔλπῃ ποτὶ δώματ᾽ ἀφῖχθαι,
καὶ τότε Φαιήκων ἴμεν ἐς πόλιν ἠδ᾽ ἐρέεσθαι
δώματα πατρὸς ἐμοῦ μεγαλήτορος Ἀλκινόοιο.

αἴγειρος, -ου [f.] poplar
ἄλσος, -εος [n.] (sacred) grove
δήω [pres. w. fut. sense] I find, I
   come upon
καθ-έζομαι, etc.   I sit down

κρήνη, -ης [f.] spring, fountain
νάω I flow
ξυν-ίημι, etc. I send together; I
   understand

1167.   NOTES

1212   ἐμέθεν: formed from (ἐ)μεῦ according to rule.
   ξυν-ίει: present imperative second singular.
1215   αἰγείρων: with ἄλσος.
1218   εἰς ὅ: "until."
1220   ἀφῖχθαι: from ἀφ-ῖγμαι, perfect of ἀφ-ικνέομαι.
1221   ἐρέεσθαι: "inquire for."

1168.   COMMENT

   1212-3 Knowing that return home is his chief desire, she is eager to help bring it about, despite the parting (perhaps only temporary!) which it implies. She is noble enough to think more of his interests than her own.

   1220 Not knowing the location of the palace, Odysseus could only estimate the time to reach it. As long, however, as he did not follow too closely or appear to have anything to do with the party of the princess, there would be no danger or arousing idle talk.

1169. MEMORIZE:

ἐυκτίμενος, -η, -ον well-built; well-tilled

ἥρως, ἥρωος [m.] [contracted gen. ἥρως] warrior [often honorary title]

θρόνος, -ου [m.] seat, chair

ὄπι(σ)θεν behind, afterward, hereafter

1170. TEXT

The Royal Household

ῥεῖα δ᾽ ἀρίγνωτ᾽ ἐστί, καὶ ἂν πάις ἡγήσαιτο
νήπιος· οὐ μὲν γάρ τι ἐοικότα τοῖσι τέτυκται
1225 δώματα Φαιήκων, οἷος δόμος Ἀλκινόοιο
ἥρωος. ἀλλ᾽ ὁπότ᾽ ἄν σε δόμοι κεκύθωσι καὶ αὐλή,
ὦκα μάλα μεγάροιο διελθέμεν, ὄφρ᾽ ἄν ἵκηαι
μητέρ᾽ ἐμήν· ἡ δ᾽ ἧσται ἐπ᾽ ἐσχάρῃ ἐν πυρὸς αὐγῇ
ἠλάκατα στρωφῶσ᾽ ἁλιπόρφυρα, θαῦμα ἰδέσθαι,
1230 κίονι κεκλιμένη· δμωαὶ δέ οἱ ἥατ᾽ ὄπισθεν.
ἔνθα δὲ πατρὸς ἐμοῖο θρόνος ποτικέκλιται αὐτῇ,
τῷ ὅ γε οἰνοποτάζει ἐφήμενος ἀθάνατος ὥς.
τὸν παραμειψάμενος μητρὸς περὶ γούνασι χεῖρας
βάλλειν ἡμετέρης, ἵνα νόστιμον ἧμαρ ἴδηαι
1235 χαίρων καρπαλίμως, εἰ καὶ μάλα τηλόθεν ἐσσί.
εἴ κέν τοι κείνη γε φίλα φρονέῃσ᾽ ἐνὶ θυμῷ,
ἐλπωρή τοι ἔπειτα φίλους τ᾽ ἰδέειν καὶ ἱκέσθαι
οἶκον ἐυκτίμενον καὶ σὴν ἐς πατρίδα γαῖαν.

ἁλιπόρφυρος, -ον dyed in sea-purple
ἀρίγνωτος, -η, -ον recognizable
δι-έρχομαι, etc. I go through
ἐλπωρη, -ης [f.] hope
ἐσχάρη, -ης [f.] hearth
ἐφ-ημαι I sit at or on
ἠλάκατα, -ων [n. pl.] yarn (spun on a distaff)

θαῦμα, -ατος [n.] wonder, marvel
κίων, -ονος [f.] pillar, column
οἰνοποτάζω I drink my wine
παρ-αμείβομαι, etc. I pass by
ποτι-κλίνω; pf. mid.: -κέκλιμαι I lean next to
στρωφάω I twist, I spin
τηλόθεν from far away

1171. NOTES

1223-4 ἀρίγνωτ' and τοῖσι: refer to δώματα πατρὸς ἐμοῦ (line 1222).

1225 οἷος: understand ἐστί.

1226 ἥρωος: the omega is shortened in scansion because of the following vowel (#564, 1, c).

1226 κεκύθωσι = κύθωσι.

1230 κεκλιμένη: from κέκλιμαι, perfect of κλίνω.

1232 τῷ: with ἐφ-ήμενος.

ὥς: when ὡς meaning "as," "how," etc., follows the word it governs, it receives a pitch-mark.

THE BANQUET HALL OF ALCINOUS

1172. COMMENT

1226 "When the entrance hall of the palace has covered you" means no more than "when you enter the palace." The entering is considered from the point of view of someone watching him from outside.

1232 He sits so majestically on the royal chair that he seems a veritable god—a description revealing Nausicaa's charming simplicity and reverent admiration of her good father.

1236 A sure indication of the elevated position and dignity of womanhood in Homeric times. With the exception of the Jews, it is doubtful if any other contemporary people had any such reverence for their women.

1237-8 The goal and consummation of all Odysseus' longings throughout twenty years!

1173. WORD STUDY

HERO, HEROINE (a man or woman of outstanding courage or character; hence, a worthy central figure of a poem or story), HEROIC; — THRONE (royal seat).

REVIEW

1174.   Go over again Lessons 198–207; make sure now that you have really mastered them. Here are a few suggestions for your review:

1. *Vocabulary:* Check your mastery of the 28 new memory words.
2. *Text:* Reread the 146 lines of text, making sure you recognize all the forms.
3. *Story:*

   a.   Summarize briefly the speech of Odysseus to Nausicaa.
   b.   What motives does Nausicaa mention for helping him?
   c.   What indications are given of Nausicaa's reaction to her acquaintance with Odysseus?
   d.   What plan is proposed for entering the city and why is it proposed?
   e.   How, according to Nausicaa, can Odysseus best secure aid?

4. *Criticism:*

   a.   Translate lines 1201–1207 into modern, idiomatic English, trying to catch the spirit of the original.
   b.   Analyze the simile in Lesson 202, showing its composition and purpose.

5. *Grammar:* Review τοιόσδε.

6. *Composition:* Put into Greek:

   a.   Such a graceful girl (as this) he thought he had never seen before.
   b.   Nausicaa led the way and Odysseus followed the wagon until they came to the well-tilled fields.
   c.   Should the much-enduring warrior obtain a safe sending-off, he would indeed rejoice in his heart.

1175.   ONE YEAR OF GREEK HISTORY

To live in stirring times, amid the excitement of great achievements on both local and national planes, is in itself a stimulus to a fuller appreciation of life. In fifth-century Greece, history and cultural progress moved so swiftly that the whole nation seemed caught up by a spirit of buoyant enthusiasm calling men out to their limit and inspiring the boldest enterprises. Let us look at the events of a single year; say 435, at the height of the Periclean Age, twenty-five years after Pericles assumed leadership of Athens.

Within the limits of this year, as in almost any other year before or after it for generations, events enough occurred to make an ordinary lifetime memorable.

It was the year, for instance, when the greatest buildings of antiquity were going up at Athens: the Parthenon almost finished, its gleaming white-marble structure already complete, its splendid sculpture being worked into final form under the master Phidias and his brilliant assistants; the Propylaea well under way as impressive entrance to the Acropolis; beyond it, overlooking Athens, the perfect little temple of Athena Nike or "Winged Victory," a fine example of Ionic architecture; the Erechtheum just started, its porch of Maidens still a secret of the architect but soon to win fame for its originality and charm. It cannot but have made the average Athenian elated to watch these wonderful buildings rise, and to note from week to week the new features and refinements going into their making. It gave the whole city an air of growth, progress, firm grip on the future.

The Athenian Empire, too, was growing. Under Pericles' skilful policy, peace was continuing as it had for the past eleven years, and the city at last seemed permanently secure, now that the third of the great 'Long Walls' connecting it with the sea four miles away had just been completed. There remained, however, the thrill of political warfare against distant potential foes, and the steady consolidation of Athens' naval supremacy and her control over many important allies. The citizens of Athens could glow with a sense of national power, feel like men sitting on the top of the world. They could listen with excitement, but no perturbation for their own safety, to all the latest news about the battles going on between nearby Corinth and Corcyra over Epidamnus and to the report of the Corinthian naval defeat off Actium. The air was tense, but with eagerness and confident ambitions, not fear or strife. Athens was in her prime, and enjoying it.

THE ACROPOLIS AT ATHENS

By the fourth century B.C. the hill dominating Athens from its center had been covered with splendid buildings of the finest marble, designed and built with supreme skill. In this view from the NW of the accurate model, the little Ionic Temple of Victory is at front right. Opposite at bottom center is the Pinakotheke (Art Gallery), attached to the Propylaea (formal entrance). Beyond at the right are the Sanctuary of Artemis Brauronia and the Armory (Chalkotheke). The Parthenon rises majestically over all. The elegant Ionic Erechtheum is near the wall's edge at left center. Altogether an impressive ensemble.

Culturally, too, the city was at its peak. Though Aeschylus was dead (but not forgotten), the drama was still in full glory, for Sophocles was writing play after play and Euripides too was in his best period. The tragic competitions this year would be lively and brilliant, with these two masters vying for the honors, and a host of other excellent playwrights also. In comedy, the great pioneer Cratīnus, still witty and original, was likely to walk off again with the prizes this spring, though he would have his rivals. And sitting in the audience, gathering ideas and technique for surpassing the old poet, would be the youthful Eupolis—and young Aristophanes, greatest of them all.

Herodotus, delightful storyteller and shrewd historian, was living at Thurii, completing his inimitable book on the Persian Wars and their background. The memory of his fascinating lectures ten years ago still lived at Athens, and the people looked forward to the publication of the whole. The chronicler Hellanīcus was writing too, telling the story of Athens' rise to splendor. Thucydides, greatest of ancient historians, was also to be met on the street these days, and Xenophon too. The city was full of brilliant writers whose works the world would admire down the centuries.

In oratory, three famous names stood out: Antiphon, Lysias, and the sophist Gorgias, all greatly admired, each with his own distinctive style. Greece loved eloquence, and the display this year left little to be desired. The marvelous advances in medicine being made by Hippocrates over in Cos have aroused the enthusiasm of all Greece, while the scientific theories of Anaxagoras, Empedocles, and Democritus are hotly debated in many learned and even popular gatherings, especially Democritus' idea that all the universe is made up of tiny particles which he calls 'atoms' and by whose various combinations he claims are explained the nature and qualities of all things.

Most stirring discussion-topic of the year, though, was the activity of Socrates, that amazing, curious fellow always going about asking insistent questions on the ultimate nature of some virtue or moral principle, embarrassing the most brilliant men in Athens by showing up their ignorance of such things in public, but always apologizing humbly for the discomfiture and saying he had only hoped to find the answer to these vital problems which constantly weighed on his mind. He makes people think, all right, but there is no end to his questioning once you let him start on you. The Sophists are furious at him for the way he is forever backing them into intellectual corners and exposing their shallowness or ignorance—they, the teachers of Greece! Why, just this year, wasn't it, he tied up the great Protagoras in a subtle discussion of virtue, as to whether or not it is teachable and what are its parts and divisions, making the learned sophist contradict himself before the debate was over; and this in the presence of other sophists, Prodicus and Hippias, and many of their pupils besides. The entire city is talking about it, and is violently divided over the merits of Socrates' method and this new thing 'Philosophy' which he is always proposing as the one true guide to life and happiness. The whole situation sets one's head spinning.

In the arts, at least, there is no such turmoil, but certainly great activity and daily progress. One hears all year long of new triumphs in sculpture, by Phidias or Myron or Kresilas or Polyclitus, and Athens is studded with their latest masterpieces. Vase painting is at a new high right now, with marvelous refinement in design and draughtsmanship giving this year's vases a beauty never known before in this field, so that people are everywhere buying them for ornaments of their homes more than for actual utility. Most artists have now adopted the new process of vase painting, drawing in the background instead of the figures, leaving the latter in the natural red of the baked clay for greater realism, and the technique has revolutionized the whole industry, supplanting earlier methods. In the art of painting on wood and canvas, Apollodorus has recently introduced a new spirit which aims less to tell a story than to create a vision of beauty, and his rivals Zeuxis and Parrhasius are now surpassing him with their even finer skill in coloring, lines, and the capturing of human emotions, while Timanthes of Sicyon is a constant threat to their present preeminence. It brings all Greece an added zest for life just to realize how many great men and movements are now active in the nation. The times are vigorous, dynamic, inspiring. One is proud to be a Greek.

Such, in rapid summary, is the picture of a single year during the golden age of Greece. It brings out some of the reasons why Greek civilization has been universally recognized as one of the glories and "miracles" of human history. So rich a concentration at one time of great geniuses in all branches of endeavor the world has never since seen. Periclean Greece remains a phenomenon; unique; still unsurpassed.

1176. | MEMORIZE:

θαυμάζω, θαυμάσσομαι, θαύμασα   I
marvel at

πολύμητις, -ιος [m. or f.]   of many
counsels

Following in detail the advice of Nausicaa, Odysseus easily wins the sympathy of her mother, the queen, and shortly afterwards that of all the Phaeacian nobles. They entertain him royally and force him to relate all the many adventures that befell him on his way from Troy. He tells them, too, of his wife and child, and of his longing to be reunited to them at last. Touched by his sufferings and in admiration at his resourcefulness, the Phaeacians quickly vote to take him home, loaded with presents of friendship. At dawn the following morning, picked sailors go down to the sea and prepare their speediest ship. Meanwhile Odysseus has delayed at the palace to bid adieu to his kind hosts.

1177. TEXT

Such Sweet Sorrow

αὐτὰρ ἐπεί ῥ᾽ ἐπὶ νῆα κατήλυθον ἠδὲ θάλασσαν,
1240   νῆα μὲν οἵ γε μέλαιναν ἁλὸς βένθοσδε ἔρυσσαν,
ἐν δ᾽ ἱστόν τ᾽ ἐτίθεντο καὶ ἱστία νηὶ μελαίνῃ,
ἠρτύναντο δ᾽ ἐρετμὰ τροποῖς ἐν δερματίνοισιν,
πάντα κατὰ μοῖραν, ἀνά θ᾽ ἱστία λευκὰ πέτασσαν.
οἱ τάδε· Ναυσικάα δὲ θεῶν ἄπο κάλλος ἔχουσα
1245   στῆ ῥα παρὰ σταθμὸν τέγεος πύκα ποιητοῖο,
θαύμαζεν δ᾽ Ὀδυσῆα ἐν ὀφθαλμοῖσιν ὁρῶσα,
καί μιν φωνήσασ᾽ ἔπεα πτερόεντα προσηύδα·
"χαῖρε, ξεῖν᾽, ἵνα καί ποτ᾽ ἐὼν ἐν πατρίδι γαίῃ
μνήσῃ ἐμεῦ,—ὅτι μοι πρώτῃ ζωάγρι᾽ ὀφέλλεις."
1250   τὴν δ᾽ ἀπαμειβόμενος προσέφη πολύμητις Ὀδυσσεύς·
"Ναυσικάα θύγατερ μεγαλήτορος Ἀλκινόοιο,
οὕτω νῦν Ζεὺς θείη, ἐρίγδουπος πόσις Ἥρης,
οἴκαδέ τ᾽ ἐλθέμεναι καὶ νόστιμον ἦμαρ ἰδέσθαι·
τῷ κέν τοι καὶ κεῖθι θεῷ ὣς εὐχετάοιμην
1255   αἰεὶ ἤματα πάντα· σὺ γάρ μ᾽ ἐβιώσαο, κούρη."

ἀρτύνω, —, ἄρτυνα   I put together,
  I fasten
βένθος, -εος [n.]   depth
βιόω, —, βιωσάμην   I give life, I save
δερμάτινος, -η, -ον   of hide, leather
ἐρίγδουπος, -ον   heavy-thundering
ζωάγρια, -ων [n. pl.]   life-forfeits [the
  reward for saving a life]

Ἥρη, -ης   Hera [wife of Zeus]
κεῖθι   there
ὀφέλλω   I owe
ποιητός, -ή, -όν   made
πύκα [adv.]   firmly, solidly
τέγος, -εος [n.]   roof; roofed hall
τρόπος, -ου [m.]   thong, strap

1178.   NOTES

> 1241   ἐτίθεντο: imperfect of τίθημι.
>
> 1244   οἱ: some verb of "doing" is understood.
>
> 1246   ἐν: "with her eyes"—a way of expressing her rapt attention.
>
> 1248   χαῖρε: "may joy be with you," "fare thee well."
>
> ἵνα: a purpose clause is used instead of the expected imperative. She joins her wishes for his good fortune with her own hope of being affectionately remembered.
>
> 1252   οὕτω = οὕτως.
>
> 1253   ἐλθέμεναι: understand ἐμέ. This line explains οὕτω above.

1179.   COMMENT

1245   As Odysseus is about to enter the hall where the king and his nobles are gathered, he encounters Nausicaa waiting for him.

1248   Her goodbye is simple—and a little pathetic. She had realized very soon from his impersonal courtesy and his plainly expressed devotion to his distant wife that her incipient love could never be reciprocated. Yet, she would never forget him, and it would be some consolation to know that she has helped him and that he remembered her. How different is her sensible, realistic attitude from the passionate emotionalism of Dido under similar circumstances!

1251   He addresses her with great courtesy, using her full title, and he promises her far more than the mere remembrance she had asked. Even as a god, would her memory be kept alive and sacred in his heart all his days. Yet, he makes clear, his motive is gratitude—nothing more. He will not take advantage of or amuse himself with the love that he must have seen in her shining eyes. Whatever attraction he may have felt towards her he is not free to indulge in or to express.

1180.   WORD STUDY

DERMATOLOGIST (a physician who specializes in treating diseases of the skin); HYPODERMIC (an injection 'under the skin').

1181. MEMORIZE:

ἄκοιτις, -ιος [f.] wife
αὖθι there, here
κρείων, -οντος [m.] ruler, prince

νοστέω, νοστήσω, νόστησα I return (home)

1182. TEXT

Farewell to Phaeacians

1256 αἶψα δὲ Φαιήκεσσι φιληρέτμοισι μετηύδα,
      Ἀλκινόῳ δὲ μάλιστα πιφαυσκόμενος φάτο μῦθον·
      "Ἀλκίνοε κρεῖον, πάντων ἀριδείκετε λαῶν,
      πέμπετέ με σπείσαντες ἀπήμονα, χαίρετε δ' αὐτοί.
1260 ἤδη γὰρ τετέλεσται, ἅ μοι φίλος ἤθελε θυμός,
      πομπή καὶ φίλα δῶρα, τά μοι θεοὶ Οὐρανίωνες
      ὄλβια ποιήσειαν· ἀμύμονα δ' οἴκοι ἄκοιτιν
      νοστήσας εὕροιμι σὺν ἀρτεμέεσσι φίλοισιν.
      ὑμεῖς δ' αὖθι μένοντες ἐυφραίνοιτε γυναῖκας
1265 κουριδίας καὶ τέκνα· θεοὶ δ' ἀρετὴν ὀπάσειαν
      παντοίην, καὶ μή τι κακὸν μεταδήμιον εἴη."

ἀριδείκετος, -ον distinguished, illustrious
ἀρτεμής, -ές safe and sound
ἐϋφραίνω I cheer
μετα-δήμιος, -ον among the people

οἴκοι [adv.] at home
Οὐρανίωνες, -ων (inhabitants) of heaven
φιλήρετμος, -ον oar-loving, sea-loving

1183. NOTES

1259 πέμπετε: plural because Alcinous is addressed merely as leader of the whole assembly.
1260 τετέλεσται: from τετέλεσμαι, perfect of τελέω.
1261 τά: relative, object of ποιήσειαν.

1184. COMMENT

1258 ff. Briefly but thoroughly, he shows his appreciation for the good things they have given him or are making possible for him, and thanks them by wishing them complete domestic and civic bliss. The speech is a model of courtesy, gratitude, and a pervasive religious outlook which brings strength and joyous confidence to future hopes because basing them on reliance on divine power and justice.

1260-3 A short but highly significant summary of Odysseus' whole character and life-ideals.
1265 He thus includes Nausicaa and her mother in his gratitude.

LESSON 211

1185. MEMORIZE:

ἵππος, -ου [m.]	horse	*πρήσσω, πρήξω, πρῆξα* I pass (over);
πεδίον, -ου [n.]	plain	I accomplish, I do
πορφύρεος, -η, -ον gleaming, bright		*τάμνω, —, τάμον* I cut

1186. TEXT

The Day of Return — and Happy Ending

ἡ δ', ὥς τ' ἐν πεδίῳ τετράοροι ἄρσενες ἵπποι
πάντες ἅμ' ὁρμηθέντες ὑπὸ πληγῇσιν ἱμάσθλης
ὑψόσ' ἀειρόμενοι ῥίμφα πρήσσουσι κέλευθον,
1270   ὣς ἄρα τῆς πρύμνη μὲν ἀείρετο, κῦμα δ' ὄπισθεν
πορφύρεον μέγα θῦε πολυφλοίσβοιο θαλάσσης·
ἡ δὲ μάλ' ἀσφαλέως θέεν ἔμπεδον· οὐδέ κεν ἴρηξ
κίρκος ὁμαρτήσειεν, ἐλαφρότατος πετεηνῶν·
ὣς ἡ ῥίμφα θέουσα θαλάσσης κύματ' ἔταμνεν,
1275   ἄνδρα φέρουσα θεοῖς ἐναλίγκια μήδε' ἔχοντα,
ὃς πρὶν μὲν μάλα πολλὰ πάθ' ἄλγεα ὃν κατὰ θυμόν,
ἀνδρῶν τε πτολέμους ἀλεγεινά τε κύματα πείρων·
δὴ τότε γ' ἀτρέμας εὗδε λελασμένος ὅσσ' ἐπεπόνθει.

ἀσφαλέως surely, straight on	*ὁμαρτέω, —, ὁμάρτησα* I go equally
ἀτρέμας [adv.] motionless, quietly	swift, I keep up with
ἐλαφρός, -ή, -όν swift, quick	*πετεηνά, -ῶν* [n. pl.] winged things,
ἐναλίγκιος, (-η), -ον like to	birds
θύω I run, I surge	*πληγή, -ῆς* [f.] blow, stroke
ἱμάσθλη, -ης [f.] whip	*πολύφλοισβος, -ον* loud-roaring,
ἴρηξ, -ηκος [m.] (a bird) of the	booming
falcon kind	*πρύμνη, -ης* [f.] aft, stern
κίρκος, -ου [m.] hawk	*τετράορος, -ον* joined four together
μῆδος, -εος [n.] thought, plan	

1187. NOTES

1267 *ἡ:* the ship.

1268 *ὁρηθέντες:* from *ὁρμήθην,* aorist passive of *ὁρμάω.*

1271 *μέγα:* adverbial, "vehemently."

1278 *λελασμένος:* from *λέλασμαι,* perfect of *λανθάνω.*
     ἐπεπόνθει: from *πέπονθα,* perfect of *πάσχω.*

1188. COMMENT

1267 After his farewell to Alcinous and his court, Odysseus embarks at once and the waiting ship leaps forward.

1270 The prow is forced down and the stern raised rhythmically by the mighty pull of the expert Phaeacian rowers and the great sail. The speed and up-and-down motion thus produced reminds Homer of the galloping of a horse.

1271 The mouth-filling, ear-tickling epithet, "polyphloisboisterous," shows Homer at his onomatopoetic best. It has been humorously used to describe Homer himself in the anonymous verses:

> Polyphloiboisterous Homer of old
> Threw all his augments into the sea,
> Although he had often been courteously told
> That perfect imperfects begin with an e
> But the poet replied with a dignified air,
> "What the Digamma does any one care?"

1273 The Phaeacians were famous for their seamanship; and besides, their ships had been given certain preternatural powers by the gods. Hence their extraordinary speed.

1276 With these lines, similar to those which long ago introduced the story to us, we come to the end of our selections from the *Odyssey*.

A PHAEACIAN CLIPPER

THE REUNION OF ODYSSEUS AND PENELOPE

A terracotta plaque from the island Melos in mid-fifth century B.C. shows Odysseus in the guise of a beggar trying to convince Penelope that he is really her beloved husband finally returned after twenty years away. She is cautious and still sceptical.

We have tried to share with Odysseus in the strange and varied adventures that he was forced to pass through to win his weary way home. We have tried to appreciate as we watched him his manly, vigorous, noble character. Of all the hundreds of soldiers that set out with him from Ithaca and adjacent islands for the Trojan war, he alone is left, though no one else fought as bravely as he, volunteered for as many hazardous enterprises, or passed through dangers calling for more resourcefulness and self-discipline. At last, in the twentieth year after his setting forth, he has been given his heart's desire. We see him now resting peacefully among his friends as he is being rushed back to his dearly-beloved family and the homeland of which he was ever a part.

He knows from the prophecy of Tiresias that he must yet face and punish the insolent suitors who have been tormenting his wife, and that he must go on a pilgrimage to be reconciled with Poseidon. But he knows, too, that the rest of a long life will be spent with his wife and son in the priceless bliss of a love sorely tested but not found wanting; that his days will be passed amid the plaudits and service of his happy and prosperous subjects.

As he looks forward to the happiness soon to be his, all the toils and sufferings of twenty years seem a small enough price to pay. Already even their memory is beginning to fade away, as he stretches out his limbs and allows peaceful sleep to assert its dominion over him — with his last thought, perhaps, a silent acknowledgment that after all life is good.

1189.   WORD STUDY

PHILIP ('lover of horses'); HIPPOPOTAMUS ('river-horse'); HIPPODROME (a place where 'horses run,' a race-course); — PURPLE (the 'gleaming' color).

182

To round out and climax our course in Homeric Greek, the remaining selections in this book will be from Homer's earlier poem, the *Iliad.*

Like the *Odyssey,* the *Iliad* is an immortal picture of life—life written in large figures against a vivid background of action, excitement, and human character. It is a more dynamic picture than even the *Odyssey,* because its theme is not peaceful travel and adventure but the fury of a great war and the vehement inner struggles that rack the soul of its central hero, Achilles.

Homer's Achilles is a most extraordinary man. Son of a noble Greek prince, Peleus, and the goddess Thetis, he is gifted by nature with a flaming ardor of spirit that makes him no man for half-measures or commonplace ideals. Whatever he feels or does, he throws his whole soul into it. He is the personification of youthful vigor, earnestness, idealism. He is human nature at its energetic peak, life at its fulness of vibrant enthusiasm. In him, Homer has concentrated all the elements of greatness: some already refined and obvious, others potential or in the rough. How he rises to full stature, to the noble flowering of his highest manhood and character, is the splendid theme of the *Iliad.*

Having been offered by the gods the choice of a long life of quiet happiness at home or a short career of immortal glory and adventure, Achilles had seized upon the latter, and gone off to the great war at Troy to win undying fame by deeds of valor. Fiery spirit that he was, he soon became the greatest warrior of all, whose mere name brought admiration to the Greeks and terror to every Trojan. The fury of his onslaught no one had ever long resisted, and the list of his martial triumphs mounted daily. Yet Troy held out in its practically impregnable stronghold, and the war dragged on for ten bloody, wearying years.

Achilles too grew weary—not of battle and the tang of danger, but of the small-minded arrogance of Agamemnon, commander of the army, and his selfish monopoly of all major booty, credit, and preeminence. Achilles is shocked and disgusted; his lofty ideals of manly character and honest worth survive the scandal unlowered, but he feels himself out of place, unjustly thrust into the background, disillusioned in his assumption of a high idealism and nobility like his own on the part of all the Greeks in the pursuance of the war. Finally, he will endure such scorn and insults no longer. He withdraws from the campaign and leaves his unappreciative chief to lord it over those who will put up with his tyranny, and to suffer disaster from the unchecked might of the Trojans.

Brooding bitterly on the injuries to his honor, and wrapping himself in furious self-pity, Achilles soon wrenches his noble but immature and overly self-centered character into a white-hot hate, even to the point of exulting in the misery and ruin of his former friends. Soured, disillusioned, morbidly absorbed with self, his character deteriorates as joy and generous idealism fade from his life.

Suddenly, he is plunged into a new sorrow when Hector, greatest of Trojan warriors, slays in combat Achilles' dearest friend and lifelong constant companion, Patroclus, precious to him as life itself. With all the intensity of his great soul, Achilles writhes in an agony of grief. Then his whole immense energy of spirit is focused on one maddening desire, to show his love for his friend and avenge his death by crushing every Trojan in Hector's army and above all Hector himself. Every fiber of his being is steeped in flaming hatred for Hector, who becomes in his eyes the incarnation of everything that is evil, vicious, and foul. He lives only to trample Hector in the dust and to throw his cursed body to the dogs for food. . . .

Meanwhile Homer shows us Hector in another light—not in the baneful distorting glare of Achilles' blind hate, but in the soft gentle glow of his own noble and manly character. The real Hector is a man of the most estimable qualities. Courageous, upright, honest, a great leader and splendid patriot, he is also remarkably gentle and refined, a man of the deepest human sympathy and love, sensitive to every emotion, full of dignity and high-mindedness, loyal to duty and his friends. Homer has created no more admirable character, and it is doubtful if anyone else has either. Yet he is human, with his human faults—a certain narrowness of outlook limited to his own immediate friends and interests, and a tendency to vanity which he strives nobly to suppress. We cannot but love and admire the man, and see in him Homer's ideal of the type of man who is mellowed and refined by human virtues in balanced blend, even though no genius nor a brilliant meteor like Achilles. Hector, the perfect gentleman and loving family man—how real and warmly appealing Homer makes him!

We look in now on the lives and inmost characters of these two great men, and on the mighty struggles in their souls as they are drawn irresistibly together for the final clash—that fateful crisis which will work Hector's pathetic death and begin the remaking of Achilles, the sublimation of his fiery character to levels at last worthy of his grandeur and his spirit.

The scene opens quietly enough, with Hector just leaving his splendid home in Troy, where he has been looking for his dearly loved wife Andromache, before returning, for what he senses will be the last time, to the field of battle and his destiny. . . .

THE YOUTHFUL ACHILLES
A modern attempt to portray the fiery hero's youth and idealism. Painted in 1810 by Michel-Martin Drölling.

1190. MEMORIZE:

ἀστήρ, -έρος [m.] [dat. pl. ἀστράσι] star

Ἕκτωρ, -ορος [m.] Hector [most distinguished warrior of Trojans]

Ἠετίων, -ωνος [m.] Eetion [father of Andromache]

κόλπος, -ου [m.] fold; bosom; bay

1191. TEXT

The Family

ἦ ῥα γυνὴ ταμίη, ὁ δ᾽ ἀπέσσυτο δώματος Ἕκτωρ

1280 τὴν αὐτὴν ὁδὸν αὖτις ἐυκτιμένας κατ᾽ ἀγυιάς.

εὖτε πύλας ἵκανε διερχόμενος μέγα ἄστυ,

Σκαιάς, τῇ ἄρ᾽ ἔμελλε διεξίμεναι πεδίονδε,

ἔνθ᾽ ἄλοχος πολύδωρος ἐναντίη ἦλθε θέουσα

Ἀνδρομάχη, θυγάτηρ μεγαλήτορος Ἠετίωνος—

1285 Ἠετίων, ὃς ἔναιεν ὑπὸ Πλάκῳ ὑληέσσῃ,

Θήβῃ ὑποπλακίῃ, Κιλίκεσσ᾽ ἄνδρεσσιν ἀνάσσων·

τοῦ περ δὴ θυγάτηρ ἔχεθ᾽ Ἕκτορι χαλκοκορυστῇ.

ἥ οἱ ἔπειτ᾽ ἤντησ᾽, ἅμα δ᾽ ἀμφίπολος κίεν αὐτῇ

παῖδ᾽ ἐπὶ κόλπῳ ἔχουσ᾽ ἀταλάφρονα, νήπιον αὔτως,

1290 Ἑκτορίδην ἀγαπητόν, ἀλίγκιον ἀστέρι καλῷ,

τόν ῥ᾽ Ἕκτωρ καλέεσκε Σκαμάνδριον, αὐτὰρ οἱ ἄλλοι

Ἀστυάνακτ᾽· οἶος, γὰρ ἐρύετο Ἴλιον Ἕκτωρ.

ἀγαπητός, -ή, -όν beloved
ἀλίγκιος, -ον like to
Ἀνδρομάχη, -ης Andromache [wife of Hector]
ἀντάω, —, ἄντησα I meet with
Ἀστυάναξ, -ακτος [m.] Astyanax [lit. "Lord of the City"]
ἀταλάφρων, -ον young-hearted, gleeful
δι-έξ-ειμι I pass (through and emerge)
δι-έρχομαι, etc. I come through
Ἑκτορίδης, -αο [m.] Hector's son
ἐναντίος, -η, -ον opposite; in order to meet
εὖτε when

Κίλικες, -ων [m. pl.] Cilicians
ναίω I dwell
Πλάκος, -ου [f.] Mt. Placus
πολύδωρος, -ον richly dowered; beautiful
Σκαιός, -ή, -όν left; Western
Σκαμάνδριος, ὀυ Scamandrius
ταμίη, -ης [f.] housekeeper
ὑλήεις, -εσσα, -εν woody, covered w. woods
ὑποπλάκιος, -η, -ον at foot of Mt. Placus
χαλκοκορυστής, -αο armed with bronze

A WARRIOR'S FAREWELL

This archaic plaque of thin bronze hammered over a wooden model represents a warrior climbing into his chariot after taking leave of a woman and her child. It is very likely an early illustration, around 600 B.C. from Olympia, of the memorable parting of Hector from his wife Andromache and son Astyanax.

1192. NOTES

1191 ἡ: "thus spoke."

1280 ὁδόν: an accusative is sometimes used to express the way along which one goes.

1287 ἔχεθ': i.e., as wife.

1288 ἅμα: with αὐτῇ.

1289 νήπιος: here in its original meaning, "a child, infant." Transl.: "mere infant that he was."

1193. COMMENT

1279 Not wishing to stay away from the battle any longer than necessary, Hector had given up the idea of looking about the city for Andromache on being told by the housekeeper that she is out searching for him. However, she had apparently seen him coming and ran to meet him.

1286 There were two Thebes frequently mentioned in Greek literature: one was in northern Greece; the other in Asia Minor not a great distance from Troy. It is to the latter, of course, that reference is made here.

1290 Poets are hard put to it to describe the wondrous beauty of a small child. "Mighty like a rose" has become famous, and this line, too, has been admired for the charm of its sound, its tenderness, and its suggestive imagery. A bright star is a beautiful symbol of glowing purity.

1291 The Scamander was the river of Troy. For this reaon Hector had named his son Scamandrius; but it was not long before the people found a nickname for him. This son of the fearless warrior, to whose leadership and protection all Troy looked, should be called, they insisted, "Astyanax" ("Lord of the City").

1194. WORD STUDY

ASTER (a 'star' flower); ASTERISK; ASTEROID (one of the small 'star-like' fragmentary planets between Mars and Jupiter).

HECTOR AND ANDROMACHE

This simple but tender rendition by the English Classicist artist John Flaxman in the early nineteenth century takes its cues from the text of Homer, but the temple in the background is imaginary and out of place.

1195. MEMORIZE:

'Aχιλ(λ)εύς, -ῆος [m.]   Achilles [greatest warrior of Greeks; hero of *Iliad*]

δαιδάλεος, -η, -ον   cunningly wrought

δαιμόνιος, -η   strange (one) [whose actions are unaccountable, wonderful, or super-human]

ἔντεα, -ων [3 decl. n. pl.]   arms, armor; utensils

σιωπή, -ῆς [f.]   silence

φύω, φύσω, φῦσα and φῦν   I produce; [3 aor., pf., and in pass.:]   I grow; [w. ἐν]   I cling to

1196.   TEXT

War, Hateful to Women

ἦ τοι ὁ μὲν μείδησεν ἰδὼν ἐς παῖδα σιωπῇ·
Ἀνδρομάχη δέ οἱ ἄγχι παρίστατο δάκρυ χέουσα,
1295   ἔν τ' ἄρα οἱ φῦ χειρί, ἔπος τ' ἔφατ' ἔκ τ' ὀνόμαζεν·
"δαιμόνιε, φθίσει σε τὸ σὸν μένος, οὐδ' ἐλεαίρεις
παῖδά τε νηπίαχον καὶ ἔμ' ἄμμορον, ἣ τάχα χήρη
σεῦ ἔσομαι· τάχα γάρ σε κατακτενέουσιν Ἀχαιοὶ
πάντες ἐφορμηθέντες· ἐμοὶ δέ κε κέρδιον εἴη
1300   σεῦ ἀφαμαρτούσῃ χθόνα δύμεναι· οὐ γὰρ ἔτ' ἄλλη
ἔσται θαλπωρή, ἐπεὶ ἂν σύ γε πότμον ἐπίσπῃς,
ἀλλ' ἄχε'· οὐδέ μοι ἔστι πατὴρ καὶ πότνια μήτηρ.
ἦ τοι γὰρ πατέρ' ἀμὸν ἀπέκτανε δῖος Ἀχιλλεύς,
ἐκ δὲ πόλιν πέρσεν Κιλίκων ἐὺ ναιεταούσαν,
1305   Θήβην ὑψίπυλον· κατὰ δ' ἔκτανεν Ἠετίωνα,
οὐδέ μιν ἐξενάριξε, σεβάσσατο γὰρ τό γε θυμῷ,
ἀλλ' ἄρα μιν κατέκηε σὺν ἔντεσι δαιδαλέοισιν
ἠδ' ἐπὶ σῆμ' ἔχεεν· περὶ δὲ πτελέας ἐφύτευσαν
νύμφαι ὀρεστιάδες, κοῦραι Διὸς αἰγιόχοιο.

ἄμμορος, -ον ill-fated, unfortunate
ἀμός, -ή, -όν our
Ἀνδρομάχη, -ης Andromache [wife of Hector]
ἀπο-κτείνω, etc. I kill
ἀφ-αμαρτάνω, etc. I miss; I am deprived of
θαλπωρή, ῆς [f.] comfort
κατα-καίω, etc. I burn (down)
Κίλικες, -ων [m. pl.] Cilicians
μειδάω, —, μείδησα I smile

νηπίαχος, -ον infant, helpless
ὀρεστιάς, -άδος [adj.] of the mountains
παρ-ίστημι, etc. I stand beside
πέρθω, —, πέρσα I sack, I ravage
πτελέη, -ης [f.] elm
σεβάζομαι, —, σεβασσάμην I consider it shameful to do
ὑψίπυλος, -ον with high gates, high gated
φυτεύω, —, φύτευσα I plant
χήρη, -ης [f.] widowed; a widow

ARES AT REST

The War God was not a frequent object of Greek art. This statue, showing the style and influence of Scopas, humanizes Ares. The cupid teasing him is a Hellenistic addition aimed at symbolizing the struggle of Love to tame War and violence.

1197. NOTES

1299   ἐφορμηθέντες: aorist passive of ἐφ-ορμάω.

1300   δύμεναι: "to put on the earth" (as garment), a vivid way of expressing death and burial.

1301   ἔσται: shortened from ἔσεται.

      ἐπίσπῃς: from ἐφ-έπω.

1302   ἄχε': depends on ἔσται.

1304   ἐκ: adverbial, merely intensifying πέρσεν.

1308   ἐπί: (adv.) "thereon."

      περί: adverbial.

1198. **COMMENT**

1293 ff. Lines of great poetic art in their touching tenderness and emotional reality.

1296 δαιμόνιε: This is a difficult word to translate correctly. In general it means that the one so described is under superhuman influence, that his or her actions are strange, unaccountable, or wonderful. If may be used in stern remonstrance, or very gently and tenderly, perhaps coming down in some cases to expressing merely affection. What makes translation of the word in this line practically impossible is that all the meanings mentioned seem in some way contained in it. There simply is no English equivalent which carries all these emotional undertones.

1299 πάντες ἐφορμηθέντες: An artful touch, flowing from Homer's insight into human nature. In her loving admiration for her husband's prowess, Andromache assumes that only the joined forces of the whole Greek army could subdue her Hector. But she is afraid the enemy realizes this, and will try it.

1303 The awful suffering he had caused to people like Andromache had up to this time never really occurred to the self-centered Achilles. But he will learn, taught by his own sorrow.

1305 Thebes was just one of the twenty-three cities allied to Troy that "swift-footed" Achilles and his Commando-type raiding forces had captures during the long siege, as Homer tells in other parts of the *Iliad*.

1306 To strip a fallen foe of his armor was accepted and expected Homeric practice. Achilles' reverence for King Eetion gives us an indication of the high-minded nobility of his character.

1307 The custom of burying armor with the body represents perhaps an earlier time when the carefully preserved body was buried intact in the earth and given its weapons to equip it for life beyond the grave. Later, when cremation became the universal Greek practice, the custom, somewhat illogically, was still continued.

1199. **WORD STUDY**

APOSIOPESIS (a sudden 'falling off into silence,' a figure of speech in which the thought is abruptly suspended, leaving the reader to gather from context what was to follow, e.g., "He has a pleasing enough personality, but as for his character —").

ACHILLES' NEW ARMOR
When Hector slew Patroclus, who was wearing Achillles' special armor, Thetis, the divine mother of Achilles, went to god Hephaestus and had him make replacements. She is shown here seated while finishing touches are being made — and using the opportunity to admire herself reflected in the shiny shield.

1200. MEMORIZE:

ἄλκιμος, -ον mighty, valiant
ἄποινα, -ων [n. pl.] ransom, recompense

ποδάρκης, -ες swift-footed
πύργος, -ου [m.] tower

1201. TEXT

Have Pity!

1310
οἳ δέ μοι ἑπτὰ κασίγνητοι ἔσαν ἐν μεγάροισιν,
οἱ μὲν πάντες ἰῷ κίον ἤματι Ἄιδος εἴσω·
πάντας γὰρ κατέπεφνε ποδάρκης δῖος Ἀχιλλεὺς
βουσὶν ἐπ' εἰλιπόδεσσι καὶ ἀργεννῇς ὀίεσσιν.
μητέρα δ', ἣ βασίλευεν ὑπὸ Πλάκῳ ὑληέσσῃ,

1315
τὴν ἐπεὶ ἂρ δεῦρ' ἤγαγ' ἅμ' ἄλλοισι κτεάτεσσιν,
ἂψ ὅ γε τὴν ἀπέλυσε λαβὼν ἀπερείσι' ἄποινα,
πατρὸς δ' ἐν μεγάροισι βάλ' Ἄρτεμις ἰοχέαιρα.
Ἕκτορ, ἀτὰρ σύ μοί ἐσσι πατὴρ καὶ πότνια μήτηρ
ἠδὲ κασίγνητος, σὺ δέ μοι θαλερὸς παρακοίτης·

1320
ἀλλ' ἄγε νῦν ἐλέαιρε καὶ αὐτοῦ μίμν' ἐπὶ πύργῳ,
μή παῖδ' ὀρφανικὸν θήῃς χήρην τε γυναῖκα·
λαὸν δὲ στῆσον παρ' ἐρινεόν, ἔνθα μάλιστα
ἀμβατός ἐστι πόλις καὶ ἐπίδρομον ἔπλετο τεῖχος·
τρὶς γὰρ τῇ γ' ἐλθόντες ἐπειρήσανθ' οἱ ἄριστοι

1325
ἀμφ' Αἴαντε δύω καὶ ἀγακλυτὸν Ἰδομενῆα
ἠδ' ἀμφ' Ἀτρεΐδας καὶ Τυδέος ἄλκιμον υἱόν·
ἤ πού τίς σφιν ἔνισπε θεοπροπίων ἐὺ εἰδώς,
ἤ νυ καὶ αὐτῶν θυμὸς ἐποτρύνει καὶ ἀνώγει."

ἀγακλυτός, -ον famous, glorious
Αἴας, -αντος [m.] Ajax [two Greek heroes bore this name]
ἀμβατός, -όν scalable, pregnable
ἀπερείσιος, -ον countless, untold
ἀπο-λύω, etc. I loose, I set free
ἀργεννός, -ή, -όν white, shining
Ἀτρεΐδης, -αο [m.] Atreus' son [Agememnon or Menelaus]
βασιλεύω I rule, I am ruler
εἰλίπους, -οδος rolling-gaited; trailing-footed
ἐπίδρομος, -ον able to be climbed over, assailable
ἐρινεός, -οῦ [m.] (wild) fig tree

θεοπρόπιον, -ου [n.] prophecy, oracle
Ἰδομενεύς, -ῆος [m.] Idomeneus [a Greek leader]
κτέαρ, -ατος [pl. only] [n.] goods; spoils
ὀρφανικός, -ή, -όν orphaned, fatherless
παρακοίτης, -αο [m.] husband
Πλάκος, -ου [m.] Mt. Placus
Τυδεύς, -έος [m.] Tydeus [Greek hero who fought against Thebes, father of Diomēdes]
ὑλήεις, -εσσα, -εν woody, covered w. woods
χήρη, -ης [f.] widowed; a widow

HEROIC ACHILLES
This mid-fifth-century amphora found at Vulci gives a noble image of the famous hero standing armed and holding a long spear. Details are especially well drawn.

1202. NOTES

1310   *οἵ:* relative; the antecedent is *οἱ* in the next line.

1311   *ἰῷ:* a rare variant for *ἑνί,* from stem *ἰ-*

1314   *μητέρα:* object of *βάλ᾽* below.

1321   *θήῃς:* second aorist subjunctive of *τίθημι;* "I cause (to be) = I make."

1324   *τῃ:* there.

1327   *θεοπροπίων:* verbs of hearing, learning, knowing, etc., sometimes take a kind of partitive genitive.

1203. COMMENT

1317   See explanation in note on line 556.

1318-9   Considering not only the strong love that this young mother would naturally have for her heroic husband but also the terrible sorrow and loneliness caused by the tragic deaths of her whole family, we do not find it hard to sympathize with the desperate way she clings to him and fears for his safety. We can appreciate, too, the ardor of her splendid outburst of affection in stating what he means to her.

1322   The wild fig-tree she mentions must have been a well-known landmark. It apparently stood near a place where the towering walls were weakest. Such experienced enemy leaders as the two Ajaxes and Diomedes had already picked it out as the point of several attacks. This was, no doubt, the part built by the mortal Aeacus who, according to the legend, had assisted Apollo and Poseidon in raising the walls of Troy. There was a prophecy that the city would be taken at this point, and Andromache suggests that some seer knew of the legend and had divined the spot.

1204. MEMORIZE:

ἄρνυμαι, ἀρέομαι, ἀρόμην I win; I strive
to win
δακρυόεις, -εσσα, -εν tearful
κλέος, κλέ(ε)ος [n.] fame, renown

κορυθαίολος, -ον w. glancing helm
νόσφι(ν) [adv.] apart (from), away
(from)
χαλκοχίτων, -ωνος bronze-clad

1205. TEXT

Code of the Warrior

τὴν δ' αὖτε προσέειπε μέγας κορυθαίολος Ἕκτωρ·
1330 "ἦ καὶ ἐμοὶ τάδε πάντα μέλει, γύναι· ἀλλὰ μαλ' αἰνῶς
αἰδέομαι Τρῶας καὶ Τρῳάδας ἑλκεσιπέπλους,
αἴ κε κακὸς ὣς νόσφιν ἀλυσκάζω πολέμοιο·
οὐδέ με θυμὸς ἄνωγεν, ἐπεὶ μάθον ἔμμεναι ἐσθλὸς
αἰεὶ καὶ πρώτοισι μετὰ Τρώεσσι μάχεσθαι,
1335 ἀρνύμενος πατρός τε μέγα κλέος ἠδ' ἐμὸν αὐτοῦ.
εὖ γὰρ ἐγὼ τόδε οἶδα κατὰ φρένα καὶ κατὰ θυμόν—
ἔσσεται ἦμαρ, ὅτ' ἄν ποτ' ὀλώλῃ Ἴλιος ἱρὴ
καὶ Πρίαμος καὶ λαὸς ἐϋμμελίω Πριάμοιο.
ἀλλ' οὔ μοι Τρώων τόσσον μέλει ἄλγος ὀπίσσω,
1340 οὔτ' αὐτῆς Ἑκάβης οὔτε Πριάμοιο ἄνακτος
οὔτε κασιγνήτων, οἵ κεν πολέες τε καὶ ἐσθλοὶ
εν κονίῃσι πέσοιεν ὑπ' ἀνδράσι δυσμενέεσσιν,
ὅσσον σεῦ, ὅτε κέν τις Ἀχαιῶν χαλκοχιτώνων
δακρυόεσσαν ἄγηται, ἐλεύθερον ἦμαρ ἀπούρας.

ἀλυσκάζω I shrink from
ἀπούρᾱς [aor. ptc. of defective verb]
  having taken away
Ἑκάβη, -ης [f.] Hecabe [wife of Priam
  and mother of Hector]

ἐλεύθερος, -η, -ον free, of freedom
ἑλκεσίπεπλος, -ον with trailing robes
ἐϋμμελίης, -ίω with fine ashen spear
ἱρός = ἱερός
Τρῳάς, -άδος [f.] Trojan woman

1206. NOTES

1331 αἰδέομαι: "I feel shame before."
1333 ἄνωγεν: understand ἀλυσκάζειν.
1335 αὐτοῦ: agrees with ἐμοῦ implied in ἐμόν.
1339 τόσσον . . . ὅσσον: adverbial with μέλει.
1342 πέσοιεν . . . ἄγηται: the difference of mood shows how much more vividly he feels the
approaching doom of his wife.
1343 σεῦ: understand ἄλγος.

1207. COMMENT

1331-5. To a professional soldier, honor means more than life itself. Hector speaks as a true warrior and man of spirit.

1339 ff. Hector is nobly appealing in his poignant sympathy for his people, his family, and most especially for his ill-fated wife. His heartbreaking presentiment of the disgrace and degradation that awaits his royal, dearly-beloved spouse, who means everything to him and who would soon have become queen of mighty Troy, is surely one of the most touching passages in literature.

HECTOR AT TROY

The famous 'Francois Vase' now in Florence dates to around 570 B.C. It has many scenes from Homeric stories. This detail shows Hector leaving Troy by one of its many gates, accompanied by his brother Polites. (Names are written). To the left, King Priam is seated on an official bench, listening to the Trojan nobleman Antenor, no doubt discussing the status of the war.

1208. MEMORIZE:

ἀμῡνω, ἀμυνέω, ἄμῡνα   I ward off; I defend, I aid
βοή, -ῆς [f.]   shout, cry

ἱππόδαμος, -ον   horse-taming
κόρυς, -υθος [f.]   helmet
νεύω, νεύσω, νεῦσα   I nod

1209. TEXT

From Queen to Slave

1345 καί κεν ἐν Ἄργει ἐοῦσα πρὸς ἄλλης ἱστὸν ὑφαίνοις,
     καί κεν ὕδωρ φορέοις Μεσσηίδος ἢ Ὑπερείης
     πόλλ᾽ ἀεκαζομένη, κρατερὴ δ᾽ ἐπικείσετ᾽ ἀνάγκη·
     καί ποτέ τις εἴπῃσιν ἰδὼν κατὰ δάκρυ χέουσαν·
     ‘ Ἕκτορος ἥδε γυνή, ὃς ἀριστεύεσκε μάχεσθαι
1350 Τρώων ἱπποδάμων, ὅτε Ἴλιον ἀμφεμάχοντο.’
     ὣς ποτέ τις ἐρέει, σοὶ δ᾽ αὖ νέον ἔσσεται ἄλγος
     χήτεϊ τοιοῦδ᾽ ἀνδρός, ἀμύνειν δούλιον ἦμαρ.
     ἀλλά με τεθνηῶτα χυτὴ κατὰ γαῖα καλύπτοι,
     πρίν γέ τι σῆς τε βοῆς σοῦ θ᾽ ἑλκηθμοῖο πυθέσθαι.”
1355   ὣς εἰπὼν οὗ παιδὸς ὀρέξατο φαίδιμος Ἕκτωρ·
     ἂψ δ᾽ ὁ πάις πρὸς κόλπον ἐυζώνοιο τιθήνης
     ἐκλίνθη ἰάχων, πατρὸς φίλου ὄψιν ἀτυχθείς,
     ταρβήσας χαλκόν τε ἰδὲ λόφον ἱππιοχαίτην,
     δεινὸν ἀπ᾽ ἀκροτάτης κόρυθος νεύοντα νοήσας.
1360 ἐκ δ᾽ ἐγέλασσε πατήρ τε φίλος καὶ πότνια μήτηρ

ἀεκαζόμενος, -η, -ον   against one's will
ἀμφι-μάχομαι, etc.   I fight around
ἀριστεύω   I am best, I am preeminent
Ἄργος, -εος [n.]   Argos [an important
  Greek city; sometimes used for all
  Greece]
ἀτύζομαι, —, ἀτύχθην   I am frightened
  at
γελάω, —, γέλασ(σ)α   I laugh
δούλιος, -η, -ον   slavish, of slavery
ἑλκηθμός, -οῖο [m.]   being dragged away
ἐπί-κειμαι, ἐπι-κείσομαι   I am laid on
ἐΰζωνος, -ον   well-girdled, fair-
  girdled

ἱππιοχαίτης, -ες   of horse-hair
Μεσσηίς, -ίδος [f.]   Messeis [a spring
  in southern Greece]
ὀρέγω, ὀρέξω, ὄρεξα   I reach out (for)
  [w. gen.]
ὄψις, -ιος [f.]   sight, appearance
ταρβέω, —, τάρβησα   I fear
τιθήνη, -ης [f.]   nurse
Ὑπερείη, -ης [f.]   Hypereia [a spring in
  Thessaly
φορέω   I bear
χῆτος, -εος [n.]   want, lack
χυτή, -ῆς [adj.]   heaped up

1210.   NOTES

1345   *πρός:* "at the bidding of."
         ἱστόν: here means that which was placed on the loom, viz., the "web."

1347   *ἐπικείσετ':* understand *σοί.*

1348   *εἴπῃσιν:* Homer sometimes uses the subjunctive even in independent clauses to express vivid future supposition.
         κατά: adverbial.

1349   *ἥδε:* understand *ἐστί.*
         μάχεσθαι: explanatory, "in fighting."

1353   *βοῆς . . . ἑλκηθμοῖο:* hendiadys (the use of two words connected by a conjunction to express a single complex idea)—"the cry of your being carried away."

1355   *οὗ = ἕου.*

1357   *ἐκλίνθη:* aorist passive of *κλίνω,* with active sense.

1359   *δεινόν:* adverbial with *νεύοντα.*
         νοήσας: the object is *λόφον.*

CAPTIVE ANDROMACHE

Lord Leighton has skilfully represented the pathos of Homer's story. Andromache in widow's black and wrapped in her memories waits her turn to get water from the fountain for household needs. After Hector's death and Troy's she was a slave of Pyrrhus, son of Achilles; but on his death was married by Helenus, a prince of Troy who survived the war. Aeneas visits her at Buthrotum in SW Italy (*Aeneid* 3.294--). As Hector had foreseen, she is humiliated by her slavery and the women's comments.

HYPEREIA SPRING TODAY

Velestinon in Thessaly is on the site of Homer's Pherai, and the spring Hypereia in the center of town is where Hector foretold to Andromache that she would go to draw water when a slave to some foreign lord. The water is still clear and abundant.

1211. COMMENT

1346 Messeis would be the scene of her labor if she should be awarded as a slave to Menelaus; Hypereia, if Achilles should carry her off.

1346 Strabo (9.5.6) says that both these springs were in Thessaly, near Pharsala. The modern town Velestinon in that area, on the site of ancient Pherai, still claims these names for its fine springs. In legend, Andromache became the slave of Neoptolemos, son of Ach., and after his death the wife of Helenos, prince of Troy. (cp. Vergil, *Aen.* 3.294--)

1355 ff. Amid the grim realities of war, Homer finds place for this marvelously human scene of family experience. Even Achilles, if he were looking on, could not help but admit that these are real, lovable human beings.

1212. WORD STUDY

ZONE (a 'belt' or area characterized by some distinctive feature, as the 'torrid zone' around the equator, a 'safety zone' in a street, etc.); — OPTICAL (pertaining to 'sight' or vision); OPTICS (the science of light, vision, and the laws of visible appearance).

LESSON 217

1213. | MEMORIZE:

κυνέω, κυνήσομαι, κύσ(σ)α I kiss   πάλλω, —, πῆλα I shake; I dandle

1214. TEXT

A Father's Prayer

1361 αὐτίκ' ἀπὸ κρατὸς κόρυθ' εἵλετο φαίδιμος Ἕκτωρ,
καὶ τὴν μὲν κατέθηκεν ἐπὶ χθονὶ παμφανάουσαν,
αὐτὰρ ὅ γ' ὃν φίλον υἱὸν ἐπεὶ κύσε πῆλέ τε χερσίν,
εἶπεν ἐπευξάμενος Διί τ' ἄλλοισίν τε θεοῖσιν·

1365 "Ζεῦ, ἄλλοι τε θεοί, δότε δὴ καὶ τόνδε γενέσθαι
παῖδ' ἐμόν, ὡς καὶ ἐγώ περ, ἀριπρεπέα Τρώεσσιν,
ὧδε βίην τ' ἀγαθὸν καὶ Ἰλίου ἶφι ἀνάσσειν·
καί ποτέ τις εἴποι 'πατρός γ' ὅδε πολλὸν ἀμείνων'
ἐκ πολέμου ἀνιόντα· φέροι δ' ἔναρα βροτόεντα

1370 κτείνας δήιον ἄνδρα, χαρείη δὲ φρένα μήτηρ."
ὣς εἰπὼν ἀλόχοιο φίλης ἐν χερσὶν ἔθηκεν
παῖδ' ἐόν· ἡ δ' ἄρα μιν κηώδεϊ δέξατο κόλπῳ
δακρυόεν γελάσασα· πόσις δ' ἐλέησε νοήσας,
χειρί τέ μιν κατέρεξεν, ἔπος τ' ἔφατ' ἔκ τ' ὀνόμαζεν·

ἀμείνων, -ον better, braver
ἄν-ειμι I go up, I come back
ἀριπρεπής, -ές very conspicuous,
    illustrious
βροτόεις, -εσσα, -εν gory, bloody
γελάω, —, γέλασ(σ)α I laugh
δήιος, -η, -ον destructive, hostile
ἔναρα, -ων [n. pl.] spoils

ἐπ-εύχομαι, etc. I pray to; I exult
ἶφι [adv.] with might, by force
κατα-ρέζω, —, κατά-ρεξα I stroke
    (caressingly)
κηώδης, -ες fragrant
παμφανάων, -ουσα, -ον gleaming,
    shimmering

1215. NOTES

1362 ἐπεί: postponed from its natural position after αὐτάρ.
1365 δότε: "grant," followed by accusative and infinitive.
1366 παῖδ': accusative subject of γενέσθαι.
      Τρώεσσιν: "among the Trojans."
1367 βίην: accusative of specification.
1369 ἀν-ιόντα: agreeing with μίν understood as object of εἴποι = "may say of him coming back."
1373 δακρθόεν: (adv.) "tearfully," "through her tears."

1216. COMMENT

1369 It would be monotonous and distracting to try to call one's attention to all the literary devices of Homer. Still, we should make it our business to notice from time to time the means he uses to secure his effects. One of the important characteristics of his style is illustrated here — his constant striving to make us *see,* not just hear about, what is taking place. He wants us to see the helmet of Hector as he takes it off, that helmet with its shimmering horse-hair plume. And he wants it to lie there on the ground shining so brilliantly that we can't help but see it, too.

1365 ff. Hector's prayer is beautiful in its simplicity and paternal pride; yet it is only too indicative of his narrow vision of life, limited to his own people and city and to the worldly power and glory of ruling and defending them.

1370 Andromache will rejoice, not in the bloody spoils as such, but in her son's daring and prowess to which they will bear stark witness.

1371 "Laughing through her tears" — a deft touch which perfectly completes the whole wonderful scene, so simple and real, so deeply true to life. This artful phrase has become a world possession through centuries of admiring repetition.

1374 ἔπος τ᾿ ἔφατ᾿ ἔκ τ᾿ ὀνόμαζεν: Notice how this interesting expression always carries a connotation of tenderness and intimacy (see lines 1187, 1295).

HELMET WITH CREST
The crest (usually of horse hair) was meant to make the enemy more terrified by its waving, as it emphasized the power and vehemence of the wearer.

1217. | **MEMORIZE:**

αἶσα, -ης [f.]   (allotted) measure, fate   *ἀνδροφόνος, -ον*   man-slaying

1218. **TEXT**

Farewell Forever

1375   "δαιμονίη, μή μοί τι λίην ἀκαχίζεο θυμῷ·
οὐ γάρ τίς μ᾽ ὑπὲρ αἶσαν ἀνὴρ Ἄιδι προϊάψει·
μοῖραν δ᾽ οὔ τινά φημι πεφυγμένον ἔμμεναι ἀνδρῶν,
οὐ κακόν, οὐδὲ μὲν ἐσθλόν, ἐπὴν τὰ πρῶτα γένηται.
ἀλλ᾽ εἰς οἶκον ἰοῦσα τὰ σ᾽ αὐτῆς ἔργα κόμιζε,
1380   ἱστόν τ᾽ ἠλακάτην τε, καὶ ἀμφιπόλοισι κέλευε
ἔργον ἐποίχεσθαι· πόλεμος δ᾽ ἄνδρεσσι μελήσει
πᾶσιν, ἐμοὶ δὲ μάλιστα, τοὶ Ἰλίῳ ἐγγεγάασιν."
ὣς ἄρα φωνήσας κόρυθ᾽ εἵλετο φαίδιμος Ἕκτωρ
ἵππουριν· ἄλοχος δὲ φίλη οἰκόνδε βεβήκει
1385   ἐντροπαλιζομένη θαλερὸν κατὰ δάκρυ χέουσα.
αἶψα δ᾽ ἔπειθ᾽ ἵκανε δόμους ἐὺ ναιετάοντας
Ἕκτορος ἀνδροφόνοιο, κιχήσατο δ᾽ ἔνδοθι πολλὰς
ἀμφιπόλους, τῇσιν δὲ γόον πάσῃσιν ἐνῶρσεν.
αἱ μὲν ἔτι ζωὸν γόον Ἕκτορα ᾧ ἐνὶ οἴκῳ·
1390   οὐ γάρ μιν ἔτ᾽ ἔφαντο ὑπότροπον ἐκ πολέμοιο
ἵξεσθαι προφυγόντα μένος καὶ χεῖρας Ἀχαιῶν.

ἀκαχίζω I grieve
ἐγ-γίγνομαι, etc. I am born in
ἔνδοθι within
ἐν-όρνυμι, etc. I stir up among
ἐν-τροπαλίζομαι I keep turning to
    look back
ἐπ-οίχομαι I come to, I attend to

ἠλακάτη, -ης [f.] spindle
ἵππουρις [acc. -ιν] with horse-hair plume
προ-ιάπτω, προ-ιάψω I hurl forth, I
    send off
προ-φεύγω, etc. I escape, I elude
ὑπό-τροπος, -ον returning

1219.   NOTES

1375   μοί: the so-called "ethical dative," showing the speaker's personal concern.

1376   ὑπὲρ αἶσαν: "over my fate" — "before my time."

1377   πεφυγμένον ἔμμεναι: a periphrastic (round-about) construction "to have escaped." πεφυγμένον is perfect of φεύγω.

1378   τὰ πρῶτα γένηται: "once he is born."

1379   αὐτῆς: agreeing with σεῦ implied in σά.

1385   κατά: with χέουσα.

1387   κιχήσατο: a variant aorist of κιχάνω.

1389   γόον: a variant second aorist of γοάω.
        ᾧ = ἑῷ.

FRIGHTENED ANDROMACHE
This terracotta statuette of a woman with terrified look holding an infant in her arms as she takes refuge at an altar, where they should be untouched under threat of sacrilege, likely represents Andromache with little Astyanax.

1220.   COMMENT

1376   Throughout the ages, the constant danger of death has created in soldiers a kind of fatalism as a defense mechanism against hysteria. The soldier tells himself that he cannot be killed until his thread of life is used up, or until the bullet comes that has his number on it, or until his luck runs out. Others abandon themselves to Providence. However expressed, the psychological necessity seems the same.

1379   With pathetic but masculine brusqueness, Hector brings their tragic final farewell to a close.

1385   A shrewd realistic detail which completes the human interest of the picture and lingers in the memory.

1390   Hector's feeling that his death was only a matter of time was shared by his wife and servants who, in fact, considered the day to be already at hand.

LESSON 219

REVIEW

1221. Go over again Lessons 209–218; make sure now that you have really mastered them. Here are a few suggestions for your review:

1. *Vocabulary:* Check your mastery of the 40 new memory words.
2. *Text:* Reread the 153 lines of text, making sure you recognize all the forms.
3. *Story:*

   a. Describe the journey of Odysseus to Ithaca from the land of the Phaeacians.
   b. What is the general situation at the beginning of Lesson 212?
   c. Why, according to Andromache, is she so vitally concerned with the life of Hector?
   d. How does Hector answer her? (Cp. also Lesson 218)
   e. What is the name of their son and how is he mentioned in the story?

4. *Criticism:*

   a. Do you like the mood in which the adventures of Odysseus come to an end? Why?
   b. List some of the qualities of Hector revealed in these lessons.
   c. Do you think Homer succeeds in making Hector and Andromache seem like real human beings? Explain.

5. *Composition:* Put into Greek:

   a. Now the man of many counsels is returning home, there to see his dear wife and child whom he left behind just an infant.
   b. When Hector had kissed his child and dandled him, he prayed to Zeus, ruler of all the gods.
   c. She clung to his hand, trying to restrain his manly courage.

1222. HOMER, SCHLIEMANN, AND ARCHAEOLOGY

Up to 1870, it had been almost universally assumed for many decades that there was no historical foundation for Homer's story of the Trojan War, unless, perhaps, it could be admitted that an actual city, Ilium, once existed. The *Iliad* was considered sheer imagination and myth, the rich fruit of a poet's fancy. How one man's indomitable conviction to the contrary overturned long-standing views of the world's leading scholars and spurred archaeology into becoming a real science of vast historical importance forms the absorbing story of Heinrich Schliemann.

Born in Germany in 1822, he often heard his father tell the story of the great war at Troy, and at the age of eight set his mind on some day going to Troy itself and exploring its remains. Later, when fourteen, while working as a grocer's apprentice, he listened with utmost excitement to a traveling stranger recite aloud, with fine spirit and interpretation, a hundred lines of Homer in Greek. Though not understanding a word of the language, he was fascinated by the sound and rhythm. "Three times," he wrote in his memoirs at sixty, "I made him repeat the divine lines, recompensing him with three drinks, which I gladly paid for with the few pennies I possessed. From that moment onwards, I never stopped praying that by God's favor it might one day be my good fortune to be permitted to learn Greek." (!)

Deciding that to carry out his plans for exploring Homer's Troy he would need much money and a special education, he worked energetically for twenty-seven years, and succeeded in making a huge fortune in the indigo business in Russia. Meanwhile, he mastered many languages: English, French, Dutch, Spanish, Italian, Portuguese, Swedish, Polish, Latin, Arabic, modern Greek, classical Greek—putting off the last to the end, as he explained, for fear that he might fall under the spell of Homer, neglect his business, and so ruin his whole life work!

Meanwhile, he had become an American citizen while visiting California, and had traveled widely in Europe. In 1863 he gave up his business, took a journey around the world, then studied archaeology for two years in Paris. He went to Greece in 1868 to visit the actual sites of the events narrated in the *Odyssey* and *Iliad,* forming in the process the suspicion that the location of Homeric Troy was near the Turkish village Hissarlik rather than at Bunarbashi many miles away, where scholars put it—when they agreed to give it any historical reality at all. Returning to Germany, he wrote up his theories in a book (composed in English), and his life story (written in classical Greek). After receiving a Doctorate at the University of Rostock for his great classical knowledge, he returned to Greece and began his series of revolutionary excavations.

From 1870–1873, he dug up the ruins near Hissarlik, laying bare great stone walls, fortifications, and other remains of an ancient city obviously destroyed by burning, and discovered a treasure of gold jewelry thousands of years old. Elated with this confirmation of his theory, he eagerly proclaimed to an excited world that he had found the very city of Priam, just as de-

A MYCENAEAN PRIESTESS

Found in 1971 at Mycenae on the wall of a house from around the time of the Trojan War, this fresco is remarkably refined and skillful. The woman fearlessly holding a serpent is likely a priestess in some religious ritual. Note details of face and hand.

scribed in the *Iliad*. He then went to old Mycenae and after much trouble with the authorities succeeded in excavating most of that ancient sity of Agamemnon, discovering the famous shaft graves of the kings and finding in them an immense hoard of gold, silver, bronze, and finely wrought works of stone and ivory—the richest treasure ever found on any archaeological expedition (see samples, pp. 10, 69, 204).

Twice more he dug at Troy, uncovering further remnants of ancient cities—for it seems from the ruins that at least nine different cities were built on the same site, each atop the ruins of its predecessor, dating from far before the Trojan War up to the second century A.D. or later. The remains of each period are distinctive and can be dated with relative accuracy. The sixth and seventh levels from the bottom show all the characteristics of the period around 1200 B.C. when the Trojan War probably took place. Investigation of these remains indicates that many little features of plan, terrain, and surroundings described in the *Iliad* actually existed, so that the Troy immortalized by Homer and Vergil is far from being purely a creature of the poet's imagination. Thus, Schliemann's boyhood dream came true, and gave new interpretation to much in Homer's poems.

Schliemann's further excavations, at Orchomenus, Ithaca, and Tiryns, were less spectacular, though the last was important for laying bare the complete ground-plan of a Greek city in the heroic age about which Homer wrote. Spurred on by Schliemann's work, other archaeologists excavated many other ancient sites and improved the techniques of searching, digging, and identification to their present highly scientific level.

Modern archaeology has been of the greatest historical value. Much of its eminence is due to the burning lifelong love of Homer that over a century ago took hold of a small German boy and made him eager to look with his own eyes on the famous scenes the poet had described.

MYCENAEAN GOLD ORNAMENTS

Homer speaks of Mycenae, Agamemnon's capital, as "rich in gold." Schliemann's excavations and later finds justify the poet's praise. Here are some small circular ornaments of pure gold, embossed with varied patterns, from a tomb dating to the late sixteenth century B.C.

WALLS AND GATE AT TROY

Though now in ruins, the walls of Troy were once massive and believed impregnable (Apollo and Poseidon had helped build them). Some 30 feet high and 15 feet thick, they surrounded the upper level of the hill on which the city was built. At intervals they were pierced by a gate protected by added defense structures. It is at such a gate that we are to visualize the moving farewell of Hector and Andromache—which will continue to arouse admiration even when the walls have eventually crumbled to dust.

THE TOMB OF ATREUS AT MYCENAE

Shaped like a bee-hive, or half of a football, Mycenaean 'tholos' tombs are great monuments from the heroic age. This huge one is plausibly thought to have been constructed for Atreus, father of Agamemnon and Menelaos, in the early 13th century B.C. The 'dromos' entry-way leads to a great door, the lintel of which across the top is made of two enormous slabs of rock, the inner one weighing nearly 120 tons! The triangular area above was to lighten pressure on the lintel; it was covered by a facing panel. Inside, the corbelled ceiling rises cone-like in diminishing layers of stone to a peak of 43 feet. The burial chamber is an adjoining room off to the right of the door. These tholoi are a Mycenaean parallel to the even greater Pyramids of Egypt.

1223. | MEMORIZE:

αἰχμή, -ῆς [f.] spear-point

ἀντίκρυ [adv.] straight on or against
 (w. gen.)

αὐχήν, -ένος [m.] neck

ἔγχος, -εος [n.] spear

εἴκω, εἴξω, (ἔ)ειξα I yield, I give way

ὁρμάω, ὁρμήσω, ὅρμησα I arouse
 [mid. or pass.:] I start, I rush (forward)

σάκος, -εος [n.] shield

στέρνον, -ου [n.] chest, breast

Outside the city, the battle continues with unabated fierceness. Gradually the other Trojans drop back behind the city walls, but Hector, carried away with enthusiasm, remains fighting outside. Then Achilles, who has been seeking Hector in the confusion of fighting men, catches sight of the object of his quest. In a blaze of hatred and fury, he hurls himself to the assault. For a time Hector avoids him, but finally he stops, and the two champions confront each other. There is an exchange of verbal recriminations; then Hector advances to the attack.

Μαχεόμενοι

1224. TEXT

Hector Fights Achilles

ὣς ἄρα φωνήσας εἰρύσσατο φάσγανον ὀξύ,
τό οἱ ὑπὸ λαπάρην τέτατο μέγα τε στιβαρόν τε.
οἴμησεν δὲ ἀλεὶς ὥς τ᾽ αἰετὸς ὑψιπετήεις,

1395 ὅς τ᾽ εἶσιν πεδίονδε διὰ νεφέων ἐρεβεννῶν
ἁρπάξων ἢ ἄρν᾽ ἀμαλὴν ἢ πτῶκα λαγωόν·
ὣς Ἕκτωρ οἴμησε τινάσσων φάσγανον ὀξύ.
ὡρμήθη δ᾽ Ἀχιλεύς, μένεος δ᾽ ἐμπλήσατο θυμὸν
ἀγρίου, πρόσθεν δὲ σάκος στέρνοιο κάλυψεν

1400 καλὸν δαιδάλεον, κόρυθι δ᾽ ἐπένευε φαεινῇ
τετραφάλῳ· καλαὶ δὲ περισσείοντο ἔθειραι
χρύσεαι, ἃς Ἥφαιστος ἵει λόφον ἀμφὶ θαμειάς.
οἷος δ᾽ ἀστὴρ εἶσι μετ᾽ ἀστράσι νυκτὸς ἀμολγῷ
ἕσπερος, ὃς κάλλιστος ἐν οὐρανῷ ἵσταται ἀστήρ,

1405 ὣς αἰχμῆς ἀπέλαμπ᾽ εὐήκεος, ἣν ἄρ᾽ Ἀχιλεὺς
πάλλεν δεξιτερῇ φρονέων κακὸν Ἕκτορι δίῳ,
εἰσοράων χρόα καλόν, ὅπη εἴξειε μάλιστα.
τῇ ῥ᾽ ἐπὶ οἷ μεμαῶτ᾽ ἔλασ᾽ ἔγχεϊ δῖος Ἀχιλεύς,
ἀντικρὺ δ᾽ ἀπαλοῖο δι᾽ αὐχένος ἤλυθ᾽ ἀκωκή.

1410 οὐδ᾽ ἄρ᾽ ἀπ᾽ ἀσφάραγον μελίη τάμε χαλκοβάρεια,
ὄφρα τί μιν προτιείποι ἀμειβόμενος ἐπέεσσιν.
ἤριπε δ᾽ ἐν κονίης· ὁ δ᾽ ἐπεύξατο δῖος Ἀχιλεύς.

αἰετός, -οῦ [m.] eagle
ἀκωκή, -ῆς [f.] point
ἀμαλός, -ή, -όν tender
ἀμολγός, -οῦ [n.] darkness
ἀπαλός, -ή, -όν soft, tender
ἀπο-λάμπω I shine forth from
ἀσφάραγος, -ου [m.] windpipe
δεξιτερός, -ή, -όν right (hand)
ἔθειραι, -άων [f. pl.] horse-hair plume
ἐπ-εύχομαι, etc. (I pray to); I exult
ἐπι-νεύω I nod (forward)
ἐρεβεννός, -ή, -όν gloomy, dark
ἐρείπω, —, ἔριπον I dash down; I fall
ἕσπερος, -ον (of) evening
εὐήκης, -ες well-pointed, sharp
Ἥφαιστος, -ου [m.] Hephaestus [god of fire and metal-work]

θαμεῖαι, -άων [adj., pl. only] crowded, thick
λαγωός, -οῦ [m.] hare, rabbit
λαπάρη, -ης [f.] flank, side
μελίη, -ης [f.] ash, ashen-spear
οἰμάω, —, οἴμησα I rush on, I swoop
ὅπη where
περι-(σ)σείομαι I shake or wave around
προτί-ειπον I address
πτώξ, πτῶκος [adj.] cowering, trembling
τετράφαλος, -ον four-horned
τινάσσω, τινάξω, τίναξα I brandish
ὑψιπετήεις, -εσσα, -εν high-soaring
χαλκοβαρής, -εῖα, -ές [f. as if from -βάρυς] heavy with bronze

1225. **NOTES**

1392 ειρύσσατο: augmented εἰ- for ἠ-, as εἶχον, etc.

1393 τέτατο: "had been stretched out" — "hung."

1394 οἴμησεν: i.e., Hector.

ἀλείς: aorist passive participle from εἰλ(έ)ω.

ὥς: has a borrowed pitch-mark. If two words without pitch-marks come together, the first is given an acute.

1398 ὡρμήθη: aorist passive of ὁρμάω.

ἐμπλήσατο: "filled full of."

1399 ἀγρίου: scan as three long syllables.

κάλυψεν: "put as a covering."

1402 ἀμφί: adverb, with ἵει.

1405 ἀπέλαμπ': impersonal; transl.: "a light shone forth from."

1406 φρονέων: "planning."

1408 οἱ: notice the pitch-mark, indicating that it is reflexive. As Hector rushed at him, Achilles drove at him with his spear.

1410 ἀπ': adverbial, with τάμε—"cut away."

1411 ὄφρα: gives the purpose not of the spear, of course, but of Fate which is directing the spear.

1226. **COMMENT**

1395 The eagle soars to tremendous heights, then when its telescopic eyes have spotted a fish or small animal, it seems to gather itself together, and, as Tennyson puts it, "like a thunderbolt he falls."

1399 ἀγρίου: The emphatic position of the word shows its significance. Now that at last he faces his hated foe, he is filled with an anger that is wild, savage, and brutal.

1402 Hephaestus, the god of metalwork, had made Achilles' armor, as a favor to the young warrior's goddess-mother, Thetis.

1409 It is significant that Homer does not make this a long, drawn-out, exciting battle. He almost seems to hurry over it in order to deal with its more important spiritual implications.

1412 A wild exultation seizes Achilles as he sees the slayer of Patroclus crumble to the ground.

1227. **WORD STUDY**

HORMONE (a chemical secretion of various glands, 'arousing' the heart or other organs to intensified activity).

1228. **MEMORIZE:**

ἅλις [adv.]   in abundance; in great
   numbers
κύων, κυνός [m., f.]   dog
λαγχάνω, λάξομαι, (λέ)λαχον   I get by
   lot; I am assigned by lot; I give one
   [acc.] his due of

οἰωνός, -οῦ [m.]   bird
τίκτω, τέξω, τέκον   I beget, I bear
τοκεύς, τοκῆος [m., f.]   parent
ὑπόδρα [adv.]   w. a scowl

1229.   TEXT

Inhuman Rage

τὸν δ᾽ ὀλιγοδρανέων προσέφη κορυθαίολος Ἕκτωρ·

"λίσσομ᾽ ὑπὲρ ψυχῆς καὶ γούνων σῶν τε τοκήων

1415   μή με ἔα παρὰ νηυσὶ κύνας καταδάψαι Ἀχαιῶν,

ἀλλὰ σὺ μὲν χαλκόν τε ἅλις χρυσόν τε δέδεξο

δῶρα, τά τοι δώσουσι πατὴρ καὶ πότνια μήτηρ,

σῶμα δὲ οἴκαδ᾽ ἐμὸν δόμεναι πάλιν, ὄφρα πυρός με

Τρῶες καὶ Τρώων ἄλοχοι λελάχωσι θανόντα."

1420   τὸν δ᾽ ἄρ᾽ ὑπόδρα ἰδὼν προσέφη πόδας ὠκὺς Ἀχιλλεύς·

"μή με, κύον, γούνων γουνάζεο μηδὲ τοκήων·

αἲ γάρ πως αὐτόν με μένος καὶ θυμὸς ἀνείη

ὤμ᾽ ἀποταμνόμενον κρέα ἔδμεναι, οἷά μ᾽ ἔοργας,

ὡς οὐκ ἔσθ᾽, ὃς σῆς γε κύνας κεφαλῆς ἀπαλάλκοι,

1425   οὐδ᾽ εἴ κεν δεκάκις τε καὶ εἴκοσι νήριτ᾽ ἄποινα

στήσωσ᾽ ἐνθάδ᾽ ἄγοντες, ὑπόσχωνται δὲ καὶ ἄλλα·

οὐδ᾽ εἴ κεν σ᾽ αὐτὸν χρυσῷ ἐρύσασθαι ἀνώγοι

Δαρδανίδης Πρίαμος, οὐδ᾽ ὣς σέ γε πότνια μήτηρ

ἐνθεμένη λεχέεσσι γοήσεται, ὃν τέκεν αὐτή,

1430   ἀλλὰ κύνες τε καὶ οἰωνοὶ κατὰ πάντα δάσονται."

ἀν-ίημι [2 aor. opt. *ἀν-είην*]   I send up;
   I drive
ἀπ-αλέξω, —, ἀπ-άλαλκον   I ward off
   (from)
ἀπο-τάμνω   I cut (off)
γουνάζομαι   I beseech
Δαρδανίδης, -āο [m.]   Dardanus'
   descendant
δατέομαι, δάσομαι   I divide among
   ourselves
δεκάκις [adv.]   ten times, tenfold

εἴκοσι   twenty; [here]   twenty-fold
ἐν-τίθημι [2 aor. ptc. *ἐν-θέμενος*]
   I place on
κατα-δάπτω, —, κατά-δαψα   I tear in
   pieces
νήριτος, -ον   countless, immense
ὀλιγοδρανέω   I am able to do little,
   I am feeble
προσ-έφη   he addressed, he said
ὑπ-ίσχομαι, —, ὑπ-ισχόμην   I promise,
   I vow
ὠμός, -ή, -όν   raw

GREEK INFLUENCE ON MODERN ARCHITECTURE
Many fine buildings around the country are in the Classical tradition. Notable examples are in Washington, D.C.—the Supreme Court Building, Jefferson Memorial, etc. One of the most impressive is the National Archives, shown here, with its neo-Corinthian pillars, sculptured pediment over the front, decorative details. The effect is one of grandeur, majesty, awesome beauty.

1230. NOTES

1414   *ὑπέρ:* "over," "in the name of."

1416   *δέδεξο:* from *δέδεγμαι,* perfect of *δέχομαι.*

1417   *δῶρα:* (pred.) "as gifts."

1418   *δόμεναι:* as imperative. (2 aor. act. inf. of *δίδωμι.*)

1421   *γουνάζεο:* meant originally to beseech by taking hold of the knees. Hence, the genitive may follow the verb to express that in whose name the plea is made.

1422   *αἴ γάρ:* introduces a wish, "if only!" (106, a.)

1423   *οἷά μ᾽ ἔοργας:* "such things you have done to me!"—an exclamation equivalent to a subordinate clause, "because you" etc. *ἔοργας* is the perfect of *ἔρδω.*

1424   *ὡς οὐκ ἔστι:* "as (surely as) there is no man."

1426   *στήσωσ᾽: ἵστημι* sometimes has the technical sense, "I put in the balance"—"I weigh (out)."

1427   *ἐρύσασθαι:* used likewise in the technical sense of dragging down the scale—'if he should offer your weight in gold.'

1430   *κατά:* adverbial, intensifying *πάντα:* "every last bit."

210

1231. COMMENT

1414-9. It is altogether in keeping with the sensitive character of Hector that his dying thought should be for the sorrow that is about to come upon those who love him. He is willing to humble himself before his enemy in an effort to alleviate their sorrow through the comfort they will feel in being able to pay his dead body their last services and reverence and thereby through burial of the ashes ease his lot in the world beyond. He promises that great treasure will be given in exchange for his body, a ransom which Achilles would be under a certain religious obligation not to refuse.

1421-30 With shocking brutality, caused by the flaming grief burning deep in his heart, Achilles scorns his fallen foe. His hatred is so intense, he says, that he would wish to be able to tear Hector's flesh to shreds with his own teeth to obtain some satisfaction for what Hector has done in slaying Patroclus. Since that is impossible, he will assure him of this: there will be no one who will be able to prevent the dogs from doing so, no matter what ransom is offered by his friends. Never, he taunts, will his parents have the consolation of at least giving him a decent burial, such as the lowliest of men deserve. Hatred can go no further.

1232. WORD STUDY

CYNIC, CYNICAL (with sneering upturned lip like a snarling dog); — ICOSIHEDRON (a 'twenty-sided' plane figure).

PUTTING ON ARMOR

The rather complicated procedure of arming a warrior is several times described in detail in the *Iliad*. Here we see the fitting of the cuirass and shoulder guards. Greaves protecting the lower leg are already in place. Athena stands by with helmet, spear, and shield. Or perhaps it is Achilles putting on the new armor made for him by Hephestus (recall illustration of that on p. 188), and his mother Thetis standing by, with Nestor or some other hero watching on the left.

1233. | MEMORIZE:

ἀέκων, -ουσα unwilling

δίφρος, -ου [m.] chariot (platform); seat

ἕλκω I drag

πάρος [adv.] before, formerly

τέλος, -εος [n.] end, fulfillment

HECTOR DISHONORED
A vivid black-figured vase illustration, of about 505 B.C., of Hector's body being dragged in disgrace around the walls of Troy by the chariot of the savagely vehement Achilles in revenge for Hector's killing of Patroclus in battle. The inhuman violence shocked the gods (note Athena at the left), who insisted with Achilles that he stop his cruelty—a powerful lesson in civilizing humans which is one of the aims of Homer in the *Iliad*.

1234. TEXT

The Desecration of Hector's Body

1431 τὸν δὲ καταθνήσκων προσέφη κορυθαίολος Ἕκτωρ·
"ἦ σ' ἐὺ γιγνώσκων προτιόσσομαι, οὐδ' ἄρ' ἔμελλον
πείσειν· ἦ γὰρ σοί γε σιδήρεος ἐν φρεσὶ θυμός.
φράζεο νῦν, μή τοί τι θεῶν μήνιμα γένωμαι
1435 ἤματι τῷ, ὅτε κέν σε Πάρις καὶ Φοῖβος Ἀπόλλων
ἐσθλὸν ἐόντ' ὀλέσωσιν ἐνὶ Σκαιῇσι πύλῃσιν."
ὣς ἄρα μιν εἰπόντα τέλος θανάτοιο κάλυψεν,
ψυχὴ δ' ἐκ ῥεθέων πταμένη Ἀϊδόσδε βεβήκει
ὃν πότμον γοάουσα, λιποῦσ' ἀνδροτῆτα καὶ ἥβην.
1440 τὸν καὶ τεθνηῶτα προσηύδα δῖος Ἀχιλλεύς·
"τέθναθι· κῆρα δ' ἐγὼ τότε δέξομαι, ὁππότε κεν δὴ
Ζεὺς ἐθέλῃ τελέσαι ἠδ' ἀθάνατοι θεοὶ ἄλλοι."
ἦ ῥα καὶ Ἕκτορα δῖον ἀεικέα μήδετο ἔργα.
ἀμφοτέρων μετόπισθε ποδῶν τέτρηνε τένοντε
1445 ἐς σφυρὸν ἐκ πτέρνης, βοέους δ' ἐξῆπτεν ἱμάντας,
ἐκ δίφροιο δ' ἔδησε, κάρη δ' ἕλκεσθαι ἔασεν·
ἐς δίφρον δ' ἀναβὰς ἀνά τε κλυτὰ τεύχε' ἀείρας
μάστιξέν ῥ' ἵππους, τὼ δ' οὐκ ἀέκοντε πετόνθο.
τοῦ δ' ἦν ἑλκομένοιο κονίσαλος, ἀμφὶ δὲ χαῖται
1450 κυάνεαι πίτναντο, κάρη δ' ἅπαν ἐν κονίῃσι
κεῖτο πάρος χαρίεν· τότε δὲ Ζεὺς δυσμενέεσσιν
δῶκεν ἀεικίσασθαι ἑῇ ἐν πατρίδι γαίῃ.

ἀεικής, -ές unseemly, shameful
ἀεικίζω, —, ἀεικισσάμην I treat unseemly, I outrage
ἀνδροτής, -ῆτος [f.] manly strength
βόεος, -η, -ον (of) oxhide
ἐξ-άπτω, etc. I attach
ἥβη, -ης [f.] youthful vigor
ἱμάς, -άντος [m.] strap, thong
κονίσαλος, -ου [m.] cloud of dust
μαστίζω, —, μάστιξα I whip
μήνιμα, -ατος [n.] cause of wrath
Πάρις, -ιος [m.] Paris [son of Priam,
   abductor of Helen]

πίτναμαι I am spread out; I wave
προσ-έφη he addressed, he said
προτι-όσσομαι I gaze upon
πτέρνη, -ης [f.] heel
ῥέθεα, -ων [n. pl.] limbs, body
Σκαιός, -ή, -όν left; Western
σφυρόν, -οῦ [n.] ankle
τένοντε [m.] [dual] tendons
τετραίνω, —, τέτρηνα I bore through,
   I pierce
Φοῖβος, -ου [m.] Phoebus, the Bright
   One [epithet of Apollo]
χαίτη, -ης [f.] hair

1235.　NOTES

> 1438 　'Αιδόσδε: recall that δῶμα is understood with 'Αιδός in this expression. The special ending -δε should be added to the accusative, but since in this case the accusative δῶμα is not expressed, -δε is added to 'Αιδός instead.
>
> 1439 　ἀνδροτῆτα: the first syllable is treated as short in scansion, the mute-and-liquid (δρ) functioning as a single consonant metrically (#564, 1, c.). This particular combination of consonants is in fact easy and fast to pronounce.
>
> 1441 　τέθναθι: perfect imperative of θνήσκω—"lie dead!"
>
> 1443 　μήδετο: takes double accusative here.
>
> 1448 　τώ: (dual) the two horses.

1236.　COMMENT

> 1432 　Sadly and resignedly, Hector acknowledges that he had not expected the iron heart of Achilles to soften. Then, as his soul begins to slip from his body, he prophesies the future. He sees the death that will soon come upon Achilles through the poisoned arrow of Paris, and he dies with the knowledge that the gods will soon demand a full account from Achilles for this outrage.
>
> 1451 　πάρος χαρίεν: These two words have been rightly considered a masterly touch of sheer pathos.
>
> 1452 　When Hector appears to Aeneas in the second book of the *Aeneid* (270-279), he is described as he looked after being thus treated:

> > raptatus bigis, ut quondam, aterque cruento
> > pulvere perque pedes traiectus lora tumentes.
> > Ei mihi, qualis erat! quantum mutatus ab illo
> > Hectore, qui redit exuvias indutus Achilli
> > vel Danaum Phrygios iaculatus puppibus ignes!
> > squalentem barbam et concretos sanguine crines
> > vulneraque illa gerens, quae circum plurima muros
> > accepit patrios.

1237. | MEMORIZE:

ἀγγέλλω, ἀγγελέω, ἄγγειλα   I announce   ὅμῑλος, -ου [m.]   throng; tumult
κραδίη, -ης [f.]   heart

1238.   TEXT

Andromache's Sorrow

ὣς τοῦ μὲν κεκόνιτο κάρη ἅπαν· ἡ δέ νυ μήτηρ
τίλλε κόμην, ἀπὸ δὲ λιπαρὴν ἔρριψε καλύπτρην

1455   τηλόσε, κώκυσεν δὲ μάλα μέγα παῖδ᾿ ἐσιδοῦσα.
ᾤμωξεν δ᾿ ἐλεεινὰ πατὴρ φίλος, ἀμφὶ δὲ λαοὶ
κωκυτῷ τ᾿ εἴχοντο καὶ οἰμωγῇ κατὰ ἄστυ.

ὣς οἱ μὲν στενάχοντ᾿ ἄλοχος δ᾿ οὔ πώ τι πέπυστο
Ἕκτορος· οὐ γάρ οἵ τις ἐτήτυμος ἄγγελος ἐλθὼν

1460   ἤγγειλ᾿, ὅττι ῥά οἱ πόσις ἔκτοθι μίμνε πυλάων,
ἀλλ᾿ ἥ γ᾿ ἱστὸν ὕφαινε μυχῷ δόμου ὑψηλοῖο.
κωκυτοῦ δ᾿ ἤκουσε καὶ οἰμωγῆς ἀπὸ πύργου·
τῆς δ᾿ ἐλελίχθη γυῖα, χαμαὶ δέ οἱ ἔκπεσε κερκίς.
αὐτίκα δὴ μεγάροιο διέσσυτο μαινάδι ἴση

1465   παλλομένη κραδίην· ἅμα δ᾿ ἀμφίπολοι κίον αὐτῇ.
αὐτὰρ ἐπεὶ πύργον τε καὶ ἀνδρῶν ἷξεν ὅμιλον,
ἔστη παπτήνασ᾿ ἐπὶ τείχεϊ, τὸν δὲ νόησεν
ἑλκόμενον πρόσθεν πόλιος· ταχέες δέ μιν ἵπποι
ἕλκον ἀκηδέστως κοίλας ἐπὶ νῆας Ἀχαιῶν.

1470   τὴν δὲ κατ᾿ ὀφθαλμῶν ἐρεβεννὴ νὺξ ἐκάλυψεν.
ἤριπε δ᾿ ἐξοπίσω, ἀπὸ δὲ ψυχὴν ἐκάπυσσεν.
τῆλε δ᾿ ἀπὸ κρατὸς βάλε δέσματα σιγαλόεντα,
ἄμπυκα κεκρύφαλόν τε ἰδὲ πλεκτὴν ἀναδέσμην
κρήδεμνόν θ᾿, ὅ ῥά οἱ δῶκε χρυσέη Ἀφροδίτη

1475   ἤματι τῷ, ὅτε μιν κορυθαίολος ἠγάγεθ᾿ Ἕκτωρ
ἐκ δόμου Ἠετίωνος, ἐπεὶ πόρε μυρία ἕδνα.

ἀκηδέστως [adv.] w. no care, mercilessly
ἄμπυξ, -υκος [m.] diadem [an ornament worn in the hair, as symbol of
  royal blood]
ἀνα-δέσμη, -ης [f.] fillet, headband
Ἀφροδῑ́τη, -ης Aphrodite [goddess of
  love and beauty]
δέσματα, -ων [n. pl.] headdress
δια-σεύομαι, etc. I rush through [gen.]
ἐκ-πίπτω, etc. I fall (from)
ἔκτοθι [adv.] outside (of)
ἐλεεινός, -ή, -όν pitiable, piteous
ἐλελίζω, aor. pass.: ἐλελίχθην I shake,
  I make tremble
ἐξοπίσω [adv.] backward
ἐρεβεννός, -ή, -όν gloomy, dark, black
ἐρείπω, —, ἔριπον I dash down; I fall
ἐτήτυμος, -ον true, trustworthy

ἵκω, —, ἷξον I come
καλύπτρη, -ης [f.] veil
καπύω, —, κάπυσσον I breathe (forth)
κεκρύφαλος, -ου [m.] (woman's) hair-net
κερκίς, -ίδος [f.] shuttle [a long rod
  used in weaving]
κονίω, pf. mid.: κεκόνῑμαι I cover with
  dust
κωκῡτός, -οῦ [m.] wailing
κωκύω, —, κώκῡσα I shriek, I wail
μαινάς, -άδος [f.] mad woman
μυχός, -οῦ [m.] innermost part, corner
οἰμωγή, -ῆς [f.] lamentation
πλεκτός, -ή, -όν plaited, twisted
τηλόσε [adv.] to a distance, far off
τίλλω I tear out, I pluck
χαμαί [adv.] to the ground, on the
  ground

1239. NOTES

1457 εἴχοντο: they were "held" or "possessed" with grief.
1458 πέπυστο: from πέπυσμαι, perfect of πεύθομαι.
1460 ὅττι: a less frequent form of ὅτι, "that, because."
1461 ἱστόν: i.e., what was on the loom, the "web."
1467 τόν: i.e., Hector.
1470 κατά: with the sense here: "came down upon and covered."

1240. COMMENT

1435 Hector's father and mother have come to the walls from which they can clearly see—with what poignant grief!—their son being dragged behind the speeding chariot of Achilles.

1460 Recall that the other Trojan warriors had withdrawn to the protection of the walls when the raging Achilles approached. Andromache naturally supposed that her husband had come in with them.

1462 Her first intimation that some tragedy has occurred is the sound of the wailing rising up all over the city. With her heart already heavy with apprehension and dread, her intuition tells her at once that *Hector* must somehow be involved. Hardly daring to think what it may be, she drops her work and rushes madly to the tower.

1467 She reaches the wall and the weeping throng gathered there. Wildly she looks towards the plain, and her heart breaks as she beholds her dearly beloved husband dead and being dragged mercilessly in the dust toward the Greek camp.

1471 ψυχήν: The shock was so great that she lost consciousness. It does not mean that she died; she had only fainted.

1475 By describing the way her veil and headdress are thrown off in her fall, Homer is able to mention by way of pathetic contrast the happy day on which Hector and Andromache were married.

1241. WORD STUDY

CHAMELEON ('ground-lion,' a lizard with power to change its color to blend with various backgrounds).

1242.   MEMORIZE:

ἀμφίς [adv.]   apart; around
θεοειδής, -ές   godlike

ἵζω   I make to sit; I sit (down)
ἰθύς [adv.]   straight (towards) [w. gen.]

Achilles has had his revenge to the full, yet his spirit is still restless with hatred and fury. Again and again, for twelve mad days, he drags around Patroclus' tomb the body of Hector — preserved from corruption by the dismayed and pitying gods. Still Achilles' sorrow burns on without abating.

Then the extraordinary happens. Old King Priam himself, guided by Hermes, steals through the Greek camp at night and right into Achilles' quarters, in a daring attempt to win his mercy and ransom back Hector's body!

1243.   TEXT

Priam's Daring

ὣς ἄρα φωνήσας ἀπέβη πρὸς μακρὸν Ὄλυμπον
Ἑρμείας· Πρίαμος δ᾽ ἐξ ἵππων ἆλτο χαμᾶζε,
Ἰδαῖον δὲ κατ᾽ αὖθι λίπεν· ὁ δὲ μίμνεν ἐρύκων
1480   ἵππους ἡμιόνους τε. γέρων δ᾽ ἰθὺς κίεν οἴκου,
τῇ ῥ᾽ Ἀχιλεὺς ἵζεσκε διίφιλος. ἐν δέ μιν αὐτὸν
εὖρ᾽, ἕταροι δ᾽ ἀπάνευθε καθείατο· τὼ δὲ δύ᾽ οἴω,
ἥρως Αὐτομέδων τε καὶ Ἄλκιμος ὄζος Ἄρηος,
ποίπνυον παρεόντε· νέον δ᾽ ἀπέληγεν ἐδωδῆς
1485   ἔσθων καὶ πίνων· ἔτι καὶ παρέκειτο τράπεζα.
τοὺς δ᾽ ἔλαθ᾽ εἰσελθὼν Πρίαμος μέγας, ἄγχι δ᾽ ἄρα στὰς
χερσὶν Ἀχιλλῆος λάβε γούνατα καὶ κύσε χεῖρας
δεινὰς ἀνδροφόνους, αἵ οἱ πολέας κτάνον υἷας.
ἔνθ᾽ Ἀχιλεὺς θάμβησεν ἰδὼν Πρίαμον θεοειδέα·
1490   θάμβησαν δὲ καὶ ἄλλοι, ἐς ἀλλήλους δὲ ἴδοντο.
τὸν καὶ λισσόμενος Πρίαμος πρὸς μῦθον ἔειπε·
"μνῆσαι πατρὸς σοῖο, θεοῖς ἐπιείκελ᾽ Ἀχιλλεῦ,
τηλίκου, ὥς περ ἐγών, ὀλοῷ ἐπὶ γήραος οὐδῷ.
καί μέν που κεῖνον περιναιέται ἀμφὶς ἐόντες

PRIAM IN ACHILLES' TENT

A fine red-figured skyphos (cup with horizontal handles at top) by the 'Brygos Painter' in early fifth century B.C. illustrates the dramatic moment when old Priam, at risk of his life, approaches Achilles to ask for the body of Hector for proper funeral rites. Achilles does not dare look the heroic king in the eyes, but moved by divine influences agreed to the request. Hector's body is seen under Achilles' couch.

1495   *τείρουσ᾽, οὐδέ τις ἔστιν ἀρὴν καὶ λοιγὸν ἀμῦναι.*

           ἀλλ᾽ ἦ τοι κεῖνός γε σέθεν ζώοντος ἀκούων

           χαίρει τ᾽ ἐν θυμῷ ἐπί τ᾽ ἔλπεται ἤματα πάντα

           ὄψεσθαι φίλον υἱὸν ἀπὸ Τροίηθεν ἰόντα·

Ἄλκιμος, -ου [m.] Alcimus [a Myrmidon, a companion of Achilles]
ἄλλομαι, —, ἄλμην [athematic] I leap, I jump
ἀπο-βαίνω, etc. I go away
ἀπο-λήγω, —, ἀπό-ληγα I cease from
ἀρή, -ῆς [f.] calamity, evil
Ἄρης, -ηος [m.] Ares [god of war]
Αὐτομέδων, -οντος [m.] Automedon [charioteer of Achilles]
ἐπι-είκελος, -ον like to
διΐφιλος, -ον dear to Zeus

Ἑρμείας, -αο [m.] Hermes [son of Zeus and Maia]
Ἰδαῖος, -ου [m.] Idaeus [herald of Trojans]
κάθ-ημαι I sit down
λοιγός, οῦ [m.] destruction, ruin
ὄζος, -ου [m.] branch; scion
παρά-κειμαι I lie near
περι-ναιέτης, -αο [m.] neighbor
ποιπνύω I pant; I am busy
τηλίκος, -η, -ον of such age, so old
χαμᾶζε [adv.] to the ground

1244. NOTES

1482 *τώ:* dual.

1488 *υἷας:* irregular acc. plural.

1496 *σέθεν:* "of you."

1497 *ἐπί:* he "keeps on" hoping.

1245. COMMENT

1477 Hermes has just revealed his identity to Priam and given him advice on how to win Achilles' sympathy.

1478 Priam was not on horseback; he jumped from the horse-drawn chariot.

1487 There is real drama in this scene of Priam kissing the terrible hands of Achilles, grim objects of his loathing and his fears. We can sense the tension and the dreadful moment of Achilles' decision—will he slay the old king or spare him?

1492 ff. Priam, the once proud and powerful ruler, comes to Achilles a grief-stricken old man. On that fact he bases his plea, reminding Achilles that his own father is in the same condition. His appeal is solely to their common humanity and their common suffering.

1246. MEMORIZE:

ἄλλοτε   at another time   πάτρη, -ης [f.] fatherland
ἵμερος, -ου [m.] yearning, desire   προπάροιθε(ν) before, in front of

1247. TEXT

The Humanizing of Achilles

αὐτὰρ ἐγὼ πανάποτμος, ἐπεὶ τέκον υἷας ἀρίστους
1500   Τροίῃ ἐν εὐρείῃ, τῶν δ' οὔ τινά φημι λελεῖφθαι.
πεντήκοντά μοι ἦσαν, ὅτ' ἤλυθον υἷες Ἀχαιῶν·
τῶν μὲν πολλῶν θοῦρος Ἄρης ὑπὸ γούνατ' ἔλυσεν·
ὃς δέ μοι οἶος ἔην, εἴρυτο δὲ ἄστυ καὶ αὐτούς,
τὸν σὺ πρῴην κτείνας ἀμυνόμενον περὶ πάτρης
1505   Ἕκτορα. τοῦ νῦν εἵνεχ' ἱκάνω νῆας Ἀχαιῶν,
λυσόμενος παρὰ σεῖο, φέρω δ' ἀπερείσι' ἄποινα.
ἀλλ' αἰδεῖο θεούς, Ἀχιλεῦ, αὐτόν τ' ἐλέησον
μνησάμενος σοῦ πατρός· ἐγὼ δ' ἐλεεινότερός περ,
ἔτλην δ', οἷ' οὔ πώ τις ἐπιχθόνιος βροτὸς ἄλλος,
1510   ἀνδρὸς παιδοφόνοιο ποτὶ στόμα χεῖρ' ὀρέγεσθαι."
   ὣς φάτο, τῷ δ' ἄρα πατρὸς ὑφ' ἵμερον ὦρσε γόοιο·
ἁψάμενος δ' ἄρα χειρὸς ἀπώσατο ἦκα γέροντα.
τὼ δὲ μνησαμένω ὁ μὲν Ἕκτορος ἀνδροφόνοιο
κλαῖ' ἀδινά, προπάροιθε ποδῶν Ἀχιλῆος ἐλυσθείς,
1515   αὐτὰρ Ἀχιλλεὺς κλαῖεν ἑὸν πατέρ', ἄλλοτε δ' αὖτε
Πάτροκλον· τῶν δὲ στοναχὴ κατὰ δώματ' ὀρώρει.

ἀπερείσιος, -η, -ον countless
ἀπ-ωθέω, etc. I push away
Ἄρης, -ηος [m.] Ares [god of war]
εἰλύω,   aor. pass.: ἐλύσθην I bend
   over
ἐλεεινός, -ή, -όν pitiable, piteous
ἐπι-χθόνιος, -ον on the earth
ἦκα [adv.] gently
θοῦρος, -ου [adj.] rushing, impetuous
ὀρέγω I stretch out

παιδοφόνος, -οιο [m.] killer of (my)
   sons
πανάποτμος, -ον all hapless, wholly
   ill-fated
Πάτροκλος, -ου [m.] Patroclus [dearest
   friend of Achilles]
πεντήκοντα fifty
πρῴην [adv.] lately
στοναχή, -ῆς [f.] groan, moan

1248. NOTES

1500 λελεῖφθαι: from λέλειμμαι, perfect of λείπω.

1502 ὑπό: adverbial—"loosening the knees" was a sort of euphemism for killing.

1503 εἴρῦτο: pluperfect of ἐρύομαι, with imperfect force.

αὐτούς: i.e., the people themselves.

1507 αὐτόν: understand ἐμέ.

1511 ὑφ᾽: adverbial—"in the depths of his soul."

πατρός: genitive after γόοιο—"lamentation for his father."

1513 τώ: dual nominative, in apposition to ὁ and Ἀχιλλεύς, each of which has its own verb.

1249. COMMENT

1499 He is the most wretched of all, and just because he suffers most, he deserves the most compassion, even from his enemy.

1500 Priam is not absolutely accurate in saying that all his sons have been killed. Paris, Polites, and possibly a few others were still living. However, the loss of Hector who meant more to him than all the others together has been such a shock that he considers himself completely bereaved.

1508 Again he reminds him that as a man he is no different from Peleus—except that his sorrow is even more pitiable yet.

1510 Touching one's chin was another conventional act of a suppliant.

1511 ff. Suddenly there comes to Achilles a new experience. He understands completely the sufferings of another, and through that understanding he feels a deep sense of sympathy and union. Both men are broken with sorrow, which puts them together on the same human plane. Inevitably, Achilles' hatred melts away in the crucible of their common suffering.

1250. WORD STUDY

PENTECOST (a religious festival occurring on the 'fiftieth day' after Easter).

THE TROJAN HORSE

This is the earliest illustration known of the Wooden Horse which Odysseus thought up as a ruse for taking Troy. It is on the neck of a large pithos (storage jar) decorated in relief. It dates to around 675 B.C. The primitive unsophisticated style, charming in its naivete, is unintentionally humorous. Greeks hidden inside are seen looking through portholes or hatches. The warriors above and below may be Trojans testing the strange monster, or meant to show the Greeks, under Odysseus' leadership, already outside the horse and set for battle. Note the wheels under the legs, to help in moving.

1251. TEXT

Achilles Comforts the King

αὐτὰρ ἐπεί ῥα γόοιο τετάρπετο δῖος Ἀχιλλεύς,
καί οἱ ἀπὸ πραπίδων ἦλθ᾽ ἵμερος ἠδ᾽ ἀπὸ γυίων
αὐτίκ᾽ ἀπὸ θρόνου ὦρτο, γέροντα δὲ χειρὸς ἀνίστη,

1520 οἰκτείρων πολιόν τε κάρη πολιόν τε γένειον,
καί μιν φωνήσας ἔπεα πτερόεντα προσηύδα·
"ἆ δείλ᾽, ἦ δὴ πολλὰ κάκ᾽ ἄνσχεο σὸν κατὰ θυμόν.
πῶς ἔτλης ἐπὶ νῆας Ἀχαιῶν ἐλθέμεν οἶος,
ἀνδρὸς ἐς ὀφθαλμούς, ὅς τοι πολέας τε καὶ ἐσθλοὺς

1525 υἱέας ἐξενάριξα; σιδήρειόν νύ τοι ἦτορ.
ἀλλ᾽ ἄγε δὴ κατ᾽ ἄρ᾽ ἕζευ ἐπὶ θρόνου, ἄλγεα δ᾽ ἔμπης
ἐν θυμῷ κατακεῖσθαι ἐάσομεν ἀχνύμενοί περ·
οὐ γάρ τις πρῆξις πέλεται κρυεροῖο γόοιο.
ὣς γὰρ ἐπεκλώσαντο θεοὶ δειλοῖσι βροτοῖσι,

1530 ζώειν ἀχνυμένοις· αὐτοὶ δέ τ᾽ ἀκηδέες εἰσίν.
δοιοὶ γάρ τε πίθοι κατακείαται ἐν Διὸς οὔδει
δώρων, οἷα δίδωσι, κακῶν, ἕτερος δὲ ἑάων·
ᾧ μέν κ᾽ ἀμμίξας δώῃ Ζεὺς τερπικέραυνος,
ἄλλοτε μέν τε κακῷ ὅ γε κύρεται, ἄλλοτε δ᾽ ἐσθλῷ·

1535 ᾧ δέ κε τῶν λυγρῶν δώῃ, λωβητὸν ἔθηκε,
καί ἑ κακὴ βούβρωστις ἐπὶ χθόνα δῖαν ἐλαύνει,
φοιτᾷ δ᾽ οὔτε θεοῖσι τετιμένος οὔτε βροτοῖσιν.

ἆ [exclamation] ah!
ἀκηδής, -ές free from care
ἀμ-μίσγω, etc. I mingle, I mix
ἀν-ίστημι [impf. 3 sg. -ίστη] I raise up
βούβρωστις, -ιος [f.] famine; misery
γένειον, -ου [n.] chin
δοιοί, -αί, -ά two
ἑαί, ἑάων [f. pl.] good things, blessings
ἐπι-κλώθω, —, ἐπί-κλωσα I spin to,
    I allot to
κατά-κειμαι I lie down, I rest
κρυερός, -ή, -όν icy, chill
κύρω I fall in with, I light upon

λωβητός, -ή, -όν outraged, object of
    abuse
οἰκτείρω I pity
οὖδας, -εος [n.] ground, floor
πίθος, -ου [m.] jar
πραπίδες, -ων [f. pl.] diaphragm, heart
πρῆξις, -ιος [f.] accomplishment, good
    (result), use
σιδήρειος = σιδήρεος
τερπικέραυνος, -ου hurler of thunder-
    bolt [epithet of Zeus]
τίω: pf. M.-P.: τέτῑμαι I honor

1252.   NOTES

1517   *τετάρπετο:* 2 aor. mid. of *τέρπω.*

1519   *χειρός:* "by the hand." Notice that the Greeks tended to use a partitive genitive for the point or part at which something is taken hold of, even when, as here, the verb of grasping is merely implied.

1532   *δίδωσι:* third singular present indicative of *δίδωμι.*
ἕτερος: to be understood before *κακῶν* also—"one . . . another."

1533   *ἀμμίξας:* the object is understood from *κακῶν* and *ἐάων.*

1535   *ἔθηκε:* understand *μιν;* "he causes him to be."

1536   *ἐπὶ:* "across."

1253.   COMMENT

1519   With a feeling of pity and reverence and almost friendship, Achilles raises the old man gently from the ground.

1522 ff.   How different is this Achilles from the one we have seen before: His angry, ruthless hate has given way to kindness and gentleness. Both men have suffered beyond all power to tell, and in that suffering they have come to realize the supreme fact of their common humanity, a clear basis of mutual respect, sympathy, and understanding.

1529-36   At last Achilles is learning resignation. Imperfectly and vaguely, it is true, but none the less with fundamental truth, he has come to realize that man cannot have peace until he humbles his will to the gods and learns to accept life's hardships and bitter moments with manly patience and calm.

1531-2   A striking poetic image, characteristic of Achilles' vivid way of conceiving things, as Homer everywhere represents him.

THE SACK OF TROY

The 'Brygos Painter' in the early fifth century B.C. decorated the sides of a large kylix with scenes from the taking of Troy, including this strong picture of the violence involved.

1254. | **MEMORIZE:**

καίνυμαι, [pf. w. pres. sense:] *κέκασμαι*   *μάχη, -ης* [f.] battle, fight
    I surpass   *τηλόθι* afar, far (from)

1255.   TEXT

The Glory of the World Passes

ὣς μὲν καὶ Πηλῆι θεοὶ δόσαν ἀγλαὰ δῶρα
ἐκ γενετῆς· πάντας γὰρ ἐπ' ἀνθρώπους ἐκέκαστο
1540 ὄλβῳ τε πλούτῳ τε, ἄνασσε δὲ Μυρμιδόνεσσι,
καί οἱ θνητῷ ἐόντι θεὰν ποίησαν ἄκοιτιν.
ἀλλ' ἐπὶ καὶ τῷ θῆκε θεὸς κακόν, ὅττι οἱ οὔ τι
παίδων ἐν μεγάροισι γονὴ γένετο κρειόντων,
ἀλλ' ἕνα παῖδα τέκεν παναώριον· οὐδέ νυ τόν γε
1545 γηράσκοντα κομίζω, ἐπεὶ μάλα τηλόθι πάτρης
ἧμαι ἐνὶ Τροίῃ σέ τε κήδων ἠδὲ σὰ τέκνα.
καὶ σέ, γέρον, τὸ πρὶν μὲν ἀκούομεν ὄλβιον εἶναι·
ὅσσον Λέσβος ἄνω, Μάκαρος ἕδος, ἐντὸς ἐέργει
καὶ Φρυγίη καθύπερθε καὶ Ἑλλήσποντος ἀπείρων,
1550 τῶν σε, γέρον, πλούτῳ τε καὶ υἱάσι φασὶ κεκάσθαι.
αὐτὰρ ἐπεί τοι πῆμα τόδ' ἤγαγον Οὐρανίωνες,
αἰεί τοι περὶ ἄστυ μάχαι τ' ἀνδροκτασίαι τε.
ἄνσχεο, μηδ' ἀλίαστον ὀδύρεο σὸν κατὰ θυμόν·
οὐ γάρ τι πρήξεις ἀκαχήμενος υἷος ἑῆος,
1555 οὐδέ μιν ἀνστήσεις· πρὶν καὶ κακὸν ἄλλο πάθῃσθα."

ἀκαχήμενος, -η, -ον grieving for [w. gen.]
ἀλίαστος, -ον unyielding, incessant
ἀνδροκτασίη, -ης [f.] slaying of men
ἄνω [adv.] up(wards); towards the sea
γενετή, -ῆς [f.] birth
γηράσκω I grow old
γονή, -ῆς [f.] offspring
ἕδος, -εος [n.] seat
Ἑλλήσποντος, -ου [m.] Hellespont
ἐντός [adv.] within
ἐύς, ἐύ (gen. *ἑῆος*) good, valiant
καθύπερθε(ν) [adv.] above; yonder
κήδω I trouble, I distress

Λέσβος, -ου [f.] Lesbos [island in the Aegean]
Μάκαρ, -αρος [m.] Macar [king of Lesbos]
Μυρμιδόνες, -ων [m. pl.] Myrmidons [a people of Greece]
Οὐρανίωνες, -ων [m. pl.] the heavenly gods
παναώριος, -ον doomed to early death
Πηλεύς, -ῆος [m.] Peleus [king of Myrmidons, father of Achilles]
πλοῦτος, -ου [m.] wealth, riches
Φρυγίη, -ης [f.] Phrygia [a district of Asia Minor]

1256. NOTES

1539 ἐπί: adverbial, merely strengthening the verb.

1544 ἀλλ᾽: "except that."

1547 τὸ πρίν: (idiom) "formerly."

1548 ὅσσον: agrees according to sense with τῶν, which is the object of κεκάσθαι. Transl.: "they say that you surpassed all those people whom Lesbos, etc."

1552 μάχαι: understand εἰσί.

1555 πάθησθα = πάθης, used with future meaning.

1257. COMMENT

1543 Peleus seemed to have everything necessary for happiness, but to him, too, came grievous sorrow.

1546 Previously, Achilles had exulted in wreaking ruin on the Trojans. Now he sees the matter more fully, and from their angle. After all, he now realizes, they too are human and can feel suffering — a thing Achilles at last understands in all its bitterness. There is the implication in his words, Why should I be here at all putting these human beings to all this needless misery? War has henceforth lost for Achilles its superficial glamor and nobility. Suffering has opened his eyes to deeper human issues; it has mellowed, transformed, inexpressibly refined his character. Such is the tremendous theme of the *Iliad,* the core of its timeless humanizing message for all men who will but read it.

1547 Like Peleus, Priam for years has been blessed with all that the world has to offer, but now he too has been humbled to the dust.

1553 With newfound insight, Achilles concludes that all men must suffer and that the only road to peace is by way of endurance and resignation.

1555 He means that before Priam can bring Hector back to life by weeping, he himself must suffer another evil, namely death.

ACHILLES AND BRISEIS
This painting from Pompeii is a copy of a Greek original showing Agamemnon's heralds leading away Briseis, as told in Book I of the *Iliad*. This caused Achilles' fury and withdrawal from the battle, from which flows the poem's whole theme.

1258. | MEMORIZE:

π(τ)ολεμίζω, π(τ)ολεμίξω   I wage war,   *χόλος, -ου* [m.]   wrath
   I fight (with)

1259.   TEXT

The Body Is Ransomed

1556   δμωὰς δ᾽ ἐκκαλέσας λοῦσαι κέλετ᾽ ἀμφί τ᾽ ἀλεῖψαι,
νόσφιν ἀειράσας, ὡς μὴ Πρίαμος ἴδοι υἱόν,
μὴ ὁ μὲν ἀχνυμένῃ κραδίῃ χόλον οὐκ ἐρύσαιτο
παῖδα ἰδών, Ἀχιλῆι δ᾽ ὀρινθείη φίλον ἦτορ

1560   καί ἑ κατακτείνειε, Διὸς δ᾽ ἀλίτηται ἐφετμάς.
τὸν δ᾽ ἐπεὶ οὖν δμῳαὶ λοῦσαν καὶ χρῖσαν ἐλαίῳ,
ἀμφί δέ μιν φᾶρος καλὸν βάλον ἠδὲ χιτῶνα,
αὐτὸς τόν γ᾽ Ἀχιλεὺς λεχέων ἐπέθηκεν ἀείρας,
σὺν δ᾽ ἔταροι ἤειραν ἐυξέστην ἐπ᾽ ἀπήνην.

1565   ᾤμωξέν τ᾽ ἄρ᾽ ἔπειτα, φίλον δ᾽ ὀνόμηνεν ἑταῖρον·
"μή μοι, Πάτροκλε, σκυδμαινέμεν, αἴ κε πύθηαι
εἰν Ἀιδός περ ἐών, ὅτι Ἕκτορα δῖον ἔλυσα."
   τὸν δ᾽ ἠμείβετ᾽ ἔπειτα γέρων Πρίαμος θεοιδής·
"εἰ μὲν δή μ᾽ ἐθέλεις τελέσαι τάφον Ἕκτορι δίῳ,

1570   ὧδέ κέ μοι ῥέζων, Ἀχιλεῦ, κεχαρισμένα θείης.
οἶσθα γὰρ ὡς κατὰ ἄστυ ἐέλμεθα, τηλόθι δ᾽ ὕλη
ἀξέμεν ἐξ ὄρεος, μάλα δὲ Τρῶες δεδίασιν.
ἐννῆμαρ μέν κ᾽ αὐτὸν ἐνὶ μεγάροις γοάοιμεν,
τῇ δεκάτῃ δέ κε θάπτοιμεν δαινῦτό τε λαός,

1572   ἑνδεκάτῃ δέ κε τύμβον ἐπ᾽ αὐτῷ ποιήσαιμεν,
τῇ δὲ δυωδεκάτῃ πολεμίζομεν, εἴ περ ἀνάγκη."

ἀλιταίνω, —, ἄλιτον   I transgress
δυωδέκατος, -η, -ον   twelfth
ἐκ-καλέω, etc.   I call out
ἐνδέκατος, -η, -ον   eleventh
ἐπι-τίθημι, etc.   I place on [gen.]
ἐφετμή, -ῆς [f.]   behest, command
θάπτω   I bury

ὀνομαίνω, —, ὀνόμηνα   I call by name
Πάτροκλος, -ου [m.]   Patroclus [dearest
   friend of Achilles]
σκυδμαίνω   I am angry (with)
τάφος, -ου [m.]   burial
τύμβος, -ου [m.]   mound

1260. NOTES

1558 &ὁ: i.e., Priam.

    ἐρύσαιτο: "keep back."

1559 *ὀρινθείη:* from *ὀρίνθην,* aorist passive of *ὀρίνω.*

1560 *ἀλίτηται:* more vividly conceived, as being more important to avoid.

1561 *τόν:* i.e., Hector.

1563 *λεχέων:* the funeral bier on which the body was carried.

1570 *ὧδε:* refers to what follows.

    κεχαρισμένα: perfect participle of *χαρίζομαι.*

1571 *ἐέλμεθα:* perfect passive of *εἴλω.*

1572 *ἀξέμεν:* an explanatory infinitive dependent on *τηλόθι* and referring to the wood they were about to bring for the funeral rites of Hector.

1574 *δαινῦτο:* present optative of *δαίνυμαι.*

1261. COMMENT

1556 ff. The change in Achilles is now complete. Through fellowship in suffering the true nobility of his character has been developed and perfected. He no longer thinks of himself; his anxiety now is for Priam. For Priam's sake, even the dead Hector will be given all the consideration in his power!

1560 As a proof of the sincerity of the change, we see Achilles carefully avoiding any situation in which his terrible anger might escape the control of his new wisdom.

He would violate the behests of Zeus by harming a suppliant; further, he had received intimations through his goddess mother that Zeus willed that he return the body for burial.

1563 Notice that it is Achilles himself who lifts the once-hateful body and places it on the wagon.

1566 He recognizes now that mercy towards Priam takes precedence over even his loyalty to Patroclus. His eagerness to explain and justify to Patroclus his changed attitude toward Hector is pathetically moving in its hints of interior struggle and of determination to stand by his new ideals of manliness.

1569 Encouraged by the astounding sympathy and generosity of Achilles, Priam makes bold to suggest that his people be given time to give their prince a fitting burial.

1576 The sadness of all wars echoes through this line.

1262. WORD STUDY

EPITAPH (a burial inscription); — TOMB (a vault or grave to cover the dead).

FUNERAL MOURNERS

On a special type of vase used in burial rites (loutrophoros), the artist has depicted women wailing and tearing their hair in grief over the dead man lying on a funeral couch. This ritual was common in Mediterranean and Near Eastern countries.

1263. MEMORIZE:

αἶθοψ, -οπος sparkling   **διοτρεφής, -ές** Zeus-cherished
ἄσπετος, -ον immeasurable, vast   **ἐυκνήμῑς, -ῑδος** well-greaved

1264. TEXT

The Burial of Horse-taming Hector

τὸν δ' αὖτε προσέειπε ποδάρκης δῖος Ἀχιλλεύς·
"ἔσται τοι καὶ ταῦτα, γέρον Πρίαμ', ὡς σὺ κελεύεις·
σχήσω γὰρ πόλεμον τόσσον χρόνον, ὅσσον ἄνωγας."
1580 ἐννῆμαρ μὲν τοί γε ἀγίνεον ἄσπετον ὕλην·
ἀλλ' ὅτε δὴ δεκάτη ἐφάνη φαεσίμβροτος ἠώς,
καὶ τότ' ἄρ' ἐξέφερον θρασὺν Ἕκτορα δάκρυ χέοντες,
ἐν δὲ πυρῇ ὑπάτῃ νεκρὸν θέσαν, ἐν δ' ἔβαλον πῦρ.
ἦμος δ' ἠριγένεια φάνη ῥοδοδάκτυλος ἠώς,
1585 τῆμος ἄρ' ἀμφὶ πυρὴν κλυτοῦ Ἕκτορος ἤγρετο λαός.
αὐτὰρ ἐπεὶ ῥ' ἤγερθεν ὁμηγερέες τε γένοντο,
πρῶτον μὲν κατὰ πυρκαϊὴν σβέσαν αἴθοπι οἴνῳ
πᾶσαν, ὁπόσσον ἐπέσχε πυρὸς μένος· αὐτὰρ ἔπειτα
ὀστέα λευκὰ λέγοντο κασίγνητοί θ' ἕταροί τε
1590 μυρόμενοι, θαλερὸν δὲ κατείβετο δάκρυ παρειῶν.
καὶ τά γε χρυσείην ἐς λάρνακα θῆκαν ἑλόντες,
πορφυρέοις πέπλοισι καλύψαντες μαλακοῖσιν·
αἶψα δ' ἄρ' ἐς κοίλην κάπετον θέσαν, αὐτὰρ ὕπερθεν
πυκνοῖσιν λάεσσι κατεστόρεσαν μεγάλοισι·
1595 ῥίμφα δὲ σῆμ' ἔχεαν· περὶ δὲ σκοποὶ εἴατο πάντῃ,
μὴ πρὶν ἐφορμηθεῖεν ἐυκνήμιδες Ἀχαιοί.
χεύαντες δὲ τὸ σῆμα πάλιν κίον· αὐτὰρ ἔπειτα
εὖ συναγειρόμενοι δαίνυντ' ἐρικυδέα δαῖτα
δώμασιν ἐν Πριάμοιο διοτρεφέος βασιλῆος.
1600 ὣς οἵ γ' ἀμφίεπον τάφον Ἕκτορος ἱπποδάμοιο.

ἀγῑνέω I drive; I fetch, I carry
ἀμφι-έπω I handle; I conduct
βασιλεύς, -ῆος [m.] king
ἐκ-φέρω I bear out
ἐπ-έχω, etc. I reach
ἐρικῡδής, -ές splendid, sumptuous
θρασύς, -εῖα, -ύ bold
κάπετος, -ου [f.] ditch, grave
κατα-στορέννῡμι, —, κατα-στόρεσα
  I spread, I cover up
κατ-είβομαι I fall from
λάρναξ, -ακος [f.] chest, urn
λέγω I collect
μύρομαι I shed tears, I weep

νεκρός, -οῦ [m.] corpse
ὀμηγερής, -ές gathered together
ὀπόσσος, -η, -ον as much as
παρειαί, -άων cheeks
πέπλος, -ου [m.] cloth; robe
πυρκαιή, -ῆς [f.] funeral-pyre
σβέννῡμι, —, σβέσα I put out, I quench
σκοπός, -οῦ [m.] watcher, look-out
συν-αγείρω I gather together
τάφος, -ου [m.] burial
τῆμος [adv.] then
ὕπατος, -η, -ον topmost
φαεσίμβροτος, -ον giving light to
  mortals

1265. NOTES

1578 ἔσται: shortened from ἔσεται.

1585 ἤγρετο: from ἐγείρω—"they bestirred themselves."

1586 ἤγερθεν: irregular third plural aorist passive (with intransitive force) of ἀγείρω.

1587 κατά: adverbial.

1595 ἔχεαν: shortened from ἔχευαν. εἴατο: 3 pl. impf. of ἧμαι.

1596 ἐφορμηθεῖεν: from ἐφ-ορμήθην, aorist passive of ἐφ-ορμάω.

1266. COMMENT

1578 Even this extraordinary request for a truce the new, magnanimous Achilles will not refuse; in fact, he is willing to grant even more time if it is needed.

1580 According to the custom of the time, the Trojans will burn the body of Hector. The long time spent in collecting wood bespeaks their determination to make everything about his funeral more magnificent than that of other mortals, in token of their loving admiration for the great hero.

1582 During the nine days of preparation, Hector had been laid out in state where all his family and friends might come to keep vigil and to weep for him.

HECTOR'S FUNERAL PYRE

231

1587-94 After the body is consumed and the funeral pyre burnt down, they quench the remaining hot embers with sparkling wine. Then the bones are collected and placed reverently in a golden casket, which in turn is buried in the ground, and a great mound of earth and stones built up over it.

1595 The Trojans can hardly believe the generosity of the Greeks in granting them such a favor. If they could have appreciated the new spiritual stature of Achilles, they would not have had the slightest fear, unless that some other Greek might break Achilles' truce.

1598 The funeral feast, which perhaps strikes us rather oddly, was part of the funeral ritual, and partaken of in that spirit, as a symbol of unity.

1600 With this "long-leaping" line our selections, and the whole *Iliad,* come to a close. It is in truth a summary and a symbol of the transformation of Achilles. This splendid funeral of Hector was possible only because of the human understanding and sympathy that came to Achilles through his bitter draft of sorrow.

The war, indeed, must go on to its cruel end. Achilles must still fight and slay. But we cannot believe that he will ever again be the same. In the few short months left to him of life, there will be no more place for the passionate hatred that formerly dominated him. The human personality in him has triumphed over all the brutalizing, inhuman influences of war and wild emotions. With resignation and peace he can now meet his death and pass to the world beyond. He has found the meaning of life, insofar as merely natural meaning goes. He is a nobler, far greater man than before. Sorrow has been a blessing in disguise.

As for his fame, which he longed for so ardently, it is worldwide and immortal. Homer has seen to that.

A MUSIC LESSON
The celebrated musician Linus is teaching Iphicles, half-brother of Hercules, how to play the lyre. This graceful painting, done about 470 B.C., is by the famous artist Pistoxenos, who has signed it at the top: πιστοξενος εποιησεν. The two figures are also named: ΛΙΝΟΣ and ΙΦΙΚΛΕ (written from top to center).

REVIEW

1267. Go over again Lessons 220–229; make sure now that you have really mastered them. Here are a few suggestions for your review:

   1. *Vocabulary:* Check your mastery of the 40 new memory words.
   2. *Text:* Reread the 209 lines of text, making sure you recognize all the forms.
   3. *Story:*

      a. Describe the death of Hector.
      b. How did Achilles mistreat his body?
      c. How did Andromache learn of her husband's death?
      d. On what grounds does Priam base his appeal to Achilles?
      e. What is the result of Priam's plea?

   4. *Criticism:*

      a. The scene in the quarters of Achilles is one of the most famous in all literature. Can you suggest any reasons why it should be so considered?
      b. Why did Homer think that the change wrought in Achilles was of tremendous significance for human living?
      c. Would you agree that the spirit of the *Iliad* is much more intense and profound than that of the *Odyssey*? Explain.

   5. *Composition:* Put into Greek:

      a. He was unwilling to give Hector his due of honor.
      b. It is said that Achilles surpassed all others in love and in wrath.
      c. Two great men were Achilles and Hector, but only in death (= having died) did they find peace and friendship.

1268. BENEFITS PAST AND FUTURE

   With this 230th lesson you have come to the end of *A Reading Course in Homeric Greek*. But not to the end of its many benefits. In mastering the basics of the Homeric language, and in reading 1600 lines from the two great epics which lie at the roots of European literature and culture, you have not only learned Greek and enjoyed the satisfaction of firsthand communication with one of the world's greatest writers (ample enough rewards for the effort spent!), but you have also gained lasting deeper insight into the functioning of human language and into the workings of English too. You have gained a clear understanding of the origin and specific meaning of nearly a thousand English words derived from Greek—important words that many people do not accurately know 'from the inside.' You have learned how to read a text with careful analysis of the words themselves and of their relation to one another—a valuable skill that will carry over into your reading and personal use of English. You have developed a richer appreciation of fine literature and its artistic secrets, with a resulting elevated taste and sharpened critical standards. From Homer's brilliant treatment of human ideals, motivations, and interactions you have gained new insight into the real people you know and those you will still meet. And from the Readings and Essays you have been introduced to the remarkable variety and continuing relevance of ancient thought and cultural heritage. All of this—and the fun of it too!

Even if you do not take more Greek, you have been richly repaid already for your efforts, and will go away pleased and full of good memories, as if from some fine banquet. Your education has progressed notably on several levels during this experience with Homer and his marvelous language.

But even better if you do go on! With this start, you could move along strongly and with ever-growing competence and enjoyment into the great wealth of later Greek literature—the fascinating Lyric Poets, great prose artists like Herodotus and Plato, the world-famous tragedies of Aeschylus, Sophocles, and Euripides and the brilliant comedies of Aristophanes, the interesting lives of ancient leaders by Plutarch, Lucian's clever satires and fantasies, and many other poets and writers across the wide range of ancient Greek literature. Then there is the special satisfaction of being able to read the New Testament in its original Greek, and the stirring spiritual writings of the Fathers of the Church. The ability to read Greek opens the way to a splendid literary adventure. Your knowledge of Homer has already provided you the key to that great experience. Do take advantage of it!

An aid to this progress into later Greek literature is the *Transition to Attic Greek* (Appendix F). With its help you can easily and confidently move from Homeric dialect to the later forms of Greek met in other authors. The differences are really few—statistically fifteen percent at most.

But before moving into Classical authors, you should seriously consider reading *more Homer* first. With the background in this Course, you already know some ninety percent of Homeric grammar, and a substantial number of the 1823 words that occur ten times or oftener in the whole *Iliad* and *Odyssey*. With the help of a dictionary, you can read more Homer with ease—and that is a high delight.

Students who have finished this Course before the end of the semester or term are well advised to use the remaining classes in *rereading* the Homer selections in the two books. They will come now more easily, and with new enjoyment and impact. Or the time could be well spent in going through Appendix F, *Transition to Attic Greek*, in preparation for your next instalment in the high adventure. In any case, *εἰς καλά.*

SUMMARY OF GRAMMAR

DECLENSION ENDINGS

	FIRST DECLENSION		SECOND DECLENSION		THIRD DECLENSION	
	βι-	*γαι-*	*θε-*	*δωρ-*	*ἄναξ, ἀνακτ-*	*ἔπος, ἐπε-*
N.	*-η*	*-α*	*-ος*	*-ον*	----	----
G.	*-ης*	*-ης*	*-ου, οιο*	*-ου, οιο*	*-ος*	*-ος*
D.	*-η*	*-η*	*-ῳ*	*-ῳ*	*-ι*	*-ι*
A.	*-ην*	*-αν*	*-ον*	*-ον*	*-α, (-ν)*	----
N.	*-αι*		*-οι*	*-α*	*-ες*	*-α*
G.	*-ᾱων*		*-ων*	*-ων*	*-ων*	*-ων*
D.	*-ησ(ι)*		*-οισ(ι)*	*-οισ(ι)*	*-(εσ)σι*	*-(εσ)σι*
A.	*-ᾱς*		*-ους*	*-α*	*-ας*	*-α*

Gender: all f.	*Gender:* all m., except a few f.	*Gender:* all n.	*Gender:* stems ending in:

Gender: stems ending in:

(1) *ατ-, αρ-, α-, ε-* are *n.*

(2) *δ-, ι-, θ-, ιτ-, τητ-* are *f.*

(3) rest are *m.*

(4) Some exceptions.

Note:

(1) *acc. sg.* ends in *-ν* for *ι-* and *υ-* stems; in *-υν* for m. adj. w. nom. *-υς.*

(2) *dat. pl.* = nom. sg. + *ι* when stem ends in *κ, γ, χ, π, β,* or *φ;* final *τ, δ, θ, ν* of stem drop before *-σι;* stems in *-εντ-* have dat. pl. *-εντεσσι* or *-εισι,* stems in *-οντ-* have *-οντεσσι* or *-ουσι.*

ADJECTIVE AND PARTICIPLE TYPES

(1) First and second decl.: *-ος, (-η), -ον*

(2) First and third decl.:
-υς, -εια, -υ (m.-n. gen. *ε-ος*)

-εις, { *-εσσα* / *-εισα* } *εν* (m.-n. gen. *εντ-ος*)

-ων, -ουσα, -ον (m.-n. gen. *οντ-ος*)
-ᾱς, -ᾱσα, -αν (m.-n. gen. *αντ-ος*)
-ως, -υια, -ος (m.-n. gen. *οτ-ος*)

(3) Third decl. only:
-ης, -ες (gen. *ε-ος*)
-ων, -ον (gen. *ον-ος*)

(4) Single termination: treated as nouns.

COMPARISON OF ADJECTIVES

(1) Adj. in *ος,* w. last syllable of stem long, add *-οτερος, -οτατος* to stem (*δικαι-ότερος, δικαι-ότατος*).

(2) Adj. in *-ος,* w. last syllable of stem short, add *-ωτερος, -ωτατος* to stem (*χαλεπ-ώτερος, χαλεπ-ώτατος*).

(3) Adj. in *-ων* add *-εστερος, -εστατος* to stem (*ἀφρον-έστερος, ἀφρον-έστατος*).

(4) Adj. in *-ης* and some in *-υς* add *-τερος, -τατος* to neuter nom. sg. (*ἀληθέσ-τερος, ὠκύ-τατος*).

IRREGULAR COMPARISON

ἀγαθός	*ἀρείων*	*ἄριστος*
καλός	*καλλίων*	*κάλλιστος*
μέγας	*μείζων*	*μέγιστος*
πολλός	*πλείων*	*πλεῖστος*
φίλος	*φίλτερος*	*φίλτατος*
ταχύς	*θάσσων*	*τάχιστος*

VOCATIVE

Same as nom. except:

(a) 2 decl. m. sg. *-ε* (*φίλε*)

(b) 3 decl. *-ευς, -ις* drop *-ς* (*Ζεῦ, πόλι*)

(c) 3 decl. long vowel of nom. shortens if it also does in gen. (*πάτερ*)

(d) Special: *θεός, γύναι.*

SPECIAL CASE ENDINGS

(1) *-δε* added to acc. = *place to which* (*οἰκόν-δε*); *-δε* blends w. *ς* into *-ζε* (*θυράζε*).

(2) *-θεν* added to gen. minus *ς* or *υ* = *place from which, source, separation* (*οὐρανό-θεν*).

(3) *-φι(ν)* added to gen. minus *ς* or *υ* = *by, at, from, with, on, in* (*βίηφι, θύρηφιν*).

(4) DUAL: 2 decl. *-ω,* 3 decl. *-ε* (*χεῖρε ἐμῶ*).

VERB ENDINGS: ACTIVE AND AORIST PASSIVE

	PRESENT A. λυ-	FUTURE A. λυσ-	1 AOR. A. λυσ-	2 AOR. A. ἰδ-	3 AOR. A. βη-	PF. ACT. A. λελυκ-	PF. MID. M.P. λελυ-	AOR. PASS. P. λυθ-
INDICATIVE	-ω	-ω			(Note: some verbs have ω or ῡ in place of η, and οι or υι in place of αι. See Lessons 42-3)	-α		
	-εις	-εις				-ας		
	-ει	-ει				-ε(ν)		
	-ομεν	-ομεν				-αμεν		
	-ετε	-ετε				-ατε		
	-ουσι(ν)	-ουσι(ν)				-ασι(ν)		
	----------					----------		
	(IMPF.)					(PLPF.)		
	-ον		-α	-ον	-ν	-εα, -η		-ην
	-ες		-ας	-ες	-ς	-ης		-ης
	-ε(ν)		-ε(ν)	-ε(ν)	—	-ει		-η
	-ομεν		-αμεν	-ομεν	-μεν	-εμεν		-ημεν
	-ετε		-ατε	-ετε	-τε	-ετε		-ητε
	-ον		-αν	-ον	-σαν	-εσαν		-ησαν
SUBJUNCTIVE	-ω		-ω	-ω	-ω	-ω		-ω
	-ης		-ης	-ης	-ης	-ης		-ης
	-η		-η	-η	-η	-η		-η
	-ωμεν		-ωμεν	-ωμεν	-ωμεν	-ωμεν		-ωμεν
	-ητε		-ητε	-ητε	-ητε	-ητε		-ητε
	-ωσι(ν)		-ωσι(ν)	-ωσι(ν)	-ωσι(ν)	-ωσι(ν)		-ωσι(ν)
OPTATIVE	-οιμι		-αιμι	-οιμι	-αιην*	-οιμι		-ειην
	-οις		-ειας	-οις	-αιης	-οις		-ειης
	-οι		-ειε(ν)	-οι	-αιη	-οι		-ειη
	-οιμεν		-αιμεν	-οιμεν	-αιμεν	-οιμεν		-ειμεν
	-οιτε		-αιτε	-οιτε	-αιτε	-οιτε		-ειτε
	-οιεν		-ειαν	-οιεν	-αιεν	-οιεν		-ειεν
IMPT	-ε		-ον	-ε	-θι	-ε		-ηθι
	-ετε		-ατε	-ετε	-τε	-ετε		-ητε
INF	-ειν	-ειν		-(ε)ειν				-ηναι
	-(ε)μεν	-(ε)μεν	-αι	-(ε)μεν	-ναι	-εναι		-ημεναι
	-(ε)μεναι	-(ε)μεναι		-(ε)μεναι		-εμεν(αι)		
PTC					β-* γν-*			
	-ων	-ων	-ᾱς	-ων	-ᾱσ -ους	-ως		-εις
	-ουσα	-ουσα	-ᾱσα	-ουσα	-ᾱσα -ουσα	-υια		-εισα
	-ον	-ον	-αν	-ον	-αν -ον	-ος		-εν

Note: the Subj. 3 sg. ending is sometimes -ησι, the 2 sg. sometimes -ησθα.   *Incorporating the stem vowel (see #302)

VERB ENDINGS: MIDDLE AND PASSIVE

	PRESENT M.P. λυ-	FUTURE M.P. λυσ-	1 AOR. M. λυσ-	2 AOR. M. ἰδ-	3 AOR. A. βη-	PF. ACT. A. λελυκ-	PF. MID. M.P. λελυ-	AOR. PASS. P. λυθ-
INDICATIVE	-ομαι -εαι -εται -ομεθα -εσθε -ονται	-ομαι -εαι -εται -ομεθα -εσθε -ονται					-μαι -σαι -ται -μεθα -σθε -αται	
	(IMPF.) -ομην -εο -ετο -ομεθα -εσθε -οντο		-αμην -αο -ατο -αμεθα -ασθε -αντο	-ομην -εο -ετο -ομεθα -εσθε -οντο			*(PLPF.)* -μην -σο -το -μεθα -σθε -ατο	
SUBJUNCTIVE	-ωμαι -ηαι -ηται -ωμεθα -ησθε -ωνται		-ωμαι -ηαι -ηται -ωμεθα -ησθε -ωνται	-ωμαι -ηαι -ηται -ωμεθα -ησθε -ωνται				
OPTATIVE	-οιμην -οιο -οιτο -οιμεθα -οισθε -οιατο		-αιμην -αιο -αιτο -αιμεθα -αισθε -αιατο	-οιμην -οιο -οιτο -οιμεθα -οισθε -οιατο				
IMPT	-εο, -ευ -εσθε		-αι -ασθε	-εο, -ευ -εσθε			-σο -σθε	
INF	-εσθαι	-εσθαι	-ασθαι	-εσθαι			-σθαι	
PTC	-ομενος -η -ον	-ομενος -η -ον	-αμενος -η -ον	-ομενος -η ον			-μενος -η -ον	

Note: (1) In the 1 pl., -μεσθα may be used for -μεθα.   (2) The Subj. 2 sg. -ηαι may contract to -η.
(3) In the Ind. and Opt. 3 pl., -αται and -ατο may be used instead of -νται and -ντο.

SPECIAL VERB FORMS*

	εἰμί I am		ἵημι I send forth	δίδωμι I give	τίθημι I put	οἶδα I know
Ind. Pres.	εἰμί ἐσσί, (εἰς) ἐστί(ν)	εἰμέν ἐστέ εἰσί(ν)			---- ---- [τίθησθα] ---- ---- ----	(PF. ENDINGS) οἶδα ἴδμεν οἶσθα ἴστε οἶδε ἴσᾱσι
Impf.	ἦα ἦσθα ἦεν, (ἦν, ἔην)	ἦμεν ἦτε ἦσαν, (ἔσαν)	ἵειν ---- ἵεις ---- ἵει ----		---- ---- ---- ---- τίθει ----	(PLPF. ENDINGS) ἤδεα ἴδμεν ἤδης ἴστε ἤδη ἴσαν
Fut.	ἔσ(σ)ομαι ἔσ(σ)εαι ἔσ(σε)ται	ἐσ(σ)όμεθα ἔ(σ)εσθε ἔσ(σ)ονται				εἰδήσω etc.
Aor.				2 AOR. ---- ---- ---- ---- ---- [δόσαν]	2 AOR. ---- ---- ---- ---- ---- θέσαν	
Subj.	ὦ ᾖς ᾖ	ὦμεν ἦτε ὦσι(ν)		2 AOR. [δῶ] ---- ---- ---- δώῃ ----		
Opt.	εἴην εἴης εἴη	εἶμεν εἶτε εἶεν		2 AOR. δοίην δοῖμεν δοίης δοῖτε δοίη δοῖεν	2 AOR. θείην θεῖμεν θείης θεῖτε θείη θεῖεν	
Impt.				2 AOR. δός δότε		ἴσθι ἴστε
Inf.	εἶναι ἔμμεν(αι)	Fut.: ἔσεσθαι				ἴδμεν(αι)
Ptc.	Pres.: ἐών, ἐοῦσα, ἐόν Fut.: ἐσόμενος, η, ον				2 AOR. MID. [θέμενος, η, ον]	εἰδώς, υἶα, ός

	φημί I speak				
	IMPF. ACT.		IMPF. MID	
	φῆν φαμέν		φάμην φάμεθα	
	φῆς φατέ		φάο φάσθε	
	φῆ φά(σα)ν		φάτο φάντο	

ITERATIVE FORMS

Expanded forms of impf. or aor., to emphasize *repeated* or *customary* action.

Formed by inserting -(ε)σκ- or -(α)σκ- between impf. or aor. stem and regular impf. or 2 aor. endings (even w. 1 aor. stems); -ασκ- is used mostly w. 1 aor. or α-stems. (ἐχ-έσκ-ετο κρυπτ-άσκ-ε).

*Cp. #470.   Forms enclosed in [ ] are not assigned for memory.

PRONOUNS

RELATIVE: ὅς, ἥ, ὅ   *who, which, that*
         ὁ, ἡ, τό   *who, which, what*

INTENSIVE: αὐτός, -ή, -ό   (*him*) *self, same, very*
(Occasionally unintensive, a simple *him, her, it*)

DEMONSTRATIVE: κεῖνος, -η, -ο   *that*
               ὁ, ἡ, τό   *that,* (*the*)
               ὅδε, ἥδε, τόδε   *this*

ὁ	ἡ	τό
τοῦ, τοῖο	τῆς	τοῦ, τοῖο
τῷ	τῇ	τῷ
τόν	τήν	τό
ταί(οι)	ταί (αι)	τά
τῶν	τάων	τῶν
τοῖσ(ι)	τῇσ(ι)	τοῖσ(ι)
τούς	τάς	τά

Use: (1) Demonstrative when modifying a noun.

      (2) Relative when following definite antecedent.

      (3) Third personal pronoun when standing in place of a noun already mentioned.

INDEFINITE

τις	τι
τευ	τευ
τεω, τω	τεω, τω
τινα	τι
τινες	τινα
τεων	τεων
τεοισι	τεοισι
τινας	τινα

INTERROGATIVE

τίς	τί
τεῦ	τεῦ
τέῳ, τῷ	τέῳ, τῷ
τίνα	τί
τίνες	τίνα
τέων	τέων
τέοισι	τέοισι
τίνας	τίνα

INDEF. AND INTERROG. REL.
ὅς τις, ἥ τις, ὅ τι (ὅττι)

Usually written as two words in nom. and acc., both parts declined; in gen. and dat., occasionally in nom. and acc., written as one word, last part declined.

FIRST PERSONAL		SECOND PERSONAL		THIRD PERSONAL (Reflexive when with pitch-mark)	
ἐγώ(ν)	ἡμεῖς (ἄμμες)	σύ	ὑμεῖς	----	----
μευ (ἐμεῖο)	ἡμέων	σεῦ (σεῖο)	ὑμέων	ἑο	σφεων
ἐμοί, μοι	ἡμῖν (ἄμμιν)	σοί (τοι)	ὑμῖν	οἱ	σφι(ν), (σφισι)
ἐμέ, με	ἡμέας (ἄμμε)	σέ	ὑμέας	μιν, ἑ	σφεας

also: ὁ, ἡ, τό; ὅδε, ἥδε, τόδε; κεῖνος, -η, -ο; αὐτός, -ή, -ό.

N.B. A pronoun may assume adjectival force and modify a noun or another pronoun, as in Latin.

PREPOSITIONS

	WITH GENITIVE	WITH DATIVE	WITH ACCUSATIVE
ἄγχι	near, close by: ἄγχι Τροίης		
ἅμα		at same time: ἅμα νυκτί together with: ἅμα ἑταίροις	
ἀμφί		on both sides: ἀμφὶ οἴκῳ around: ἀμφὶ νηῷ concerning: ἀμφὶ δώροις	on both sides: ἀμφὶ οἶκον around: ἀμφὶ νηόν concerning: ἀμφὶ δῶρα
ἀνά	on(to): ἀνὰ νεῶν	on [at rest]: ἀνὰ νηί	on(to): ἀνὰ νῆα over: ἀνὰ γαῖαν
ἀπάνευθε	away (from): ἀπάνευθε οἴκου apart (from): ἀπάνευθε πόνου afar (from): ἀπάνευθε φίλων		
ἀπό	away from: ἀπὸ πέτρης from: ἀπὸ ψυχῆς		
διά	through: διὰ πυρός		through: διὰ πῦρ among [motion]: διὰ ἑταίρους on account of : διὰ χρυσόν
ἐγγύς	near: ἐγγὺς θαλάσσης		
εἵνεκα	on account of : εἵνεκα πολέμου for sake of: εἵνεκα σεῦ		
εἰς			into: εἰς γαῖαν to: εἰς θάλασσαν
ἐκ, ἐξ	out of: ἐκ πέτρης from: ἐξ ἀρχῆς		
ἐν		in: ἐν ψυχῇ on: ἐν πέτρῃσι among: ἐν φίλοις	
ἐπί	upon: ἐπὶ πέτρης	on: ἐπὶ πέτρῃ at, beside: ἐπὶ θαλάσσῃ	to, towards: ἐπὶ πέτρας after [in search]: ἐπὶ δόξαν
κατά	down (from): κατὰ πέτρης		down (along): κατὰ ποταμόν according to: κατὰ δίκην throughout: κατὰ γαῖαν
μέτα		among: μετὰ δενδρέοισι with: μετὰ ἀγάπῃ	into the midst: μετὰ ξείνους after: μετὰ πτόλεμον
παρά	from [side of]: παρὰ φίλων	at, beside: παρὰ ποταμῷ	to: παρὰ θάλασσαν along (side): παρὰ ποταμόν
περί	about: περὶ βουλῆς excelling: περὶ πάντων	about: περὶ σώματι for: περὶ δώροις	about: περὶ σῶμα for: περὶ δῶρα
πρός	from (side of): πρὸς ἄνακτος	on: πρὸς γαίῃ at: πρὸς θαλάσσῃ	to, towards: πρὸς θάλασσαν
σύν		with: σὺν σοφοῖσι	
ὑπέρ	over: ὑπὲρ θύρης		over: ὑπὲρ πόντον
ὑπό	from under: ὑπὸ πέτρης by: ὑπὸ ψυχῆς	under [at rest]: ὑπὸ πέτρῃ	under [motion to]: ὑπὸ πέτρην

Position of preposition:

(1) Ordinarily: before its object or object's modifier (πρός με, σὺν πολλοῖς ἑταίροις).
(2) For poetic purposes: after its object, or between modifier and object (χειρὸς ἄπο, πολλοῖς σὺν ἑταίροις).
(3) In compound words: directly joined (προσ-φέρω).
(4) As adverb: detached (ἀμφί ῥα πάντες ἔστησαν).

VARIA

NU MOVABLE

ν may be added before a vowel, at end of sentence, occasionally before a consonant, to the final *σι* of the 3 pl. or dat. pl. and to the final *-ε* of the 3 sg.; also in a few other words ending in *-σι* or *-ε*.

ELISION

For easier pronunciation, a short final vowel (except *υ*), and sometimes a final *-αι* or *-οι* may drop out before an initial vowel or diphthong and in compounds (*ἀπ' ἀρχῆς, πάρ-ην*).

Elision does *not* occur in the dat. pl. of the 3 decl., or in *περί, πρό, ὅτι, τι,* or in words which take *ν* movable.

When elision brings *π, τ,* or *κ* before a rough breathing, they change to *φ, θ, χ (ἀφ-αιρέω).*

DISTINCTION OF *οὐ* AND *μή*

οὐ negatives statements of concrete fact, *μή* the others — possibility, condition, general, wish, supposition, etc.

ADVERBS

Formation:

(1) By adding *-ως* to neuter stem (*καλ-ῶς, ταχέ-ως*).
(2) Simple n. acc., sg. or pl. (*πρῶτον*).
(3) Special: *νῦν, τότε,* etc.
(4) Prepositions used adverbially.

Comparison:

n. acc. sg. of the comparative adj. (*θᾶσσον*),
n. acc. pl. of supl. adj. (*τάχιστα*).

DEPONENT VERBS

Have mid. or pass. endings only, but w. act. force (*μάχομαι*).
The mid. of deponent and of many active verbs often is *intransitive* (*τρέπομαι* I turn).

-MI VERBS

Irregular only in pres. and 2 aor. systems, where they lack the thematic vowel, have some special endings.

Subj. mid., however, retains the usual long thematic vowel, which absorbs a final *α* or *ε* of stem and contracts with a final *o* to *ω*.

AUGMENT IN PAST INDICATIVE

(1) Stems beginning w. consonant(s) prefix *ἐ* (*λύω: ἔ-λῦσα*). Initial *ρ* often doubles (*ἔρρεε*).
(2) Stems beginning w. a short vowel or a diphthong which is not the reduplication lengthen the initial vowel (*οἰκέω: ᾤκεον*).
Initial *ἐ* lengthens to *ἠ;* but to *εἰ* in the following: *ἔχω, ἐάω, ἕπομαι, ἕλκω, ἕρπω, ἑρπύζω, ἕλον.*
(3) Stems beginning w. a long vowel (*ἠσάμην*) or a vowel-reduplication (*ἔγνωσμαι*) take no augment.

CONSONANT CHANGES

In dat. pl.:

$\kappa, \gamma, \chi + \sigma = \xi$

$\pi, \beta, \varphi + \sigma = \psi$

$\tau, \delta, \theta, \nu$ drop before σ

When both *ντ* drop, the preceding *ε* lengthens to *ει,* o lengthens to *ου.*

In pf. mid. of consonant stems:

Principal part ending in:

,,	$\mu + \sigma = \psi$
,,	$\mu + \tau = \pi\tau$
,,	$\mu + \sigma\theta = \varphi\theta$
,,	$\mu + \nu\tau = \varphi\alpha\tau$
,,	$\gamma + \sigma = \xi$
,,	$\gamma + \tau = \kappa\tau$
,,	$\gamma + \sigma\theta = \chi\theta$
,,	$\gamma + \nu\tau = \chi\alpha\tau$
,,	$\sigma + \sigma = \sigma$
,,	$\sigma + \tau = \sigma\tau$
,,	$\sigma + \sigma\theta = \sigma\theta$
,,	$\sigma + \nu\tau = \theta\alpha\tau$

VOWEL CONTRACTIONS

(1) *αε* becomes *ᾱ, αει* becomes *ᾳ.*
(2) *αο, αω, αου* become *ω.*
(3) *εε, εει* become *ει.*
(4) *εο, εου* become *ευ.*
(5) *οε, οο* become *ου.*

REDUPLICATION IN PF. STEM

(1) Stems beginning w. single consonant prefix initial consonant w. *ε* (*λύω: λέ-λυκα*).
(2) Stems beginning w. 2 consonants simply prefix *ἐ* (*στέλλω: ἔ-σταλκα*).
(3) Stems beginning w. short vowel or w. diphthong lengthen initial vowel (*ἁμαρτάνω: ἡμάρτηκα; αἱρέω: ᾕρηκα*).
(4) Stems beginning w. mute plus liquid (*π, β, φ, κ, γ, χ, τ, δ, θ* plus *λ, μ, ν,* or *ρ*) prefix the mute w. *ε* (*γράφω: γέ-γραφα*).
   (a) But initial *γν* follows rule 2.
   (b) Initial *φ, χ, θ* become *π, κ, τ* in reduplicating (*φιλέω: πε-φίληκα*).
(5) Some reduplications irregular.

SYNTAX OF THE NOUN (#18)

1. NOMINATIVE: case of subject of a finite verb.

   a. *Note* (#53): a neuter plural subject ordinarily takes a singular verb.

      δῶρα ἐστὶ καλά.   The gifts are beautiful.

2. GENITIVE: basic meaning—*of; from:*

   a. Types: possessive, partitive, contents, material; separation; w. certain verbs, adjectives; w. prepositions.

3. DATIVE: basic meanings—*to, for; by, with; in, on:*

   a. Types: personal (indirect object, reference, possession: #502); instrumental (means, manner); locative (where, when); w. certain verbs, adjectives; w. prepositions.

4. ACCUSATIVE: case of object of action, motion, thought:

   a. Types: direct object; place to which; subject of infinitive depending in indirect discourse on verb of thinking, saying, perceiving; w. prepositions.

   b. Special uses: *cognate:* #600 (governed by an intransitive verb of related meaning: *μακρὴν ὁδὸν ἤλθομεν. We came a long journey.*); specification: #643 (specifying in what respect the idea contained in an accompanying word is true: *νόον ἐσθλός noble-minded*).

5. VOCATIVE: case of direct address.

SYNTAX OF THE VERB BY MOODS

1. INDICATIVE (tenses indicate time, as well as kind, of action):

   a. *Statements of fact* (#91)—past, present, future: simple, continuous, completed. Negative *οὐ.*

ἔρχεται.	*ἔρχετο.*	*ἦλθεν.*	*ἐώρᾶται.*	*οὐ λέξω.*
He comes.	*He was coming.*	*He came.*	*He has been seen.*	*I shall not say.*

   b. *Past contrary-to-fact* (#91): impf. or aor. ind. in both clauses, *ἄν* or *κε(ν)* in conclusion. Neg. *μή* in if-clause, *οὐ* in conclusion.

      εἰ μὴ τόδε πίνεν, οὐκ ἄν θάνεν
      If he had not drunk this, he would not have died.

2. SUBJUNCTIVE (tenses indicate kind of action, not time);

   a. *Hortatory* (#98): requested or proposed actions referring to the speaker himself: first person, sg. or pl. Neg. *μή.*

      μὴ τῇδε μένωμεν, ἑταῖροι, ἀλλὰ φύγωμεν.
      Let us not remain here, comrades, but let us flee.

   b. *Present purpose* (#98): to express intended action, after *primary* main verb; introduced by *ἵνα, ὡς, ὅπως, ὄφρα.* Neg. *ἵνα μή,* etc., rarely *μή* alone.

      πεύθομαι ἵνα γιγνώσκω, ὄφρα μὴ νήπιος ὦ.
      I inquire that I may know, in order that I may not be simple.

      N.B. The subj. is occasionally used to indicate *pres.* purpose after a secondary main verb.

   c. *Vivid future* (#244): to express a probable future supposition; often takes *ἄν* or *κε(ν).* Neg. *μή.*

      εἰ (κεν) ἔλθη, δέξομαί μιν πρόφρων.
      If he comes, I shall receive him eagerly.

d. *Present general* (#244): to indicate repeated occurrence in the present; may take *ἄν* or *κε(ν)*. Neg. *μή*.

> *ὅτε (ἄν) βούληται, ἐπὶ θάλασσαν ἔρχεται.*
> *Whenever he wishes, he goes to the sea.*

N.B. The main verb is regularly pres. ind., neg. *οὐ*.

3. OPTATIVE (tenses indicate kind of action, not time):

a. *Wishes* (#106): to express possible and impossible wishes (often equivalent to a polite imperative); may be introduced by *εἰ, εἴθε, εἰ γάρ* ("if only," "would that"), especially if an impossible wish. Neg. *μή*.

> *πολλά γε μανθάνοιμι·   εἴθε μὴ χαλεπὸν εἴη.*
> *Many things at least may I learn—if only it were not difficult!*

b. *Past purpose* (#106): to express intended action after *secondary* main verb; introduced by *ἵνα, ὡς, ὅπως, ὄφρα*. Neg. *ἵνα μή*, etc., rarely *μή* alone.

> *θάνε αὐτὸς ὄφρα σώζοι ἡμέας, ἵνα μὴ ἀπ-ολοίμεθα.*
> *He himself died to save us, in order that we might not perish.*

c. *Vague future* ("should-would) (#281): to indicate a less likely future supposition (should, happen to . . .) and its assumed consequences; both clauses may take *ἄν* or *κε(ν)*. Neg. of supposition is *μή*, of conclusion *οὐ*.

> *εἰ (κε) μὴ ἔλθοις, οὐκ (ἄν) ἐθέλοιμι ἔρχεσθαι αὐτός.*
> *If you should not go, I would not wish to go myself.*

N.B. The conclusion may sometimes not be vague but definite—an ordinary impt. or hortatory subj.

d. *Potential* (#281): to express an opinion as to what might, could, or would happen if certain unstated circumstances should prevail; usually takes *ἄν* or *κε(ν)*. Neg. *οὐ*. (This construction = the conclusion of a "should-would" sentence of which the condition is not expressed).

> *μὴ βῆτε· κτείνειε γάρ (κεν) ὑμέας πάντας.*
> *Do not go—for he would kill all of you!*

e. *Expectation* (#522): simply a potential opt. w. special force, indicating what one expects or desires to happen under assumed circumstances, and equivalent to English "can, will," rather than "could, would, might." Same rule as Potential Opt.

> *εὕρωμέν τινα ὃς ἄν ἡμῖν ὁδὸν φαίνοι.*
> *Let us find someone who can show us the way.*

f. *Past general* (#478): to indicate repeated occurrence in the past. Neg. *μή*.

> *ὅτε βούλοιτο, ἐπὶ θάλασσαν ἔρχετο.*
> *Whenever he wished, he came to the sea.*

N.B. The main verb is ordinarily impf. ind., rarely aor.; neg. *οὐ*.

g. *Indirect questions* (#463): the verb within a question depending on a *secondary* main verb of asking, knowing, etc. ordinarily shifts from the ind. (or subj.) of the direct question into the corresponding tense of the opt., though it may stay unchanged. Neg. as in direct-question form.

> *ἔρετο τίς ἡμέας πέμψειεν (πέμψεν).*
> *He asked who sent us.*

4. IMPERATIVE (tenses indicate kind of action, not time):

    a. *Commands* (#114): to express what one desires or orders another to do. Neg. *μή*.

    > μὴ εὕδετε· μανθάνειν γε πειράετε.
    > *Do not sleep; try at least to learn.*

5. INFINITIVE (tenses indicate kind of action except in indirect discourse):

    a. *After certain verbs:* (#114): (wishing, planning, bidding, etc.), to complete their sense. Neg. *μή*.

    > κελεύει ἡμέας δίκη πάντας φιλέμεν, καὶ μή τινα μισέειν.
    > *Justice orders us to love all and not to hate anyone.*

    b. *Explanatory* (#586): to explain the sense of another word and fill out its meaning. Neg. *μή*.

    > χαλεπὸν μὲν ἔρδειν, αἰσχρὸν δὲ μὴ ἔρξαι.
    > *It is difficult, indeed, to do, but it is shameful not to do.*

    c. *Purpose* (#586): to explain why an action is done. Neg. *μή*.

    > πέμψε σφέας ὕδωρ ζητέειν.
    > *He sent them to seek water.*

    d. *As noun* (#414): subject or object of another verb. Neg. *μή*.

    > φαγέμεναι καὶ ἀνάγκη ἐστὶ καὶ ἡδονή.
    > *Eating is both a necessity and a pleasure.*

    e. *As imperative* (#148): to express command. Neg. *μή*.

    > τὰ γιγνώσκεις, λέγειν.
    > *Say what you know.*

    f. *With accusative in indirect discourse* (#114): to express an action depending on a main verb of saying, thinking, perceiving, etc. Tense by Relation (pres. inf. for action going on at same time as that of main verb, aor. inf. for an earlier action, future for a later action than main verb). Neg. *οὐ*.

    > ἔφη πατέρα ἑὸν χρήματά ποτε σχέθειν πολλά,
    >   νῦν δὲ οὐκ ἔχειν οὐδὲ αἶψα σχήσειν.
    > *He said that his father once had many possessions,*
    >   *but that he did not now have nor would he quickly have many.*

6. PARTICIPLE (tenses indicate time of action):

    a. *Circumstantial* (#114): to indicate cause, condition, manner, or circumstances attending the action of the main verb. Neg. *οὐ* if fact, otherwise *μή*.

    > εὕδων ἐπὶ γαῖαν πέσε καὶ ἀπ-όλετο.
    > *While sleeping, he fell to the earth and was killed.*

    b. *Adjectival* (#114): modifying a noun or pronoun. Neg. *οὐ*.

    > τὸν μὲν φεύγοντα ὁράω, ἄνακτα δὲ διώκοντα.
    > *That man indeed I see fleeing, but the king I see pursuing.*

SYNTAX OF THE VERB BY CONSTRUCTIONS

(Note: relative, temporal, and conditional clauses all follow the same rules in each type of construction.)

1. CIRCUMSTANTIAL (#114): the ptc. indicates the circumstances under which the main action takes place. Neg. οὐ if fact, otherwise μή.

    > μαχεόμενος θάνεν.
    > *While fighting, he died.*

2. COMMANDS (#114, 148, 106): expressed by impt., inf., occasionally opt. (= "please . . . "). Neg. μή.

    > τὰ γιγνώσκεις λέγε (λέγειν, λέγοις).
    > *Say (please) what you know.*

3. CONTRARY-TO-FACT IN PAST (#91): impf. or aor. ind. in both clauses, ἄν or κε(ν) in conclusion. Neg. μή in if-clause, οὐ in conclusion.

    > εἰ μὴ τόδε πῖνεν, οὐκ ἄν θάνεν.
    > *If he had not drunk this, he would not have died.*

4. EXPECTATION (#522): of what can or will follow if certain assumed circumstances should prevail (merely a special kind of potential construction): opt., usually w. ἄν or κε(ν). Neg. οὐ.

    > εὕρωμέν τινα ὅς ἄν ἡμῖν ὁδὸν φαίνοι.
    > *Let us find someone who can show us the way.*

5. EXPLANATORY (#586): inf. filling out sense of main word. Neg. μή. Also, by ἐπεί or ὅτι w. ind. Neg. οὐ.

    > χαλεπὸν νοῆσαι.   ὅτι σε φιλῶ, ἤλυθον.
    > *It is difficult to perceive.   I came because I love you.*

6. FACT (#91): ind., proper tense to indicate both time and kind of action. Neg. οὐ.

    > ἔρχεται.   ἔρχετο.   ἦλθεν.   οὐ λέξω.
    > *He comes.   He was coming.   He came.   I shall not say.*

7. FUTURE SUPPOSITION:

    a. *Vivid future* (#244): indicating a probable supposition; subj., often w. ἄν or κε(ν), main verb in fut. ind. or in impt. Neg. of subj. and impt. μή, of ind. οὐ.

    > εἰ (κεν) ἔλθῃ, δέξομαί μιν· εἰ δὲ μὴ χρυσὸν ἔχῃ,
    > πόρε οἱ σύ, ὄφρα ἐλθεῖν δυνατὸς ᾖ.
    > *If he comes, I shall receive him; but if he has no gold,*
    >   *you give him some, so that he may be able to come.*

    b. *Vague future* (#281): ("should-would"), indicating a less likely supposition and its assumed consequences: both clauses opt. (either may take ἄν or κε). Neg. of supposition μή, of conclusion οὐ.

    > εἰ (κε) μὴ ἔλθοις, οὐκ (ἄν) ἐθέλοιμι ἔρχεσθαι αὐτός.
    > *If you should not go, I would not wish to go myself.*

8. GENERAL, repeated occurrence:

    a. *Present* (#244): subj., may take ἄν or κε(ν). Neg. μή. Main verb is regularly present ind., neg. οὐ.

    > ὅτε (ἄν) βούληται, ἐπὶ θάλασσαν ἔρχετο.
    > *Whenever he wishes, he goes to the sea.*

b. *Past* (#478): opt. Neg. μή. Main verb is ordinarily impf. ind., rarely aor.; neg. οὐ.

> ὅτε βούλοιτο, ἐπὶ θάλασσαν ἔρχετο.

9. HORTATORY (#98): subj., 1 sg. or pl. Neg. μή.

> μὴ τῇδε μένωμεν, ἑταῖροι, ἀλλὰ φύγωμεν.
> *Let us not remain here, comrades, but let us flee.*

10. INDIRECT DISCOURSE (#114): after main verb of saying, knowing, perceiving, etc., the dependent verb goes into inf. of corresponding tense. Neg. οὐ.

> ἔφη σφέας δέξασθαι τάδε δῶρα ἀπὸ ἄνακτος.
> *He said that they had received these gifts from the king.*

11. INDIRECT QUESTIONS (#463): after *primary* main verb of asking, knowing, etc., the verb within the question itself remains in the ind. (or subj.) unchanged; after a *secondary* main verb, the dependent verb ordinarily shifts into the corresponding tense of the opt., though it may stay unchanged. Negative as in direct-question form.

> εἴρεται τίς ἡμέας πέμψεν.   ἔρετο τίς ἡμέας πέμψειεν (πέμψεν).
> *He asks who sent us.*   *He asked who sent us.*

12. POTENTIAL (#281): expressing an opinion as to what might or could happen if certain assumed but unexpressed circumstances should prevail (= conclusion of "should-would" sentence): opt., usually w. ἄν or κε(ν). Neg. οὐ.

> μὴ βῆτε· κτείνειε γάρ (κεν) ὑμέας πάντας.
> *Do not go—for he would kill all of you!*

13. PURPOSE (introduced by ἵνα, ὡς, ὅπως, ὄφρα. Neg. ἵνα μή, etc., rarely μή alone):

a. *Present* (#98), after primary (occasionally secondary) main verb: subj.

> πεύθομαι ἵνα γιγνώσκω, ὄφρα μὴ νήπιος ὦ.
> *I inquire that I may know, in order that I may not be simple.*

b. *Past* (#106), after secondary main verb: opt.

> θάνε αὐτὸς ὄφρα σῴζοι ἡμέας, ἵνα μὴ ἀπ-ολοίμεθα.
> *He himself died to save us, in order that we might not perish.*

14. SHOULD-WOULD: see above, number 7b.

15. WISHES (#106), both possible and impossible of fulfilment: opt., often w. εἰ, εἴθε, εἰ γάρ ("if only," "would that")—especially if an impossible wish. Neg. μή.

> πολλά γε μανθάνοιμι· εἴθε μὴ χαλεπὸν εἴη.
> *Many things at least may I learn—if only it were not difficult!*

SUMMARY OF ADDITIONAL GRAMMAR SEEN IN BOOK TWO

DECLENSION

MASC. NOUNS OF THE FIRST DECLENSION (#779):

Same as fem., except in sg. nom., gen., voc.:

	NOM.	GEN.	VOC.
κυβερνή	-της	āο (εω, ω)	α
Ἀίδ	-ης	āο (εω, ω)	η
Ἑρμεί	-ᾱς	āο (εω, ω)	ᾱ

DATIVE PLURAL IN -σσι(ν) (#786):

Occasional substitute for -σι or -εσσι.

E.g.: λέχεσσι, ποσσίν

SPECIAL FORMS OF βοῦς (#850):

Besides those regularly formed on stem βο-:

Acc. sg.: βοῦν (for βόα)
Acc. pl.: βοῦς (for βόας)
Dat. pl.: βουσί (for βόεσσι)

PECULIAR PERFECT PARTICIPLES (#798):

A few may retain ω: τεθνηῶτος, μεμαῶτα

USE OF CASES

GENITIVE OF COMPARISON (#955):

(Instead of ἤ and nom. or acc., use gen.)

οὐδεὶς πατέρος μοι φίλτερος.
No one is dearer to me than my father.

DATIVE OF CAUSE (#804):

φιλότητι   *out of friendship*
ὄλβῳ   *because of wealth*

ACCUSATIVE OF EXTENT (TIME OR SPACE) (#785):

νύκτας εὕδουσι.
They sleep through the night

VERBS

ἦμαι I SIT (#835):

Non-thematic, may drop sigma; in 3 pl., root-vowel is either ἠ- or εἰ-.

PRES.	IMPF.
ἦμαι	ἤμην
ἦσαι	ἧσο
ἧσται	ἧστο
ἤμεθα	ἤμεθα
ἧσθε	ἧσθε
ἧνται, εἴαται	ἧντο, εἴατο

IRREG. FORMS OF εἶμι I GO, I SHALL GO (#861):

Ind. 3 sg.: εἶσι(ν) he goes, he will go; Inf.: ἴμεν(αι) to go; Ptc.: ἰών going.

USES OF TENSES

GNOMIC AORIST (#923):

To express general truths or proverbs.
νοῦσος ἐξείλετο θυμόν.
Disease takes away life.

FUTURE PARTICIPLE OF PURPOSE (#910)

To express the reason for an action.
εἵματα ἄγομαι πλυνεοῦσα.
I am bringing the clothes to wash them.

PRONOUNS

οὗτος, αὕτη, τοῦτο: THIS (#935)

οὗτος	αὕτη	τοῦτο
τούτου, οιο	ταύτης	τούτου, οιο
τούτῳ	ταύτῃ	τούτῳ
τοῦτον	ταύτην	τοῦτο
οὗτοι	αὗται	ταῦτα
τούτων	ταυτάων	τούτων
τούτοισ(ι)	ταύτῃσ(ι)	τούτοισ(ι)
τούτους	ταύτας	ταῦτα

USE: (1) referring to connection with person addressed: τοῦτο γέρας = *This prize* (of yours).
(2) referring back: ταῦτα εἶπε = *he said this* (which I reported).

τοιοῦτος, τοιαύτη, τοιοῦτον: SUCH (#941):

τοι- plus regular οὗτος forms (without initial τ), but n. nom. and acc. sg. add ν. E.g.: τοιοῦτον, τοιαῦτας.

τοιόσδε, τοιήδε, τοιόνδε: SUCH AS (#1149):

τοι- and -δε not decline; -οσ-, -η-, -ον- declined as usual. E.g., τοιῇδε, τοιῶδε.

SPECIAL CORRELATIVES

IDIOMATIC USES (#855):

ἕτερος . . . ἕτερος = *the one . . . the other.*
ἄλλοθεν ἄλλος = *one from one direction, others from other directions.*
ἄλλοτε . . . ἄλλοτε = *at one time . . . at another.*

CRASIS

Fusion of two words by contraction of adjacent vowels (#1050): τἄλλα (= τὰ ἄλλα), προὔφαινον (= πρὸ ἔφαινον).

APPENDIX B

REVIEW VOCABULARY LIST BY LESSONS

6	**10**	**14**	108 μή	143 δοκέω	**25**
1 ἀπό	36 αἶψα	72 αὐτός	109 μηδέ	144 ὄμβρος	180 ἀμείβομαι
2 γάρ	37 εἰ	73 ἐγγύς	110 φέρω	145 οὐδέ	181 γέ
3 ἐκ	38 εἰμί	74 ἕτερος	111 φιλέω	146 παντοῖος	182 δείδω
4 ἐν	39 εἰς	75 ἡμέτερος	112 ὡς	147 πάρ-ειμι	183 εἴρομαι
5 ἐπί	40 κατά	76 καρπός		148 πίπτω	184 ἱερός
6 καί	41 λέγω	77 κεῖνος	**18**	149 που	185 νηός
7 σύν	42 ποτε	78 ὅς	113 ἐννέπω	150 ποῦ	186 πεύθομαι
8 ὑπό	43 πρός	79 ὀφθαλμός	114 ἐπεί	151 σπεύδω	187 πρῶτος
	44 φίλη	80 πολλός	115 ἔχω	152 τρέφω	188 σώζω
7		81 πόνος	116 ἵνα	153 φρονέω	
9 ἀληθείη	**11**	82 ποταμός	117 κεύθω		**26**
10 ἀρετή	45 ἄνθρωπος	83 Χριστός	118 ὅπως	**22**	189 ἀπ-ολλύω
11 βίη	46 θεός		119 ὅτι	154 ἀέξω	190 ἐμός
12 δίκη	47 ἰητρός	**15**	120 ὄφρα	155 αἰτέω	191 ἔρχομαι
13 εἰρήνη	48 λόγος	84 βροτός	121 παρ-έχω	156 ἥδομαι	192 ζωή
14 κᾱλή	49 μοῦνος	85 ἑός	122 ῥέζω	157 λαμβάνω	193 κασιγνητός
15 πέτρη	50 νήπιος	86 θησαυρός		158 μαχ(έ)ομαι	194 οὐρανός
16 φιλεομένη	51 σοφός	87 θνητός	**19**	159 μετά	195 παρ-έρχομαι
17 ψῡχή	52 ὑψηλός	88 κρατερός	123 ἀδικέω	160 οὖν	196 πῶς
	53 φίλος	89 νόος	124 διώκω	161 πλησίος	197 πως
8		90 νοῦσος	125 εἴθε	162 τρέπω	198 σῖτος
18 ἀλλά	**12**	91 ὁ, ἡ, τό	126 ἐσθίω		
19 γαῖα	54 βίος	92 πονηρός	127 ἱκάνω	**23**	**27**
20 δόξα	55 δένδρεον	93 χαλεπός	128 κελεύω	163 ἀν-έχομαι	199 ἄναξ
21 ἡδεῖα	56 δίκαιος		129 ποιέω	164 γίγνομαι	200 ἀνήρ
22 θάλασσα	57 εἵνεκα	**16**	130 φοιτάω	165 ἑταῖρος	201 ἕκαστος
23 μὲν...δέ	58 ἔργον	94 αἰσχρός		166 ἠέλιος	202 ἤ
24 οὐ	59 θάνατος	95 γιγνώσκω	**20**	167 μῑσέω	203 ἤ...ἤ
25 οὔτε	60 κακός	96 λίθος	131 ἐθέλω	168 ὀρθός	204 μέτρον
26 οὔτε...οὔτε	61 ὁμοῖος	97 λύω	132 ἔφη	169 πῑνω	205 παῖς
27 φιλέουσα	62 π(τ)όλεμος	98 ὄλβος	133 ζώω	170 ὤ	206 περ
	63 χρῡσός	99 ὁράω	134 ἠδέ		207 φύσις
9		100 ῥηίδιος	135 νοέω	**24**	208 φαίνω
28 ἀγαθή	**13**	101 χρόνος	136 παρά	171 ἄπ-ειμι	
29 αἰεί	64 δῶρον		137 φεύγω	172 αὐτάρ	**28**
30 ἀνάγκη	65 ἐσθλός	**17**	138 χρή	173 δυνατός	209 διά
31 ἀρχή	66 θῡμός	102 ἄγω		174 μέλλω	210 ἔπος
32 δή	67 ξεῖνος	103 ἄν	**21**	175 ὄφρα	211 κῆρ
33 νῦν	68 ὀλίγος	104 εὕδω	139 ἀθάνατος	176 πέλω	212 μῆκος
34 οὕτως	69 σχέτλιος	105 θνήσκω	140 ἁμαρτάνω	177 πέμπω	213 πρᾶγμα
35 φωνή	70 τε	106 κε(ν)	141 διδάσκω	178 σός	214 πῦρ
	71 τε...τε	107 μανθάνω	142 δίς	179 τοί	215 σῶμα

216 τῇ	*33*	*39*	*47*	358 βοῦς	395 ὠκύς
217 τῇδε	255 δέχομαι	292 ἄκρος	326 εἶπον	359 θυγάτηρ	
218 φάος	256 εὑρίσκω	293 ἄλληλοι	327 κεῖμαι	360 νόστιμος	*71*
219 χρῆμα	257 εὐρύς	294 ἅμα	328 κρύπτω	361 ὀλλύω	396 ἅλς
	258 λαός	295 ἔπειτα	329 τότε	362 Ὑπερίων	397 ἕζομαι
29	259 ὁδός	296 κόσμος			398 ἑξῆς
220 αἱρέω	260 οἶνος	297 μακρός	*48*	*64*	399 ἐρετμόν
221 ἀληθής	261 πόθεν		330 ἀμφί	363 ἀτάρ	400 καθ-ίζω
222 ἡδονή	262 σύ	*40*	331 κτείνω	364 ἔδω	401 κληΐς
223 ἡδύς		298 αὐλή	332 μήτηρ	365 εἶδαρ	402 πολιός
224 κρίνω	*34*	299 ἔλπω	333 πατήρ	366 ἐννῆμαρ	403 τύπτω
225 μάκαρ	263 γόνυ	300 εὔχομαι		367 ἐπι-βαίνω	
226 πρόφρων	264 εἰσ-έρχομαι	301 ποιμήν	*49*	368 Λωτοφάγοι	*73*
227 πτερόεις	265 ἐντολή		334 δεύτερος	369 ὀλοός	404 ἦμος
228 χρηστός.	266 ζητέω	*41*	335 Ζεύς		405 ἠριγένεια
	267 πύλη	302 ἀπάνευθε		*65*	406 Ἠώς
30	268 υἱός	303 περί	*50*	370 ἀφύσσω	407 μίμνω
229 ἅπας		304 πόρον	336 δέκατος	371 δεῖπνον	408 ῥοδοδάκτυλος
230 εἷς	*35*	305 τελέω	337 μέγας	372 ἔνθα	
231 ἥμισυς	269 Ἀπόλλων		338 νύξ	373 θοός	*74*
232 μηδείς	270 δύω	*42*	339 οἰκέω		409 ἄγριος
233 οὐδείς	271 ἐπήν	306 βαίνω		*67*	410 ἀνά, ἄμ
234 πᾶς	272 ἦν	307 ῥέω	*51*	374 δίδωμι	
235 πειράω	273 μάλα	308 στῆν	340 ἅζομαι	375 ἵημι	*75*
236 πατρίς	274 ὅτε	309 τλάω	341 μέλος	376 ἰών	411 ἄγχι
	275 τεύχω		342 χείρ	377 ὀπάζω	412 αἴξ
31		*43*		378 πατέομαι	413 ἀφ-ικνέομαι
237 ἄνεμος	*36*	310 ἄλγος	*52*	379 προ-ίημι	414 ὄϊς
238 ἄρα, ῥα	276 βουλεύω	311 λείπω	343 ἀνα-βαίνω	380 χθών	415 σπέος
239 ἔρδω	277 βουλή	312 ὀΐω	344 κέρδιον		416 χῶρος
240 ἔτι	278 γαμέω	313 ποθέω	345 λιλαίομαι	*68*	
241 νέκταρ	279 θέμις			381 λωτός	*76*
242 ὅς τις	280 λανθάνω	*44*	*53*	382 μήδομαι	417 ἀπόπροθεν
243 πείθω	281 πω	314 βάλλω	346 ἀλέομαι	383 ὄλεθρος	418 ἰδέ
244 τις		315 εὖ	347 θύρη		419 οἶος
245 τίς	*37*	316 μένω	348 κράτος	*69*	420 πελώριος
	282 βασιλείη	317 σάρξ	349 νηῦς	384 αὐτοῦ	
32	283 ἐάω		350 οὖλος	385 μελιηδής	*77*
246 ἄλλος	284 πάσχω	*45*		386 νέομαι	421 ἀρνειός
247 βούλομαι	285 πονέομαι	318 ἀγάπη	*61*	387 τίθημι	422 θυρεός
248 γλυκύς	286 χάρις	319 γυνή	351 Τροίη		423 ἵστημι
249 ἐγώ(ν)		320 δόλος		*70*	424 ὄρος
250 ἔνθεν	*38*	321 ἔοικα	*62*	388 γλαφυρός	
251 μίσγω	287 ἀείρω		352 ἄστυ	389 δέω	*79*
252 Μοῦσα	288 ἦμαρ	*46*	353 (ἐ)ρύομαι	390 ἐρίηρος	425 ἀγλαός
253 ὕδωρ	289 μῆλον	322 μέσ(σ)ος	354 νόστος	391 ἐρύω	426 ἄμαξα
254 φρήν	290 πιστεύω	323 οἶκος	355 πόντος	392 κέλομαι	427 ἀσκός
	291 χαίρω	324 πάλιν	356 ὡς, ὥς	393 κλαίω	428 μέλας
		325 σφέτερος	357 ἀφ-αιρέομαι	394 οἶδα	429 ὑψόσε

80
430 ἄλοχος
431 ἀμφίπολος
432 δμώς
433 ἑπτά
434 εὐ-εργής
435 κρητήρ

81
436 ἀγήνωρ
437 ἀπ-έχω
438 αὐτίκα
439 ἐμ-πίπλημι
440 ἐπ-έρχομαι
441 θεσπέσιος
442 χέω

82
443 ἄντρον
444 ἄρνες
445 ἔνδον
446 καρπάλιμος
447 πίων
448 σηκός
449 τυρός

83
450 αἴνυμαι
451 ἁλμυρός
452 ἤ
453 λίσσομαι
454 ξείνιον
455 πολύς

85
456 ἀπο-σεύω
457 ἔντοσθεν
459 ἤμενος
459 ἧος
460 καίω
461 νέμω
462 ὄβριμος
463 ὕλη

86
464 ἀμέλγω
465 ἄρσην
466 βαθύς
467 ἐλαύνω
468 ἐπι-τίθημι
469 ὅσ(σ)ος
470 τόσ(σ)ος

87
471 αὖτε
472 εἰσ-οράω
473 ἔμβρυον
474 κατα-τίθημι
475 λευκός
476 μοῖρα

88
477 ἀλάομαι
478 ἦτορ
479 κέλευθος
480 οἶος
481 πλέω
482 ὑγρός
483 ὑπέρ
484 φημί
485 φθόγγος

89
486 Ἀγαμέμνων
487 Ἀχαιοί
488 λαῖτμα
489 οἴκαδε
490 π(τ)όλις
491 προσ-εῖπον

91
492 αἰδέομαι
493 ἱκεταί
494 ἱκνέομαι
495 κιχάνω
496 νηλ(ε)ής
497 ὄπ(π)ῃ

92
498 αἰγίοχος
499 ἆσσον
500 δύναμαι
501 Κύκλωψ
502 σχεδόν

93
503 αἰπύς
504 μάρπτω
505 μηρός
506 πεῖραρ
507 Ποσειδάων

94
508 ἀνδρόμεος
509 δόρπον
510 κρέα
511 ξίφος
512 ὁπλίζω
513 ὀστέον

95
514 δῖος
515 ἐπι-μαίομαι
516 μεγαλήτωρ
517 ὅθι
518 ὀξύς
519 στενάχω

97
520 Ἀθήνη
521 ἄψ
522 κλυτός
523 τίνω

98
524 ἐλαΐνεος
525 ἱστός
526 παρ-ίσταμαι
527 χλωρός

99
528 ἀνώγω
529 μοχλός
530 ὕπνος

100
531 αἷμα
532 ὄνομα
533 τρίς

101
534 αὖ
535 ἐλεέω
536 προσ-αυδάω

103
537 αἰνῶς
538 ἄρουρα
539 αὖτις
540 τεός

104
541 μειλίχιος
542 Οὖτις
543 παχύς
544 πρόσθε(ν)

105
545 ἅπτω
546 δαίμων
547 Ἦ
548 ἐκ-σεύω
549 τάχα

106
550 ἀϋτμή
551 βλέφαρον
552 δόρυ
553 ὀφρύς

107
554 ἰάχω
555 οἰμώζω
556 ὧδε

109
557 ἄλλοθεν
558 βοάω
559 Πολύφημος
560 ῥίπτω

110
561 ἀμύμων
562 βιάζω
563 στείχω

111
564 ἐγγύθεν
565 πετάννυμι
566 ὑφαίνω

112
567 ἀκέων
568 ὕστατος

113
569 γαστήρ
570 νῶτον
571 φώς

115
572 θῆλυς
573 πυκ(ι)νός
574 τείρω

116
575 δαμάζω
576 λυγρός
577 σταθμός

117
578 μένος
579 τῷ

118
580 γοάω
581 λίην
582 καὶ λίην

119
583 γεγωνέω
584 ἔσθω

121
585 Αἴολος
586 δώδεκα
587 ἕξ
588 μέγαρον
589 ναίω
590 νῆσος
591 τεῖχος
592 χάλκεος

122
593 αἰδοῖος
594 δαίνυμι
595 δῶμα
596 λέχος
597 μῦρίος

123
598 ἠμέν
599 Ἴλιος
600 κατα-λέγω
601 Κρονίων
602 μήν
603 ὄρνῦμι
604 παύω
605 πομπή

124
606 ἄημι
607 ἀργύρεος
608 ἐκ-τελέω
609 Ζέφυρος
610 φαεινός

125
611 ἀγορεύω
612 ἄργυρος
613 ἤδη
614 κάμνω
615 λεύσσω
616 νωμάω
617 πούς

126
618 πόποι
619 φιλότης
620 χαρίζομαι

127
621 ἁρπάζω
622 ἐγείρω
623 ζωός
624 θύελλα
625 μερμηρίζω
626 νῑκάω
627 ὀρούω

128
628 ἤπειρος
629 καλύπτω
630 κῆρυξ
631 τέκος

129
632 ἀπο-πέμπω
633 ἄχνυμαι
634 ἐνδυκέως
635 ἐρέω
636 θαμβέω
637 Ὀδυσ(σ)εύς
638 οὐδός

130
639 ἀλεγεινός
640 βαρύς
641 δόμος
642 κομίζω
643 μαλακός
644 μῦθος

132
645 δάκρυον
646 δεινός
647 ἐϋπλόκαμος
648 θαλερός
649 ἱστίον
650 κατ-έρχομαι
651 Κίρκη
652 κυανόπρωρος
653 οὖρος

133
654 ἀγυιά
655 δύω
656 ἧμαι
657 κυβερνήτης

134
661 ἀήρ
662 ἀστερόεις
663 δειλός
664 νεφέλη
665 ὁπ(π)ότε
666 ῥόος
667 φράζω

135
668 βόθρος
669 Εὐρύλοχος
670 νέκῡς

136
671 ἀγείρω
672 γουνόομαι
673 ἔθνος
674 ἱερεύω
675 Ἰθάκη
676 κάρηνα
677 κατα-θνήσκω
678 κελαινεφής
679 πυρή
680 Τειρεσίης

137
681 γέρων
682 δέος
683 εἶμι
684 νύμφη
685 οὐτάω
686 τεύχεα
687 χαλκήρης

138
688 Ἀίδης
689 δέρω
690 ἐπ-οτρύνω
691 ἴφθῑμος
692 κατά-κειμαι
693 Περσεφόνεια
694 πρίν

658 ὅπλον
659 τείνω
660 Ὠκεανός

139
697 ἀχε(ύ)ω
698 Θηβαῖος
699 κατα-λείπω
700 πρότερος
701 σκῆπτρον
702 χρύσε(ι)ος

140
703 δῖογενής
704 δύστηνος
705 Λᾱερτιάδης
706 μάντις
707 νημερτής
708 πολυμήχανος
709 τίπτε
710 φάσγανον

141
711 αἰ
712 ἀργαλέος
713 βόσκω
714 ἐννοσίγαιος
715 ἐρύκω
716 ἴφιος
717 πελάζω
718 φαίδιμος
719 χώομαι

143
720 ἀλύσκω
721 ἀντίθεος
722 βίοτος
723 ἕδνα, ἔεδνα
724 μνάομαι
725 πῆμα
726 ὑπερφίαλος

144
727 εὐήρης
728 μνηστήρ

145
729 γῆρας

695 σφάζω
696 χαλκός

730 εἴρω
731 ἑκατόμβη
732 ἐξείης
733 κάπρος
734 λιπαρός
735 ὄλβιος
736 πήγνῡμι
737 σῆμα
738 σῦς
739 τοῖος
740 ὦμος

146
741 ἀτρεκέως

147
742 ἔ(ι)σω
743 ἔμπεδος
744 θέσφατος
745 ὀλοφύρομαι
746 ὀπίσ(σ)ω

148
747 ἐνθάδε
748 πεζός
749 περάω
750 τέκνον

149
751 ἀγανός
752 Ἄρτεμις
753 βέλος
754 ἐπ-οίχομαι
755 ἕπομαι
756 ἰοχέαιρα
757 κατά-πεφνον
758 κήρ
759 νύ
760 ὀϊζύς
761 Τρῶες
762 χρε(ι)ώ

150
763 γέρας
764 πότν(ι)α
765 φθί(ν)ω
766 φυλάσσω

151	156	162	178
767 ἀγρός	807 ἀνάσσω	844 δεσμός	881 Σκύλλη	912 ἀράομαι
768 αὐτόθι	808 ἄφαρ	845 θεά	882 ὦκα	913 Ὄλυμπος
769 δαίς	809 ἐξ-εναρίζω	846 λειμών		914 ὄρνις
770 εἷμα	810 θήβη	847 μετ-αυδάω	170	915 σκέπας
771 ἔκηλος		848 μῦθέομαι	883 ἑτέρωθι	
772 ἕννῦμι	157	849 πιέζω	884 κοῖλος	179
773 εὐνή	811 δηλέομαι	850 Σειρήν	885 κῦάνεος	916 χολόω
774 Ἶσος	812 κατα-κτείνω		886 κυκάω	
775 καλέω	813 πῶυ	163		180
776 σῖγαλόεις	814 χέρσος	851 ἀν-ίστημι	171	917 ἐΰσσελμος
777 τέμενος		852 ἀπήμων	887 ἀσπαίρω	918 εὐχετάομαι
778 χλαῖνα	158	853 ἐπ-είγω	888 δηϊοτής	919 κνίση
779 χρώς	815 ἀφνειός	854 κοιμάω	889 ἰχθύς	920 ὀβελός
	816 γάμος	855 κῦμα	890 κλάζω	921 πείρω
152	817 οἰκτρός	856 πιφαύσκω	891 ὕπερθεν	922 σπένδω
780 ἀλωή	818 τράπεζα	857 τόφρα		923 τῆλε
781 ἐφ-έπω	819 ὑσμίνη		173	
782 κλίνω	820 φόνος	165	892 αὔτως	181
783 μάλιστα		858 ἀλείφω	893 γυῖον	924 ἄγγελος
784 πάντη	159	859 ἀοιδή	894 κάματος	925 ἀμφίελισσα
785 πένθος	821 ἀεικής	860 αὐγή	895 κλύω	926 ἄτη
786 πότμος	822 αἰνός	861 ἰαίνω	896 σιδήρεος	927 θίς
787 στυγερός	823 ἀκούω	862 κηρός		928 κίω
788 τέθηλα, τέθαλα	824 ἔξοχα	863 ὁμοῦ	174	
789 φύλλον	825 ἐρείδω	864 οὖας	897 ἀέκητι	182
	826 κουρίδιος	865 ῥίμφα	898 αἰνέω	929 κεάζω
154	827 ὄψ	866 στιβαρός	899 Νότος	930 κεραυνός
790 ἀγαυός	828 πόσις			931 οἶνοψ
791 ἀμφότερος	829 προτί, ποτί	166	176	932 φαείνω
792 ἄχος	830 Πρίαμος	867 δεῦρο	900 βρώμη, βρῶσις	
793 γόος	831 στόμα	868 κῦδος	901 ἐδητύς	183
794 ἐφ-ορμάω	832 τοιοῦτος	869 μογέω	902 ἔρος	933 νεικέω
795 μέμαα			903 λιμήν	
796 ὀδύρομαι	160	168	904 ὄμνῦμι	184
797 ὄνειρος	833 γλυκερός	870 (ἐ)έργω	905 ὅρκος	934 ἄμυδις
798 ὀτρύνω	834 μενεαίνω	871 εἰλ(έ)ω	906 πόσις	935 ἀπο-αίνυμαι
799 πέτομαι	835 μήν	872 ἐκτός	907 τελευτάω	936 ἐλίσσω
800 τέρπω	836 νέφος	873 ἐπι-τέλλω		937 θέω
801 φωνέω	837 σκιόεις	874 κεῖσε	177	938 κατα-χέω
		875 μιμνήσκω	908 ἀγορή	939 κεφαλή
155	161	876 σκόπελος	909 λαῖλαψ	940 πλήσσω
802 αἰθόμενος	838 κάρη		910 νεφεληγερέτα	941 ῥήγνῦμι
803 ἠΰτε	839 κονίη	169	911 χορός	
804 ἴς	840 κυλίνδω	877 θωρήσσω		185
805 μετόπισθε(ν)	841 λᾶας	878 ἴκρια		942 Καλυψώ
806 οὗτος	842 λόφος	879 ὄσσε		943 στῆθος
	843 ὠθέω	880 παπταίνω		944 Ὠγυγίη

187
945 ἀγγελίη
946 ἄμβροτος
947 ἀτρύγετος
948 σχεδίη

188
949 ἀδινός
950 Ἀλκίνοος
951 γηθέω
952 ἐνοσίχθων
953 νήχω
954 ὀρίνω
955 Φαίηκες

189
956 ἀμβρόσιος
957 ἀπείρων
958 (ἐ)είδομαι

190
959 ἀπήνη
960 ἀραρίσκω
961 ἡμίονος
962 μέλω
963 τρεῖς

191
964 ἐδωδή
965 ἔλαιον
966 ἐσθής
967 ἐΰξεστος
968 ζεύγνῡμι
969 ἡνία
970 θάλαμος
971 κούρη

192
972 ἔρις
973 καθαίρω
974 λοέω
975 περικαλλής
976 σεύω
977 χρίω

193
978 γλαυκῶπις
979 δμωή

980 ἔλαφος
981 ἡγέομαι
982 κρήδεμνον
983 λευκώλενος
984 Ναυσικάα
985 πτύσσω
986 ῥεῖα

194
987 ἀϋτή
988 ἀΰω
989 ὁρμαίνω

195
990 ἀλκή
991 ἅλμη
992 ἄντα
993 δαίω
994 δείχνῡμι
995 λέων
996 σμερδαλέος

196
997 εἶδος
998 ναιετάω

198
999 δήν
1000 κῆδος
1001 νέος
1002 πάροιθε(ν)

199
1003 ἀντίος
1004 δυσμενής
1005 ἐλεαίρω
1006 ἔμπης

201
1007 δηρόν
1008 φᾶρος
1009 χιτών

202
1010 κάλλος
1011 κόμη
1012 χαρίεις

203
1013 ἀνδάνω
1014 πολύτλας
1015 τοιόσδε

204
1016 ἀλεείνω
1017 δαΐφρων
1018 ἡγεμονεύω
1019 ὀνομάζω

205
1020 πλάζω
1021 νεμεσ(σ)άω

206
1022 τυγχάνω

207
1023 ἐϋκτίμενος
1024 ἥρως
1025 θρόνος
1026 ὄπι(σ)θεν

209
1027 θαυμάζω
1028 πολύμητις

210
1029 ἄκοιτις
1030 αὖθι
1031 κρείων
1032 νοστέω

211
1033 ἵππος
1034 πεδίον
1035 πορφύρεος
1036 πρήσσω
1037 τάμνω

212
1038 ἀστήρ
1039 Ἕκτωρ
1040 Ἠετίων
1041 κόλπος

213
1042 Ἀχιλ(λ)εύς
1043 δαιδάλεος
1043 δαιμόνιος
1045 ἔντεα
1046 σιωπή
1047 φύω

214
1048 ἄλκιμος
1049 ἄποινα
1050 ποδάρκη
1051 πύργος

215
1052 ἄρνυμαι
1053 δακρυόεις
1054 κλέος
1055 κορυθαίολος
1056 νόσφι(ν)
1057 χαλκοχίτων

216
1058 ἀμύνω
1059 βοή
1060 ἱππόδαμος
1061 κόρυς
1062 νεύω

217
1063 κυνέω
1064 πάλλω

218
1065 αἶσα
1066 ἀνδροφόνος

220
1067 αἰχμή
1068 ἀντικρύ
1068 αὐχήν
1070 ἔγχος
1071 εἴκω
1081 ὁρμάω
1082 σάκος
1083 στέρνον

221
1084 ἅλις
1085 κύων
1086 λαγχάνω
1087 οἰωνός
1088 τίκτω
1089 τοκεύς
1090 ὑπόδρα

222
1091 ἀέκων
1092 δίφρος
1093 ἕλκω
1094 πάρος
1095 τέλος

223
1096 ἀγγέλω
1097 κραδίη
1098 ὅμιλος

224
1099 ἀμφίς
1100 θεοειδής
1101 ἵζω
1102 ἰθύς

225
1103 ἄλλοτε
1104 ἵμερος
1105 πάτρη
1106 προπάροιθεν

227
1107 καίνυμαι
1108 μάχη
1109 τηλόθι

228
1110 π(τ)ολεμίζω
1111 χόλος

229
1112 αἶθοψ
1113 ἄσπετος
1114 διοτρεφής
1115 ἐϋκνήμῑς

ALPHABETICAL LIST OF DERIVATIVES SEEN IN BOOK II
The numerals refer to the section in which the words are explained.

actinic 845
air 845
ambrosial 1093
analysis 997
analytical 997
anarchy 1112
aposiopēsis 1199
apostrophe 971
archbishop 1112
archconspirator 1112
archenemy 1112
architect 1112
architecture 1112
Aspasia 961
aster 1194
asterisk 1194
asteroid 1194
astronomy 1040
Atlantic 1077
Atlas 1077
atmosphere 1117
autocephalous 1072

brontosaurus 1072

calliope 961
cataleptic 871
catalepsy 871
categorical 805
category 805
chameleon 1241
chest 1102
chlorophyl 928
choral 1040
chorus 1040
chrism 1107
clinic 928
coma 981
comet 1150
cosmopolite 1159
cyanide 1011
cylinder 971
cynic 1232
cynical 1232

democracy 845
democrat 845
dermatologist 1180
Dodecanese 780
dome 787

dynamite 823

ectoderm 1002
emetic 1011
endemic 845
Eolian Harp 780
epidemic 845
epistemology 1035
epitaph 1262
eristic 1107
esoteric 905
ether 942
ethereal 942
ethnic 856
ethnology 856
etesian 1084
exegesis 1112

gymnasium 1122
gymnastics 1122

hebdomadal 1067
hegemony 1112
hemorrhage 1072
hero 1173
heroic 1173
heroine 1173
hex- 780
hippodrome 1189
hippopotamus 1189
homonym 810
hormone 1227
hyacinth 1150
hypodermic 1180

iconoclast 1024
icosihedron 1232

kerosine 988
kudos 993

melon 966
myriad 787
myth 828
mythology 828

necromancy 876
nemesis 1164
nymph 862

Olympian 1045
oneiromancy 936
optical 1212
optics 1212
ornithology 1045

panacea 823
panegyric 856
panoply 840
pause 793
Peloponnesus 780
Pentecost 1250
phenol 799
Philip 1189
pomp 793
pore 1016
pterodactyl 891
purple 1189

rhinoceros 1016

sceptic 1016
sceptre 871
Sebastian 1133
semantics 896
semaphore 896
Sevastopol 1133
siren 976
sphere 1117
squirrel 936
sycamore 966
sycophant 966
symbol 896
symbolic 896
symbolism 896

tantalize 966
tapestry 787
technical 1150
technician 1150
technique 1150
throne 1173
tomb 1262
trapeze 956
trapezium 956
trapezoid 956

zephyr 799
zeugma 1102
zone 1212

ODYSSEUS' ROUTE

The geographical identification of places along Odysseus' route home from Troy cannot always be determined, and has for centuries been a source of puzzlement and controversy. In ancient times, Crates of Mallos, director in the second century B.C. of the great library at Pergamum, maintained that all Odysseus' adventures occurred in Outer Ocean (the Atlantic) beyond the Pillars of Hercules (that is, West of Gibraltar). The great scholar Eratosthenes, head of the library in Alexandria a century earlier, had rejected any validity in identifying particular places with what Homer relates, and held that all the locations were imaginary. He tartly said "You will find the route of Odysseus when you have found the fellow who sewed up that bag of winds." The Greek historian Polybius also doubted the reality of specific geographical identifications for sites in the poem. But the learned geographer Strabo in the early first century A.D. stoutly defended old popular and local traditions on Odyssean sites as worthy of cautious consideration. He said that these ancient traditions should not be pressed to give accurate information in all instances; but neither should they be brushed aside as baseless and ungrounded in realities of the Mediterranean world.

Some places mentioned by Homer are clearly historical and certain, such as Troy itself and Cape Maleia on the SE tip of Greece. Some are obviously imaginary, such as the 'floating island' home of Aeolus. But most can be plausibly located within the context of the Mediterranean shores and islands, though details are often poetic invention and distances and directions between sites are frequently unreal—it is not likely that Homer had accurate knowledge or reports of all places he associates with Odysseus' travels, or even cared for such accuracy; he was, after all, a creative poet, not a scientist or research scholar. Besides, the story is full of fantastic tales and events and is meant to be thought of as happening, at least in part, in an unreal fairyland beyond the known world familiar to its hearers.

Many modern scholars have attempted to locate the Odyssean sites, notably Bérard, Lessing, Bradford, Moulinier, Obregon, Luce (cp. Appendix E #5). Some places all agree upon, others are variously interpreted—sometimes quite implausibly. The map offered here, at the beginning of the Homer readings in Lesson 61 and again at the front of Book II, corresponds with these scholars' identifications of some sites but not all. It is *based on the actual data provided by the poem* and on the realities of Mediterranean geography, always with the assumption that what Homer says will not fit the topographical facts in every case, and that where he does locate adventures in places that can be identified, his statements of direction and distance and mutual relationship may not always be accurate in detail. Homer had no map to rely on, and travellers' reports about places West of Greece were often vague and confused. And some scenes of action were conscious imaginative creations of the poet.

Troy is firmly enough located, since Schliemann rediscovered it. From there, the first place visited is the land of the *Cicones* and their town Ismaros, where Maron gave Odysseus the rich wine by which he later drugged the Cyclops (*Od.*9.39–66, 196–198). Herodotus located the Cicones on the coast of Thrace, NW of Troy.

From there, Odysseus is blown by a wind from the North (*Od.* 9.67–) to the SE tip of Greece, *Cape Maleia,* and around the S edge of Cythera island (Od.9.80–81). He intended to sail northward home to Ithaca, but a strong wind from the N blew the ships for nine days, bringing them to the land of the *Lotus Eaters* (*Od.*9.79–85). The distance and direction locates this on the western coast of North Africa, very plausibly the small island of Djerba off modern Tunisia, where Strabo put it, following an ancient tradition.

Next they sail on to the land of the *Cyclopes,* with its moutains and caves and the nearby wooded island where Polyphemus lived (*Od.*9.105–119). In view of where Odysseus came from and next went, the Cyclopes are best located at the Western edge of Sicily—not, as many do, on the Eastern coast near Mt. Etna.

Aeolus' realm is described as a "floating island, with sheer rocky cliffs and on all sides an unbreakable bronze wall" (*Od.*10.1-4). This is patently imaginary with no real existence or location. Since it is visited after the Cyclops episode and before the journey toward Ithaca, it must be visualized as lying South of Sicily. The route described in the *Odyssey* does not allow placing Aeolia North of Sicily, among the Aeolian Islands (Stromboli, etc.), which would require Odysseus to pass Scylla and Charybdis on his way from it to Ithaca—which he does not do. But Stromboli's conical shape and actively volcanic nature may have served as a model of the imaginary Island of the Winds.

Aeolus has all the winds except that from the West tied up in a bag, so that Odysseus may be blown homeward—clearly to the East and far away, as the voyage took nine days and nights (*Od.*10.25-28). The *Ithaca* which he seeks to reach is best identified with the island still so named, off the West coast of central Greece. Attemps to locate it elsewhere are not convincing, and the centuries-long tradition must be honored.

When the curious sailors untie the bag of winds and all are blown back to Aeolia (*Od.*10.47-55) the route again is clear and direct. Rejected by Aeolus, they row without help of any wind for six days and nights to *Laestrygonia,* with its deep harbor protected by high enfolding cliffs, in a distant region where the paths of day and night come close together (*Od.*10.76-91). This too is a land of mystery, and will not match the location for it which some propose in Eastern Sicily or in Italy SW of Rome. It can plausibly be placed at Bonifacio in Southern Corsica, where there is a fine enclosed harbor far out of the usual Greek sailor's world.

Only Odysseus' ship escapes the fierce battle with the Laestrygonians, and reaches *Aiaia,* Circe's island (*Od.*10.135-136), described as lying low in the endless sea where all directions are confused (*Od.*10.190-196). The ancients associated this with the heights lying off the West coast of Italy still called Monte Circeo, North of Terracina. Homer likely had no particular place in mind. The witch Circe suitably lived in some hidden area away from human abodes.

On Circe's urging, Odysseus goes to the edge of *Hades,* to consult the ghost of the prophet Tiresias. This is only one day's sail, with a stiff wind from the North (*Od.*10.507; 11.11). It is in the territory of the *Cimmerians,* who live in perpetual mist and darkness, never seeing the sun—perhaps a reference to copper miners working underground in central Italy (*Od.*11.14-22). The location and distance would fit Lake Avernus near Naples, where Vergil clearly places the entry to Hades in Book VI of the *Aeneid.* But Homer's description of the area, along the distant stream of Ocean, seems influenced by the shrine of the Dead in Thesprotia, Western upper Greece, where the river Acheron was traditionally located. We should not look too hard for the Land of the Dead among the living. There is no reason from Homer's text to place Hades beyond the straits of Gibraltar in the far West, and that location will not fit the account of the short trip Southward from Circe's isle.

Odysseus returns without problem from the edge of Hades to *Aiaia* (*Od.*12.1-17), where Circe instructs him on his further voyaging. She says he will pass the island of the *Sirens,* where he must not land (*Od.*12.38-55). This has since ancient times been identified with the small I Galli islets in the Gulf of Salerno a bit South of Capri and Sorrento. It is therefore on his way to Sicily. He reaches it after a short voyage.

Circe tells Odysseus that after escaping the seductive Sirens he has the choice of two routes: either past the Wandering Rocks, whose sheer cliffs are pounded by the roaring sea and belch fire; or through the narrows where on one side dreadful *Charybdis* sucks whole ships into her whirlpool and destruction, while on the other side gruesome snaky-headed *Scylla* snatches sailors from the ships passing by (*Od.*12.56-126). This sounds like alternative ways of getting around Sicily from a Northern approach—but highly colored with fantastic details and fairyland flavor. The Wandering Rocks, with their destructive fire, may hint at volcanic Stromboli and its companion Aeolian Islands off the North coast of Eastern Sicily. There is archaeological evidence that Mycenean Age Greeks visited that area to get its valuable obsidian deposits. But some of the description, and the mention that Jason and the ship Argo passed there, imports details from a different site, associated with the Bosporos entry into the Black Sea NE of Greece. A clear example of Homeric conflation of facts and legends. This route would take Odysseus along the Northern edge of Sicily and to a swing Southward and then Eastward past the big island in a homeward direction for Ithaca. Odysseus chooses the shorter, more direct route down the East coast of Sicily opposite lower Italy. Charybdis is on the Sicilian side, and the sea currents are still strong there, changing direction several times a day under influence of the powerful tides. A rock opposite jutting out from Italy well locates the cave of ravenous Scylla, and is still named after her. Vergil and other post-Homeric authors place Scylla and Charybdis here, between Sicily and Italy at the narrowest point.

After escaping these monstrous dangers, Odysseus arrives "at once" at the Island of the Sun God Hyperion, *Thrinakia,* as Circe had said and where she sternly warned him not to harm the Sun God's splendid cattle (*Od.*12.127–141). This must therefore be off the East coast of Sicily not far from the Northern tip. The name comes from Θρῖναξ, 'trident'. It was latter called Trinakria, 'triple heights'. It is *not* Sicily itself, as often supposed, for which Homer uses the old designation Sikanie (*Od.*24.307), after the historic early inhabitants there, the Sicani. Held on Thrinakia a whole month by winds always blowing from the East or South (therefore pushing a ship away from Ithaca, not toward it; and indicating that Thrinakia is W of their goal and that Ithaca lies to the East), the restless and starving men defy the prohibition of Circe and kill and eat some of the cattle of the Sun. In punishment they are all slain, only Odysseus escaping, since he did not share in their sacrilegious guilt (*Od.*12.271–419).

Odysseus clung to the mast and keel of his shattered ship and was carried by the South wind back to *Scylla and Charybdis,* barely escaping once more with his life (*Od.*12.420–446).

From there, still clinging to part of his ship's wreckage, Odysseus is blown for nine days and nights until he is cast up on *Ogygia,* Calypso's isle (*Od.*12.447–449). This island is described as heavily wooded and "lying at the navel (i.e., center) of the sea" (*Od.*1.50–51). Though its direction from Scylla is not indicated, it seems to be Eastward and somewhat to the North, since the last-mentioned wind was from the South (*Od.*12.427) and it lies on his way home to Ithaca, as subsequent data reveal. If imagined to be below the 'heel' of Italy, it fits these criteria, including being at the center of the whole Mediterranean sea. No actual island exists there. Like Calypso herself, her island is "hidden away' (καλύπτεται) and is legendary.

After being kept on Ogygia for seven years, Odysseus is finally released by direct command of Zeus, acting under pressure from Odysseus' patron goddess Athena (*Od.*1.44–88). With Calypso's help, he builds a sturdy raft, on which he sails for seventeen days until reaching the proximity of *Scheria,* land of the Phaeacians. Poseidon then wrecks his raft in a great storm and the hero has to swim in mighty waves for two days and nights and is dashed against harsh cliffs, but eventually with the help of Athena, who calms all the winds except that from the North, lands on a smoother shore and climbs out of the sea to sleep in exhaustion, till wakened by Nausicaa and her companions and taken to the palace where he is welcomed, honored, and given passage home to Ithaca (*Od.*5.30–42, 268–493). The Phaeacians' island has since ancient times been identified with Kerkyra, modern Corfu, off the West coast of upper Greece. Thucydides (1.25) reports that the inhabitants claimed descent from the legendary Phaeacians and had inherited their skill with ships. The fact that Odysseus steered his raft on the long voyage by always keeping the constellation Bear or Wagon (our 'Big Dipper') on his left, as instructed by Calypso to do (*Od.*5.273–280) shows that he was travelling basically Eastward. He would have missed Scheria, passing too far to the North, except for Athena's intervention in having the North wind blow him Southward to land. The island is described as looking "like a shield lying on the sea" (*Od.*5.281)—which is apt for Kerkyra seen from the NW. Plausible locations on Corfu have been found for the various scenes and events mentioned in the poem. It seems to be the basis for that part of Homer's story.

Finally, Odysseus is taken home to *Ithaca* in a speedy Phaeacian clipper (*Od.*13.70–138), deposited asleep near the bay of Phorcys, from which he goes up to a familiar cave of the local nymphs (*Od.*13.96–199; 344–360), then to his farm and his palace, where he takes vengeance on the Suitors who have been seeking to win Penelope, and is happily reunited with his loyal family. Places for all these events have been found in modern Ithaki, which claims by a firm tradition down the centuries to have been Odysseus' kingdom.

continued on next page

Just as he took some realities of the Trojan War and imaginatively expanded on them into the brilliant story of the *Iliad,* so also Homer took various legends and sagas of heroic adventures in the Mediterranean area and infused them with his extraordinary poetic style to create the *Odyssey,* which is a *poem,* therefore *something made*—a mixture of fact and fancy, in a setting sometimes real but often imaginary and fanciful. Our map of Odysseus' travels has to be a similar combination of geographic realities and poetic fiction. It is *Homer's* map, the only kind suited to be a context and guide to Homer's story.

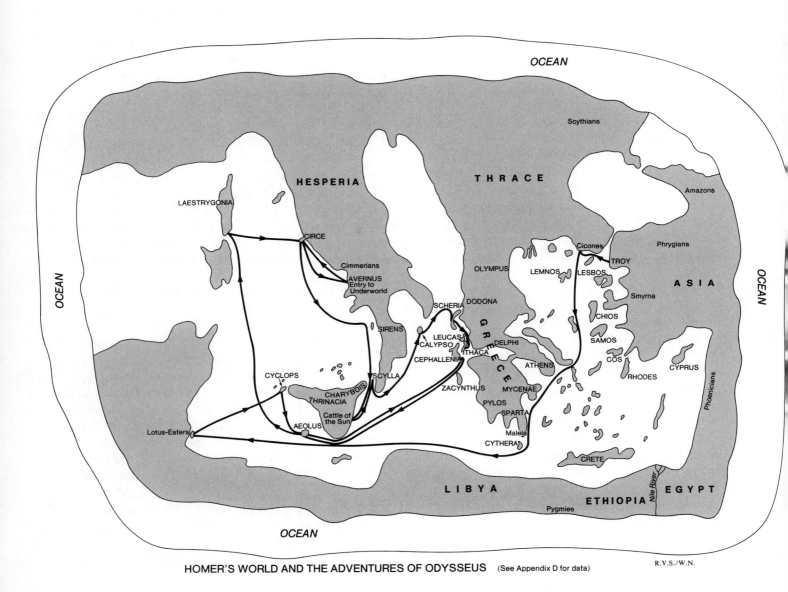

HOMER'S WORLD AND THE ADVENTURES OF ODYSSEUS   (See Appendix D for data)   R.V.S./W.N.

FOR FURTHER READING

Your introduction to Homer and to various facets of general Greek culture has likely stirred an interest for more contact with these fascinating subjects. The following list of books is highly selective — just a few from a vast number. They are recommended as especially useful for broadening your background in Greek literature, art, and civilization. Good libraries have most of them.

1. HOMER IN GENERAL

BASSETT, SAMUEL E., *The Poetry of Homer* (University of California Press, 1938): fine literary analysis.

BEYE, CHARLES R., *The* Iliad, *the* Odyssey, *and the Epic Tradition* (New York, Doubleday, 1966): excellent short introduction to Homeric poems and technique.

BOWRA, C. M., *Homer* (London, Duckworth, 1972): general appreciative study.

JAEGER, WERNER, "Homer the Educator": pp. 35–56 in vol. 1 of his *Paideia* (Harvard University Press, 1944): Homer's unique impact on ancient education.

KIRK, G. S., *The Songs of Homer* (Cambridge University Press, 1962): epic composition, characteristics.

KNIGHT, W. F. JACKSON, *The Many-Minded Homer* (London, Allen & Unwin, 1969): penetrating literary and stylistic appraisal.

LUCE, J. V., *Homer and the Heroic Age* (London, Thames & Hudson, 1975): the world which Homer depicts and our other knowledge of it.

SCOTT, JOHN A., *Homer and His Influence* (Boston, Marshall Jones, 1925): later writers' knowledge and use of Homer.

VIVANTE, PAOLO, *The Homeric Imagination: Homer's Poetic Perception of Reality* (Indiana University Press, 1970): literary analysis.

WACE, ALAN J. B. and FRANK STUBBINGS, *A Companion to Homer* (London, Macmillan, 1962): a survey of all major aspects of Homeric studies — language, authorship of the poems, oral composition, geographical background, archaeogical data, social conditions, religion, armor, food, crafts, etc.

WHITMAN, CEDRIC H., *Homer and the Heroic Tradition* (Harvard University Press, 1958): origins of Homeric epic stories, style, structure.

2. THE *ODYSSEY*

AUSTIN, NORMAN, *Archery at the Dark of the Moon: Poetic Problems in the* Odyssey (University of California Press, 1975): technical analysis of style, use of formulas and patterned themes.

CLARKE, HOWARD W., *The Art of the* Odyssey (New Jersey, Prentice-Hall, 1967): good literary analysis.

COOK, ALBERT, *Homer: The* Odyssey (New York: Norton, 1967): excellent translation. Other good translations are by Lattimore, Rieu, Rouse, Shewring.

FINLEY, JOHN H., *Homer's* Odyssey (Harvard University Press, 1978): fine general study.

FINLEY, M. I., *The World of Odysseus* (New York, Viking, revised edition 1965): study of the social world and daily life portrayed in the poem.

STANFORD, W. B., *The* Odyssey *of Homer* (London, Macmillan, 1965), 2 vols.): complete Greek text with commentary.

STANFORD, W. B., *The Ulysses Theme* (New York, Barnes & Noble, 1963): the story as treated in post-Homeric literature and art down the ages.

TAYLOR, CHARLES H. (editor), *Essays on the* Odyssey (Indiana University Press, 1963): appreciative essays by seven different authors.

3. THE *ILIAD*

ATCHITY, KENNETH J., *Homer's* Iliad: *The Shield of Memory* (Southern Illinois University Press, 1977): Homeric imagery, characters, poetic power.

MONRO, D. B., *Homer:* Iliad (Oxford, Clarendon Press, 4th edition 1897; 2 vols.): complete Greek text with commentary.

RIEU, E. V., *Homer: The* Iliad (Baltimore, Penguin Books, 1950): careful, lively prose translation. Other good translations by Lattimore, Rouse, Chase & Perry.

SCOTT, JOHN A., *The Unity of Homer* (University of California Press, 1921): vigorous defense of the single authorship of the *Iliad* and *Oddysey*.

SHEPPARD, J. T., *The Pattern of the* Iliad (London, Methuen, 1922): unity of design.

WILLCOCK, M. M., *A Commentary on Homer's* Iliad (London, Macmillan, 1970–, 4 vols.): explains forms, grammar, names and objects.

4. ARCHAEOLOGY, BACKGROUND

LORIMER, H. L., *Homer and the Monuments* (London, Macmillan, 1950): a detailed study of archaeological evidence for way of life in the Heroic Age.

MCDONALD, WILLIAM A., *Progress into the Past* (Indiana University Press, 1967): interesting account of archaeological discoveries of Schliemann, Evans, Blegen, others which have illuminated the Homeric world.

NILSSON, M. P., *Homer and Mycenae* (London, Methuen, 1933): brilliant analysis of background of epic world and poetic composition and religious outlook.

PALMER, L. R., *The Interpretation of Mycenean Greek Texts* (Oxford, Clarendon Press, 1963): light thrown on realities of the Heroic Age by the recently deciphered 'Linear B' texts.

WEBSTER, T. B. L., *From Mycenae to Homer* (London, Methuen, 1958): historical data behind Homeric poetry and epic civilization.

5. GEOGRAPHY OF THE *ODYSSEY*

BENY, ROLOFF, *A Time of Gods* (London, Studio, 1962): 'arty' photographs of places he associates with Odysseus' wanderings.

BÉRARD, VICTOR, *Les Navigations d'Ulysse* (Paris, Colin, 1929), 4 vols.): an attempt to identify all places in the poem with actual sites in Mediterranean world.

BRADFORD, ERNLE, *Ulysses Found* (London, Hodder & Stoughton, 1963): effort by a sailor familiar with Mediterraen area to locate Odyssean sites; illustrated.

LESSING, ERICH, *The Voyages of Ulysses* (Freiburg, Herder, 1965): striking photographs of assumed Odyssean sites, with commentary by Michel Gall.

MOULINIER, LOUIS, *Quelques Hypothèses relatives à la Géographie d'Homère dans l'*Odyssée (Aix-en-Provence, Ophrys, 1958): theories on location of episodes in the *Odyssey*.

OBREGON, MAURICIO, *Ulysses Airborne* (New York, Harper & Row, 1971): photographs, many from the air, of assumed Odyssean places.

ROUSSEAU-LIESSENS, A., *Géographie de l'*Odyssée (Bruxelles, Brepols, 1961–, 4 vols.).

STANFORD, W. B., and J. V. LUCE, *The Quest for Ulysses* (London, Phaidon, 1974): chapter six, by Luce, on "The Wanderings of Ulysses," with fine photographs.

6. HOMERIC LANGUAGE

AUTENRIETH, G., *Homeric Dictionary* (1886, reissued 1970 by University of Oklahoma Press): shorter treatment not as detailed or useful as Cunliffe; illustrated.

BENNER, ALLEN R., *Selections from Homer's* Iliad (New York, Appleton-Century, 1903): passages from whole poem, with good notes; short, clear summary of grammar.

CHANTRAINE, P., *Grammaire Homérique* (Paris, 1953, 2 vols.): full data and analysis.

CUNLIFFE, RICHARD J., *A Lexicon of the Homeric Dialect* (London, Blackie, 1924): very intelligent and complete treatment of all Homeric vocabulary, with citation of passages illustrating given meanings and reference of difficult forms to their root word. The best general Homeric dictionary.

DUNBAR, HENRY, *A Complete Concordance to Homer's* Odyssey *and Hymns* (Oxford University Press, 1880): same arrangement as Prendergast.

GEHRING, A., *Index Homericus* (Hildesheim, Olms, 1895), reissued 1970): complete alphabetical list of all words in both poems, broken down into their main forms and compounds, with citation of every place where each form occurs.

LIDDELL, HENRY G. and R. SCOTT and H. S. JONES, *A Greek-English Lexicon* (Oxford, Clarendon Press, 1940, with Supplement 1968): the complete dictionary of ancient Greek, giving all Homeric words at beginning of each entry.

MONRO, D. B., *Grammar of the Homeric Dialect* (Oxford University Press, 2nd edition 1891): good for collation of passages illustrating specific usage; not complete, or always clear.

OWEN, WILLIAM B. and E. J. GOODSPEED, *Homeric Vocabularies* (new edition by University of Oklahoma Press, 1969): very useful lists of all words that occur ten times or oftener in both poems, arranged by categories and frequency.

PHARR, CLYDE, *Homeric Greek* (Boston, Heath, 1924): good detailed presentation of grammar in appendix; rest of book is text of *Iliad* I, with commentary.

PRENDERGAST, G. L., *Concordance to the* Iliad (Oxford University Press, 1875): a list of every word in the poem by way of its context—each line is given complete in which the word occurs, except that very-frequently-occurring words are listed only once.

SEYMOUR, THOMAS D., *Homeric Language and Verse* (Boston, Ginn, 1890): handy summary, not always accurate in statistics, and partly out of date.

SMYTH, HERBERT W., *Greek Grammar* (Harvard University Press, 1920): best complete synthesis of Greek grammar, admirably clear, organized, precise; has special Homeric forms and usage in footnotes; very useful grammatical index.

STANFORD, W. B., *The* Odyssey *of Homer* (London, Macmillan, 1964), 2 vols.): useful short digest of epic grammar in Introduction.

VAN LEEUWEN, J. and M. B. MENDES DA COSTA, *Enchiridion Dictionis Epicae* (Amsterdam, Sijthoff, 1918): philological and comparative treatment, with some radical theories not accepted by all scholars.

7. GENERAL GREEK CULTURE

AGARD, WALTER, *The Greek Mind* (Princeton, Van Nostrand, 1957): aspects of Greek outlook, with illustrative passages from ancient writers.

AMOS, H. D. and A. G. P. LAND, *These Were the Greeks* (England, Hulton, 1979): brief account, illustrated.

ARIAS, P. E., *A History of Greek Vase Painting* (London, Thames & Hudson, 1962): rich survey of all styles, types, artists, beautifully illustrated.

AUDEN, W. H. (editor), *The Portable Greek Reader* (New York, Viking, 1948): selections in translation of all major Greek authors, arranged by themes.

AVERY, CATHERINE, *The New Century Classical Handbook* (New York, Appleton-Century, 1962): encyclopedic coverage of historical persons, writers, mythological figures, religious themes, geographical areas and places.

BERVE, H. and G. GRUBEN, *Greek Temples, Theaters, and Shrines* (New York, Abrams, 1962): elaborate photos, plans, data of outstanding architectural structures.

BIERS, WILLIAM R., *The Archaeology of Greece* (Cornell University Press, 1980): a survey of ancient Greek art, architecture, cultural monuments, arranged by chronological periods. Many illustrations.

BOWDER, DIANA (editor), *Who Was Who in the Greek World* (Cornell University Press, 1982): short data on 750 writers, statesman, artists, historic figures; many illustrations.

BOWRA, C. M. *Classical Greece* (New York, Time-Life Books, 1965): attractive general account of Greek history, culture, art, scenery; fine photographs.

BOWRA, C. M., *The Greek Experience* (London, World, 1957): appreciative essay on the achievements and impact of Greek culture.

BURY, J. B., and R. MEIGGS, *A History of Greece* (London, Macmillan, 4th edition 1975): a full account from beginnings through Alexander the Great.

CHAMOUX, FRANÇOIS, *The Civilization of Greece* (New York, Simon & Schuster, 1965): synthesis of history, art, literature, richly illustrated.

FINLEY, M. I., *The Legacy of Greece* (Oxford, Clarendon Press, 1981): similar in plan to Livingstone, from more recent perspective; adds essays on education, biography, myths, city planning, Greek influence down the ages.

FLACELIÈRE, ROBERT, *A Literary History of Greece* (London, Elek, 1964): shorter survey of all major writers.

FLACELIÈRE, ROBERT, *Daily Life in Greece at the Time of Pericles* (London, Weidenfeld & Nicolson, 1965).

GRAVES, ROBERT, *Greek Myths: Illustrated Edition* (London, Cassell, 1981): a shorter recasting of Graves' retelling of the myths, giving all the main stories; illustrated with over 100 representations of the myths in ancient art exclusively.

GREEN, PETER, *A Concise History of Ancient Greece* (London, Thames & Hudson, 1973): lively treatment, 200 illustrations.

HAMMOND, N. G. L. and H. H. SCULLARD (editors), *The Oxford Classical Dictionary* (Oxford, Clarendon Press, 2nd edition 1970): encyclopedia on all areas and aspects of Greek civilization and heritage.

HARVEY, PAUL, *The Oxford Companion to Classical Literature* (Oxford, Clarendon Press, 1937): very handy summaries of all major literary works and the lives of authors, and main persons in Greek literature and myths.

HOLMS, BRYAN, *Bulfinch's Mythology: The Greek and Roman Fables Illustrated* (New York, Viking, 1979): a retelling of the myths, with hundreds of illustrations from Renaissance artists.

KRAAY, C. M., *Greek Coins* (New York, Abrams, 1966): splendid large photographs, detailed descriptions, a survey of whole range and history of Greek coinage.

LAWRENCE, A. W., *Greek Architecture* (Baltimore, Penguin Books, 1957): full description of construction and styles, and data on major buildings.

LESKY, ALBIN, *A History of Greek Literature* (London, Methuen, 1966): full account of all authors, works, literary genres, with documentation from ancient sources.

LEVI, PETER, *Atlas of the Greek World* (Oxford, Phaidon, 1980): 87 maps of various areas, cities, periods, and 325 illustrations, with extended text on history, ancient Greek culture.

LIVINGSTONE, *The Legacy of Greece* (Oxford University Press, 1921): essays by various authors on Greek religion, philosophy, mathematics, astronomy, science, medicine, literature, political thought,art.

LULLIES, R., *Greek Sculpture* (London, Thames & Hudson, 1960): selected study of major artists and works, in full detail and fine photographs.

MACKENDRICK, PAUL, *The Greek Stones Speak* (New York, St. Martin's Press, 1962): the story of Greek archaeological discoveries; many illustrations.

RICHTER, GISELA, *A Handbook of Greek Art* (London, Phaidon, 1969 6th edition): a textbook covering all periods and areas of Greek art; many illustrations.

ROSE, H. J., *A Handbook of Greek Literature* (New York, Dutton, 1960): detailed data and appraisal.

ROSE, H. J., *Ancient Greek Religion* (London, Hutchinson, 1946): short survey.

ROSSITER, STUART, *Greece: The Blue Guide* (London, Benn, 1977 3rd edition): good description of all areas, places in Greece today, with archaeological data, maps.

SCHODER, RAYMOND V., *Ancient Greece from the Air* (London, Thames & Hudson, 1974): air photos and identification charts of all major archaeological sites in Greece and the islands, with historical data, bibliographical guide to fuller information.

SCHODER, RAYMOND V., *Masterpieces of Greek Art* (Chicago, Ares, 3rd edition 1975): 108 color photos of great examples of every type and period of Greek art, with facing artistic analysis; bibliography of detailed studies in each area of Greek art. Introductory history of Greek art styles.

SEVERY, MERLE (editor), *Greece and Rome: Builders of Our World* (Washington, National Geographic Society, 1968): splendidly illustrated with over 500 photographs, mostly in color; treats key periods and historical persons as representative of general Greek and Roman life and ideals.

STARR, CHESTER G., *The Ancient Greeks* (Oxford University press, 1971): short survey, with many illustrations.

A GOD LEADS THE WAY

Dionysus' transit from Asia Minor to mainland Greece, here depicted by the great vase painter Exekias, symbolizes the ambitious student's transition from an early (Epic/Homeric) form of the Greek language to a later (Attic) usage of Classical authors and to the Koine usage of late Hellenistic and early Christian times. New adventures and discoveries beckon!

TRANSITION TO ATTIC GREEK

If you continue your reading of Greek beyond Homer—as is strongly recommended for educational advantage and intellectual and literary enjoyment—you will find some differences in forms, vocabulary, and grammatical rules. The Lyric Poets and Herodotus are closer to Homeric usage, but the later authors in the Classical Age and beyond use a form of Greek (known as the Attic dialect, because centered in Athens) which has enough differences from Homeric language to require some orientation of the student—which is what this Appendix provides.

The differences are really much fewer than is commonly believed. By actual statistical analysis, Attic Greek is about eighty-five percent identical with Homeric. Of the fifteen percent that is different, half is merely the contraction of vowels in the spelling of words or the dropping out of use of some Homeric forms and vocables. The other eight percent consists of new words and forms and syntax rules. Therefore, when you read later authors, most of the language will be familiar or within the framework of patterns you have already learned. New words can be solved by use of a dictionary. The notes to most student editions of Greek writers usually identify and explain unusual or strange forms and syntax, and classroom teachers will help over problems met. If you intend to read fairly extensively, you will need to have at hand a grammar of Attic Greek—such as the form-charts and summary of rules in the appendix to Crosby and Schaeffer or other similar introductory books which use Attic language as their base, or the fuller grammars by Goodwin and Gulick or H. W. Smyth. But the following pages will simplify the transition by pointing out *only the new or different matter not already learned* for Homer.

It is not necessary to memorize all this. But you should go over it carefully, more than once, to be familiar with the main principles and to know where to look up special Attic forms and rules which you come across in reading the post-Homeric authors. This Appendix F therefore is mainly for *reference* as you need it.

The material in this summary of Attic forms and rules will also serve for reading the post-Classical *Koine* writers, such as the New Testament, Christian Fathers, Plutarch, etc. Greek in that period is basically like Attic, but more simplified in verb forms and grammar, and with some new words or new meanings.

PART I: GENERAL PRINCIPLES

A. STRESS: The rules for emphasis in pronouncing Greek words, which you learned in #8 for reading Homer, can be used also for later writers, in prose as well as poetry. By keeping a clear distinction between short and long syllables even in prose, you will be closer to ancient usage than if you treat the pitch-marks as signs of stress. However, many people insist on stressing the marked syllables, and you may elect to do so also—but keep all *long* syllables long, do not run over them as rapidly as short syllables. That is essential to pronouncing ancient Greek of any dialect and period.

B. AUGMENT: Homer uses augmented forms of the past tenses of the indicative (#387) about half the time. In Attic prose the augmented forms are *always used*. For this reason the third principal part of verbs is usually given in its augmented form: λύω, λύσω, ἔλυσα. ἔγνων. ἔβην, etc. Remember that the augment is omitted in the subjunctive, optative, imperative, infinitive, and participle.

C. CONTRACTION: contraction of contiguous vowels is occasional in Homer, almost universal in Attic. The rules already learned for Homer (#395) apply also in Attic—except that ε + o, which contract to ευ in Homer, become ου in Attic.

PART II: DECLENSION

A. FIRST DECLENSION:

1. All nouns, adjectives, participles take *-ων in the genitive plural and -αις in the dative plural:* δίκων, δίκαις (Hom: δικάων, δίκησι).

2. Nouns ending in *-a* (or *-ας*) preceded by ε, ι, or ρ *keep the a throughout* the singular.

3. Adjectives and participles have *-a in the nom. sg.* after ε, ι, or ρ and keep it throughout the sg.; otherwise, they have *-η*.

4. Masculine nouns take *-ου in the genitive sg.*

5. Many vowel combinations are *contracted*, especially after ε-, a-, or o- ending a stem.

    Note: in all following lists and charts, * *indicates a new or non-Homeric form,*
       [ ] means that that Homeric form is *not used in Attic.*

Attic examples:

ἡδεία, *ἡδείας, *ἱδείᾳ, ἡδείαν,   ἡδείαι, *ἡδείων, *ἡδείαις, ἡδείας.
ναύτης, *ναύτου (Hom: -αο, -εω), *ναύτων, *ναύταις.

B. SECOND DECLENSION:

1. *-οιο is not used* in the genitive sg., *nor is -οισι used* in the dative pl.

2. All participles with stems in a-, ε-, or o- contract. Other contractions occur.

Attic examples:

θεός, θεοῦ, θεῷ, θεόν,   θεοί, θεῶν, θεοῖς, θεούς.
*ὁρώμενος, -η, -ον (Hom: ὁραόμενος, -η, -ον).

C. THIRD DECLENSION:

1. The *shortened form of dative pl.* is always used: ἄναξι (Hom. [ἀνάκτεσσι], ἄναξι).

2. *-ς is used for -ας in acc. pl.* of stems ending in υ-: *ἰχθῦς (Hom: ἰχθύας).

3. Nouns with stems in ι-, and some with stems in υ-, *change the stem-vowel* to ε except in acc. sg.; and they *lengthen the gen. sg. ending* (cp. example πόλις).

4. Nouns with stems in ευ- *change the stem-vowel* to ε- except in dat. pl.; and they *lengthen the gen. sg. ending.* (cp. example βασιλεύς).

Attic examples:

πόλις, *πόλεως, πόλει, πόλιν,   *πόλεις, *πόλεων, *πόλεσι, πόλεις.
ἄστυ, *ἄστεως, ἄστει, ἄστυ,   *ἄστη, ἄστεων, ἄστεσι, *ἄστη.
βασιλεύς, *βασιλέως, *βασιλεῖ, *βασιλέα   *βασιλεῖς, *βασιλέων, *βασιλεῦσι, *βασιλέας
βοῦς, βοός, βοΐ, βοῦν,   βόες, βοῶν, βουσί, βοῦς
*ναῦς, *νεώς, νηΐ, *ναῦν,   νῆες, νεῶν, *ναυσί, *ναῦς.
πατήρ, πατρός, πατρί, πατέρα,   πατέρες, πατέρων, πατράσι, πατέρας.

PART III. PRONOUNS

A. **DEFINITE ARTICLE:** in Homer, ὁ, ἡ, τό is mostly a weak demonstrative pronoun 'That'. In Attic, it is the definite article 'The', identifying nouns and participles with which it is used: ὁ ἄναξ 'The king', ὁ λέγων 'The one speaking', etc. The Homeric forms τοῖο, τοί, ταί, τάων, τῇσι, τοῖσι are not used.

Attic article:

ὁ	ἡ	τό		οἱ	αἱ	τά
τοῦ	τῆς	τοῦ		τῶν	τῶν	τῶν
τῷ	τῇ	τῷ		τοῖς	ταῖς	τοῖς
τόν	τήν	τό		τούς	τάς	τά

B. **PERSONAL PRONOUNS:** These use ου instead of ευ, and show contraction often. In Attic prose, the third person is usually expressed by αὐτός in its various forms. Attic poetry however frequently uses the older forms.

Attic first person: ἐγώ, *(ἐ)μοῦ, (ἐ)μοί, (ἐ)μέ,   ἡμεῖς, *ἡμῶν, ἡμῖν, *ἡμᾶς

Attic second person: σύ, *σοῦ, σοί, σέ,   ὑμεῖς, *ὑμῶν, ὑμίν, *ὑμᾶς

Attic third person: αὐτός, αὐτή, αὐτά, etc.

> *Note:* μου, μοι, με, σου, σοι, σε are enclitic (Book I, Appendix G.6).

C. **INDEFINITE AND INTERROGATIVE PRONOUNS:** The indefinite τις, τι and the interrogative τίς, τί are the same in form, being distinguished only by the pitch-mark of the interrogative. They have the regular endings added to the stem τιν-, but also shortened forms in genitive and dative sg. The indefinite relative pronoun ὅστις, ἥτις, ὅ τι (also functioning as an indirect interrogative, commonly used in indirect questions) is a combination of ὅς, ἥ, ὅ and τις, τι. Both parts are declined, except in the shortened forms; ἄττα is a substitute for ἅτινα. The indefinite pronoun is enclitic.

Attic forms:

τίς	τί	ὅστις	ἥτις	ὅ τι
τίνος, τοῦ	τίνος, τοῦ	οὗτινος, ὅτου	ἥστινος	οὗτινος, ὅτου
τίνι, τῷ	τίνι, τῷ	ᾧτινι, ὅτῳ	ᾗτινι	ᾧτινι, ὅτῳ
τίνα	τί	ὅντινα	ἥντινα	ὅ τι
τίνες	τίνα	οἵτινες	αἵτινες	ἅτινα, ἅττα
τίνων	τίνων	ὧντινων, ὅτων	ὧντινων	ὧντινων, ὅτων
τίσι	τίσι	οἷστισι, ὅτοις	αἷστισι	οἷστισι, ὅτοις
τίνας	τίνα	οὕστινας	ἅστινας	ἅτινα, ἅττα

PART IV: CONJUGATION

A. THE REGULAR VERB: endings are the same as in Homer, except that:

1. Attic makes a clear distinction between the future middle and the *future passive*—whose forms are constructed thus: aorist passive stem + -ησ- + future middle endings *λυθ-ήσ- ομαι I shall be loosed; γνωσθ-ησ- όμεθα We shall be known; ὀφθ-ήσ- ονται They will be seen;* etc.
2. Attic uses a *future optative,* formed from the future stem + the present optative endings:

   fut. *act.* opt.: *λύσ-οιμι, λύσ-οις,* etc.
   fut. *mid.* opt.: *λυσ-οίμην, λύσ-οιο,* etc.
   fut. *pass.* opt.: *λυθ-ησ-οίμην, λυθ-ήσ-οιο,* etc.
3. *Contraction* occurs:

   a. In second person sg. of the *middle:* pres./fut. indic.: *λύ-ει* or *-ῃ* (Hom: *-εαι*); impf./2 aor. indic.: *λύ-ου* (Hom: *-εο*); 1 aor. indic.: *λύ-σω* (Hom: *-αο*); pres./aor. subj.: *λύ-ῃ* (Hom: *-ηαι*); pres./2 aor. impt.: *λύ-ου* (Hom: *-εο, -ευ*).
   b. In the 3 aor. subj. active: *βῶ, βῇς,* etc. (Hom: *βή-ω, βή-ῃς,* etc.).
   c. In the plpf. active 1 sg.: *λελύκ-η* (Hom: *-εα*).
4. The *longer forms of the infinitive* are not used.
5. The *3 pl. of mid./pass. indic. pf.* is *-νται,* of *plpf.* is *-ντο* (Hom: *-αται, -ατο*).

B. CONTRACT VERBS: When a verb-stem ends in *ε-, α-,* or *ο-,* these vowels usually contract with the initial vowel or diphthong of the ending according to the usual rules for contraction (above, Part I.C.). E.g., *τιμά-ουσι* becomes *τιμῶσι, ἐφίλε-ον* becomes *ἐφίλουν,* etc. However, the infinitive ending *-ειν* is already the result of a contraction from *-εεν,* and therefore contracts with a stem-final *α* to *-ᾶν* (*α + ε + εν = ᾶν*): *τιμά-ειν = τιμᾶν,* and contracts with *ο* to *-οῦν* (*ο + ε + εν = ουν*): *δηλό-ειν = δηλοῦν*).

Note: Charts of all contract verb forms may be found in the standard Attic grammars.

C. -MI VERBS: Some seventy-seven verbs (in the whole of Greek literature) have certain peculiarities in common. They are called "non-thematic verbs" because they add the verb-ending without the intervening 'thematic' vowel (e.g., *δύνα-μαι I can,* instead of *δυνά-ομαι*), or "-MI verbs" because their first principle part (act.) ends in *-μι* instead of the usual *-ω.* -MI verbs are *irregular only in the present system;* the middle has the usual endings but without a thematic vowel between stem and ending; their *stem vowel is shortened,* except in the act. indic. sg. and the impt. sg.

Seven -Mi verbs need special attention: *τίθημι I place, δίδωμι I give, ἵημι I send, φημί I say, εἰμί I am, εἶμι I shall go, ἧμαι I sit.* You have seen some of their forms in ##470, 471, 483, and in Appendix A "Special Verb Forms." The following *charts of their Attic forms* are for reference, and need not be memorized. They provide the context for those individual -MI forms which you now and then meet in Attic authors.

Note that *φημί is not used in the middle* in Attic Greek, although it is in Homer. The impt. sg. is *φά-θι; φῇς* is sometimes written *φής.*

ἧμαι is deponent. In Attic it is usually found in its compound form *κάθημαι* and is even augmented as though a simple verb, e.g., *ἐκαθήμην.* It takes middle endings without the thematic vowel, except in the subj. and opt., where the regular endings are added and absorb the stem vowel, as is seen in its chart.

			ἵημι, τίθημι, δίδωμι **ACTIVE**			
		PRESENT SYSTEM		**2ND AORIST SYSTEM**		
	ἵημι *ἱη-, ἱε-*	*τίθημι* *τιθη-, τιθε-*	*δίδωμι* *διδω-, διδο-*	*ἵημι* *ἑ-*	*τίθημι* *θε-*	*δίδωμι* *δο-*
I N D I C A T I V E	*ἵη-μι* *ἵη-ς* *ἵη-σι* *ἵε-μεν* *ἵε-τε* *ἱᾶσι*	*τίθη-μι* *τίθη-ς* *τίθη-σι* *τίθε-μεν* *τίθε-τε* § *τιθέ-ᾱσι*	*δίδω-μι* *δίδω-ς* *δίδω-σι* *δίδο-μεν* *δίδο-τε* § *διδό-ᾱσι*	(Note: *ἑ-* is augmented to *εἱ-*.)		
	(IMPF.) *ἵη-ν* § *ἵεις* § *ἵει* *ἵε-μεν* *ἵε-τε* *ἵε-σαν*	(IMPF.) *ἐτίθη-ν* # *ἐτίθεις* § *ἐτίθει* *ἐτίθε-μεν* *ἐτίθε-τε* *ἐτίθε-σαν*	(IMPF.) § *ἐδίδουν* § *ἐδίδους* § *ἐδίδου* *ἐδίδο-μεν* *ἐδίδο-τε* *ἐδίδο-σαν*	# *ἧκα* # *ἧκας* # *ἧκε* *εἷ-μεν* *εἷ-τε* *εἷ-σαν*	# *ἔθηκα* # *ἔθηκας* # *ἔθηκε* *ἔθε-μεν* *ἔθε-τε* *ἔθε-σαν*	# *ἔδωκα* # *ἔδωκας* # *ἔδωκε* *ἔδο-μεν* *ἔδο-τε* *ἔδο-σαν*
S U B J	*ἱ-ῶ* *ἱ-ῇς* *ἱ-ῇ* *ἱ-ῶμεν* *ἱ-ῆτε* *ἱ-ῶσι*	*τιθ-ῶ* *τιθ-ῇς* *τιθ-ῇ* *τιθ-ῶμεν* *τιθ-ῆτε* *τιθ-ῶσι*	*διδ-ῶ*[1] *διδ-ῷς* *διδ-ῷ* *διδ-ῶμεν* *διδ-ῶτε* *διδ-ῶσι*	*ὧ* *ᾗς* *ᾗ* *ὧ-μεν* *ἧτε* *ὧσι*	*θ-ῶ* *θ-ῇς* *θ-ῇ* *θ-ῶμεν* *θ-ῆτε* *θ-ῶσι*	*δ-ῶ*[1] *δ-ῷς* *δ-ῷ* *δ-ῶμεν* *δ-ῶτε* *δ-ῶσι*
O P T	*ἱείην* *ἱείης* *ἱείη* *ἱεῖμεν* *ἱεῖτε* *ἱεῖεν*	*τιθείην* *τιθείης* *τιθείη* *τιθεῖμεν* *τιθεῖτε* *τιθεῖεν*	*διδοίην* *διδοίης* *διδοίη* *διδοῖμεν* *διδοῖτε* *διδοῖεν*	*εἵην* *εἵης* *εἵη* *εἷμεν* *εἷτε* *εἷεν*	*θείην* *θείης* *θείη* *θεῖμεν* *θεῖτε* *θεῖεν*	*δοίην* *δοίης* *δοίη* *δοῖμεν* *δοῖτε* *δοῖεν*
I M P T	§ *ἵει* *ἵέ-τε*	§ *τίθει* *τίθε-τε*	§ *δίδου* *δίδο-τε*	# *ἕς* *ἕ-τε*	# *θέ-ς* *θέ-τε*	# *δό-ς* *δό-τε*
I N F	*ἱέ-ναι*	*τιθέ-ναι*	*διδό-ναι*	# *εἷναι*	# *θεῖναι*	# *δοῦναι*
P T C	*ἱείς* *ἱεῖσα* *ἱέν*	*τιθείς* *τιθεῖσα* *τιθέν*	*διδούς* *διδοῦσα* *διδόν*	*εἵς* *εἷσα* *ἕν*	*θείς* *θεῖσα* *θέν*	*δούς* *δοῦσα* *δόν*
	§ These forms do not follow *ἵστημι*. [1] Contract according to rule.			# These 2nd aor. forms do not follow the present system form.		

ἵημι, τίθημι, δίδωμι
MIDDLE

	PRESENT SYSTEM			2ND AORIST SYSTEM		
	ἵημι ἱε-	τίθημι τιθε-	δίδωμι διδω-, διδο-	ἵημι ἑ-	τίθημι θε-	δίδωμι δο-
I N D I C A T I V E	ἵε-μαι ἵε-σαι ἵε-ται ἱέ-μεθα ἵε-σθε ἵε-νται	τίθε-μαι τίθε-σαι τίθε-ται τιθέ-μεθα τίθε-σθε τίθε-νται	δίδο-μαι δίδο-σαι δίδο-ται διδό-μεθα δίδο-σθε δίδο-νται	(Note: ἑ- is augmented to εἱ-.)		
	(IMPF.) ἱέ-μην ἵε-σο ἵε-το ἱέ-μεθα ἵε-σθε ἵε-ντο	(IMPF.) ἐτιθέ-μην ἐτίθε-σο ἐτίθε-το ἐτιθέ-μεθα ἐτίθε-σθε ἐτίθε-ντο	(IMPF.) ἐδιδό-μην ἐδίδο-σο ἐδίδο-το ἐδιδό-μεθα ἐδίδο-σθε ἐδίδο-ντο	εἵ-μην εἷ-σο εἷτο εἵ-μεθα εἷ-σθε εἷ-ντο	ἐθέ-μην # ἔθου ἔθε-το ἐθέ-μεθα ἔθε-σθε ἔθε-ντο	ἐδό-μην # ἔδου ἔδο-το ἐδό-μεθα ἔδο-σθε ἔδο-ντο
S U B J	ἱ-ῶμαι ἱ-ῇ ἱ-ῆται ἱ-ώμεθα ἱ-ῆσθε ἱ-ῶνται	τιθ-ῶμαι τιθ-ῇ τιθ-ῆται τιθ-ώμεθα τιθ-ῆσθε τιθ-ῶνται	διδ-ῶμαι[1] διδ-ῷ διδ-ῶται διδ-ώμεθα διδ-ῶσθε διδ-ῶνται	ὦμαι ᾗ ἧται ὥμεθα ἧσθε ὦνται	θ-ῶμαι θ-ῇ θ-ῆται θ-ώμεθα θ-ῆσθε θ-ῶνται	δ-ῶμαι[1] δ-ῷ δ-ῶται δ-ώμεθα δ-ῶσθε δ-ῶνται
O P T	ἱείμην ἱεῖο ἱεῖτο ἱείμεθα ἱεῖσθε ἱεῖντο	τιθείμην τιθεῖο τιθεῖτο τιθείμεθα τιθεῖσθε τιθεῖντο	διδοίμην διδοῖο διδοῖτο διδοίμεθα διδοῖσθε διδοῖντο	εἵμην εἷο εἷτο εἵμεθα εἷσθε εἷντο	θείμην θεῖο θεῖτο θείμεθα θεῖσθε θεῖντο	δοίμην δοῖο δοῖτο δοίμεθα δοῖσθε δοῖντο
I M P T	ἵε-σο ἵε-σθε	τίθε-σο τίθε-σθε	δίδο-σο δίδο-σθε	οὗ ἕ-σθε	θοῦ θέ-σθε	δοῦ δό-σθε
I N F	ἵε-σθαι	τίθε-σθαι	δίδο-σθαι		θέ-σθαι	δό-σθαι
P T C	ἱέ-μενος ἱε-μένη ἱέ-μενον	τιθέ-μενος τιθε-μένη τιθέ-μενον	διδό-μενος διδο-μένη διδό-μενον	ἕ-μενος ἑ-μένη ἕ-μενον	θέ-μενος θε-μένη θέ-μενον	δό-μενος δο-μένη δό-μενον

[1] Contract according to rule.

These 2nd aor. forms do not follow the presen system form.

	-MI VERBS				IRREGULAR – MI VERBS	
	δείκνῡ-μι PRES. ACT.	ἵστη-μι PRES. ACT.	δείκνῡ-μι PRES. MID.	ἵστη-μι PRES. MID.	φη-μί PRES. ACT. (No middle)	κάθ-ημαι PRES. MID. (Deponent)
I N D I C A T I V E	δείκνῡ-μι δείκνῡ-ς δείκνῡ-σι δείκνυ-μεν δείκνυ-τε δεικνύ-ᾱσι	ἵστη-μι ἵστη-ς ἵστη-σι ἵστα-μεν ἵστα-τε ἵστᾶσι²	δείκνυ-μαι δείκνυ-σαι δείκνυ-ται δεικνύ-μεθα δείκνυ-σθε δείκνυ-νται	ἵστα-μαι ἵστα-σαι ἵστα-ται ἱστά-μεθα ἵστα-σθε ἵστα-νται	φη-μί φή-ς⁴ φη-σί φα-μέν φα-τέ φᾱ-σί⁵	κάθη-μαι κάθη-σαι κάθη-ται καθή-μεθα κάθη-σθε κάθη-νται
	(IMPF.) ἐδείκνῡ-ν ἐδείκνῡ-ς ἐδείκνῡ ἐδείκνυ-μεν ἐδείκνυ-τε ἐδείκνυ-σαν	(IMPF.) ἵστη-ν ἵστη-ς ἵστη ἵστα-μεν ἵστα-τε ἵστα-σαν	(IMPF.) ἐδεικνύ-μην ἐδείκνυ-σο ἐκείκνυ-το ἐδεικνύ-μεθα ἐδείκνυ-σθε ἐκείκνυ-ντο	(IMPF.) ἱστά-μην ἵστα-σο ἵστα-το ἱστά-μεθα ἵστα-σθε ἵστα-ντο	(IMPF.) ἔφη-ν ἔφη-ς⁶ ἔφη ἔφα-μεν ἔφα-τε ἔφα-σαν	(IMPF.) ἐκαθή-μην ἐκάθη-σο ἐκάθη-το ἐκαθή-μεθα ἐκάθη-σθε ἐκάθη-ντο
S U B J	δεικνύ-ω δεικνύ-ῃς δεικνύ-ῃ δεικνύ-ωμεν δεικνύ-ητε δεικνύ-ωσι	ἱστ-ῶ ἱστ-ῇς ἱστ-ῇ ἱστ-ῶμεν ἱστ-ῆτε ἱστ-ῶσι	δεικνύ-ωμαι δεικνύ-ῃ δεικνύ-ηται δεικνυ-ώμεθα δεικνύ-ησθε δεικνύ-ωνται	ἱστ-ῶμαι ἱστ-ῇ ἱστ-ῆται ἱστ-ώμεθα ἱστ-ῆσθε ἱστ-ῶνται	φ-ῶ φ-ῇς φ-ῇ φ-ῶμεν φ-ῆτε φ-ῶσι	καθ-ῶμαι καθ-ῇ καθ-ῆται καθ-ώμεθα καθ-ῆσθε καθ-ῶνται
O P T	δεικνύ-οιμι δεικνύ-οις δεικνύ-οι δεικνύ-οιμεν δεικνύ-οιτε δεικνύ-οιεν	ἱσταίην³ ἱσταίης ἱσταίη ἱσταίμεν ἱσταῖτε ἱσταῖεν	δεικνυ-οίμην δεικνυ-οιο δεικνυ-οιτο δεικνυ-οίμεθα δεικνυ-οισθε δεικνυ-οιντο	ἱσταίμην ἱσταῖο ἱσταῖτο ἱσταίμεθα ἱσταῖσθε ἱσταῖντο	φαίην φαίης φαίη φαῖμεν φαῖτε φαῖεν	καθ-οίμην καθ-οῖο καθ-οῖτο καθ-οίμεθα καθ-οῖσθε καθ-οῖντο
I M P T	δείκνῡ δείκνυ-τε	ἵστη ἵστα-τε	δείκνυ-σο δείκνυ-σθε	ἵστα-σο ἵστα-σθε	φά-θι φά-τε	κάθη-σο κάθη-σθε
I N F	δεικνύ-ναι	ἱστά-ναι	δείκνυ-σθαι	ἵστα-σθαι	φά-ναι	καθῆ-σθαι
P T C	δεικνῡ́ς¹ δεικνῦσα δεικνύν	ἱστάς¹ ἱστᾶσα ἱστάν	δεικνύ-μενος δεικνυ-μένη δεικνύ-μενον	ἱστά-μενος ἱστα-μένη ἱστά-μενον	φάς¹ φᾶσα φάν	καθή-μενος καθη-μένη καθή-μενον

¹Compensative lengthening.
²Contraction of ἱστα-ασι.
³Compare 3rd aor. act.

⁴Also written φής.
⁵Contraction of φα-ασι.
⁶Sometimes ἔφησθα.

IRREGULAR -MI VERBS

εἰμί *I am*

εἰμί has the stem ἐσ- which frequently drops the σ and then undergoes various changes—some regular (like the contraction of the subj. and ptc., and the augment of the impf.), others irregular. The future ἔσομαι is regular except for the shortened 3rd person sg., ἔσται. The starred forms in this chart are those which are new to you.

IND. PRES.	IND. IMPF.	SUBJ.	OPT.	IMPT.	INF.	PTC.
εἰμί	*ἦ or ἦν	ὦ	εἴην			
*εἶ	ἦσθα	ᾖς	εἴης	*ἴσθι		*ὤν
ἐστί	ἦν	ᾖ	εἴη		εἶναι	*οὖσα
*ἐσμέν	ἦμεν	ὦμεν	εἶμεν			*ὄν
ἐστέ	ἦτε	ἦτε	εἶτε	*ἔστε		
εἰσί	ἦσαν	ὦσι	εἶεν			

εἶμι *I shall go*

εἶμι is present in form but in the present indicative *has future meaning*. It is usually used in Attic as the future of ἔρχομαι *I come, I go*. (Notice that its first two forms are the same as those of εἰμί *I am*.) There are two stems: εἰ- (augmented regularly) and ἰ-. The subj., opt., and ptc. are regular. You have already learned the inf., ptc., and pres. ind. 3 sg. (#861).

IND. PRES.	IND. IMPF.	SUBJ.	OPT.	IMPT.	INF.	PTC.
εἶμι	ᾖ-α, ᾔειν	ἴ-ω	ἴ-οιμι			
εἶ	ἴη-εις	ἴ-ῃς	ἴ-οις	ἴ-θι		ἰ-ών
εἶ-σι	ᾔ-ει	ἴ-ῃ	ἴ-οι		ἰ-έναι	ἰ-οῦσα
ἴ-μεν	ᾖ-μεν	ἴ-ωμεν	ἴ-οιμεν			ἰ-όν
ἴ-τε	ᾖ-τε	ἴ-ητε	ἴ-οιτε	ἴ-τε		
ἴ-ᾱσι	ᾖ-σαν	ἴ-ωσι	ἴ-οιεν			

D. οἶδα *I know*

This irregular verb is not a -MI verb; it uses three different stems and follows no recognizable system. It is classified as a *perfect in form but is present in meaning*. The starred forms are those which differ from the Homeric forms you have already learned (#489).

IND. PRES.	IND. IMPF.	SUBJ.	OPT.	IMPT.	INF.	PTC.
οἶδα	*ᾔδη	εἰδῶ	εἰδείην			
οἶσθα	*ᾔδησθα	εἰδῇς	εἰδείης	ἴσθι		εἰδώς
οἶδε	*ᾔδει	εἰδῇ	εἰδείη		*εἰδέναι	εἰδυῖα
*ἴσμεν	*ᾔδεμεν	εἰδῶμεν	εἰδεῖμεν			εἰδός
ἴστε	*ᾔδετε	εἰδῆτε	εἰδεῖτε	ἴστε		
ἴσᾱσι	*ᾔδεσαν	εἰδῶσι	εἰδεῖεν			

E. **VERBS WITH "IRREGULAR" PRINCIPAL PARTS.** In the course of your further study of Greek you will sometimes hear verbs like *γιγνώσκω* or *ὁράω* referred to as "irregular" verbs. They are so called because their principal parts change too radically to be predicted from the present. The endings added to the stem of these principal parts are the usual ones.

F. **FURTHER VERB ENDINGS**

DUAL: In #457 you learned the special endings for the Dual in nouns, adjectives, participles. In Attic the Dual of verbs is fairly frequently used also, both in second person ("we two") and in third person ("they two"). You will recognize these Duals by their characteristic endings: *-τον, -την, -των, -σθον, -σθην, -σθων.* Dual forms occur in the Ind., Subj., Opt., Impt.

THIRD PERSON IMPERATIVE: Most imperatives are in the second person, sg. or pl., expressing commands to the person(s) spoken to. But there are also third person imperatives, referring to someone not being addressed ("Let him bring it." "They must bring it," etc.). These forms end in *-τω* and *-ντων* (*φερέτω, φερόντων,* etc.). Thus, 'Let there be light!' = *γενέσθω φῶς.*

AN ANCIENT CHARIOT RACE

PART V: SYNTAX

A. THE DEFINITE ARTICLE

In Homer *ὁ, ἡ, τό* was a weak demonstrative pronoun or adjective. In Attic Greek it became so unemphatic as to be nearly equivalent to the English definite article, *the,* and is usually translated as such in English. Note the following points.

1. The earlier, Homeric, force of *ὁ, ἡ, τό* is still sometimes apparent in Attic, especially when used in combination with *δέ.* For example:

ὁ μὲν . . . ὁ δέ	*the one . . . the other*
πρὸ τοῦ	*before this*
ὁ δέ	*but he*

2. It is sometimes used in Attic prose contrary to the English usage.

    a. Predicate nouns do not take the article, even where the English uses it, unless for some special reason.

    Πάντων μέτρον ἄνθρωπός ἐστιν.   *Man is the measure of all things.*

    b. Proper nouns sometimes take the article to indicate that the person is well known.

ὁ Σωκράτης	*Socrates*
αἱ τοῦ Ὀδυσσέως νῆες	*the boats of Odysseus*

    c. Abstract nouns often take the article.

    ἀεὶ φιλεῖτε τὴν ἀλήθειαν.   *Always love truth.*

    d. Possessive pronouns may take the article when modifying a noun referring to a definite thing.

τὸ ἐμὸν ξίφος	*my sword* (I have a definite one in mind)
ἐμὸν ξίφος	*a sword of mine* (any one of several)

    e. The article sometimes takes the place of an unemphatic possessive pronoun when the meaning is clear.

    πάντα εἶπε τοῖς ἑταίροις.   *He told his comrades everything.*

    f. The infinitive used as a noun may take the neuter article.

    παισὶ τὸ πείθεσθαι τοῦ κελεύειν ἄρειόν ἐστιν.
    Obedience is better for children than commanding.

3. By means of the article, a noun in the genitive, an adverb, a prepositional phrase, etc., can be used like an adjective to quality a noun.

οἱ Ὀδυσσέως ἑταίροι	*the companions of Odysseus*
οἱ νῦν (ἄνδρες)	*the men of today* (The noun may be omitted.)
οἱ παρὰ ἄνακτος ἄγγελοι	*the messengers from the king*

4. The position of the article is important.

    a. *Attributive position:* an article immediately preceding a qualifying expression is said to put the expression in the attributive position. This is the ordinary position and has no special significance.

    ὁ σοφὸς ἀνήρ or *ὁ ἀνὴρ σοφός*   *the wise man*

    b. *Predicate position:* an article following a qualifying expression or separated from it by intervening words is said to put the expression in the predicate position. This position gives emphasis and is frequently equivalent to a clause.

    σοφὸς ὁ ἀνήρ or *ὁ ἀνὴρ σοφός*   *The man (is) wise.*

c. The demonstrative adjectives *οὗτος, ὅδε,* and *ἐκεῖνος* take the predicate position in Attic prose.

> *οὗτος ὁ ἀνήρ* or *ὁ ἀνὴρ οὗτος*   *this man*

d. *αὐτός* in the attributive position means *same:* in the predicate position, *self.*

> *ὁ αὐτὸς ἀνήρ*   *the same man*
> *ὁ ἀνὴρ αὐτός* or *αὐτὸς ὁ ἀνήρ*   *the man himself*

B. THE RELATIVE PRONOUN

The general rule for all relative pronouns is that they agree with their antecedents in gender and number but their case depends on the construction of their own clause. However, in Attic Greek two peculiar uses must be noted.

1. *Assimilation:* a relative pronoun in the accusative case is sometimes assimilated to the case of its antecedent, provided that this antecedent is itself in the genitive or dative.

> *πρὸ τῶν κακῶν ἃ οἶδα* (*instead of the evils which I know*) may be written:
> *πρὸ τῶν κακῶν ὧν οἶδα*
>
> *αἰνῶ σε ἐπὶ τούτοις ἃ λέγεις* (*I praise you for these things which you say*) may be written:
> *αἰνῶ σε ἐπὶ τούτοις οἷς λέγεις.* Moreover, the pronominal antecedent may be dropped, as in English: *αἰνῶ σε ἐφ' οἷς λέγεις* (*I praise you for what you say*).
>
> *κάλλιστή ἐστι πασῶν ἃς ἑώρακα* (*She is the most beautiful of all the women whom I have seen*) *may be written: κάλλιστή ἐστι πασῶν ὧν ἑώρακα.*

2. *Attraction:* the opposite of assimilation is called attraction. The antecedent is sometimes attracted to the relative clause and takes the case of the relative pronoun. (Recall Vergil's use: "urbem, quam statuo, vestra est" instead of the ordinary "urbs, quam statuo, vestra est"—*the city which I am founding is yours.*)

> *αἱ γυναῖκες ἃς ὁρᾷς ἔρχονται* (*The women whom you see are coming*) may be written:
> *τὰς γυναῖκας ἃς ὁρᾷς ἔρχονται.*
>
> *ὁ ἀνὴρ οὗτος, ὃν ἐζητεῖτε, ἐνθάδε ἐστίν.* (*This man, whom you were seeking, is here*) may be written: *τὸν ἄνδρα τοῦτον, ὃν ἐζητεῖτε, ἐνθάδε ἐστίν.*

C. SYNTAX OF THE NOUN

Note: the *numbers starred* contain data not met in Homer or different from Homeric usage.

I. Nominative

1. In Attic a neuter plural subject practically always takes a singular verb. (Cf. #53).

*2. *Nominative with infinitive*—in Greek, unlike Latin, the subject of the infinitive after a main verb of saying, thinking, etc., is not necessarily in the accusative. When the subject of the infinitive is the same as that of the main verb, it is omitted but is considered to be in the nominative. Hence any modifiers will remain in the nominative case.

> *οἶμαι γνῶναι.*   *I think I know.*
> *ἔφη εἶναι κρατερός.*   *He said he was strong.*
> *ἐνομίσατε ἔσεσθαι ὄλβιοι.*   *You thought you would be happy.*

II. Genitive

1. *Agency*—personal agency is regularly expressed in Attic by ὑπό + genitive (rarely by the dative alone).

*2. *Price or value*—the value of something or the price for which one gives or does anything is expressed by the genitive.

φίλος ἐστὶ χρηστὸς πολλοῦ.　*A friend is worth much.*

ἀπο-δίδομαι οἶνον ἀργύρου.　*I sell wine for silver.*

πόσου διδάσκει;　*For how much does he teach?*

*3. *Cause*—with verbs of emotion the genitive may denote the cause.

ἐχολωσάμην σοι δόλου.　*I was angry with you because of your trickery.*

ἐθαύμασε τῆς χάριτος αὐτῆς.　*He marveled at her beauty.*

αἰνήσω ὑμᾶς τῆς ἀρετῆς.　*I will praise you for your manliness.*

*4. *Time*—the partitive genitive is used to denote a time of which only a part is of interest, that is, a *time within which* an action took place.

ἦλθε τῆς νυκτός.　*He came during the night.*

θανοῦμαι τοῦ λοιποῦ.　*I shall die in the future.*

Note: The *dative of time* denotes a definite point of time *at which* an action occurred, and usually contrasts one point of time with another.

τῇ δευτέρᾳ ἡμέρᾳ　*on the second day*

τρίτῳ μηνί　*in the third month*

The *accusative of time* implies that the action of the verb covers the entire period.

ἔμειναν ἑπτά ἡμέρας.　*They remained seven days.*

*5. *Genitive absolute*—a circumstantial participle agreeing with a noun or pronoun (not referring to a person or thing mentioned in the main clause) may stand in the genitive absolute. (Compare the ablative absolute in Latin.)

τούτων λεχθέντων, ἀν-έστησαν.　*When this was said, they stood up.*

καὶ μετα-πεμπομένου αὐτοῦ,　*Even though he is sending for me,*

οὐκ ἐθέλω ἐλθεῖν.　*I am unwilling to go.*

III. Dative

*1. *Place where*—in poetry the dative alone is permitted, but in Attic prose the addition of the preposition ἐν is usually required.

*2. *Agency*—if the agent is nonliving, the dative is used; if the agent is living, the dative is used only with passive verbs in the perfect or pluperfect. (Otherwise, use ὑπό + genitive.)

ἐμοὶ πέπρακται.　*It has been done by me.*

ἐπειδὴ αὐτοῖς παρ-εσκεύαστο.　*When it had been prepared by them.*

*3. *Degree of difference*—with expressions of comparison, the dative is used to mark the degree by which one thing differs from another.

πολλαῖς ἡμέραις ὕστερον ἦλθεν.　*He arrived many days later.*

πολλῷ ἀρείων ἐστίν.　*He is much braver.*

κεφαλῇ ἐλάττων ἐστίν.　*He is a head shorter.*

*4. *Respect*—the dative is sometimes used instead of the accusative of specification. There is no noticeable difference in meaning.

> ἀσθενὴς ἦν τῷ σώματι.   *He was weak in body.*
> τῇ φωνῇ τραχὺς ἐστιν.   *He is harsh of voice.*

IV. Accusative

*1. *Place to which*—in poetry the accusative alone is permitted to express place to which; in Attic prose a preposition *must* accompany the accusative.

*2. *Accusative absolute*—the participles of *impersonal* verbs are used absolutely in the accusative instead of in the genitive. (Among the common impersonal verbs are: ἔξ-εστι *it is possible*, δεῖ *it is necessary*, μέλει *it concerns*.)

> ἐξ-ὸν ἐλθεῖν, οὐκ ἤθελεν.   *Although it was possible to go, he was unwilling.*
> δέον αἱρεῖσθαι, τόδε αἱρῶ.   *Since it is necessary to choose, I take this.*

*3. *With adverbs of swearing*—νή, introducing an affirmative oath, and μά, introducing a negative oath, are followed by the accusative.

> νὴ τὸν Δία.   *(yes) by Zeus!*
> μὰ τοὺς θεούς.   *(no) by the gods!*

D. SYNTAX OF THE VERB BY CONSTRUCTIONS

Note: the *numbers starred* contain data not met in Homer or different from Homeric usage.

1. *Commands:*

   a. Imperative: cf. #114.   b. Infinitive: cf. #148.   c. Optative: cf. #106.

   *d. The aorist subjunctive may be used for negative commands.

   > μὴ ποιήσῃς.   *Do not do this.*
   > μὴ ἀπ-έλθητε.   *Do not go away.*

*2. *Conditions or Suppositions*—the various types of conditional sentences are arranged graphically in the following chart, and an example is given of each type in Attic Greek. Remember that temporal and relative clauses follow the same constructions as conditional clauses, ὅτε *when* and ὅς *who* taking the place of εἰ *if*. (ὅτε + ἄν = ὅταν.)

CONDITIONAL SENTENCES IN ATTIC GREEK

TIME	FORM	"IF"-CLAUSE (Neg. μή)	CONCLUSION (Neg. οὐ)
Present	1. Factual *2. Contrary-to-fact *3. General Supposition	εἰ + ind. (pres. or pf.) εἰ + impf. ind. ἐάν + subj.	ind. (pres. or pf.) ἄν with impf. ind. pres. ind.
Past	4. Factual *5. Contrary-to-fact 6. General Supposition	εἰ + ind. (impf., aor., plpf.) εἰ + aor. ind. εἰ + opt.	ind. (impf., aor., or plpf.) ἄν with aor. ind. impf. ind.
Future	*7. Vivid Supposition *8. Vague Supposition	ἐάν + subj. εἰ + opt.	fut. ind. (or equivalent) ἄν with opt.

Examples in Attic Greek

1. εἰ ταῦτα λέγει, ἀληθῆ λέγει.
   If he says this, he speaks the truth.

2. εἰ ταῦτα ἔλεγον, οὐκ ἂν ἀληθῆ ἔλεγεν.
   If he were saying this (now), he would not be speaking the truth (now).

3. ἐάν τι λέγῃ (λέξῃ), ἀληθῆ λέγει.
   If he (ever) says anything, he (always) speaks the truth.

4. εἰ ταῦτα ἔλεξεν, ἀληθῆ ἔλεξεν.
   If he said this, he spoke the truth.

5. εἰ ταῦτα ἔλεξεν, οὐκ ἂν ἀληθῆ ἔλεξεν.
   If he had said this (then), he would not have spoken the truth (then).

6. εἴ τι λέγοι (λέξειεν), ἀληθῆ ἔλεγεν.
   If he (ever) said anything, he (always) spoke the truth.

7. ἐὰν ταῦτα λέγῃς (λέξῃς), ἀληθῆ λέξεις.
   If you say this, you will speak the truth.

8. εἰ ταῦτα λέγοις (λέξειας), ἀληθῆ ἂν λέγοις (λέξειας).
   If you should say this, you would speak the truth.

*3. *Deliberative questions* — the subjunctive of the first person may be used in a purely rhetorical question. Neg. μή.

τί ποιῶμεν;	*What shall we do?*
εἰπῶμεν ἢ σιγῶμεν;	*Shall we speak or keep silence?*
μὴ ταῦτα φῶμεν;	*Shall we not say this?*

4. *Expectation* (optative) — cf. #522.

5. *Explanatory* (infinitive) — cf. #586.

6. *Fact* (indicative) — cf. #91.

7. *Hortatory* (subjunctive) — cf. #98

8. *Indirect discourse* — when one reports the words of another, not directly (with quotation marks) but according to sense, he uses what is called indirect discourse. Latin regularly uses but one construction for this: the accusative with infinitive. Greek, however, offers two other choices: the participial construction and ὅτι with a finite verb.

  a. Accusative with infinitive: cf. #114.

*b. Participial construction: the participle sometimes takes the place of the infinitive and is in the same tense as the infinitive would be if used.

ὁρῶμεν πάντα ἀληθῆ ὄντα.	*We see that everything is true.*
οὐκ ἔγνωσαν αὐτὸν τεθνηκότα.	*They did not know that he was dead.*
ἤκουσα τοὺς ἄνδρας οὐκ ἀφ-ιξομένους.	*I heard that the men would not arrive.*

*c. ὅτι with a finite verb: this construction is very close to the English usage. After a primary main verb, the original mood and tense of the dependent verb are retained.

λέγει ὅτι οἱ ἄνδρες οὐκ ἀφ-ίξονται.　*He says that the men will not arrive.*
λέγει ὅτι οἱ ἄνδρες οὐκ ἀφ-ίκοντο.　*He says that the men did not arrive.*

After a secondary main verb, the dependent verb *may sometimes* be changed to the optative, the tense remaining the same if possible. The negative always remains the same.

ἔλεξεν ὅτι οἱ ἄνδρες οὐκ ἀφ-ίξοιντο.　*He said that the men would not arrive.*
ἔλεξεν ὅτι οἱ ἄνδρες οὐκ ἀφ-ίκοιντο.　*He said that the men had not arrived.*

Note: (a) most verbs of *thinking* and *believing* take acc. w. inf.
      (b) verbs of *saying* frequently take the ὅτι construction.
      (c) verbs of *knowing* and *perceiving* often take the participle.

9. *Indirect questions*—cf. #463.

*10. *Object clauses*—these are clauses which are used as the objects of verbs such as *I strive that, I take care that, I plan that,* etc. In Homer they take ὅπως with the purpose construction. In Attic also they may take the purpose construction, but more frequently they take ὅπως with the *future indicative* even after a secondary verb. Neg. μή.

βουλεύομαι ὅπως ταῦτα ποιήσομεν.　*I plan that we shall do this.*
ἐβουλευόμην ὅπως μὴ ταῦτα ποιήσομεν.　*I planned that we should not do this.*

11. *Potential* (optative)—cf. #281.

12. *Purpose*—there are four ways of expressing purpose. For example: *The king sent (sends) him to save us.*

a. Subj. or opt.:　ὁ ἄναξ πέμπει αὐτὸν ὅπως σώζῃ ἡμᾶς.

               ὁ ἄναξ ἔπεμψε αὐτὸν ἵνα σώζοι ἡμᾶς.

b. Infinitive:　ὁ ἄναξ ἔπεμψε αὐτὸν σώζειν ἡμᾶς.

c. Future ptc.:　ὁ ἄναξ ἔπεμψε αὐτὸν σώσοντα ἡμᾶς.

*d. ὅς *who* with fut. ind.:　ὁ ἄναξ ἔπεμψε αὐτὸν ὅς σώσει ἡμᾶς.

*13. *Result*—to express the result of an action, Greek has two constructions: ὥστε with the infinitive and ὥστε with the indicative. The main clause frequently has such demonstrative words as οὕτως *thus, so;* τοιοῦτος *such;* τοσοῦτος *so great.*

a. If the main clause has the emphatic idea and the result clause is added primarily to bring out this idea by showing its natural or anticipated result, though not necessarily its actual result, ὥστε is used with the inf. Neg. μή.

ἡ θύελλα τοσαύτη ἦν ὥστε ἀπ-ολέσαι τὴν ναῦν. *The storm was so great as to destroy the boat.* (The storm was violent enough to destroy the boat—though perhaps actually it did not.)

b. If the result clause expresses an important *fact* which the main clause helps to account for, ὥστε is used with the indicative. Neg. οὐ.

ἡ θύελλα τοσαύτη ἦν ὥστε ἀπ-ώλεσε τὴν ναῦν. *The storm was so great that it destroyed the boat.* (The boat was sunk—so great was the storm.)

*14. *Supplementary participle*—the participle may be used to supplement the meaning of three particular verbs to such an extent that the participle itself carries the main idea. The three verbs are: τυγχάνω *I happen;* λανθάνω *I elude, I escape (someone's notice);* φθάνω *I anticipate, I arrive before.*

ἐτύγχανε παρ-ών. *He was there by chance.* (He happened being there.)

ἔλαθον εἰσ-ελθόντες. *They came in secretly.* (They escaped notice coming in.)

ἔφθασε τὸν βασιλέα εἰς τὴν πόλιν ἀφ-ικόμενος. *He arrived at the city before the king.* (He anticipated the king, coming to the city.)

*15. *Verbs of fearing—*

a. Fear to do something: infinitive. Neg. μή.

> φοβοῦμαι ἀδικεῖν.   *I fear to do wrong.*
>
> φοβοῦμαι μὴ εἴκειν.   *I am afraid not to yield.*

b. Fear that something will happen: after primary main verb—μή with subj.; after secondary main verb—μή with subj. or opt. Neg. μὴ οὐ.

> φοβοῦμαι μὴ (οὐ) γένηται.   *I fear it may (not) happen.*
>
> ἐφοβούμην μὴ (οὐ) γένοιτο or γένηται.   *I feared it might (not) happen.*

16. *Wishes—*in Homer, wishes both possible and impossible of fulfilment are expressed by the optative, often with εἰ, εἴθε, or εἰ γάρ. In Attic the two kinds of wishes are carefully distinguished.

a. Possible wishes are expressed by the opt.; εἴθε or εἰ γάρ *may* be added. Neg. μή.

> (εἴθε, εἰ γάρ) ἔλθοι.   *May he come!*

*b. Impossible wishes have two constructions.

(1) Past tense of the indicative: impf. for present time; aor. for past time. εἴθε or εἰ γάρ *must* be added. Neg. μή.

> εἴθε μὴ ἦν οὕτως μέγας.   *Would that he were not so large!*
>
> εἰ γὰρ δίκην ἀληθῶς ἐφιλήσαμεν.   *If only we had really loved justice!*

(2) ὤφελον *I ought* with the infinitive: pres. for present time; aor. for past time. Neg. μή.

> ὤφελεν Ὀδυσσεὺς παρ-εῖναι.   *Would that Odysseus were here!*
>
> μήποτε ὠφέλομεν λιπεῖν οἶκον.   *Would that we had never left home!*

PART VI: VOCABULARY

Of the 1115 words you memorized in the *Reading Course in Homeric Greek,* the vast majority (87.5%, to be exact) undergo no changes in passing over into Attic prose. Of the remaining 139 words which do appear in a somewhat different form from that to which you are accustomed, practically all will be easily recognized. Besides, even these words frequently occur in their older form in Attic poetry. Here is a breakdown of the *139 words which are different* in Attic prose.

A. Thirty-eight are adjectives of the 1st and 2nd declensions which differ only in taking *a* in the feminine instead of *η.* This is in keeping with the Attic rule that *a* is used after *ε, ι,* or *ρ.* For example:

   δίκαιος, -α, -ον   γλυκερός, -ά, -όν

B. Twenty-three other words also change *η* to *a.* Of these, notice that twelve are 1st declension nouns whose stems end in *ε, ι,* or *ρ.*

HOMER:	ATTIC:		HOMER:	ATTIC:
ἀγγελίη	= ἀγγελία		κνίση	= κνίσα
ἀγορή	= ἀγορά		Ἀθήνη	= Ἀθηνᾶ
ἀληθείη	= ἀλήθεια		βρώμη	= βρῶμα
βασιλείη	= βασιλεία		κάρη	= κάρα
βίη	= βία		κρητήρ	= κρατήρ
θύρη	= θύρα		νηῦς	= ναῦς
κονίη	= κονία		ἰητρός	= ἰατρός
μελίη	= μελία		ἔμπης	= ἔμπας
πάτρη	= πάτρα		λίην	= λίαν
πέτρη	= πέτρα		ἀήρ, ἠέρος	= ἀήρ, ἀέρος
πυρή	= πυρά		(ἀράομαι) ἀρήσομαι	= ἀράσομαι
σχεδίη	= σχεδία			

C. Forty words undergo contraction or shortening when passing into Attic.

   1. Adjectives in *-εος* usually contract.

   ἀργύρεος, -η, -ον = ἀργυροῦς, -ᾶ, -οῦν   χάλκεος, -η, -ον = χαλκοῦς, -ῆ, -οῦν
   πορφύρεος, -η, -ον = πορφυροῦς, -ᾶ, -οῦν   χρύσεος, -η, -ον = χρυσοῦς, -ῆ, -οῦν
   σιδήρεος, -η, -ον = σιδηροῦς, -ᾶ, -οῦν   κυάνεος, -η, -ον = κυανοῦς, -ῆ, -οῦν

   2. Attic often shortens *ου* to *ο.*

   γόνυ, γούνατος = γόνυ, γόνατος   νοῦσος = νόσος
   δόρυ, δούρατος = δόρυ, δόρατος   οὐδός = ὀδός (threshold)
   κούρη = κόρη   οὖλος = ὅλος
   μοῦνος = μόνος

   3. *ει* is shortened in the following words:

   ἀεικής = αἰκής   εἵνεκα = ἕνεκα
   ἀείρω = αἴρω   εἴρομαι = ἔρομαι
   ξείνιον = ξένιον   φαείνω = φαίνω
   ξεῖνος = ξένος

4. These words contract according to the rules previously learned.

ἀέκων = ἄκων
ἀοιδή = ᾠδή
(ἐ)έργω = εἴργω
ἠέλιος = ἥλιος
νόος = νοῦς

ὀστέον = ὀστοῦν
ῥόος = ῥοῦς
φάος = φῶς
Ποσειδάων = Ποσειδῶν

5. Other words that are shortened:

αἰεί = ἀεί
αἰετός = ἀετός
κλαίω = κλάω
αὐτάρ = ἀτάρ
γαῖα = γῆ

δένδρεον = δένδρον
ἐννέπω = ἐνέπω
ἐννοσίγαιος = ἐνοσίγαιος
ἑός, -ή, -όν = ὅς, ἥ, ὅν
κληΐς = κλείς

D. Double sigma often changes to double tau in Attic.

θάλασσα = θάλαττα
θάσσων = θάττων
πλήσσω = πλήττω

φυλάσσω = φυλάττω
πρήσσω = πράττω
(σφάζω = σφάττω)

E. A few words suffer what is called a metathesis of quantity, that is, the transposition of the quantity of two vowels. Sometimes consonants are similarly changed.

ἧος = ἕως
λᾱός = λεώς

νηός = νεώς
κραδίη = καρδία

F. The remaining twenty-eight words fit into no particular classification.

ἀέξω = αὔξω
(αἰνέω) αἰνήσω = αἰνέσω
ἀλωή = ἅλως
ἄμαξα = ἅμαξα
ἀπείρων = ἄπειρος
(ἁρπάζω) ἁρπάξω = ἁρπάσω
αὖτις = αὖθις
(γίγνομαι) γέγαα = γέγονα
δεξιτερός = δεξιός
ἐλεαίρω = ἐλεέω
ἔρος = ἔρως
ζώω = ζάω
ἦμαρ = ἡμέρα
ἐπι-μάσσομαι = ἐπι-μάσομαι

Ἠώς = Ἔως
θέμις, θέμιστος = θέμις, θέμιτος
Θήβη = Θῆβαι
ἰθύς = εὐθύς
κεῖνος = ἐκεῖνος
κεῖσε = ἐκεῖσε
κιχάνω = κιγχάνω
ὅθι = οὗ
πεῖραρ = πέρας
πεύθομαι = πυνθάνομαι
(ὀλλύω) ὀλέσω = ὀλῶ
τάμνω = τέμνω
χρώς, χροός = χρώς, χρωτός
ἐύσσελμος = ἐύσελμος

Containing All Memory Words in Both Books

1. *Asterisks indicate memory words of Book One.*
2. *Number after word indicates Lesson in which the* word *is* first given for memory
3. *( ) inclose words not always needed in translating;*
4. *[ ] contain explanatory information.*

*ἀγαθός, -ή, -όν   good, brave;
   [comp.: ἀρείων, -ον; supl.: ἄριστος, -η, -ον]   9
*Ἀγαμέμνων, -ονος   Agamemnon [king of Mycenae
   and Commander-in-chief of Greeks at Troy]   89
ἀγανός, -ή, -όν   gentle   149
ἀγάπη, -ης [f.]   love, charity   45
ἀγαυός, -ή, -όν   admirable, noble   154
ἀγγελίη, -ης [f.]   message, news   187
ἀγγέλλω, ἀγγελέω, ἄγγειλα   I announce   223
ἄγγελος, -ου [m.]   messenger   181
ἀγείρω, ἀγερέω, ἄγειρα [2nd aor. mid.: ἀγερόμην]
   I gather together   136
*ἀγήνωρ, -ορος   manly, courageous   81
*ἀγλαός, -ή, -όν   splendid   79
ἀγορεύω, ἀγορεύσω, ἀγόρευσα   I speak (in assembly)   125
ἀγορή, -ῆς [f.]   assembly   177
*ἄγριος, (-η), -ον   wild, savage   74
ἀγρός, -οῦ [m.]   field, country [opp. to city]   151
ἀγυιά, -ῆς [f.]   street, way   133
*ἄγχι [adv., prep. w. gen.]   near, close by   75
*ἄγω, ἄξω, ἄγαγον   I lead;
   ἄγε(τε)   come! [impt. of ἄγω used as interjection]
   17
*ἀδικέω, ἀδικήσω, ἀδίκησα   I do wrong, I injure   19
ἀδινός, -ή, -όν   thick-thronging, vehement   188
ἀεικής, -ές   unseemly, shameful   159
*ἀείρω, —, ἄειρα   I lift up, I take up, I raise   38
ἀέκητι [adv.]   against the will of   174
ἀέκων, -ουσα   unwilling   222
*ἀέξω, ἀεξήσω, ἀέξησα   I increase;
   [in mid.:]   I increase myself, I grow   22
*ἅζομαι [pres. system only]   I respect, I revere; I hesi-
   tate to   51
ἄημι   I blow   124
ἀήρ, ἠέρος [f.]   mist   134
*ἀθάνατος, -η, -ον   immortal, eternal   21
*Ἀθήνη, -ης   Athene [a goddess, special patron of
   Odysseus]   97
αἰ [= εἰ]   if   141
*αἰγίοχος, -η, -ον   aegis-bearing   92
*αἰδέομαι, αἰδέσ(σ)ομαι, αἰδεσσάμην   I reverence,
   I respect, I feel shame before   91

Ἀΐδης [gen.:] Ἀΐδαο or Ἄιδος [m.]   Hades [ruler
   of the lower world]   138
αἰδοῖος, -η, -ον   revered, honored   122
*αἰεί   ever, always, forever   9
αἰθόμενος, -η, -ον   burning, blazing   155
αἶθοψ, -οπος   sparkling   229
*αἷμα, -ατος [n.]   blood   100
αἰνέω, αἰνήσω, αἴνησα   I praise; I consent   174
αἰνός, -ή, -όν   dreadful, terrible   159
*αἴνυμαι [pres. system only]   I seize upon, I select   83
*αἰνῶς   awfully, greatly   103
*αἴξ, αἰγός [m., f.]   goat   75
Αἴολος, -ου   Aeolus [ruler of the winds]   121
*αἰπύς, -εῖα, -ύ   steep, utter   93
*αἱρέω, αἱρήσω, ἕλον   I seize;
   [in mid.:[I pick for myself, I choose   29
αἶσα, -ης [f.]   (allotted) measure, fate   218
*αἰσχρός, -ή, -όν   shameful   16
*αἰτέω, αἰτήσω, αἴτησα   I ask, I request   22
αἰχμή, -ῆς [f.]   spear-point   220
*αἶψα   quickly, suddenly   10
*ἀκέων, -ουσα   in silence, silent(ly)   112
ἄκοιτις, -ιος [f.]   wife   210
ἀκούω, ἀκούσομαι, ἄκουσα   I hear [sometimes w.
   gen.]   159
*ἄκρος, -η, -ον   top(most), outermost, extreme; [as a
   noun:]   edge, tip   39
*ἀλάομαι [pf. w. pres. sense: ἀλάλημαι]   I wander   88
*ἄλγος, -εος [n.]   pain, distress, woe   43
ἀλεγεινός, -ή, -όν   painful, grievous   130
ἀλεείνω   I avoid, I shun   204
ἀλείφω, ἀλείψω, ἄλειψα   I anoint, I daub   165
*ἀλέομαι, —, ἀλεάμην or ἀλευάμην   I avoid; I shrink
   before   53
*ἀληθείη, -ης [f.]   truth   7
*ἀληθής, -ές   true   29
ἄλις [adv.]   in abundance, in great numbers   221
ἀλκή, -ῆς [f.] [dat. sg.: ἀλκί]   defence; prowess   195
ἄλκιμος, -ου   mighty, valiant   214
Ἀλκίνοος, -ου   Alcinoüs [king of Phaeacians]   188
*ἀλλά [conj.]   but   8
*ἄλληλοι, -ων [pl. only]   one another   39
*ἄλλοθεν   from elsewhere   109

*ἄλλος, -η, -ο   other, another, else   32
ἄλλοτε   at another time   225
ἄλμη, -ης [f.]   brine, briny crust   195
*ἁλμυρός, -ή, -όν   salty, briny   83
*ἄλοχος, -ου [f.]   wife   80
*ἅλς, ἁλός [f.]   sea   71
ἀλύσκω, ἀλύξω, ἄλυξα   I shun, I escape   143
ἀλωή, -ῆς [f.]   threshing-floor; garden   152
*ἄμ or ἀνά [adv.:]   up, back;
   [prep. w. dat. or acc.:]   on, over   74
*ἅμα [adv., prep. w. dat.]   together with, at the same
   time   39
*ἄμαξα, -ης [f.]   wagon   79
*ἁμαρτάνω, ἁμαρτήσομαι, ἅμαρτον   I fail of, I miss,
   I err   21
ἀμβρόσιος, -η, -ον   fragrant   189
ἄμβροτος, -ον   fragrant, immortal   187
*ἀμείβομαι, ἀμείψομαι, ἀμειψάμην   I (ex)change, I
   reply [sometimes used in act.: ἀμείβω, etc.]   25
*ἀμέλγω [pres. system only]   I milk   86
*ἄμμε   we [acc. pl.]   32
*ἄμμες   we [nom. pl.]   32
*ἄμμιν   to or for us [dat. pl.]   32
ἄμυδις   at the same time, together   184
*ἀμύμων, -ονος   excellent, admirable   110
ἀμύνω, ἀμυνέω, ἄμυνα   I ward off; I aid, I defend
   216
*ἀμφί [adv., prep. w. dat. or acc.]   around, on both
   sides, concerning   48
ἀμφιέλισσα, -ης   easily-directed [epithet of ships]
   181
*ἀμφίπολος, -ου [f.]   handmaid, attendant   80
ἀμφίς [adv.]   apart; around   224
ἀμφότερος, -η, -ον   both   154
*ἄν   untranslatable particle giving a theoretical, gen-
   eral, expected, or contrary-to-fact coloring to the
   thought. [See appendix, p. 245]   17
*ἀνά or ἄμ [adv., prep.]
   [adv.:]   up, back;
   [w. gen:]   on (to)
   [w. dat.:]   on (at rest)
   [w. acc.:]   over, on (to)   74
*ἀνα-βαίνω, ἀνα-βήσομαι, ἀνά-βην, ἀνα-βέβηκα   I
   go up, I ascend   52
*ἀνάγκη, -ης [f.]   necessity, need   9
*ἄναξ, ἄνακτος [m.]   king, lord   27
ἀνάσσω, ἀνάξω, ἄναξα   I am lord (of), I reign   156
ἀνδάνω, ἀδήσω, ἄδον   I am pleasing (to)   203
*ἀνδρόμεος, -η, -ον   human [referring always to a
   man's flesh]   94
ἀνδρόφονος, -ον   man-slaying   218
*ἄνεμος, -ου [m.]   wind   31
*ἀν-έχομαι   I hold up under, I endure   23
*ἀνήρ, ἀνέρος or ἀνδρός [m.] [dat. pl.: ἄνδρεσσι or
   ἀνδράσι]   man, male   27
*ἄνθρωπος, -ου [m.]   man   11

ἀν-ίστημι   I stand up   163
ἄντα [adv., prep. w. gen.]   before, opposite   195
ἀντίθεος, -η, -ον   godlike   143
ἀντῑκρύ [adv.]   straight on or against [w. gen.]   220
ἀντίος, -η, -ον   opposite, towards; in reply   199
*ἄντρον, -ου [n.]   cave   82
*ἀνώγω, ἀνώξω, ἄνωξα, ἄνωγα [pf. has pres. sense;
   plpf. has impf. sense]   I urge, I command   99
ἀοιδή, -ῆς [f.]   song   165
ἀπαλός, -ή, -όν   soft, tender   220
*ἀπάνευθε [adv., prep. w. gen.]   away (from), apart
   (from), afar   41
*ἅπᾱς, ἅπᾱσα, ἅπαν   all, the whole   30
*ἄπ-ειμι   I am away   24
ἀπείρων, -ον   boundless   189
*ἀπ-έχω   I hold back from, I refrain from   81
ἀπήμων, -ον   safe, propitious   163
ἀπήνη, -ης [f.]   wagon   190
*ἀπό [adv., prep. w. gen.]   away from, from   6
ἀπο-αίνυμαι   I take away   184
ἄποινα, -ων [n. pl.]   ransom, recompense   214
*ἀπ-ολλύω, ἀπ-ολέσω, ἀπ-όλεσ(σ)α, ἀπ-όλωλα,
   [2 aor. mid.: ἀπ-ολόμην]   I kill;
   [in pf. and mid.:]   I perish, I am lost   26
*Ἀπόλλων, -ωνος   Apollo [god of light, culture,
   and prophecy]   35
ἀπο-πέμπω   I send away; I send off safely   129
*ἀπόπροθεν [adv.]   far away, aloof   76
*ἀπο-σεύω, —, ἀπο-σσύμην [non-thematic 2 aor.]   I
   rush away, I rush back (from)   85
*ἅπτω, ἅψομαι, ἅψα   I fasten;
   [in mid.:]   I lay hold of; I catch fire   105
*ἄρ(α) or ῥα [never first word; often untranslatable]
   therefore; then [not of time]   31
ἀράομαι, ἀρήσομαι, ἀρησάμην   I pray (to)   178
ἀραρίσκω, ἄρσομαι, ἄρσα or ἄραρον   I fit together;
   I am fitted with   190
ἀργαλέος, -η, -ον   hard, painful   141
ἀργύρεος, -η, -ον   of silver   124
ἄργυρος, -ου [m.]   silver   125
*ἀρείων, -ον   braver, better;
   [comp. of ἀγαθός, -ή, -όν]   50
*ἀρετή, -ῆς [f.]   manliness, virtue   7
*ἄριστος, -η, -ον   best, bravest;
   [supl. of ἀγαθός, -ή, -όν]   50
*ἀρνειός, -οῦ [m.]   ram [full-grown]   77
*ἄρνες, -ων [m. pl.]   acc. sg.: ἄρνα]   lamb(s)   82
ἄρνυμαι, ἀρέομαι, ἀρόμην   I win; I strive to win   215
ἁρπάζω, ἁρπάξω, ἅρπαξα or ἅρπασα   I snatch (up)
   or away)   127
*ἄρουρα, -ης [f.]   soil, earth   103
*ἄρσην, -ενος [m.]   male   86
Ἄρτεμις, -ιδος   Artemis [twin sister of Apollo]   149
*ἀρχή, -ῆς [f.]   beginning   9
*ἀσκός, -οῦ [m.]   bag   79
ἀσπαίρω   I gasp   171

ἄσπετος, -ον immeasurable, vast 229

*ᾶσσον [adv.] near, close [often w. gen. or dat.] 92

ἀστερόεις, -εσσα, -εν starry 134

ἀστήρ, -έρος [m.] [dat. pl.: ἀστράσι] star 212

*ἄστυ, -εος [n.] town 62

*ἀτάρ but 64

ἄτη, -ης [f.] infatuation; ruin 181

ἀτρεκέως truly, exactly 146

ἀτρύγετος, -ον barren 187

*αὖ again; but now 101

αὐγή, -ῆς [f.] light; ray 165

αὖθι there, here 210

*αὐλή, -ῆς [f.] courtyard, farmyard, fold 40

*αὐτάρ but, yet 24

*αὖτε again; on the other hand 87

ἀϋτή, -ῆς [f.] shout 194

*αὐτίκα at once 81

*αὖτις back, again 103

*ἀϋτμή, -ῆς [f.] breath; vapor; blast 106

αὐτόθι [adv.] right here; right there 151

*αὐτός, -ή, -όν self, same, very; himself, herself, itself; him, her, it [not used in nom. in last sense] 14

*αὐτοῦ [adv.] in the same place, there 69

αὔτως [adv.] in the same way; just 173

αὐχήν, -αὐχένος [m.] neck 220

ἀΰω, ἀΰσω, ἄϋσα I shout 194

*ἀφ-αιρέομαι, ἀφ-αιρήσομαι, ἀφ-ελόμην I take away 63

ἄφαρ [adv.] straightway, at once 156

*ἀφ-ικνέομαι, ἀφ-ίξομαι, ἀφ-ικόμην I come to, I arrive [w. acc.] 75

ἀφνειός, (-ή), -όν wealthy [sometimes w. dat. or gen.] 158

*ἀφύσσω, ἀφύξω, ἄφυσ(σ)α I draw, I heap up 65

*Ἀχαιοί, -ῶν Achaeans [a division of the Greeks]; also Greeks in general 89

ἀχε(ύ)ω, —, ἄκαχον I grieve 139

Ἀχιλ(λ)εύς, -ῆος Achilles [greatest warrior of Greeks and hero of Iliad] 213

ἄχνυμαι I grieve 129

ἄχος, -εος [n.] grief, pain 154

*ἄψ back, back again 97

*βαθύς, -εῖα, -ύ deep 86

*βαίνω, βήσομαι, βῆν, βέβηκα I go 42

*βάλλω, βαλέω, βάλον I throw, I strike 44

βαρύς, -εῖα, -ύ heavy, dire 130

*βασιλείη, -ης [f.] kingdom 37

βέλος, -εος [n.] missile, arrow 149

*βιάζω I use violence against, I constrain 110

*βίη, -ης [f.] force 7

*βίος, -ου [m.] life, way of living 12

βίοτος, -ου [m.] living, possessions 143

*βλέφαρον, -ου [n.] eyelid 106

*βοάω, βοήσω, βόησα I shout, I roar 109

βοή, -ῆς [f.] shout, cry 216

βόθρος, -ου [m.] hole, pit 135

βόσκω, βοσκήσω, βόσκησα I pasture, I feed 141

*βουλεύω, βουλεύσω, βούλευσα I plan, I consider whether to or how to [w. inf. or ὅπως and purpose constr.] 36

*βουλή, -ῆς [f.] plan, advice, will 36

*βούλομαι, βουλήσομαι, βουλόμην I desire, I prefer 32

*βοῦς, βοός [m., f.] [dat. pl. also: βουσί] ox, cow 63

*βροτός, -ή, -όν mortal, human 15

βρώμη, -ης [f.] or βρῶσις, -ιος [f.] food 176

*γαῖα, -ης [f.] earth, land 8

*γαμέω, γαμέω, γάμησα or γῆμα I marry 36

γάμος, -ου [m.] marriage, marriage-feast 158

*γάρ [conj., never first word] for; εἰ γάρ if only, would that [w. opt. in impossible wish] 6

*γαστήρ, γαστέρος or γαστρός [f.] belly 113

*γε at least, in fact 25

*γέγαα = pf. of γίγνομαι 23

*γεγωνέω, γεγωνήσω, γεγώνησα, γέγωνα [pf. with pres. meaning] I shout, I make myself heard 19

γέρας, -αος [n.] prize (of honor); estate 150

γέρων -οντος [m.] old man 137

γηθέω, γηθήσω, γήθησα I rejoice (at) 188

γῆρας, -αος [n.] old age 145

*γίγνομαι, γενήσομαι, γενόμην, γέγαα I am born, I become, I am; I happen 23

*γιγνώσκω, γνώσομαι, γνῶν, ἔγνωκα, ἔγνωσμαι, γνώσθην I know 16

γλαυκῶπις, -ιδος flashing-eyed [epithet of Athene] 193

*γλαφυρός, -ή, -όν hollow 70

γλυκερός, -ή, -όν sweet 160

*γλυκύς, -εῖα, -ύ sweet, delightful 32

*γοάω, γοήσομαι, γόησα I weep (for) [w. acc.], I mourn 118

*γόνυ, γούνατος or γουνός [n.] knee 34

γόος, -ου [m.] groan, lamentation 154

γουνόομαι I supplicate 136

*γυνή, γυναικός [f.] woman, wife 45

γυῖον, -ου [n.] limb 173

δαιδάλεος, -η, -ον cunningly wrought 213

δαιμόνιος, -η strange (one) [whose actions are unaccountable, wonderful, or superhuman] 213

*δαίμων, -ονος [m., f.] a divinity, a superhuman being 105

δαίνυμι, δαίσω, δαῖσα I give a feast; [mid.:] I feast 122

δαίς, δαιτός [f.] feast; portion 151

δαΐφρων, -ον sagacious 204

δαίω I light up; [pass.:] I blaze 195

δακρυόεις, -εσσα, -εν tearful 215

δάκρυον, -ου [n.] or δάκρυ, -υος [n.]   tear   132
*δαμάζω, δαμάω, δάμασσα I tame, I overpower   116
*δέ   but, while, then (not of time), on the other hand
   [sometimes indicating contrast with an earlier idea
   introduced by μέν; often not to be translated]   8
*δείδω, δείσομαι, δεῖσα, δείδια [pf. w. pres. sense]
   I fear [w. inf. or μή w. purpose construction]   25
δείκνῡμι, δείξω, δεῖξα I show   195
δειλός, -ή, -όν cowardly, luckless   134
δεινός, -ή, -όν awe-inspiring, dreadful   132
*δεῖπνον, -ου [n.]   dinner, meal   65
*δέκατος, -η, -ον tenth   50
*δένδρεον, -ου [n.]   tree   12
δέος, δέεος [f.]   fear, terror   137
δέρω, δερέω, δεῖρα I flay   138
δεσμός, -οῦ [m.]   bond   162
δεῦρο [adv.]   hither   166
*δεύτερος, -η, -ον second   49
*δέχομαι, δέξομαι, δεξάμην I receive, I accept   33
*δέω, δήσω, δῆσα I tie, I fasten   70
*δή indeed, clearly, now [not of time]   9
δηιοτής, -ῆτος [f.]   strife   171
δηλέομαι, δηλήσομαι, δηλησάμην I harm   157
δῆμος, -ου [m.]   realm, people   134
δήν [adv.]   long   198
δηρόν [adv.]   long   201
*διά [adv., prep.]
   [w. gen.:]   through (the midst of);
   [w. acc.:]   through(out), among, on account of   28
*διδάσκω, διδάξω, δίδαξα I teach   21
*δίδωμι, δώσω, δῶκα   I give [see appendix p. 238
   for irreg. forms]   67
*δίκαιος, -η, -ον just, honorable   12
*δίκη, -ης [f.]   justice, custom   7
διογενής, -έος sprung from Zeus   140
*δῖος, -α, -ον bright, glorious; [f. usually keeps α
   throughout sg.]   95
διοτρεφής, -ές Zeus-cherished   229
*δίς twice, a second time   21
δίφρος, -ου [m.]   chariot (platform), seat   222
*διώκω, διώξω, δίωξα I pursue   19
δμωή, -ῆς [f.]   handmaid   193
*δμώς, -ωός [m.]   servant (male)   80
*δοκέω, δοκήσω, δόκησα I seem, I appear   21
*δόλος, -ου [m.]   cunning, craftiness, trickery; bait
   for catching fish   45
δόμος, -ου [m.]   house, room   130
*δόξα, -ης [f.]   opinion; glory   8
*δόρπον, -ου [n.]   supper   94
*δόρυ, δούρατος or δουρός [n.]   beam, plank; spear
   106
*δῦν, 3 aor. of δύω I go down
*δύναμαι, δυνήσομαι, δυνησάμην I can, I am able
   [w. inf.]   92
*δυνατός, -ή, -όν able, possible   24

δυσμενής, -ές hostile   199
δύστηνος, -ον wretched, unfortunate   140
*δύω or δύο [indecl.]   two   35
δύω, δύσομαι, δῡσάμην or δῦν   I enter; I put (on);
   I sink; I set [of the sun]   133
δώδεκα [indecl.]   twelve   121
δῶμα, -ατος [n.]   house, hall   122
*δῶρον, -ου [n.]   gift   13

*ἑ   him, her [acc. sg. of 3 pers. pron.]   34
*ἐάω, ἐάσω, ἔᾱσα I allow, I leave (alone)   37
*ἐγγύθεν [adv.]   from close at hand, near   111
*ἐγγύς [adv., prep. w. gen.]   near   14
ἐγείρω, ἐγερέω, ἔγειρα [aor. mid.: ἐγρόμην]   I
   rouse, I wake   127
*ἔγνωκα, ἔγνωσμαι = pf. of γιγνώσκω I know   16
ἔγχος, -εος [n.]   spear   220
*ἐγώ(ν) I [for forms, see appendix, p. 239]   32
ἐδητύς, -ύος [f.]   eating, food   176
*ἔδνα or ἕεδνα, -ων [n. pl.]   bride-price, dowry   143
*ἔδομαι = fut. of ἐσθίω I eat   19
*ἔδω [pres. system only]   I eat   64
ἐδωδή, -ῆς [f.]   food   191
*ἕζομαι, —, ἕσα I sit down;
   [in aor.:]   I cause to be seated   71
*ἐθέλω, ἐθελήσω, ἐθέλησα I wish   20
ἔθνος, -εος [n.]   group, band   136
*εἰ (1) if;
   (2) if only, would that [w. opt. in impossible wish];
   (3) whether [in indirect questions];
   (4) εἰ γάρ if only, would that [w. opt., in impossible
      wish];
   (5) εἰ μή unless   10
*εἶδαρ, -ατος [n.]   food   64
(ἐ)είδομαι, —, (ἐ)εισάμην I appear, I seem (like to)
   189
εἶδος, -εος [n.]   appearance, face   196
*εἴθε if only, would that;
   [w. opt., in impossible wish]   19
εἴκω, εἴξω, (ἔ)ειξα I yield, I give way   220
εἰλ(έ)ω, —, (ἔ)ελσα I confine, I check; [pass.:]   I
   throng; I crouch   168
εἷμα, -ατος [n.]   garment; [pl.:]   clothes   151
*εἰμί I am [see appendix p. 238 for forms]   10
εἶμι   I go, I shall go [see #861 for forms]   137
*εἵνεκα [prep. w. gen.]   on account of, for the sake of
   12
*εἶπον [2 aor. system]   I said, I told; [augmented
   ἔειπον, for ἔϜειπον]   47
*εἰρήνη, -ης [f.]   peace   7
*εἴρομαι, εἰρήσομαι, ἐρόμην I ask   25
εἴρω, ἐρέω I speak, I say   145
*εἷς, μία, ἕν [m.—n. gen. ἑνός]   one   30
*εἰς [adv., prep. w. acc.]   into, to, unto   10

GREEK-ENGLISH VOCABULARY

*εἰσ-έρχομαι I enter 34
*εἰσ-οράω I see, I look at 87
ἔ(ι)σω [adv.] within 147
*ἐκ [ἐξ before vowels; adv., prep. w. gen.] out of, from 6
*ἕκαστος, -η, -ον each 27
*ἑκατόμβη, -ης [f.] hecatomb [strictly, sacrifice of 100 cattle; but usually sacrifices in general] 145
ἕκηλος, -ον at rest, undisturbed 151
*ἐκ-σεύω, —, ἐκ-σσύμην [non-thematic 2 aor.] I rush out of, I pour out of [intr.] 105
ἐκ-τελέω I accomplish (completely) 124
ἐκτός [adv.] outside of, away from 168
Ἕκτωρ, -ορος Hector [most distinguished warrior of Trojans] 212
*ἐλᾴνεος, -η, -ον or ἐλᾴινος, -η, -ον (of) olive-wood 98
ἔλαιον, -ου [n.] olive-oil 191
*ἐλαύνω, ἐλάω, ἔλασ(σ)α I drive 86
ἔλαφος, -ου [f.] deer 193
ἐλεαίρω I pity 199
*ἐλεέω, —, ἐλέησα I pity, I have mercy on 101
ἑλίσσω, —, (ἐλ)έλιξα I whirl, I turn 184
ἕλκω I drag 222
*ἕλον = 2 aor. of αἱρέω I seize; [in mid.:] I pick for myself, I choose 29
*ἔλπω or ἔλπομαι [present system only] I expect, I hope, I suppose 40
*ἔλ(υ)θον = 2 aor. of ἔρχομαι I come, I go 26
*ἔμβρυον, -ου [n.] a young one [of animals] 87
*ἐμός, -ή, -όν my, mine 26
ἔμπεδος, -ον firm, unchanged 147
ἔμπης [adv.] nevertheless 199
*ἐμ-πίπλημι, ἐμ-πλήσω, ἔμ-πλησα I fill (with) 81
*ἐν [adv., prep. w. dat.] in, on, among 6
*ἔνδον [adv.] within, inside 82
ἐνδυκέως kindly 129
*ἔνεικα = aor. of φέρω I bear, I bring 17
*ἔνθα there, then 65
ἐνθάδε [adv.] here, hither 148
*ἔνθεν from there; then [of time] 32
*ἐννέπω, ἐνίψω, ἔνισπον I say, I tell 18
*ἐννῆμαρ [adv.] for nine days 64
ἐννοσίγαιος, -ου earth-shaker [epithet of Poseidon] 141
ἕννυμι, ἕσ(σ)ω, ἕσ(σ)α I clothe, I put on 151
ἐνοσίχθων, -ονος earth-shaker [epithet of Poseidon] 188
ἔντεα, -ων [n. pl.] [3 decl.] arms, armor; utensils 213
*ἐντολή, -ῆς [f.] command, order 34
*ἔντοσθε(ν) within, inside of 85
*ἐξ [used before vowels for ἐκ; adv., prep. w. gen.] out of, from 6
ἕξ [indecl.] six 121

ἐξείης [adv., = ἑξῆς] in order 145
ἐξ-εναρίζω, ἐξ-εναρίξω, ἐξ-ενάριξα I strip off; I kill 156
*ἑξῆς [adv.] in order 71
ἔξοχα [adv.] chiefly, above the rest 159
*ἕο of him, of her [gen. sg. of 3rd pers. pron.] 34
*ἔοικα [pf. w. pres. force; ἐῴκεα plpf. w. impf. force] I seem, I am like to; [in 3 sg. impers., which may govern acc. and inf. constr.:] it is fitting 45
*ἑός, -ή, -όν own, his, her 15
*ἐπεί [conj.] when; since 18
ἐπ-είγω I drive on; [mid.:] I hasten 163
*ἔπειτα then, thereupon 39
*ἐπ-έρχομαι I come to, I come upon [w. dat. or acc.] 81
*ἐπήν = contraction of ἐπεὶ ἄν 35
*ἐπί [adv., prep.]
  [w. gen.:] upon;
  [w. dat.:] on, at, beside;
  [w. acc.:] to, towards, after (i.e., in search or attack) 6
*ἐπι-βαίνω, ἐπι-βήσομαι, ἐπί-βην, ἐπι-βέβηκα I go upon, I land upon [w. gen.] 64
*ἐπι-μαίομαι, ἐπι-μάσσομαι, ἐπι-μασσάμην I seek out, I feel, I touch 95
ἐπι-τέλλω, —, ἐπί-τειλα I enjoin; I give orders to 168
*ἐπι-τίθημι, ἐπι-θήσω, ἐπί-θηκα I put on; I put in position 86
ἐπ-οίχομαι I go towards or round, I assail; I work (at) 149
ἕπομαι, ἕψομαι, ἑσπόμην I follow (with) 149
*ἔπος, -εος [n.] word 28
ἐπ-οτρύνω, ἐπ-οτρυνέω, ἐπ-ότρυνα I stir up, I compel [w. dat. or acc.] 138
*ἑπτά seven 80
*ἔργον, -ου [n.] work, deed 12
(ἐ)έργω, ἔρξω, ἔρξα I keep off; I shut up 168
*ἔρδω, ἔρξω, ἔρξα I do 31
ἐρείδω, ἐρείσω, ἔρεισα I rest; I lean; I press 159
*ἐρετμόν, -οῦ [n.] oar 71
ἐρέω I inquire 129
*ἐρίηρος, -ον [pl. follows 3 decl.: ἐρίηρες, -ων] faithful, loyal 70
ἔρις, -ιδος [f.] strife 192
ἔρος, -ου [m.] love, desire 176
ἐρύκω, ἐρύξω, ἔρυξα or ἐρύκακον I check; I guard 141
*(ἐ)ρύομαι, (ἐ)ρύσσομαι, (ἐρ)ρυσ(σ)άμην I save, I rescue, I protect 62
*ἐρύω, —, ἔρυσ(σ)α I drag, I draw 70
*ἔρχομαι, ἐλεύσομαι, ἔλ(υ)θον, εἰλήλουθα I come, I go 26
ἐσθής, -ῆτος [f.] clothing 191

287

*ἐσθίω, ἔδομαι, φάγον I eat 19

*ἐσθλός, -ή, -όν noble, excellent, brave 13

*ἔσθω [pres. system only] I eat, I devour 119

ἔσσα = aor. of ἔννῡμι I clothe, I put on 151

ἔ(ι)σω [adv.] within 147

*ἑταῖρος, -ου [m.] companion, comrade 23

*ἕταρος, -ου [m.] companion, comrade 23

*ἕτερος, -η, -ον (the) other 14

ἑτέρωθι on the other side 170

*ἔτι yet, still; οὐκ ἔτι no longer 31

*εὖ well 44

*εὕδω, εὑδήσω, εὕδησα I sleep 17

*εὐ-εργής, -ές well-made, fine 80

εὐήρης, -ες well-balanced 144

εὐκνήμις, -ῖδος well-greaved 229

εὐκτίμενος, -η, -ον well-built; well-tilled 207

εὐνή, -ῆς [f.] bed; anchor-stone 151

ἐύξεστος, (-η), -ον well-polished 191

ἐυπλόκαμος, -ον fair-tressed 132

*εὑρίσκω, εὑρήσω, εὗρον I find, I discover 33

Εὐρύλοχος, -ου Eurylochus [a companion of Odysseus] 136

*εὐρύς, -εῖα, -ύ wide, broad 33

ἐύσσελμος, -ου w. fine rowing-benches 180

εὐχετάομαι I declare myself, I exult; I pray (to) 180

*εὔχομαι, εὔξομαι, εὐξάμην I claim (to be), I boast, I exult; I pray (to), I vow [w. inf.] 40

ἐφ-έπω, ἐφ-έψω, ἐπί-σπον I meet; I drive, I pursue 152

*ἔφη [irreg.] he said, she said 20

ἐφ-ορμάω, ἐφ-ορμήσω, ἐφ-όρμησα I urge on; [mid.:] I rush forward, I am eager to 154

*ἔχω, ἕξω or σχήσω, σχόν or σχέθον I have, I hold 18

ζεύγνῡμι, ζεύξω, ζεῦξα I yoke 191

*Ζεύς, Διός or Ζηνός Zeus [father and chief of the gods] 49

Ζέφυρος, -ου Zephyrus [the west wind] 124

*ζητέω, ζητήσω, ζήτησα I seek, I search after 34

*ζωή, -ῆς [f.] life 26

ζωός, -ή, -όν alive, living 127

*ζώω, ζώσω, ζώσα I live 20

*ἤ or; than; ἤ...ἤ either...or, whether...or 27

*ἦ truly, indeed [sometimes merely introduces a question and is not to be translated] 83

*ἦ thus he spoke [3 sg. impf. of ἠμί, the only form used] 105

ἡγεμονεύω, ἡγεμονεύσω, ἡγεμόνευσα I lead (the way) 204

ἡγέομαι, ἡγήσομαι, ἡγησάμην I lead, I guide 193

*ἠδέ [conj.] and 20

ἤδη [adv.] by now, already, now 125

*ἥδομαι, ἥσομαι, ἡσάμην I am pleased (with) 22

*ἡδονή, -ῆς [f.] pleasure 29

*ἡδύς, -εῖα, -ύ sweet, pleasant 8, 29

*ἠέ = ἤ; ἦε = ἦ or ἦ 27, 83

*ἠέλιος, -ου [m.] sun 23

ἠέρος = gen. sg. of ἀήρ [f.] mist 134

Ἠετίων, -ωνος Eëtion [father of Andromache] 212

ἧμαι I sit [for forms, see appendix p. 247] 133

*ἦμαρ, ἤματος [n.] day 38

*ἡμεῖς we [for forms, see appendix p. 239] 32

ἠμέν [correlative w. ἠδέ] both 123

*ἥμενος, -η, -ον sitting, seated 85

*ἡμέτερος, -η, -ον our 14

ἡμίονος, -ου [f.] mule 190

*ἥμισυς, (-εια), -υ half 30

*ἦμος [conj.] when 73

*ἤν = contraction of εἰ ἄν 35

ἡνία, -ων [n. pl.] reins 191

*ἧος while, until [w. ind. if purely factual; w. purpose constr. if anticipatory] 85

ἤπειρος, -ου [f.] land, mainland 128

*ἠριγένεια, -ης the early-born (one) 73

ἥρως, ἥρωος [m.] [contracted gen.: ἥρως] warrior [often honorary title] 207

*ἦτορ [n., indec.] heart 88

ἠύτε as 155

*ἠώς, ἠόος [f.] dawn 73

*Ἠώς, Ἠόος [f.] Dawn [acc. sg. often contracts to Ἠῶ] 73

θάλαμος, -ου [m.] bed-room, store-room 191

*θάλασσα, -ης [f.] sea 8

θαλερός, -ή, -όν blooming, vigorous, big 132

θαμβέω, —, θάμβησα I wonder (at) 129

*θάνατος, -ου [m.] death 12

*θάσσων, -ον swifter; [comp. of ταχύς, -εῖα, -ύ] 50

θαυμάζω, θαυμάσσομαι, θαύμασα I marvel (at) 209

θεά, -ᾶς [f.] goddess [keeps ᾱ throughout sg.] 162

*θέμις, -ιστος [f.] a right, custom; θέμις ἐστί it is right, lawful 36

θεοειδής, -ές godlike 224

*θεός, -οῦ [m., f.] god; goddess 11

*θεσπέσιος, -η, -ον heavenly, divine, unearthly 81

θέσφατος, -ον divinely decreed; divine decree 147

θέω I run 184

Θηβαῖος, -η, -ον Theban 139

Θήβη, -ης [f.] [also pl.] Thebes 158

*θῆλυς or θήλεια [adj.] female 115

*θησαυρός, -οῦ [m.] treasure 15

θίς, θινός [m.] beach 181

*θνήσκω, θανέομαι, θάνον, τέθνη(κ)α I die 17

*θνητός, -ή, -όν moral 15

*θοός, -ή, -όν swift 65

*θρέψω, θρέψα = fut. and aor. of τρέφω I nourish I feed, I rear 21

θρόνος, -ου [m.] seat, chair 207

*θυγάτηρ, θυγατέρος or θυγατρός [f.] daughter 63

θύελλα, -ης [f.] blast, storm 127

*θυμός, -οῦ [m.] heart, spirit 13

*θυρεός, -οῦ [m.] door-stone 77

*θύρη, -ης [f.] door 53

θωρήσσω, —, θώρηξα I arm 169

ἰαίνω, —, ἴηνα I warm, I melt; I cheer 165

*ἰάχω I shout, I hiss; I resound 107

*ἰδέ [= ἠδέ] and 76

ἰερεύω, ἰερεύσω, ἰέρευσα I sacrifice, I slaughter 136

*ἰερός, -ή, -όν holy, sacred 25

ἵζω I make to sit; I sit (down) 224

*ἵημι, ἥσω, ἧκα I send forth, I cast; I place 67

*ἰητρός, -οῦ [m.] physician 11

Ἰθάκη, -ης [f.] Ithaca [a small island in the Ionian Sea, home of Odysseus] 136

ἰθύς [adv.] straight (towards) [w. gen.] 224

*ἰκάνω [pres. system only] I come, I have come 19

*ἰκέται, -άων [m. pl.] suppliants 91

*ἰκνέομαι, ἵξομαι, ἰκόμην I approach, I come [w. acc.] 91

ἴκρια, -ων [n. pl.] deck 169

Ἴλιος, -ου [f.] Ilion, Troy 123

ἵμερος, -ου [m.] yearning, desire 225

*ἵνα [adv.] where;
[conj.] that, in order that, to 18

ἰοχέαιρα, -ης shooter of arrows 149

ἰππόδαμος, -ου horse-taming 216

ἵππος, -ου [m.] horse 211

ἴς, ἰνός [f.] sinew, strength 155

ἴσος, (ἐ)ἴση, ἴσον equal, fair, trim 151

*ἵστημι, στήσω, στῆσα [tr. in act.:] I put, I halt;
ἵσταμαι, στήσομαι, στῆν [intr. in mid.:] I stand 77

ἰστίον, -ου [n.] sail [pl. often used for sg.] 132

*ἰστός, -οῦ [m.] mast; loom [for weaving] 98

ἴφθιμος, -η, -ον mighty, doughty 138

ἴφιος, -η, -ον fat, strong

ἰχθύς, -ύος [m.] fish 171

*ἰών, ἰοῦσα, ἰόν going 67

*κὰδ = κατὰ before δ 10

καθαίρω, καθαρέω, κάθηρα I cleanse 192

*καθ-ίζω, —, κάθ-ισα I seat myself; I cause to be seated 71

*καί and, even, also 6

καίνυμαι, [pf. w. pres. sense: κέκασμαι] I surpass 227

*καίω, καύσω, κῆα I kindle, I burn 85

*κακός, -ή, -όν cowardly, bad, evil 12

καλέω, καλέω, κάλεσ(σ)α I call, I invite 151

κάλλος, -εος [n.] beauty 202

*κᾱλός, -ή, -όν beautiful, noble;
[compr. καλλίων, -ον; supl. κάλλιστος, -η, -ον] 7

καλύπτω, καλύψω, κάλυψα I cover 128

Καλυψώ, -όος [f.] Calypso [a nymph] 185

κάματος, -ου [m.] toil, weariness 173

κάμνω, καμέομαι, κάμον I toil, I construct; I grow weary 125

κάπρος, -ου [m.] boar 145

κάρη, καρή(α)τος or κρά(α)τος head 161

κάρηνα, -ων [n. pl.] summits, heads 136

*καρπάλιμος, -ον swift, quick 82

*καρπός, -οῦ [m.] fruit 14

*κασιγνητός, -οῦ [m.] brother 26

*κατά [adv., prep.]
[adv.:] thoroughly, completely;
[w. gen.:] down (from);
[w. acc.:] down (along), according to, throughout 10

κατα-θνήσκω I die 136

κατά-κειμαι I lie down 138

κατα-κτείνω I slay, I kill 157

κατα-λέγω I tell in order, I relate 123

κατα-λείπω I leave behind, I forsake 139

κατά-πεφνον [2 aor. only] I slay 149

*κατα-τίθημι, κατα-θήσω, κατά-θηκα I put down 87

κατα-χέω, κατα-χεύσω, κατά-χευα or κατα-χεύμην I pour down: [mid.:[I fall down 184

κατ-έρχομαι I come down 130

*κε(ν) untranslatable particle giving a theoretical, general, expected, or contrary-to-fact coloring to thought; used w. verb in indic., subj., opt., inf. [See appendix p. 245 for syntax] 17

κεάζω, κεάσω, κέασ(σ)α I shatter 182

*κεῖμαι [pf. mid. system] I have been placed, I lie down 47

*κεῖνος, -η, -ο that (one) 14

κεῖσε [adv.] thither 168

κελαινεφής, -ές cloud-wrapped, dark 136

*κέλευθος, -ου [f., but frequently n. in pl. κέλευθα, -ων] way, path, course 88

*κελεύω, κελεύσω, κέλευσα I command [w. acc., dat., inf.] 19

*κέλομαι, κελήσομαι, κεκλόμην I order 70

*κεν = κε

κέραυνος, -οῦ [m.] thunderbolt 182

*κέρδιον [comp. adv.] more beneficial, better 52

*κεύθω, κεύσω, κύθον I hide 18

κεφαλή, -ῆς [f.] head 184

κῆδος, -εος [n.] care, woe 198

*κῆρ, κῆρος [n.] heart 28

κήρ, κηρός [f.] fate, death 149

κῆρυξ, κήρυκος [m.] attendant, herald 128

Κίρκη, -ης [f.] Circe 132

*κιχάνω, κιχήσομαι, κίχον I reach, I come (by chance) 91

κίω, —, κίον I go 181

κλάζω, κλάγξω, κλάγξα I shriek 171

*κλαίω, κλαύσω, κλαῦσα I weep, I wail 70

κλέος, κλέ(ε)ος [f.] fame, renown 215

*κληΐς, κληῗδος [f.] bolt; oar-lock 71

κλίνω, κλινέω, κλῖνα I lean, I lie 152

*κλυτός, -όν famous, excellent 97

κλύω, —, (κέ)κλυον [athematic in aor. impt.] I hear (sound of), I attend to 173

κνίση, -ης [f.] fat, savor 180

κοῖλος, -η, -ον hollow 170

κοιμάω, κοιμήσω, κοίμησα I put to sleep; I calm 163

κόλπος, -ου [m.] fold; bosom; bay 212

κόμη, -ης [f.] hair 202

κομίζω, κομιέω, κόμισσα I tend; I aid; I pick up 130

κονίη, -ης [f.] dust 161

κορυθαίολος, -ον with glancing helm 161

κόρυς, κόρυθος [f.] helmet 216

*κόσμος, -ου [m.] world 39

κούρη, -ης [f.] girl, daughter 191

κουρίδιος, -η, -ον wedded 159

κραδίη, -ης [f.] heart 223

*κρατερός, -ή, -όν strong 15

*κράτος, -εος [n.] strength, power 53

*κρέα, κρεῶν [n. pl.] [3 decl.; nom. sg. *κρέας*] flesh, meat 94

κρείων, -οντος [m.] ruler, prince 210

κρήδεμνον, -ου [n.] veil 193

*κρητήρ, -ῆρος [m.] mixing-bowl 80

*κρίνω, κρινέω, κρῖνα I pick out; I separate; I judge 29

Κρονίων, Κρονίωνος [m.] Cronus's son [Zeus] 123

*κρύπτω, κρύψω, κρύψα I conceal 47

*κτείνω, κτενέω, κτεῖνα or *κτάνον* I kill 48

κύανεος, -η, -ον dark (blue) 170

κυανόπρωρος, -ον dark-prowed 132

κυβερνήτης, -αο [m.] steersman, pilot 133

κῦδος, -εος [n.] honor, glory 166

κυκάω, κυκήσω, κύκησα I stir up; I confuse 170

*Κύκλωψ, Κύκλωπος [m.] Cyclops 92

κυλίνδω I roll 161

κῦμα, -ατος [n.] wave 163

κυνέω, κυνήσομαι, κύσ(σ)α I kiss 217

κυών, κυνός [m., f.] dog 221

λᾶας, λᾶος [m.; acc.: *λᾶαν*] stone 161

λαγχάνω, λάξομαι, (λέ)λαχον I get by lot; I am assigned by lot; I give one [acc.] his due of 221

Λᾱερτιάδης, -εω [m.] Laertes' son [Odysseus] 140

λαῖλαψ, λαίλαπος [f.] tempest 177

*λαῖτμα, -ατος [n.] gulf 89

*λαμβάνω, λήψομαι, λάβον I take, I get 22

*λανθάνω, λήσω, λάθον I elude, I escape someone's notice, I deceive; [in mid.:] I am forgetful of 36

*λᾱός, -οῦ [m.] people [a nation]; followers 33

*λέγω, λέξω, λέξα I say, I tell; I call 10

λειμών, λειμῶνος [m.] meadow 162

λείπω, λείψω, λίπον I leave [aor. mid. sometimes has pass. sense] 43

*λευκός, -ή, -όν bright, white 8

λευκώλενος, -ον white-armed 193

λεύσσω I see, I look 125

λέχος, -εος [n.] bed [pl. is often used for sg.] 122

λέων, λέοντος [m.] lion 195

*λίην exceedingly; *καὶ λίην* truly 118

*λίθος, -ου [m.] stone 16

*λιλαίομαι [pres. system only] I long [w. gen.] 52

λιμήν, λιμένος [m.] harbor 176

λιπαρός, -ή, -όν sleek; comfortable; gleaming 145

*λίσσομαι, —, λισάμην I entreat, I beg 83

*λόγος, -ου [m.] word, speech; account; reason 11

λοέω, λοέσσω, λόεσ(σ)α [frequently contracts to *λούω*, etc.] I wash 192

λόφος, -ου [m.] crest, summit 161

*λυγρός, -ή, -όν good-for-nothing; wretched 116

*λύω (ῠ), λύσω, λῦσα, λέλυκα, λέλυμαι, λύθην I loose, I release 16

*λωτός, -οῦ [m.] lotus 68

*Λωτοφάγοι, -ων [m. pl] Lotus-eaters 64

*μάκαρ, μάκαρος happy, blessed 29

*μακρός, -ή, -όν long, large 39

*μάλα very, quite, greatly; [often merely intensifies force of an adj. or adv., not to be translated separately.] 35

μαλακός, -ή, -όν soft, gentle 130

μάλιστα [supl. of *μάλα*] especially 152

*μανθάνω, μαθήσομαι, μάθον I learn 17

μάντις, μάντιος [m.] seer 140

*μάρπτω, μάρψω, μάρψα I seize 93

μάχη, -ης [f.] battle, fight 227

*μαχ(έ)ομαι, μαχήσομαι, μαχεσ(σ)άμην I fight (with) 22

*μεγαλήτωρ, μεγαλήτορος great-hearted, great 95

μέγαρον, -ου [n.] large hall; [in pl.:] halls, palace 121

*μέγας, μεγάλη, μέγα [m. acc. sg.: *μέγαν;* n. acc. sg.: *μέγα;* rest 2nd decl. on stem: *μεγαλ-*] great, large big; [comp.: *μείζων, -ον;* supl.: *μέγιστος, -η, -ον*] 50

*μείζων, -ον bigger, larger [comp. of *μέγας*] 50

μειλίχιος, -η, -ον pleasing, winning, gentle 104

*μέλας, μέλαινα, μέλαν [m.—n. gen.: *μέλανος*] dark, black 79

*μελιηδής, -ές honey-sweet 69
*μέλλω, μελλήσω, μέλλησα I am about; I intend, I am destined 24
*μέλος, -εος [n.] member (of the body), limb 51
μέλω, μελήσω, μέλησα I am a care to 190
μέμαα [pf. w. pres. meaning] I am eager 154
*μέν indeed, for one thing, on the one hand, to be sure [introducing a contrast and followed by δέ; often not to be explicitly translated] 8
μενεαίνω, —, μενέηνα I desire eagerly; I rage 160
*μένος, -εος [n.] might, courage, wrath 117
*μένω, μενέω, μεῖνα I remain, I stay; I await 44
μερμηρίζω, μερμηρίξω, μερμήριξα I ponder (anxiously) 127
*μέσ(σ)ος, -η, -ον middle (of), midst (of) [followed by noun in same case; cp. Latin "in mediam urbem" = "into the middle of the city"] 46
*μετά [adv., prep.]
[w. gen. or dat.:] among, with;
[w. acc.:] into the midst, after 22
μεταυδάω I speak among 162
μετόπισθε(ν) [adv.] behind, later, after 155
*μέτρον, -ου [n.] measure 27
*μή not 17
*μηδέ and not, nor, not even 17
*μηδείς, μηδεμία, μηδέν no one, none 30
*μήδομαι, μήσομαι, μησάμην I contrive, I plan 68
*μῆκος, -εος [n.] length 28
*μῆλον, -ου [n.] sheep, flock 38
μήν [a stronger form of μέν] truly, indeed 160
μήν, μηνός [m.] month 123
*μηρός, -οῦ [m.] thigh 93
*μήτηρ, μητέρος or μητρός [f.] mother 48
μιμνήσκω, μνήσω, μνῆσα I remind; [mid.:] I remember [w. gen.] 168
*μίμνω [pres. system only] I remain, I await 73
*μιν him, her [acc. sg. of 3 pers. pron.] 34
*μίσγω, μίξω, μῖξα I mix with, I mingle with 32
*μισέω, μισήσω, μίσησα I hate 23
μνάομαι I am mindful of; I court 143
μνηστήρ, μνηστῆρος [m.] suitor 144
μογέω, —, μόγησα I toil, I suffer 166
*μοῖρα, -ης [f.] due measure; portion, fate; κατὰ μοῖραν just right; properly 87
*μοῦνος, -η, -ον alone, only 11
*Μοῦσα, -ης [f.] Muse [a goddess of poetry and art] 32
*μοχλός, -οῦ [m.] bar, stake 99
μυθέομαι, μυθήσομαι, μυθησάμην I relate, I say 162
μῦθος, -ου [m.] word, speech, saying 130
μυρίος, -η, -ον countless, measureless 122

ναιετάω I dwell, I inhabit; I am situated, I exist 196
ναίω, —, νάσσα I inhabit 121

Ναυσικάα, -ας [f.] Nausicaa 193
νεικέω, νεικέσω, νείκεσ(σ)α I quarrel with; I rebuke 183
*νέκταρ, νέκταρος [n.] nectar [special drink of the gods] 31
νέκυς, νέκυος [m.] corpse; [pl.:] the dead 135
νεμεσ(σ)άω, νεμεσ(σ)ήσω, νεμέσ(σ)ησα I am indignant with 205
*νέμω, νεμέω, νεῖμα I assign; I drive my flock; [mid.:] I possess, I feed on 85
*νέομαι [pres. system only] I return 69
νέος, -η, -ον young, fresh, new 198
νεύω, νεύσω, νεῦσα I nod 216
νεφέλη, -ης [f.] cloud 134
νεφεληγερέτα, -αο cloud-gatherer [epithet of Zeus] 177
*νέφος, -εος [n.] cloud 160
*νηλ(ε)ής, -ές pitiless, ruthless 91
νημερτής, -ές unfailing; true; clear 140
*νηός, -οῦ [m.] temple 25
*νήπιος, -η, -ον simple, foolish 11
νῆσος, -ου [f.] island 121
*νηῦς, νηός or νεός [f.] [dat. pl. also: νηυσί] [f.] ship 53
νήχω, νήξομαι, νηξάμην I swim 188
νῑκάω, νῑκήσω, νίκησα I conquer, I prevail 127
*νοέω, νοήσω, νόησα I think, I perceive 20
*νόος, -ου [m.] mind 15
νοστέω, νοστήσω, νόστησα I return (home) 210
*νόστιμος, -η, -ον of one's home-coming 63
*νόστος, -ου [m.] return (home) 62
νόσφι(ν) [adv.] apart (from), away (from) 205
Νότος, -ου [m.] Notus [the south wind] 174
*νοῦσος, -ου [f.] disease 15
νυ now [a weak temporal or inferential particle] 149
νύμφη, -ης [f.] maiden; nymph; bride 137
*νῦν now, at the present time 9
*νύξ, νυκτός [f.] night 50
νωμάω, νωμήσω, νώμησα I distribute; I control 125
*νῶτον, -ου [n.] back 113

*ξείνιον, -ου [n.] gift of hospitality; [a present given by host to guest] 83
*ξεῖνος, -ου [m.] guest, stranger 13
*ξίφος, -εος [n.] sword 94

*ὁ, ἡ, τό [pron., weak demonstrative adj.]
[when modifying a noun:] that, (the);
[w. definite antecedent:] who, which, what;
[as pron. standing alone:] he, she, it 15
ὀβελός, -οῦ [m.] spit 180
*ὄβριμος, -η, -ον heavy, mighty 85
*ὅδε, ἥδε, τόδε [demonstr. pron. & adj.] this (one); he, she, it 15

*ὁδός, -οῦ [f.] way, road; journey 33

ὀδύρομαι, ὀδὐρέομαι, ὀδῡράμην I bewail, I lament 154

Ὀδυσ(σ)εύς, -ῆος [m.] Odysseus 129

*ὅθι where 95

*οἶδα, εἰδήσω I know [irreg., see appendix p. 240 for forms] 70

ὀϊζύς, -ύος [f.] sorrow, distress 149

*οἴκαδε [adv.] homewards 89

*οἰκέω, οἰκήσω, οἴκησα I dwell, I inhabit 50

*οἶκος, -ου [m.] house, home 46

οἰκτρός, -ή, -όν [alternative superlative: οἴκτιστος] pitiful, miserable 158

*οἰμώζω, οἰμώξομαι, οἴμωξα I cry out in pain 107

*οἶνος, -ου [m.] wine 33

οἶνοψ, -οπος wine-dark 182

*οἷος, -η, -ον such as, what sort (of) 88

*οἶος, -η, -ον alone 76

*ὄϊς, ὄϊος [m., f.] [dat. pl. also: ὄεσσι; acc. always: ὄῐς] sheep 75

*οἴσω = fut. of φέρω I bear, I bring 17

*ὀΐω or ὀΐομαι, ὀΐσομαι, ὀϊσάμην I think, I suppose, I imagine 43

οἰωνός, -οῦ [m.] bird 221

ὄλβιος, -η, -ον happy, prosperous 145

*ὄλβος, -ου [m.] happiness, prosperity 16

*ὄλεθρος, -ου [m.] destruction 68

*ὀλίγος, -η, -ον small, few 13

*ὄλλῡμι, ὀλέσω, ὄλεσ(σ)α, ὄλωλα, [2 aor. mid.: ὀλόμην] I kill, I destroy, I lose; [in pf. act. and all middle:] I perish, I am lost 63

*ὀλοός, -ή, -όν destructive, deadly 64

ὀλοφύρομαι, ὀλοφύρέομαι, ὀλοφῡράμην I lament, I commiserate 147

Ὄλυμπος, -ου [m.] Olympus 178

*ὄμβρος, -ου [m.] rain, storm 21

ὅμῑλος, -ου [m.] throng, tumult 223

ὄμνῡμι, ὀμέομαι, ὄμοσ(σ)α I swear 176

*ὅμοῖος, -η, -ον like to, similar to 12

ὁμοῦ together, at the same time 165

ὄνειρος, -ου [m.] dream 154

*ὄνομα or οὔνομα, -ατος [n.] name 100

ὀνομάζω, ὀνομάσω, ὀνόμασα I name, I call (by name) 204

*ὀξύς, -εῖα, -ύ sharp, keen 95

*ὀπάζω, ὀπάσσω, ὄπασ(σ)α I send with (someone); I present 67

ὄπι(σ)θεν behind, afterwards, hereafter 207

ὀπίσ(σ)ω [adv.] behind, back, hereafter 147

*ὁπλίζω, ὁπλίσ(σ)ω, ὅπλισσα I prepare 94

ὅπλον, -ου [n.] tool, rope 133

*ὅπ(π)η where, in what direction 91

ὁπ(π)ότε when, whenever 134

*ὅπως that, in order that, to 18

*ὁράω, ὄψομαι, ἴδον, ἑώρᾱκα, ἑώρᾱμαι, ὄφθην I see, I look (at) 16

*ὀρθός, -ή, -όν straight, true 23

ὀρῑνω, —, ὄρῑνα I agitate 188

ὅρκος, -ου [m.] oath 176

ὁρμαίνω, —, ὅρμηνα I ponder 194

ὁρμάω, ὁρμήσω, ὅρμησα I arouse; [mid.:] I start, I rush (forward) 220

ὄρνις, ὄρνῑθος [m., f.] bird 178

ὄρνῡμι, ὄρσω, ὄρσα, ὄρωρα [aor. mid. also: ὀρ(ό)μην] I incite, I raise; [pf. is intrans. w. pres. meaning:] I move, I rise 123

*ὄρος, -εος [n.] mountain 77

ὀρούω, ὀρούσω, ὄρουσα I rush, I dart 127

*ὅς, ἥ, ὅ [rel. pron.] who, which, what 14

*ὅς, ἥ, ὅν [= ἑός, -ή, -όν] own, his, her 15

*ὅσ(σ)ος, -η, -ον as many as, as great as 86

ὄσσε [n. dual] eyes 169

*ὀστέον, -ου [n.] bone 94

*ὅς τις, ἥ τις, ὅ τι or ὅττι [indef. rel. pron. and adj.] whoever, whatever; [for forms, see appendix p. 239] 14

*ὅτε when, whenever 35

*ὅτι [conj.] that, because 18

ὀτρύνω, ὀτρῡνέω, ὄτρῡνα I urge on, I send 154

*οὐ [οὐκ before smooth breathing; οὐχ before rough breathing] not, no 8

οὖας, οὔατος [n.] [dat. pl. also: ὠσί] ear 165

*οὐδέ and not, nor, not even 21

*οὐδείς, οὐδεμία, οὐδέν no one, none 30

οὐδός, -οῦ [m.] threshold 129

*οὐκέτι no longer 31

*οὖλος, -η, -ον whole, entire 52

*οὖν therefore, then [not of time] 22

*οὐρανός, -οῦ [m.] heaven, sky 26

οὖρος, -ου [m.] a (fair) wind 132

οὐτάω, οὐτήσω, οὔτησα or οὖτα I wound, I pierce 137

*οὔτε and not, nor;
οὔτε . . . οὔτε neither . . . nor 8

*Οὖτις Nobody 104

οὖτος, αὕτη, τοῦτο this [for forms, see appendix p. 247] 155

*οὕτως thus, in this way, so 9

*ὀφθαλμός, -οῦ [m.] eye 14

*ὄφρα that, in order that, to [w. purpose constr.]; while, until [w. ind. if purely factual; w. purpose constr. if anticipatory] 24

*ὀφρύς, -ύος [f.] eyebrow 106

ὄψ, ὀπός [f.] voice 159

*παῖς, παιδός [m., f.] child, boy, girl 27

*πάλιν back (again), again 46

πάλλω, —, πῆλα I shake, I dandle 217

πάντῃ [adv.] on all sides, everywhere 152
**παντοῖος, -η, -ον* of all sorts 21
παπταίνω, —, πάπτηνα I look about sharply (for) 169
**παρά* [adv., prep.]
  [w. gen.:] from (the side of);
  [w. dat.:] at, beside;
  [w. acc.:] to, along (side) 20
**πάρ-ειμι* I am present 21
**παρ-έρχομαι* I go past, I pass 26
**παρ-έχω* I supply 18
**παρ-ίσταμαι, παρα-στήσομαι, παρά-στην* I stand by 98
πάροιθε(ν) before 198
πάρος [adv.] before, formerly 222
**πᾶς, πᾶσα, πᾶν* [m.–n. gen.: *παντός*] all, every, the whole 30
**πάσχω, πείσομαι, πάθον* I suffer, I experience 37
**πατέομαι, —, πασ(σ)άμην* I partake of 67
**πατήρ, πατέρος* or *πατρός* [m.] father 48
πάτρη, -ης [f.] fatherland 225
**πατρίς, -ίδος* [f.] fatherland, country; [as f. adj.: of one's fathers, ancestral 30
παύω, παύσω, παῦσα I stop; [mid.;] I cease 123
**παχύς, -εῖα, -ύ* thick, stout 104
πεδίον, -ου [n.] plain 211
πεζός, -ή, -όν on foot, by land 148
**πείθω, πείσω, πεῖσα* or *πέπιθον*, [2 aor. mid.: *πιθόμην*] I persuade, I win over; I trust [w. dat.]; [in mid.:] I am persuaded by, I am obedient to, I obey 31
**πεῖραρ, πείρατος* [n.] end, boundary; rope 93
**πειράω, πειρήσω, πείρησα* I make trial of, I attempt, I try 30
πείρω, —, πεῖρα I pierce, I stick; I pass through 180
πελάζω, πελάσω, πέλασ(σ)α I bring near to, I go near to 141
**πέλω, —, π(έ)λον* or *πέλομαι, —, πλόμην* I come to be, I am 24
**πελώριος, -η, -ον* gigantic, monstrous 76
**πέμπω, πέμψω, πέμψα* I send 24
πένθος, -εος [n.] sorrow, grief 152
**περ* surely; [w. ptc.:] though 27
περάω, περήσω, πέρησα I cross, I pass through 148
**περί* [adv., prep.]
  [adv.:] round about, especially;
  [w. gen.:] about, excelling;
  [w. dat. or acc.:] about, for 41
περικαλλής, -ές very beautiful 192
Περσεφόνεια, -ης [f.] Persephone [wife of Hades and queen of lower world] 138
**πετάννῡμι, —, πέτασ(σ)α* I spread out 111

πέτομαι, πτήσομαι, πτάμην I fly 154
**πέτρη, -ης* [f.] rock 7
**πεύθομαι, πεύσομαι, πυθόμην* I learn (by inquiry), I inquire (from), I hear (of) [object in acc. or gen.] 25
**πήγνῡμι, πήξω, πῆξα* I fix, I make fast 45
πῆμα, πήματος [n.] suffering, woe 143
πιέζω, πιέσ(σ)ω, πίεσα I press, I oppress 162
**πίνω, πίομαι, πιον* I drink 23
**πίπτω, πεσέομαι, πέσον* I fall 21
**πιστεύω, πιστεύσω, πίστευσα* I believe (in), I have faith in 38
πιφαύσκω I make known 163
**πίων, -ονος* fat, rich 82
πλάζω, πλάγξω, πλάγξα, —, —, πλάγχθην I beat; [pass.:] I wander 205
**πλεῖστος, -η, -ον* most; [supl. of *πολλός, -ή, -όν*] 50
**πλείων, -ον* more; [comp. of *πολλός, -ή, -όν*] 50
**πλέω, πλεύσομαι, πλεῦσα* I sail (over) 88
**πλησίος, -η, -ον* near, neighbor(ing) 22
πλήσσω, πλήξω, πλῆξα I smite 184
ποδάρκης, -ες swift-footed 214
**πόθεν* whence? from what source? from what place? 33
**ποθέω, ποθήσω, πόθεσα* I long for, I yearn, I miss 43
**ποιέω, ποιήσω, ποίησα* I make, I do, I produce 19
**ποιμήν, -ένος* [m.] shepherd 40
π(τ)ολεμίζω, π(τ)ολεμίξω I wage war, I fight (with) 228
**πόλεμος, -ου* [m.] war 12
**πολιός, (-ή), -όν* greyish, white 71
**πόλις, -ιος* [f.] city 89
**πολλός, -ή, -όν; [m. and n. also 3rd decl.: *πολύς, -ύ*] much, many; [comp.: *πλείων, -ον;* supl.: *πλεῖστος, -η, -ον*] 14
πολύμητις, -ιος [m. or f.] of many counsels 209
πολυμήχανος, -ον resourceful 140
**πολύς, —, -ύ* many, much 83
πολύτλας [only nom.] much-enduring 203
**Πολύφημος, -ου* [m.] Polyphemus [a Cyclops, son of Poseidon] 109
πομπή, -ῆς [f.] escort, safe sending-off 123
**πονέομαι, πονήσομαι, πονησάμην* I labor, I toil at, I am busy about 37
**πονηρός, -ή, -όν* worthless, base, wicked 15
**πόνος, -ου* [m.] toil, trouble 14
**πόντος, -ου* [m.] sea, the deep 62
πόποι oh! [a general exclamation to be trans. according to context] 126
**πόρον* [2 aor. system only] I gave 41
πορφύρεος, -η, -ον gleaming, bright 211

*Ποσειδάων, -ωνος [m.] Poseidon [brother of Zeus and god of sea] 93

πόσις, -ιος [f.] drink 176

πόσις, -ιος [m.] husband 159

*ποταμός, -οῦ [m.] river 14

*ποτέ ever, (at) some time, once, at any time 10

ποτί = πρός 159

πότμος, -ου [m.] fate, death 152

πότν(ι)α, -ης [f.] queen; [as adj.:] revered 150

*που perhaps, I suppose, no doubt, of course 21

*ποῦ where? 21

πούς, ποδός [m.] foot; sheet [a rope attached to the foot of the sail] 125

*πρᾶγμα, -ατος [n.] deed; [in pl.:] deeds; trouble 28

πρήσσω, πρήξω, πρῆξα I pass (over); I accomplish, I do 211

Πρίαμος, -ου [m.] Priam [king of Troy] 159

πρίν [adv., conj.]
  [adv.:] before, sooner;
  [conj. w. inf. or anticipatory subj.:] before, until 138

*προ-ίημι, προ-ήσω, προ-ῆκα I send forth, I cast 67

προπάροιθε(ν) before, in front of 225

*πρός [adv., prep.]
  [w. gen.:] from (the side of);
  [w. dat.:] on, at;
  [w. acc.:] to, towards, against 10

*προσ-αυδάω I address 101

*προσ-εῖπον I address, I speak to [w. acc.] 89

*πρόσθεν in front of, before 104

πρότερος, -η, -ον sooner, former 139

π(ρ)οτί = πρός 159

*πρόφρων, -ον with willing heart, kindly, eager(ly) 29

*πρῶτος, -η, -ον first 25

*πτερόεις, -εσσα, -εν winged 29

π(τ)ολεμίζω, π(τ)ολεμίξω I wage war, I fight (with) 228

*π(τ)όλεμος, -ου [m.] war 12

*π(τ)όλις, -ιος [f.] city 89

πτύσσω, πτύξω, πτύξα I fold 193

*πυκ(ι)νός, -ή, -όν thick, close; shrewd; vehement 115

*πύλη, -ης [f.] gate, entrance 34

*πῦρ, πυρός [n.] fire 28

πύργος, -ου [m.] tower 214

πυρή, -ῆς [f.] funeral-pyre, sacrificial fire 136

*πω [w. negative] never yet, in no way, not at all 36

*πως somehow, in any way 26

*πῶς how? 26

πῶυ, πώεος [n.] flock (of sheep) 157

*ῥα therefore, then 31

*ῥέζω, ῥέξω, ῥέξα I do, I sacrifice 18

ῥεῖα [adv.] easily, at ease 193

*ῥέω I flow 42

ῥήγνυμι, ῥήξω, ῥῆξα I smash, I break 184

*ῥηίδιος, -η, -ον easy 16

ῥίμφα [adv.] swiftly 165

*ῥίπτω, ῥίψω, ῥῖψα I hurl 109

*ῥοδοδάκτυλος, -ον rosy-fingered 73

ῥόος, -ου [m.] stream, current 134

*ῥύομαι, ῥύσ(σ)ομαι, ῥυσ(σ)άμην I save, I rescue, I protect 62

σάκος, -εος [n.] shield 220

*σάρξ, σαρκός [f.] flesh 44

Σειρήν, -ῆνος [f.] siren 162

σεύω, —, (σ)σεῦσα or (σ)σύμην I set in motion, I drive; [mid.:] I rush 192

*σηκός, -οῦ [m.] pen, fold 82

σῆμα, -ατος [n.] sign, mound

σϊγαλόεις, -εσσα, -εν shining 151

σιδήρεος, -η, -ον of iron 173

*σῖτος, -ου [m.] bread, food 26

σιωπή, -ῆς [f.] silence 213

σκέπας, σκέπαος [n.] shelter 178

σκῆπτρον, -ου [n.] staff [usually a symbol of office] 139

σκιόεις, -εσσα, -εν shadowy 160

σκόπελος, -ου [m.] crag 168

Σκύλλη, -ης [f.] Scylla 169

σμερδαλέος, -η, -ον frightful, terrible 195

*σός, -ή, -όν your [sg.] 24

*σοφός, -ή, -όν wise 11

σπένδω, σπείσω, σπεῖσα I pour a libation 180

*σπέος, σπέος or σπῆος [n.] cave 75

*σπεύδω, σπεύσω, σπεῦσα I hasten 21

*σταθμός, -ου [m.] door-post; farm-yard 116

*στείχω, —, στίχον I go, I proceed 110

*στενάχω [pres. system only] I groan, I lament 75

στέρνον, -ου [n.] chest, breast 220

στῆθος, -εος [n.] breast, chest 185

*στῆν [3 aor. system of ἵστημι] I stood 42

στιβαρός, -ή, -όν stout, strong 165

στόμα, -ατος [n.] mouth 159

στυγερός, -ή, -όν hateful, gloomy 152

*σύ you [sg.; for forms, see appendix p. 239] 33

*σύν [adv., prep. w. dat.] with 6

σύς, συός [m., f.] pig, swine 145

σφάζω, σφάξω, σφάξα I cut the throat, I slaughter 138

σφέας, σφέων them, of them; [acc. and gen. pl. of 3 pers. pron.] 34

*σφέτερος, -η, -ον their(s) 46

*σφι(ν) or σφισι(ν) to or for them; [dat. pl. of 3 pers. pron.] 34

σχεδίη, -ης [f.] raft 187

*σχεδόν [adv.] close by, near 92

*σχέθον = 2 aor. of ἔχω I have, I hold 18

*σχέτλιος, -η, -ον cruel, pitiless, reckless 13
*σχήσω = fut. of ἔχω I have, I hold 18
*σχόν = 2 aor. of ἔχω I have, I hold 18
*σώζω, σώσω, σῶσα I save 25
*σῶμα, -ατος [n.] body, dead body 28

τάμνω, —, τάμον I cut 211
*τάχα quickly, soon 105
*ταχύς, -εῖα, -ύ swift [comp.: θάσσων, -ον; supl.: τάχιστος, -η, -ον] 49
*τε [postpositive conj.] and, also; [often not to be translated, merely giving generalized or subordinate force to the thought, especially w. rel. pronouns and adverbs]
τε...τε, τε...καί both...and 13
τέθηλα or τέθαλα [pf. w. pres. meaning] I flourish 152
*τέθνη(κ)α= pf. of θνήσκω I die (cf. #798) 17
τείνω, τενέω, τεῖνα, τέτακα, τέταμαι I stretch 133
Τειρεσίης, -αο Tiresias [blind seer of Thebes] 136
*τείρω [pres. system only] I wear out, I distress 115
τεῖχος, -εος [n.] wall 121
τέκνον, -ου [n.] child 148
τέκος, -εος [n.] child 128
τελευτάω, τελευτήσω, τελεύτησα I bring to pass, I finish 176
*τελέω, τελέω, τέλεσα I fulfill, I accomplish, I complete 41
τέλος, -εος [n.] end, fulfillment 222
τέμενος, -εος [n.] land marked off [for a god or as private property] 151
*τεοισι = dat. pl. of τις, τι 31
*τεός, -ή, -όν your [sg.] 103
τέρπω, τέρψω, τέρψα or (τε)ταρπόμην I comfort, I cheer; [mid.:] I take my fill of 154
*τευ = gen. sg. of τις, τι 31
τεύχεα, -ων [n., pl.] [3 decl.] arms, armor 137
*τεύχω, τεύξω, τεῦξα I build, I make ready; [pf. mid.: τέτυγμαι (often = I am)] 35
*τεων = gen. pl. of τις, τι 31
*τῇ [adv.] there, where 28
*τῇδε [adv.] here 28
τῆλε far (away) 180
τηλόθι afar, far (from) 227
*τίθημι, θήσω, θῆκα I put, I cause, I make 69
τίκτω, τέξω, τέκον I beget, I bear 221
*τίνω, τίσω, τῖσα I pay; [mid.: I take vengeance upon, I punish 97
τίπτε what? why? how? 140
*τίς, τί who? which? what? [for forms, see appendix p. 239] [τί as adv. = why?] 31
*τις, τι some(one), something, one, a certain, any; [for forms, see appendix p. 239] [τι as adv. = somehow, in some respect] 31

*τλάω, τλήσομαι, τλῆν I endure patiently, I have the heart, I dare 42
*τοι [never first word] surely, you see 24
*τοι = dat. sg. of 2 pers. pron. sg. [see appendix p. 239] 33
τοῖος, -η, -ον such 145
τοιόσδε, τοιήδε, τοιόνδε such (as this, as that) 203
τοιοῦτος, τοιαύτη, τοιοῦτον such [see appendix p 247] 159
τοκεύς, τοκῆος [m., f.] parent 221
*τόσ(σ)ος, -η, -ον so many, so great 86
*τότε then 47
τόφρα so long, meanwhile 163
τράπεζα, -ης [f.] table 158
τρεῖς, τρία three 190
*τρέπω, τρέψω, τρέψα I turn 22
*τρέφω, θρέψω, θρέψα I nourish, I feed, I rear 21
*τρίς thrice, three times 100
*Τροίη, -ης [f.] Troy, Ilion 61
Τρῶες, -ων [m. pl.] Trojans 149
τυγχάνω, τεύξομαι, τύχον I happen (upon), I obtain [gen.] 206
*τύπτω, τύψω, τύψα I strike, I beat 71
*τυρός, -οῦ [m.] cheese 82
*τῷ [conj.] therefore, in that case 117

*ὑγρός, -ή, -όν fluid, watery, moist 88
*ὕδωρ, ὕδατος [n.] water 32
*υἱός, -οῦ or -εος [dat. pl.; υἱάσι] son 34
*ὕλη, -ης [f.] forest, wood 85
*ὑμεῖς you [for forms, see appendix p. 239] 33
*ὑπέρ or ὑπείρ [prep. w. gen. or acc.] over 88
ὕπερθεν above 171
*Ὑπερίων, -ονος [m.] Hyperion ["exalted one"] 63
ὑπερφίαλος, -ον overbearing 143
*ὕπνος, -ου [m.] sleep 99
*ὑπό [adv., prep.]
[w. gen.:] from under, under the influence of, by;
]w. dat.:] under (at rest);
[w. acc.:] under (motion to) 6
ὑπόδρα [adv.] with a scowl 158
ὑσμίνη, -ης [f.] battle, conflict 158
*ὕστατος, -η, -ον last 112
*ὑφαίνω, ὑφαινέω, ὕφηνα I weave, I devise 111
*ὑψηλός, -ή, -όν high 11
*ὑψόσε on high; upwards 79

*φάγον = 2 aor. of ἐσθίω I eat 19
φαεινός, -ή, -όν bright, shining 124
φαείνω I give light 182
φαίδιμος, -ον [never f.] shining; glorious 141
Φαίηκες, -ων [m., pl.] Phaeacians 188
*φαίνω, φανέω, φῆνα I show, I reveal; φαίνομαι, φανέομαι, φάνην [pass. w. act. sense] I show myself, I appear 27

*φάος, φάεος [n.] light 28

φᾶρος, -εος [n.] mantle 201

φάσγανον, -ου [n.] sword 140

*φέρω, οἴσω, ἔνεικα I bear, I bring 17

*φεύγω, φεύξομαι, φύγον I flee, I escape 20

*φημί, φήσω, φῆσα I think, I speak, I say, I tell [for impf. forms see appendix p. 238] 20, 88

φθίνω, φθίσω, φθῖσα I waste away, I pass away 150

*φθόγγος, -ου [m.] voice 88

*φιλεομένη [f. ptc.] being loved 7

*φιλέουσα f. ptc.] loving 8

*φιλέω, φιλήσω, φίλησα I love 17

*φίλος, -η, -ον dear (to), friendly (to); pleasing; own; [as noun:] friend; [comp.: φίλτερος, -η, -ον; supl.: φίλτατος, -η, -ον] 10, 11

φιλότης, -ητος [f.] love, friendship 126

*φοιτάω, φοιτήσω, φοίτησα I go (back and forth), I roam 19

φόνος, -ου [m.] death, slaughter 158

φράζω, φράσ(σ)ω, φράσ(σ)α I point out; [mid.:] I consider 134

*φρήν, φρενός [f.] mind, spirit 32

*φρονέω, φρονήσω, φρόνησα I consider, I have understanding 21

φυλάσσω, φυλάξω, φύλαξα I guard; I observe 150

φύλλον, -ου [n.] leaf 152

*φύσις, -ιος [f.] nature 27

φύω, φύσω, φῦσα I produce; φύομαι, φύσομαι, φῦν I grow; [w. ἐν:] I cling to 213

φωνέω, φωνήσω, φώνησα I lift up my voice, I utter 154

*φωνή, -ῆς [f.] voice, sound 9

*φώς, φωτός [m.] man 113

*χαίρω, χαιρήσω, χάρην [pass. w. active sense] I rejoice (in) 38

*χαλεπός, -ή, -όν difficult 15

χάλκεος, -ον bronze 125

χαλκήρης, -ες bronze-tipped 137

χαλκός, -οῦ [m.] copper, bronze 138

χαλκοχίτων, -ωνος bronze-clad 215

χαρίεις, -εσσα, -εν graceful, pleasing 202

χαρίζομαι, χαριέομαι, χαρισάμην I gratify; I give graciously 126

*χάρις, -ιτος [f.] [acc. sg.: χάριν] grace, beauty, charm; favor, kindness 37

*χείρ, χε(ι)ρός [f.] hand 51

χέρσος, -ου [f.] dry land, land 157

*χέω, χεύω, χεῦα I pour, I heap up 81

*χθών, χθονός [f.] earth 67

χιτών, -ῶνος [m.] tunic 201

χλαῖνα, -ης [f.] cloak 151

*χλωρός, -ή, -όν greenish-yellow, green 98

χόλος, -ου [m.] wrath 228

χολόω, (κε)χολώσω, χόλωσα I anger; [mid.:] I am angry [w. dat. of person; gen. of cause] 179

χορός, -οῦ [m.] dance, dancing-place 177

χρε(ι)ώ, χρε(ι)όος [f.] need, necessity 149

*χρή [impersonal] it is necessary; ought, should [acc. w. inf.] 20

*χρῆμα, -ατος [n.] possession, property; [in pl.:] wealth 28

*χρηστός, -ή, -όν worthy, good 29

*Χριστός, -οῦ [m.] Christ ["the anointed one"] 14

χρίω. χρίσομαι, χρῖσα I anoint 192

*χρόνος, -ου [m.] time 16

χρύσε(ι)ος, -η, -ον of gold 139

*χρῡσός, -οῦ [m.] gold 12

χρώς, χροός [m.] skin, body, person 151

χώομαι, χώσομαι, χωσάμην I am angry (with) 141

*χῶρος, -ου [m.] place, region 75

*ψῡχή, -ῆς [f.] soul; life 7

*ὦ O! [in direct address] 23

Ὠγυγίη, -ης Ogygia [a mythical island] 185

*ὧδε thus, so 107

ὠθέω, ὤσω, ὦσα I push 161

ὦκα quickly, swiftly 169

Ὠκεανός, -οῦ [m.] Ocean [a river encircling the earth; also personified as a god] 133

*ὠκύς, -εῖα, -ύ swift, nimble 70

ὦμος, -ου [m.] shoulder 145

*ὡς [adv., conj.] as, that, how, to 17

*ὣς, ὡς thus, so [always w. pitch-mark] 62

Containing All Memory Words in Both Books

1. ( ) *inclose words not always needed in translating.*
2. [ ] *contain explanatory information.*

able δυνατός, -ή, -όν; I am able δύναμαι, δυνήσομαι, δυνησάμην
about περί [prep. w. gen., dat., or acc.]; I am about μέλλω, μελλήσω, μέλλησα
above (all) περί [prep. w. gen.]; above ὕπερθεν
above the rest ἔξοχα [adv.]
abundance, in abundance ἅλις [adv.]
accept δέχομαι, δέξομαι, δεξάμην
accomplish τελέω, τελέω, τέλεσα; πρήσσω, πρήξω, πρῆξα; accomplish (completely) ἐκ-τελέω
according to κατά [prep. w. acc.]
account λόγος, -ου [m.]; on account of διά [prep. w. acc.]; εἵνεκα [prep. w. gen.]
Achaeans Ἀχαιοί, -ῶν [m. pl.]
Achilles Ἀχιλ(λ)εύς, -ῆος [m.]
address προσ-αυδάω; προσ-εῖπον
admirable ἀμύμων, -ονος; ἀγαυός, -ή, -όν
advice βουλή, -ῆς [f.]
aegis-bearing αἰγίοχος, -η, -ον
Aeolus Αἴολος, -ου [m.]
afar ἀπάνευθε; τηλόθι
after [in search or attack] ἐπί [w. acc.]; after [in time or position] μετά [w. acc.]
afterward ὄπι(σ)θεν; μετόπισθε(ν)
again αὖ; αὖτε; αὖτις; πάλιν
against the will ἀέκητι [adv.]
Agamemnon Ἀγαμέμνων, -ονος [m.]
agitate ὀρίνω, —, ὄρῑνα
aid ἀμύνω, ἀμυνέω, ἄμυνα; κομίζω, κομιέω, κόμισσα
Alcinoüs Ἀλκίνοος, -ου [m.]
alive ζωός, -ή, -όν
all ἅπας, ἅπᾱσα, ἅπαν; πᾶς, πᾶσα, πᾶν
allow ἐάω, ἐάσω, ἔᾱσα
alone μοῦνος, -η, -ον; οἶος, -η, -ον
along παρά [prep. w. acc.]
aloof ἀπόπροθεν [adv.]
already ἤδη [adv.]
always αἰεί
am (a) εἰμί
  (b) πέλω, —, π(έ)λον, [or mid.:] πέλομαι, —, πλόμην;
  (c) γίγνομαι, γενήσομαι, γενόμην, γέγαα
am lord ἀνάσσω, ἀνάξω, ἄναξα
among ἐν [prep. w. dat.]; μετά [prep. w. dat.]; διά [prep. w. acc.]

ancestral πατρίς, -ίδος [as f. adj.]
anchor-stone εὐνή, -ῆς [f.]
and καί; ἠδέ; ἰδέ; τε [never first word]; and not οὐδέ, μηδέ
anger [dat. of person; gen. of cause] χολόω, (κε)χολώσω, χόλωσα; I am angry [dat. of person; gen. of cause] χολόομαι, χολώσομαι, χολωσάμην
announce ἀγγέλλω, ἀγγελέω, ἄγγειλα
anoint χρίω, χρίσομαι, χρῑσάμην; ἀλείφω
any (one) τις, τι
apart (from) ἀπάνευθε [adv., prep. w. gen.] νόσφι(ν); ἀμφίς [adv.]
Apollo Ἀπόλλων, -ωνος [m.]
appear φαίνομαι, φανέομαι, φάνην; appear [= seem] δοκέω, δοκήσω, δόκησα; (ἐ)είδομαι, —, (ἐ)εισάμην
appearance εἶδος, -εος [n.]
approach ἱκνέομαι, ἵξομαι, ἱκόμην [w. acc.]
armor ἔντεα. -ων [n. pl. 3 decl.]; τεύχεα, -ων [n. pl., 3 decl.]
arms τεύχεα, -ων [n. pl. 3 decl.]; ἔντεα, -ων [n. pl., 3 decl.] I arm θωρήσσω, —, θώρηξα
around ἀμφί [adv.; prep. w. dat. or acc.]; ἀμφίς [adv.]
arouse ὀρμάω, ὀρμήσω, ὄρμησα
arrive ἀφ-ικνέομαι, ἀφ-ίξομαι, ἀφ-ικόμην
arrow βέλος, -εος [n.]
Artemis Ἄρτεμις, -ιδος [f.]
as ὡς; ἠΰτε
ascend ἀνα-βαίνω, ἀνα-βήσομαι, ἀνά-βην, ἀνα-βέβηκα
ash μελίη, -ης [f.]
ashen spear μελίη, -ης [f.]
ask αἰτέω, αἰτήσω, αἴτησα; εἴρομαι, εἰρήσομαι, ἐρόμην
assail ἐπ-οίχομαι
assembly ἀγορή, -ῆς [f.]
assign νέμω, νεμέω, νεῖμα
assigned by lot λαγχάνω, λάξομαι, (λέ)λαχον
at ἐπί; παρά; πρός [preps. w. dat.]
at another time ἄλλοτε
at ease ῥεῖα [adv.]
at least γε
at once ἄφαρ; αὐτίκα
at the same time ὁμοῦ
Athene Ἀθήνη, -ης [f.]
attempt πειράω, πειρήσω, πείρησα

attendant ἀμφίπολος, -ου [f.]; κῆρυξ, -ῦκος [m.]

attend to κλύω, —, (κέ)κλυον [athematic in aor. impt.]

avoid ἀλέομαι, —, ἀλεάμην or ἀλευάμην; ἀλεείνω

await μένω, μενέω, μεῖνα; μίμνω

away (from) ἀπό; ἀπάνευθε [advs., preps. w. gen.]; I am away ἄπ-ειμι; away (from) νόσφιν; ἐκτός [advs.]

awe-inspiring δεινός, -ή, -όν

awfully αἰνῶς

back [adv.] αὖτις; ἄψ; πάλιν; ἀνά; ὀπίσ(σ)ω; [noun] νῶτον, -ου [n.]; back again [adv.] ἄψ; πάλιν

bad κακός, -ή, -όν

bag ἀσκός, -οῦ [m.]

band ἔθνος, -εος [n.]

bait [for catching fish] δόλος, -ου [m.]

bar μοχλός, -οῦ [m.]

barren ἀτρύγετος, -ον

base πονηρός, ή, -όν

battle ὑσμίνη, -ης [f.]; μάχη, -ης [f.]

bay κόλπος, -ου [m.]

be [see "am"]

beach θίς, θῑνός [m.]

beam δόρυ, δούρατος or δουρός [n.]

bear φέρω, οἴσω, ἔνεικα; τίκτω, τέξω, τέκον [= give birth to]

beat τύπτω, τύψω, τύψα; πλάζω, πλάγξω, πλάγξα, —, —, πλάγχθην

beautiful κᾱλός, -ή, -όν [compl: καλλίων, -ον supl.: κάλλιστος, -η, -ον]

beautiful, very beautiful περικαλλής, -ές

beauty χάρις, -ιτος [f.] [acc. sg.: χάριν]; κάλλος, -εος [n.]

because ὅτι

become γίγνομαι, γενήσομαι, γενόμην, γέγαα

bed εὐνή, -ῆς [f.] ; λέχος, -εος [n.]

bed-room θάλαμος, -ου [m.]

before πρόσθε(ν); πάροιθε(ν); προπάροιθε(ν); ἄντα; πάρος; πρίν [adv.]; πρίν [conj. w. inf. or anticipatory subj.]

beg λίσσομαι, —, λισάμην

beget τίκτω, τέξω, τέκον

beginning ἀρχή, -ῆς [f.]

behind ὀπίσ(σ)ω; ὄπι(σ)θεν; μετόπισθε(ν)

believe (in) πιστεύω, πιστεύσω, πίστευσα [w. dat.]

belly γαστήρ, γαστέρος or γαστρός [f.]

beneficial, more beneficial κέρδιον [comp. adv.]

beside ἐπί; παρά [preps. w. dat.]

better κέρδιον [comp. adv.]; ἀρείων, -ον [comp. adj.]

bewail ὀδύρομαι, ὀδῡρέομαι, ὀδῡράμην

big μέγας, μεγάλη, μέγα [m. acc. sg.: μέγαν; [n. acc. sg.: μέγα; rest 2nd decl. on stem μεγαλ-; comp.: μείζων, -ον; supl.: μέγιστος, -η, -ον]; θαλερός, -ή, -όν

bird ὄρνις, ὄρνῑθος [m., f.]; οἰωνός, -οῦ [m.]

black μέλας, μέλαινα, μέλαν [m. – n. gen.: μέλανος]

blast ἀϋτμή, -ῆς [f.]; θύελλα, -ης [f.]

blaze δαίομαι

blazing αἰθόμενος, -η, -ον

blessed μάκαρ, -αρος

blood αἷμα, -ατος [n.]

blooming θαλερός, -ή, -όν

blow ἄημι

boar κάπρος. -ου [m.]

boast εὔχομαι, εὔξομαι, εὐξάμην

body σῶμα, -ατος [n.]; χρώς, χροός [m.]

bolt κληΐς, -ῖδος [f.]

bond δεσμός, -οῦ [m.]

bone ὀστέον, -ου [n.]

born, I am γίγνομαι, γενήσομαι, γενόμην, γέγαα

bosom κόλπος, -ου [m.]

both . . . and τε . . . τε, τε . . . καί; on both sides ἀμφί [adv., prep. w. dat. or acc.]; both ἀμφότερος, -η, -ον; both ἠμέν [correlative with ἠδέ]

boundary πεῖραρ, -ατος [n.]

boundless ἀπείρων, -ον

boy παῖς, παιδός [m.]

brandish τινάσσω, τινάξω, τίναξα

brave ἀγαθός, -ή, -όν [comp.: ἀρείων, -ον; supl.: ἄριστος, -η, ον]

bread σῖτος, -ου [m.]

break ῥήγνῡμι, ῥήξω, ῥῆξα

breast στέρνον, -ου [n.]; στῆθος, -εος [n.]

breath ἀϋτμή, -ῆς [f.]

bride νύμφη, -ης [f.]

bride-price ἔδνα (ἔεδνα), -ων [n. pl.]

bright δῖος, -α, -ον [f. usually keeps α throughout sg.]; λευκός, -ή, -όν; φαεινός, -ή, -όν; πορφύρεος, -η, -ον

brine ἅλμη, -ης [f.]

bring φέρω, οἴσω, ἔνεικα; bring to a halt ἵστημι, στήσω, στῆσα [transitive]; bring oneself to a halt ἵσταμαι, στήσομαι, στῆν

bring near to πελάζω, πελάσω, πέλασ(σ)α

bring to pass τελευτάω, τελευτήσω, τελεύτησα

briny ἁλμυρός, -ή, -όν

briny crust ἅλμη, -ης [f.]

broad εὐρύς, -εῖα, -ύ

bronze χαλκός, -οῦ [m.]; χάλκεος, -ον

bronze-clad χαλκοχίτων, -ωνος

bronze-tipped χαλκήρης, -ες

brother κασιγνητός, -οῦ [m.]

build τεύχω, τεύξω, τεῦξα, [pf. mid.: τέτυγμαι]

burn καίω, καύσω, κῆα [tr.]

burning αἰθόμενος, -η, -ον

busy about, I am πονέομαι, πονήσομαι, πονησάμην

but ἀλλά; αὐτάρ; δέ [never first word]; but now αὖ

by [cause or agent] ὑπό [w. gen.]
by now ἤδη [adv.]

call λέγω, λέξω, λέξα; καλέω, καλέω, κάλεσα;
  call (by name) ὀνομάζω, ὀνομάσω, ὀνόμασα
calm κοιμάω, κοιμήσω, κοίμησα
Calypso Καλυψώ, -όος [f.]
can δύναμαι, δυνήσομαι, δυνησάμην [w. inf.]
care κῆδος, -εος [n.]; I am a care to μέλω, μελήσω,
  μέλησα
cast προ-ίημι, προ-ήσω, προ-ῆκα
catch fire ἅπτομαι, ἅψομαι, ἁψάμην
cause τίθημι, θήσω, θῆκα; cause to be seated ἕσα
  [aor. of ἕζομαι]; καθ-ίζω, —, κάθ-ισα
cave σπέος, σπέος or σπῆος [n.]; ἄντρον, -ου [n.]
cease παύομαι, παύσομαι, παυσάμην
certain, a τις, τι
chair θρόνος, -ου [m.]
change ἀμείβω or ἀμείβομαι, ἀμείψομαι, ἀμειψάμην
chariot (platform) δίφρος, -ου [m.]
charity ἀγάπη, -ης [f.]
charm χάρις, -ιτος [f.]; acc. sg.: χάριν]
check ἐρύκω, ἐρύξω, ἔρυξα or ἐρύκακον; εἰλ(έ)ω,
  —, (ἔ)ελσα
cheer τέρπω, τέρψω, τέρψα or (τε)ταρπόμην; ἰαίνω,
  —, ἴηνα
cheese τῡρός, -οῦ [m.]
chest στέρνον, -ου [n.]; στῆθος, -εος [n.]
chiefly ἔξοχα
child παῖς, παιδός [m., f.]; τέκνον, -ου [n.]; τέκος,
  -εος [n.]
choose αἱρέομαι, αἱρήσομαι, ἑλόμην
Christ Χρῑστός, -οῦ [m.]
Circe Κίρκη, -ης [f.]
city π(τ)όλις, -ιος [f.]
claim to be εὔχομαι, εὔξομαι, εὐξάμην
cleanse καθαίρω, καθαρέω, κάθηρα
clear νημερτής, -ές
clearly δή
cling to φύομαι, φύσομαι, φῦν [w. -εν]
cloak χλαῖνα, -ης [f.]
close [adj.:] πυκ(ι)νός, -ή, -όν; [adv.:] ἆσσον;
  close by σχέδον [adv.]; ἄγχι [adv., prep. w. gen.]
clothe ἕννῡμι, ἕσ(σ)ω, ἕσ(σ)α
clothing ἐσθής, -ῆτος [f.]; εἶμα, -ατος [n.] [in pl.]
cloud νεφέλη, -ης [f.]; νέφος, -εος [n.]
cloud-gatherer νεφεληγερέτα, -ᾱο
cloud-wrapped κελαινεφής, -ές
come (a) ἔρχομαι, ἐλεύσομαι, ἔλ(υ)θον, εἰλήλουθα;
  (b) ἱκνέομαι, ἵξομαι, ἱκόμην; (c) ἱκάνω; (d) I
  come (by chance) κιχάνω, κιχήσομαι, κίχον;
  (e) I come to ἐπ-έρχομαι, etc.; ἀφ-ικνέομαι, etc.
  [w. acc.]; (f) I come to be πέλω, —, π(έ)λον or
  πέλομαι, —, πλόμην; γίγνομαι, γενήσομαι, γενόμην, γέγαα; (g) I come upon ἐπ-έρχομαι, etc.
  [w. dat., acc.]

come down κατ-έρχομαι, etc.
comfort τέρπω, τέρψω, τέρψα or (τε)ταρπόμην
comfortable λιπαρός, -ή, -όν
command ἀνώγω, ἀνώξω, ἄνωξα, ἄνωγα [pf. has
  pres. sense; plpf. has impf. sense]; κελεύω, κελεύσω, κέλευσα [w. acc., dat., or inf.]; a command
  ἐντολή, -ῆς [f.]
commiserate ὀλοφύρομαι, ὀλοφῡρέομαι, ὀλοφῡράμην
companion ἑταῖρος, -ου [m.]; ἔταρος, -ου [m.]
compel ἐπ-οτρύνω, -οτρῡνέω, -ότρῡνα [dat. or acc.]
complete τελέω, τελέω, τέλεσα
comrade ἑταῖρος, -ου [m.] or ἔταρος, -ου [m.]
conceal κρύπτω, κρύψω, κρύψα
concerning ἀμφί [adv., prep. w. dat. or acc.]
confine εἰλ(έ)ω, —, (ἔ)ελσα
conflict ὑσμίνη, -ης [f.]
confuse κυκάω, κυκήσω, κύκησα
conquer νῑκάω, νῑκήσω, νίκησα
consent αἰνέω, αἰνήσω, αἴνησα
consider φρονέω, φρονήσω, φρόνησα; φράζομαι,
  φράσ(σ)ομαι, φρασ(σ)άμην; consider whether to or
  how to βουλεύω, βουλεύσω, βούλευσα [w. inf.
  or ὅπως and purpose constr.]
constrain βιάζω
construct κάμνω, καμέομαι, κάμον
contrive μήδομαι, μήσομαι, μησάμην
control νωμάω, νωμήσω, νώμησα
copper χαλκός, -οῦ [m.]
corpse νέκῡς, -υος [n.]
could [= potential future supposition] expressed by
  verb in opt. w. κε(ν) or ἄν
counsels, of many counsels πολύμητις, -ιος [m. or f.]
countless μῡρίος, -η, -ον
country πατρίς, -ίδος [f.]; ἀγρός, -οῦ [m.] [opp. to
  city]
courage μένος, -εος [n.]
courageous ἀγήνωρ, -ορος
course κέλευθος, -ου [f., but frequently n. in pl.]
  of course που
court μνάομαι
courtyard αὐλή, -ῆς [f.]
cover καλύπτω, καλύψω, κάλυψα
cow βοῦς, βοός [f., m.] [dat. pl. also: βουσί]
cowardly κακός, -ή, -όν; δειλός, ή, όν
craftiness δόλος, -ου [m.]
crag σκόπελος, -ου [m.]
crest λόφος, -ου [m.]
Cronus' son Κρονίων, -ίωνος [m.]
cross περάω, περήσω, πέρησα
crouch εἰλ(έ)ομαι
cruel σχέτλιος, -η, -ον
cry βοή, -ῆς [f.]
cry out in pain οἰμώζω, οἰμώξομαι, οἴμωξα
cunning δόλος, -ου [m.]
current ῥόος, -ου [m.]

custom, δίκη, -ης [f.]; θέμις, -ιστος [f.]

cut τάμνω, —, τάμον

cut the throat σφάζω, σφάξω, σφάξα

Cyclops Κύκλωψ, -ωπος [m.]

dance χορός, -οῦ [m.]

dancing-place χορός, -οῦ [m.]

dandle πάλλω, —, πῆλα

dare τλάω, τλήσομαι, τλῆν

daring μεγαλήτωρ, -ορος

dark μέλας, μέλαινα, μέλαν [m.–n. gen.: μέλανος]; κελαινεφής, -ές; κῡάνεος, -η, -ον

dark-prowed κυανόπρῳρος, -ου

dart ὀρούω, ὀρούσω, ὄρουσα

daub ἀλείφω, ἀλείψω, ἄλειψα

daughter θυγάτηρ, θυγατέρος or θυγατρός [f.]; κούρη, -ης [f.]

dawn ἠώς, ἠόος [f.]

Dawn Ἠώς, Ἠόος [f.]

day ἦμαρ, ἤματος [n.]

dead, the dead νέκυες, -ύων [m. pl.]; I am dead τέθνηκα

deadly ὀλοός, -ή, -όν

dear φίλος, -η, -ον [comp.: φίλτερος, -η, -ον; supl.: φίλτατος, -η, -ον]

death θάνατος, -ου [m.]; κήρ, κηρός [f.]; φόνος, -ου [m.]; πότμος, -ου [m.]

deceive λανθάνω, λήσω, λάθον

deck ἴκρια, -ων [n. pl.]

declare myself εὐχετάομαι

deed ἔργον, -ου [n.]; πρᾶγμα, -ατος [n.]

deep βαθύς, -εῖα, -ύ

deer ἔλαφος, -ου [f.]

defence ἀλκή, -ῆς [f.] [dat. sg.: ἀλκί]

defend ἀμύνω, ἀμῡνέω, ἄμῡνα

delightful γλυκύς, -εῖα, -ύ

desire βούλομαι, βουλήσομαι, βουλόμην; desire eagerly μενεαίνω, —, μενέηνα; desire ἵμερος, -ου [m.]; ἔρος, -ου [m.]

destined, I am μέλλω, μελήσω, μέλλησα

destroy ὀλλύω, ὀλέσω, ὄλεσ(σ)α; ἀπ-ολλύω, etc. [= destroy utterly]

destruction ὄλεθρος, -ου [m.]

destructive ὀλοός, -ή, -όν

devise ὑφαίνω, ὑφανέω, ὕφηνα

devour ἔσθω

die θνήσκω, θανέομαι, θάνον, τέθνη(κ)α; καταθνήσκω, etc.

difficult χαλεπός, -ή, -όν

dinner δεῖπνον, -ου [n.]

dire βαρύς, -εῖα, -ύ

direction, in what direction ὅπ(π)η

discover εὑρίσκω, εὑρήσω, εὗρον

disease νοῦσος, -ου [f.]

distress ἄλγος, -εος [n.]; I distres τείρω; distress ὀιζύς, -ύος [f.]

distribute νωμάω, νωμήσω, νώμησα

divine θεσπέσιος, -η, -ον

divine decree θέσφατον, -ου [n.]

divinely decreed θέσφατος, -ον

divinity, a δαίμων, -ονος [m., f.]

do ῥέζω, ῥέξω, ῥέξα; ἔρδω, ἔρξω, ἔρξα; ποιέω, ποιήσω, ποίησα; I do wrong ἀδικέω, ἀδικήσω, ἀδίκησα; do πρήσσω, πρήξω, πρῆξα

dog κυών, κυνός [m., f.]

door θύρη, -ης [f.]

door-post σταθμός, -οῦ [m.]

door-stone θυρεός, -οῦ [m.]

doubt, no doubt που

doughty ἴφθιμος, -η, -ον

down (from) κατά [prep. w. gen.]; down (along) κατά [w. acc.]; down to κατά [w. acc.]

dowry ἔδνα or ἔεδνα, -ων [n. pl.]

drag ἐρύω, —, ἔρυσ(σ)α; ἕλκω

draw ἀφύσσω, ἀφύξω, ἄφυσ(σ)α

dreadful αἰνός, -ή, -όν; δεινός, -ή, -όν

dream ὄνειρος, -ου [m.]

drink πίνω, πίομαι, πίον

drive ἐλαύνω, ἐλάω, ἔλασ(σ)α; drive a flock νέμω, νεμέω, νεῖμα; drive ἐφ-έπω, ἐφ-έψω, ἐπί-σπον; σεύω, —, (σ)σεῦα or (σ)σύμην

drive on ἐπ-είγω

dry land χέρσος, -ου [f.]

due, give one his due of λαγχάνω, λήξομαι, (λέ)λαχον

due measure μοῖρα, -ης [f.]

dust κονίη, -ης [f.]

dwell οἰκέω, οἰκήσω, οἴκησα; ναιετάω

each ἕκαστος, -η, -ον; each other ἄλληλοι, -ων [pl. only]

eager(ly) πρόφρων, -ον; I am eager μέμαα [pf. w. pres. meaning]; I am eager to ἐφ-ορμάομαι, ἐφ-ορμήσομαι, ἐφορμησάμην

eagle αἰετός, -οῦ [m.]

ear οὖας, -ατος [n.]

early-born (one) ἠριγένεια, -ης

earth γαῖα, -ης [f.] [world, globe]; χθών, χθονός [f., ground]; ἄρουρα, -ης [f.] [soil, plowable land]

earth-shaker ἐννοσίχθων, -νος; ἐννοσίγαιος, -ου

easily ῥεῖα

easily-directed ἀμφιέλισσα, -ης

easy ῥηίδιος, -η, -ον

eat ἐσθίω, ἔδομαι, φάγον; ἔσθω; ἔδω

eating ἐδητύς, -ύος [f.]

edge ἄκρον, -ου [n.]

Eëtion Ἠετίων, -ωνος [m.]

either . . . or ἤ . . . ἤ; [after negative:] οὐδέ . . . οὐδέ

elude λανθάνω, λήσω, λάθον

end πεῖραρ, -ατος [n.]; τέλος, -εος [n.]

endure ἀν-έχομαι, etc.; endure patiently τλάω, τλήσομαι, τλῆν enjoin ἐπι-τέλλω, —, ἐπί-τειλα

enter εἰσ-έρχομαι, etc.; δύω, δύσομαι, δυσάμην or δῦν

entire οὖλος, -η, -ον

entrance πύλη, -ης [f.]

entreat λίσσομαι, —, λισάμην

equal ἶσος, (ἐ)ἴση, ἶσον

escape φεύγω, φεύξομαι, φύγον; ἀλύσκω, ἀλύξω, ἄλυξα; escape someone's notice λανθάνω, λήσω, λάθον

escort πομπή, -ῆς [f.]

especially περί [adv.]; μάλιστα

estate γέρας, -αος [n.]

eternal ἀθάνατος, -η, -ον

Eurylochus Εὐρύλοχος, -ου [m.]

even καί; not even οὐδέ, μηδέ

ever αἰεί; ποτε [= at some time]

every πᾶς, πᾶσα, πᾶν

everywhere πάντη

evil κακός, -ή, -όν

exactly ἀτρεκέως

exceedingly λίην

excellent ἐσθλός, -ή, -όν; κλυτός, -όν; ἀμύμων, -ονος

excelling περί [prep. w. gen.]

exchange ἀμείβομαι, ἀμείψομαι, ἀμειψάμην

exist ναιετάω

expect ἔλπω

experience πάσχω, πείσομαι, πάθον

extreme ἄκρος, -η, -ον

exult εὔχομαι, εὔξομαι, εὐξάμην; εὐχετάομαι

eye ὀφθαλμός, -οῦ [m.]; eyes ὄσσε [n. dual]

eyebrow ὀφρύς, -ύος [f.]

eyelid βλέφαρον, -ου [n.]

face εἶδος, -εος [n.]

fail of ἁμαρτάνω, ἁμαρτήσομαι, ἅμαρτον

fair ἶσος, (ἐ)ἴση, ἶσον

fair-tressed ἐϋπλόκαμος, -ον

faithful ἐρίηρος, -ον [pl. 3 decl.: ἐρίηρες]

faith in, I have πιστεύω, πιστεύσω, πίστευσα [w. dat.]

fall πίπτω, πεσέομαι, πέσον

fall down κατα-χέομαι, -χεύσομαι, -χευάμην or -χύμην

fame κλέος, κλέ(ε)ος [n.]

famous κλυτός, -όν

far (away) ἀπόπροθεν; τῆλε [advs.]

far (from) τηλόθι

farmyard αὐλή, ῆς [f.]; σταθμός, -οῦ [m.]

fast ταχύς, -εῖα, -ύ [comp.: θάσσων, -ον; supl.: τάχιστος, -η, -ον]

fasten ἅπτω, ἅψω, ἅψα; δέω, δήσω, δῆσα

fat πίων, -ονος; ἴφιος, -η, -ον [adjs.]; κνίση, -ης [f., noun]

fate μοῖρα. -ης [f.]; κήρ, κηρός [f.]; αἶσα, -ης [f.]; πότμος, -ου [m.]

father πατήρ, πατέρος or πατρός [m.]; of one's fathers πατρίς, -ίδος [as f. adj.]

fatherland πατρίς, -ίδος [f.]; πάτρη, -ης [f.]

fear δείδω, δείσομαι, δεῖσα, δείδια [w. inf. or μή and purpose construction; pf. has pres. sense]; δέος, δέεος [n.]

feast δαίνυμαι, δαίσομαι, δαισάμην; I give a feast δαίνῡμι, δαίσω, δαῖσα; δαίς, δαιτός [f., noun]

feed [tr.] τρέφω, θρέψω, θρέψα; βόσκω, βοσκήσω, βόσκησα; feed upon [intr.] νέμομαι, νεμέομαι, νειμάμην [w. acc.]

feel ἐπι-μαίομαι, ἐπι-μάσσομαι, -μασσάμην

fellow ἄνθρωπος, -ου [m.]

female [adj.] θῆλυς, -εος [f.]; θήλεια, -ης [f.]

few ὀλίγος, -η, -ον

field ἀγρός, -οῦ [m.]

fight μάχη, -ης [f.]

fight (with) μαχ(έ)ομαι, μαχήσομαι, μαχεσ(σ)άμην; π(τ)ολεμίζω, π(τ)ολεμίζω

fill ἐμ-πίπλημι, ἐμ-πλήσω, ἔμ-πλησα

find εὑρίσκω, εὑρήσω, εὗρον

fine ἐϋ-εργής, -ές

finish τελευτάω, τελευτήσω, τελεύτησα

fire πῦρ, πυρός [n.]

firm ἔμπεδος, -ον

first πρῶτος, -η, -ον; at first πρῶτον

fish ἰχθύς, -ύος [m.]

fit together, I am fitted with ἀραρίσκω, ἄρσομαι, ἄρσα or ἄραρον

fitting, it is ἔοικα, ἐῴκεα [in 3rd sg. impers. construction sometimes followed by acc. and inf.]

fix πήγνῡμι, πήξω, πῆξα

flashing-eyed γλαυκῶπις, -ιδος

flay δέρω, δερέω, δεῖρα

flee φεύγω, φεύξομαι, φύγον

flesh σάρξ, σαρκός [f.]; κρέα, κρεῶν [nom. sg.: κρέας] [n.]

flock μῆλον, -ου [n.]

flock of sheep πῶυ, πώεος [n.]

flourish τέθηλα or τέθαλα [pf. w. pres. meaning]

flow ῥέω

fluid ὑγρός, -ή, -όν

fly πέτομαι, πτήσομα, πτάμην

fold [for sheep, goats, or cattle] σηκός, -οῦ [m.]; αὐλή, -ῆς [f.]; fold [of a garment] κόλπος, -ου [m.]; I fold πτύσσω, πτύξω, πτύξα

follow (with) ἔπομαι, ἔψομαι, ἑσπόμην

followers λᾱός, -οῦ [m.]

food σῖτος, -ου [m.]; εἶδαρ, -ατος [n.]; ἐδωδή, -ῆς [f.]; ἐδητύς, -ύος [f.]

foolish νήπιος, -η, -ον

foot πούς, ποδός [m.]; on foot πεζός, -ή, -όν

for γάρ [conj., never first word]; for περί [prep. w. dat. or acc.]; for the sake of εἵνεκα [prep. w. gen.]

force βίη, -ης [f.]

forest ὕλη, -ης [f.]

forever αἰεί

forgetful of, I am λανθάνομαι, λήσομαι, λαθόμην

former πρότερος, -η, -ον

formerly πάρος [adv.]

forsake κατα-λείπω, etc.

fragrant ἀμβρόσιος, -η, -ον; ἄμβροτος, -ον

fresh νέος, -η, -ον

friend φίλος, -ου [m. adj. as noun]

friendly (to) φίλος, -η, -ον

friendship φιλότης, -ητος [f.]

frightful σμερδαλέος, -η, -ον

from [prep.] ἀπό; ἐκ; παρά; πρός [w. gen.]; from close at hand ἐγγύθεν; elsewhere ἄλλοθεν; from there ἔνθεν; from what place or source? πόθεν

fruit καρπός, -οῦ [m.]

fulfill τελέω, τελέω, τέλεσα

fulfillment τέλος, -εος [n.]

funeral-pyre πυρή, -ῆς [f.]

garden ἀλωή, -ῆς [f.]

garment εἷμα, -ατος [n.]

gasp ἀσπαίρω

gate πύλη, -ης [f.]

gather together ἀγείρω, ἀγερέω, ἄγειρα, [3nd aor. mid: ἀγερόμην]

gave πόρον [2nd aor. system only]

gentle ἀγανός, -ή, -όν; μαλακός, -ή, -όν

get λαμβάνω, λήψομαι, λάβον

get by lot λαγχάνω, λάξομαι, (λέ)λαχον

gift δῶρον, -ου [n.]; gift of hospitality [a present given by host to guest] ξείνιον, -ου [n.]

gigantic πελώριος, -η, -ον

girl παῖς, παιδός [f.]; κούρη, -ης [f.]

give δίδωμι, δώσω, δῶκα [see appendix for forms]; ὀπάζω, ὀπάσσω, ὀπασ(σ)α; gave πόρον [2nd aor. system only]

give graciously χαρίζομαι, χαριέομαι, χαρισάμην

give light φαείνω

give one [acc.] his due of λαγχάνω, λάξομαι, (λέ)λαχον

give orders to ἐπι-τέλλω, —, ἐπί-τειλα

give way εἴκω, εἴξω, (ἔ)ειξα

gleaming πορφύρεος, -η, -ον

gloomy στυγερός, -ή, -όν

glorious δῖος, -α, -ον [f. usually keeps α throughout sg.]; φαίδιμος, -ον [never f.]

glory δόξα, -ης [f.]; κῦδος, -εος [n.]

go βαίνω, βήσομαι, βῆν, βέβηκα; ἔρχομαι, ἐλεύσομαι, ἐλ(υ)θον, εἰλήλουθα; στείχω, —, στίχον; go past παρ-έρχομαι, etc.; go upon ἐπι-βαίνω, etc. [w. gen.]; go κίω, —, κίον; go near to πελάζω, πελάσω, πέλασ(σ)α; go towards or round ἐπ-οίχομαι

goat αἴξ, αἰγός [m., f.]

god θεός, -οῦ [m., f.]

goddess θεά, -ᾶς [f.]; θεός, -οῦ [f.]

godlike ἀντίθεος, -η, -ον; θεοειδής, -ές

going ἰών, ἰοῦσα, ἰόν

gold χρυσός, -οῦ [m.]; of gold χρύσε(ι)ος, -η, -ον

good ἀγαθός, -ή, -όν [comp.: ἀρείων, -ον; supl.: ἄριστος, -η, -ον]; χρηστός, -ή, -όν

good-for-nothing λυγρός, -ή, -όν

grace χάρις, -ιτος [f.], [acc. sg.: χάριν]

graceful χαρίεις, -εσσα, -εν

gratify χαρίζομαι, χαριέομαι, χαρισάμην

great μέγας, μεγάλη, μέγα [m. acc. sg.: μέγαν; n. acc. sg.: μέγα; rest 2nd decl. on stem: μεγαλ-; comp.: μείζων, -ον; supl.: μέγιστος, -η, -ον]; μεγαλήτωρ, -ορος [= great-hearted]; so great τόσ(σ)ος,, -η, -ον; as great as ὅσ(σ)ος,, -η, -ον

greatly μάλα; αἰνῶς

Greeks Ἀχαιοί, -ῶν [m. pl.]

green, greenish-yellow χλωρός, -ή, -όν

greyish πολιός, (-ή), -όν

grief ἄχος, -εος [n.]; πένθος, -εος [n.]

grieve ἀκαχίζω, ἀκαχήσω, ἄκαχον; ἀχε(ύ)ω, —, ἄκαχον; ἄχνυμαι [intrans.]

grievious ἀλεγεινός, -ή, -όν

groan στενάχω; γόος, -ου [m.]

group ἔθνος, -εος [n.]

grow ἀέξω, ἀεξήσω, ἀέξησα; φύομαι, φύσομαι, φῦν

guard φυλάσσω, φυλλάξω, φύλαξα; ἐρύκω, ἐρύξω, ἔρυξα

guest ξεῖνος, -ου [m.]

guide ἡγέομαι, ἡγήσομαι, ἡγησάμην

gulf λαῖτμα, -ατος [n.]

Hades [ruler of the lower world] Ἀίδης, Ἀίδαο or Ἄιδος [m.]

hair κόμη, -ης [f.]

half ἥμισυς, (-εια), -υ

hall δῶμα, -ατος [n.]; large hall μέγαρον, -ου [n.]

halt [intr.] ἵσταμαι, στήσομαι, στῆν; [tr., = bring to a halt] ἵστημι, στήσω, στῆσα

hand χείρ, χε(ι)ρός [f.]

handmaid ἀμφίπολος, -ου [f.]; δμωή, -ῆς [f.]

happen γίγνομαι, γενήσομαι, γενόμην, γέγαα; happen to [expressed by verb in opt. — in "should ... would" construction]; happen [upon] τυγχάνω, τεύξομαι, τύχον

happiness ὄλβος, -ου [m.]

happy μάκαρ, -αρος; ὄλβιος, -η, -ον

harbor λιμήν, -ένος [m.]

hard ἀργαλέος, -η, -ον

harm δηλέομαι, δηλήσομαι, δηλησάμην

harmless ἀπήμων, -ον

hasten ἐπ-είγομαι; σπεύδω, σπεύσω, σπεῦσα

hate μῑσέω, μῑσήσω, μῑσησα

hateful στυγερός, -ή, -όν

have ἔχω, ἕξω or σχήσω, σχόν or σχέθον; have mercy on ἐλεέω, —, ἐλέησα; have the heart (to) τλάω, τλήσομαι, τλῆν

he [see appendix p. 239]

head κεφαλή, -ῆς [f.]; κάρη, καρή(α)τος or κρά(α)τος [n.]; heads κάρηνα, -ων [n. pl.]

heap up χέω, χεύω, χεῦα; ἀφύσσω, ἀφύξω, ἄφυσ(σ)α

hear (of) πεύθομαι, πεύσομαι, πυθόμην; ἀκούω, ἀκούσομαι, ἄκουσα [sometimes w. gen.]; hear [sound of] κλύω, —, (κέ)κλυον [athematic in aor. impt.]

heart κῆρ, κῆρος [n.]; θῡμός, -οῦ [m.]; ἦτορ [n., indecl.]; I have the heart (to) τλάω, τλήσομαι, τλῆν; heart κραδίη, -ης [f.]

heaven οὐρανός, -οῦ [m.]

heavenly θεσπέσιος, -η, -ον

heavy ὄβριμος, -η, -ον; βαρύς, -εῖα, -ύ

hecatomb ἑκατόμβη, -ης [f.]

Hector Ἕκτωρ, -ορος [m.]

helmet κόρυς, -υθος [f.]

her (a) [pron.: see appendix p. 239]
  (b) [adj.: ἑός, -ή, -όν]
  (c) herself αὐτή

herald κῆρυξ, -ῡκος [m.]

here τῇδε; αὖθι; ἐνθάδε [advs.]

hereafter ὄπι(σ)θεν, ὀπίσ(σ)ω [advs.]

hesitate to ἅζομαι

hide κεύθω, κεύσω, κύθον

high ὑψηλός, -ή, -όν

him [see appendix p. 239]

himself, herself, itself αὐτός, -ή, -ό

his ἑός, -ή, -όν

hiss ἰάχω

hither ἐνθάδε; δεῦρο [advs.]

hold ἔχω, ἕξω or σχήσω, σχόν or σχέθον; hold back from ἀπ-έχω, etc.; hold up under ἀν-έχομαι, etc.; take hold αἴνυμαι

hole βόθρος, -ου [m.]

hollow γλαφυρός, -ή, -όν; κοῖλος, -η, -ον

holy ἱερός, -ή, -όν;

home οἶκος, -ου [m.]

home-coming, of one's νόστιμος, -η, -ον

honey-sweet μελιηδής, -ές

honor κῦδος, -εος [n.]

honorable δίκαιος, -η, -ον

honored αἰδοῖος, -η, -ον

hope ἔλπω or ἔλπομαι

horse ἵππος, -ου [m.]

horse-taming ἱππόδαμος, -ον

hostile δυσμενής, -ές

house οἶκος, -οῦ [m.]; δόμος, -ου [m.]; δῶμα, -ατος [n.]

how ὡς; how? πῶς; τίπτε

however δέ [never first word]

human [adj.:[βροτός, -ή, -όν; [in reference to a man's flesh:] ἀνδρόμεος, -η, -ον; human being ἄνθρωπος, -ου [m.]

hurl ῥίπτω, ῥίψω, ῥῖψα; ἵημι, ἥσω, ἧκα

husband πόσις, -ιος [m.]

Hyperion Ὑπερίων, -ονος [m.]

I ἐγώ(ν)

if εἰ; if only [= impossible wish] εἰ, εἰ γάρ, or εἴθε [w. opt.]; if αἰ [= εἰ]

Ilion Τροίη, -ης [f.]; Ἴλιος, -ου [f.]

imagine ὀΐω or ὀΐομαι, ὀΐσομαι, ὀϊσάμην

immeasurable ἄσπετος, -ον

immortal ἀθάνατος, -η, -ον; ἄμβροτος, -ον

in ἐν [prep. w. dat.]; in any way πως; in fact γε; in front of πρόσθε(ν); in order [adv.] ἑξῆς; in order that ἵνα, ὡς, ὅπως, ὄφρα; in silence ἀκέων -ουσα, —; in that case [conj.] τῷ; in the same place [adv.] αὐτοῦ; in great numbers ἅλις [adv.]; in abundance ἅλις [adv.]; in front of προπάροιθε(ν); in reply ἀντίος, -η, -ον

incite ὄρνῡμι, ὄρσω, ὄρσα [aor. mid. also: ὀρ(ό)μην]

increase ἀέξω, ἀεξήσω, ἀέξησα

indeed ἦ; δή; [in contrasts, followed by δέ:] μέν, μήν

indignant, I am indignant (with) νεμεσ(σ)άω, νεμεσ(σ)ήσω, νεμέσ(σ)ησα

infatuation ἄτη, -ης [f.]

inhabit οἰκέω, οἰκήσω, οἴκησα; ναιετάω; ναίω, —, νάσσα

injure ἀδικέω, ἀδικήσω, ἀδίκησα

inquire (from) πεύθομαι, πεύσομαι, πυθόμην; ἐρέω

inside (of) ἔντοσθε(ν), ἔνδον

into εἰς [prep. w. acc.]; into the midst μετά [prep. w. acc.]

invite καλέω, καλέω, κάλεσα

iron, of iron σιδήρεος, -η, -ον

island νῆσος, -ου [f.]

it [see appendix p. 239]

Ithaca Ἰθάκη, -ης [f.]

itself αὐτό

journey ὁδός. -οῦ [f.]

judge κρίνω, κρινέω, κρῖνα

just δίκαιος, -η, -ον; αὔτως [adv.]

justice δίκη, -ης [f.]

keen ὀξύς, -εῖα, -ύ

keep off (ἐ)έργω, ἔρξω, ἔρξα

kill κτείνω, κτενέω, κτεῖνα; ὀλλύω, ὀλέσω, ὀλεσ(σ)α; ἀπ-ολλύω, etc.; κατα-κτείνω, etc.; ἐξ-εναρίζω, -εναρίξω, -ξα

kindle καίω, καύσω, κῆα

kindly πρόφρων, -ον; ἐνδυκέως [adv.]

king ἄναξ, ἄνακτος [m.]

kingdom βασιλείη, -ης [f.]

kiss κυνέω, κυνήσομαι, κύσ(σ)α

knee γόνυ, γούνατος or γουνός [n.]

know γιγνώσκω, γνώσομαι, γνῶν, ἔγνωκα, ἔγνωσμαι, γνώσθην; οἶδα [see appendix p. 238]

labor at πονέομαι, πονήσομαι, πονησάμην

Laertes' son [i.e., Odysseus] Λαερτιάδης, -āο [m.]

lamb(s) ἄρνες, -ων [acc. sg.: ἄρνα] [m., f.]

lament στενάχω; ὀλοφύρομαι, ὀλοφῡρέομαι, ὀλοφῡράμην; ὀδύρομαι, ὀδῡρέομαι, ὀδῡράμην

lamentation γόος, -ου [m.]

land γαῖα, -ης [f.]; I land upon ἐπι-βαίνω, etc. [w. gen.]; by land πεζός, -ή, -όν; land ἤπειρος, -ου [f.]; χέρσος, -ου [f.]

land marked off [for a god or as private property] τέμενος, -εος [n.]

large (a) μέγας, μεγάλη, μέγα [m. acc. sg.: μέγαν; n. acc. sg.: μέγα; rest 2nd decl. on stem: μεγαλ-; comp.: μείζων, -ον; supl.: μέγιστος, μέγιστος, -η, -ον]

　　(b) μακρός, -ή, -όν

last ὕστατος, -η, -ον

later μετόπισθε(ν)

lawful, it is θέμις ἐστί

lay hold of ἅπτομαι, ἅψομαι, ἁψάμην

lead ἄγω, ἄξω, ἄγαγον; ἡγέομαι, ἡγήσομαι, ἡγησάμην; lead (the way) ἡγεμονεύω, ἡγεμενεύσω, ἡγεμόνευσα

leaf φύλλον, -ου [n.]

lean κλῑνω, κλινέω, κλῖνα; ἐρείδω, ἐρείσω, ἔρεισα

learn μανθάνω, μαθήσομαι; μάθον; I learn by inquiry πεύθομαι, πεύσομαι, πυθόμην

least, at least γε

leave λείπω, λείψω, λίπον; leave (alone) ἐάω, ἐάσω, ἔᾱσα; leave behind κατα-λείπω, etc.

length μῆκος, -εος [n.]

lest ἵνα μή, μή

let (a) let me, let us [expressed by verb in hortatory subj.];

　　(b) let him, her, it, them [expressed by verb in opt.];

　　(c) [= allow, permit] ἐάω, ἐάσω, ἔᾱσα

lie (down) κεῖμαι [pf. mid. system only]; κατά-κειμαι

lie κλῑνω, κλινέω, κλῖνα

life ζωή, -ῆς [f.]; ψῡχή, -ῆς [f.]; βίος, -ου [m.]

lift up ἀείρω, —, ἄειρα

light φάος, φάεος [n.]; αὐγή, -ῆς [f.]; I give light φαείνω

light up δαίω

like to ὁμοῖος, -η, -ον; I am like to ἔοικα, ἐῴκεα [pf. and plpf. w. pres. and impf. sense]

limb (of body) μέλος, -εος [n.]; γυῖον, -ου [n.]

lion λέων, -οντος [m.]

live ζώω, ζώσω, ζῶσα

living ζωός, -ή, -όν; βίοτος, -ου [m.]

long (a) μακρός, -ή, -όν

　　(b) I long (after) ποθέω, ποθήσω, πόθεσα;

　　(c) δήν; δηρόν [advs.]

look about sharply (for) παπταίνω, —, πάπτηνα

look (at) ὁράω, ὄψομαι, ἴδον, ἑώρᾱκα, ἑώρᾱμαι, ὄφθην; εἰσ-οράω, etc.; λεύσσω

loom [for weaving] ἱστός, -οῦ [m.]

loose λύω, λύσω, λῦσα, λέλυκα, λέλυμαι, λύθην

lord ἄναξ, ἄνακτος [m.]; I am lord ἀνάσσω, ἀνάξω, ἄναξα

lose ἀπ-ολλύω, ἀπ-ολέσω, ἀπ-όλεσ(σ)α; ὀλλύω, etc.

lotus λωτός, -οῦ [m.]

Lotus-eaters Λωτοφάγοι, -ων [m. pl.]

love ἀγάπη, -ης [f.]; I love φιλέω, φιλήσω, φίλησα; being loved [f. ptc.] φιλεομένη, -ης; loving [f. ptc.] φιλέουσα, -ης; love ἔρος, -ου [n.]; φιλότης, -ητος [f.]

loyal ἐρίηρος, -ον [pl. 3 decl.: ἐρίηρες]

luckless δειλός, -ή, -όν

maiden νύμφη, -ης [f.]

mainland ἤπειρος, -ου [f.]

make ποιέω, ποιήσω, ποίησα; make myself heard γεγωνέω, γεγωνήσω, γεγώνησα, γέγωνα [pf. with pres. meaning]

make fast πήγνῡμι, πήξω, πῆξα

make known πιφαύσκω

make to sit ἵζω

male ἄρσην, -ενος [m.]

man [= homo:] ἄνθρωπος, -ου [m.]; [= vir:] ἀνήρ, ἀνέρος or ἀνδρός [m.]; [dat. pl.: ἄνδρεσσι or ἀνδράσι]; [= person:] φώς, φωτός [m.]

manliness ἀρετή, -ῆς [f.]

manly ἀγήνωρ, -ορος

mantle φᾶρος, -εος [n.]

man-slaying ἀνδρόφονος, -ου

many πολλός, -ή, -όν [m. and n. also 3rd decl.: πολύς, -ύ; comp.: πλείων, -ον; supl.: πλεῖστος, -η, -ον] as many as ὅσ(σ)ος, -η, -ον; so many τόσ(σ)ος, -η, -ον

marriage γάμος, -ου [m.]

marriage-feast γάμος, -ου [m.]

marry γαμέω, γαμέω, γάμησα or γῆμα

marvel (at) θαυμάζω, θαυμάσσομαι, θαύμασα

mast ἱστός, -οῦ [m.]

may (I, we, you, he, she, it, they) [expressed by verb in opt.]

meadow λειμών, -ῶνος [m.]

meal δεῖπνον, -ου [n.]

meanwhile τόφρα

measure μέτρον, -ου [n.]; (due) measure μοῖρα, -ης [f.]; (allotted) measure αἶσα, -ης [f.]

measureless μῡρίος, -η, -ον

meat κρέα, κρεῶν [nom. sg.: κρέας] [n.]

meet ἐφ-έπω, ἐφ-έψω, ἐπί-σπον

melt ἰαίνω, —, ἵηνα

member [of the body] μέλος, -εος [n.]

message ἀγγελίη, -ης [f.]

messenger ἄγγελος, -ου [m.]

middle (of) μέσ(σ)ος, -η, -ον

midst of μέσ(σ)ος, -η, -ον

might [noun:] μένος, -εος [n.]; might [potential future supposition, e.g., 'he might get angry':] expressed by verb in opt. w. κε(ν) or ἄν

mighty ὄβριμος, -η, -ον; πελώριος, -η, -ον; ἄλκιμος, -ον; ἴφθιμος, -η, -ον

milk ἀμέλγω

mind νόος, -ου [m.]; φρήν, φρενός [f.]

mindful, I am mindful of μνάομαι

mine ἐμός, -ή, -όν; ἐμεῖο; μευ

miserable οἰκτρός, -ή, -όν [alternative superlative: οἴκτιστος]

miss ἁμαρτάνω, ἁμαρτήσομαι, ἅμαρτον [w. gen.]; miss (I long for) ποθέω, ποθήσω, πόθεσα

missile βέλος, -εος [n.]

mist ἀήρ, ἠέρος [f.]

mix (with) μίσγω, μίξω, μῖξα

mixing-bowl κρητήρ, -ῆρος [m.]

money χρήματα, -ων [n. pl.]

monstrous πελώριος, -η, -ον

month μήν, μηνός [m.]

mortal θνητός, -ή, -όν; βροτός, -ή, -όν

mother μήτηρ, μητέρος or μητρός [f.]

mound σῆμα, -ατος [n.]

mountain ὄρος, -εος [n.]

mourn γοάω, γοήσομαι, γόησα

mouth στόμα, -ατος [n.]

move [intr.] ὄρνυμαι, ὄρσομαι, ὀρ(ό)μην, ὄρωρα

much πολλός, -ή, -όν [m. and n. also 3rd decl.: πολύς, πολύ; comp.: πλείων, -ον; supl.: πλεῖστος, -η, -ον] much (adv.) πολύ

much-enduring πολύτλας [only nom.]

mule ἡμίονος, -ου [f.]

muse Μοῦσα, -ης [f.]

my ἐμός, -ή, -όν; ἐμεῖο; μευ

myself (a) 1st pers. pron. plus αὐτός in same case; (b) often expressed by middle voice of verb

name ὄνομα or οὔνομα, -ατος [n.]; I name ὀνομάζω, ὀνομάσω, ὀνόμασα

nature φύσις, -ιος [f.]

Nausicaa Ναυσικάα, -ας [f.]

near ἐγγύς; ἄγχι [advs., preps. with gen.]; ἆσσον; ἐγγύθεν; σχεδόν [advs.]; πλησίος, -η, -ον [adj.]

necessary, it is χρή [impersonal, w. inf., subject in acc.]

necessity ἀνάγκη, -ης [f.]; χρε(ι)ώ, -όος [f.]

neck αὐχήν, -ένος [m.]

nectar νέκταρ, -αρος [n.]

need ἀνάγκη, -ης [f.]; χρε(ι)ώ, -όος [f.]

neighbor(ing) πλησίος, -η, -ον

neither . . . nor οὔτε . . . οὔτε

never (yet) ποτε; πω [w. negative]

nevertheless ἔμπης

new νέος, -η, -ον

news ἀγγελίη, -ης [f.]

night νύξ, νυκτός [f.]

nimble ὠκύς, -εῖα, -ύ

nine days, for ἐννῆμαρ [adv.]

no, not οὐ, οὐκ [before smooth breathing], οὐχ [before rough breathing]; μή [οὐ generally is the negative of concrete fact, μή of other constructions — possibility, condition, command, general, dependence, etc.]; no doubt που; no longer οὐκ ἔτι or οὐκέτι; no one οὐδείς, οὐδεμία, οὐδέν; μηδείς, μηδεμία, μηδέν; in no way πω [w. negative]

noble ἐσθλός, -ή, -όν; καλός, -ή, -όν [comp.: καλλίων, -ον; supl.: κάλλιστος, -η, -ον]; ἀγαυός, -ή, -όν

Nobody Οὖτις [m.]

nod νεύω, νεύσω, νεῦσα

none οὐδείς, οὐδεμία, οὐδέν; μηδείς, μυδεμία, μηδέν

nor (a) οὐδέ, μηδέ;
(b) οὔτε [following a negative clause];
(c) neither . . . nor οὔτε . . . οὔτε

not [see "no"]; not at all πω [w. negative]; not even μηδέ; οὐδέ; nothing οὐδέν

nourish τρέφω, θρέψω, θρέψα

now [= at the present time] νῦν; now [not time — therefore] δή; now ἤδη [adv.]; νύ [a weak temporal or inferential particle]

nymph νύμφη, -ης [f.]

O (in direct address) ὦ

oar ἐρετμόν, -οῦ [n.]

oar-lock κληΐς, -ῖδος [f.]

oath ὅρκος, -ου [m.]

obey, am obedient to πείθομαι, πείσομαι, πιθόμην

observe φυλάσσω, φυλάξω, φύλαξα

obtain [gen.] τυγχάνω, τεύξομαι, τύχον

Ocean Ὠκεανός, -οῦ [m.]

Odysseus Ὀδυσ(σ)εύς, -ῆος [m.]

of: expressed by genitive case; of course που

offer(ed) πόρον [2 aor. system only]

Ogygia Ὠγυγίη, -ης [f.]

oh! [a general exclamation to be trans. according to context] πόποι

old age γῆρας, -αος [n.]

old man γέρων, -οντος [m.]

olive oil ἔλαιον, -ου [n.]

olive-wood, (of) ἐλάϊνεος, -η, -ον or ἐλάϊνος, -η, -ον

Olympus Ὄλυμπος, -ου [m.]

on   ἐπί; ἐν; πρός [preps. w. dat.]; ἀνά [prep. w. gen.,
   dat., acc.]; on account of   εἴνεκα [prep. w. gen.]; διά
   [prep. w. acc.]; on high   ὑψόσε; on the one hand
   μέν; on the other hand   δέ; αὖτε
on all sides   πάντη
on the other side   ἑτέρωθι
once [of indefinite time in past]   ποτε; at once   αὐτίκα
one [in number]   εἷς, μία, ἕν; one [indef. pronoun]
   τις, τι; one another   ἀλλήλοι, ων [in pl. only]
only   μοῦνος, -η, -ον
opinion   δοξα, -ης [f.]
opposite   ἀντίος, -η, -ον
oppress   πιέζω, πιέσ(σ)ω, πίεσα
or   ἤ, ἠε
order (a)   ἐντολή, -ῆς [f.];
      (b)   κέλομαι, κλήσομαι, κεκλόμην;
      (c)   in order that   ἵνα; ὡς; ὅπως; ὄφρα [neg.
         μή]; in order   ἐξείης; ἑξῆς
orders, I give orders to   ἐπι-τέλλω, —, ἐπί-τειλα
other   ἄλλος, -η, -ον; (the) other(s)   ἕτερος, -η, -ον
ought   χρή [impersonal, w. inf., subj. in acc.]
our   ἡμέτερος, -η, -ον
out of   ἐκ, ἐξ before vowels [prep. w. gen.]
outermost   ἄκρος, -η, -ον
outside of   ἐκτός [adv.]
over   ἀνά [prep. w. dat., acc.]; ὑπέρ [prep. w. gen.,
   acc.]
overbearing   ὑπερφίαλος, -ον
overpower   δαμάζω, δαμάω, δάμασσα
own   ἑός, -ή, -όν
ox   βοῦς, βοός [m.] [dat. pl. also βουσί]

pain   ἄλγος, -εος [n.]; ἄχος, -εος [n.]
painful   ἀλεγεινός, -ή, -όν; ἀργαλέος, -η, -ον
pair of [expressed by the dual]
palace   μέγαρα, -ων [n. pl.]
parent   τοκεύς, τοκῆος [m., f.]
partake of   πατέομαι, —, πασ(σ)άμην
pass   παρ-έρχομαι, etc.; pass (over)   πρήσσω, πρήξω, πρῆξα
pass away   φθί(ν)ω, φθίσω, φθῖσα
pass through   περάω, περήσω, πέρησα
pasture   βόσκω, βοσκήσω, βόσκησα
path   κέλευθος, -ου [f., but frequently n. in pl.]
pay   τίνω, τίσω, τῖσα
peace   εἰρήνη, -ης [f.]
pen   σηκός, -οῦ [m.]
people   λᾱός, -οῦ [m.]; δῆμος, -ου [m.]
perceive   νοέω, νοήσω, νόησα
perhaps   που [indef. adv.]
perish   ὀλλύομαι, ὀλέσομαι, ὀλόμην, ὄλωλα; ἀπ-
   ολλύομαι, etc.
Persephone   Περσεφόνεια, -ης [f.]
person   χρώς, χροός [m.]
persuade   πείθω, πείσω, πεῖσα or πέπιθον

Phaeacians   Φαίηκες, -ων [m. pl.]
physician   ἰητρός, -οῦ [m.]
pick for myself   αἱρέομαι, αἱρήσομαι, ἑλόμην; pick
   out   κρίνω, κρινέω, κρῖνα
pick up   κομίζω, κομιέω, κόμισσα
pierce   οὐτάω, οὐτήσω, οὔτησα or οὖτα; πείρω,
   —, πεῖρα
pig   σῦς, συός [m., f.]
pilot   κυβερνήτης, -ᾱο [m.]
pit   βόθρος, -ου [m.]
pitiful   οἰκτρός, -ή, -όν [alternative superlative: οἴκτιστος, -η, -ον
pitiless   σχέτλιος, -η, -ον; νηλ(ε)ής, -ές
pity   ἐλεέω, —, ἐλέησα; ἐλεαίρω
place   χῶρος, -ου [m.]; I place   τίθημι, θήσω, θῆκα;
   ἵημι, ἥσω, ἧκα; I have been placed   κεῖμαι [pf.
   mid. system only]
plain   πεδίον, -ου [n.]
plan   βουλή, -ῆς [f.]; I plan   βουλεύω, βουλεύσω,
   βούλευσα [w. inf., or ὅπως and purpose constr.];
   μήδομαι, μήσομαι, μησάμην
plank   δόρυ, δούρατος or δουρός [n.]
pleasant   ἡδύς, -εῖα, -ύ
please [expressed by verb in opt.]
pleased with, I am   ἥδομαι, ἥσομαι, ἡσάμην
pleasing   ἡδής, -εῖα, -ύ; μειλίχιος, -η, -ον; χαρίεις,
   -εσσα, -εν; I am pleasing (to)   ἀνδάνω, ἁδήσω,
   ἅδον
pleasure   ἡδονή, -ῆς [f.]
point   ἀκωκή, -ῆς [f.]
point out   φράζω, φράσ(σ)ω, φράσ(σ)α
pole   μοχλός, -οῦ [m.]
Polyphemus   Πολύφημος, -ου [m.]
ponder   ὁρμαίνω, —, ὅρμηνα; ponder (anxiously)
   μερμηρίζω, μερμηρίξω, μερμήριξα
portion   μοῖρα, -ης [f.]; δαίς, δαιτός [f.]
Poseidon   Ποσειδάων, -ωνος [m.]
possess   νέμομαι, νεμέομαι, νειμάμην
possession   χρῆμα, -ατος [n.]; possessions   βίοτος,
   -ου [m.]
possible   δυνατός, -ή, -όν
pour [tr.]   χέω, χεύω, χεῦσα; I pour out of [intr.]
   ἐκ-σεύω, —, ἐκ-σσύμην [non-thematic 2 aor.]
pour a libation   σπενδω, σπείσω, σπεῖσα
pour down   κατα-χέω, -χεύσω, -χεῦσα, -χεύμην
power   κράτος, -εος [n.]; a superhuman power or
   divinity   δαίμων, -ονος [m., f.]
praise   αἰνέω, αἰνήσω, αἴνησα
pray (to)   εὔχομαι, εὔξομαι, εὐξάμην; ἀράομαι, ἀρήσομαι, ἀρησάμην; εὐχετάομαι
prefer   βούλομαι, βουλήσομαι, βουλόμην
prepare   ὁπλίζω, —, ὅπλισσα; τεύχω, τεύξω, τεῦξα,
   —, τέτυγμαι
present, I am   πάρ-ειμι
present   ὀπάζω, ὀπάσσω, ὄπασ(σ)α

press πιέζω, πιέσ(σ)ω, πίεσα; ἐρείδω, ἐρείσω, ἔρεισα
prevail νῑκάω, νῑκήσω, νίκησα
Priam Πρίαμος, -ου [m.]
prince κρείων, -οντος [m.]
prize (of honor) γέρας, -αος [n.]
proceed στείχω, —, στίχον
produce ποιέω, ποιήσω, ποίησα; φύω, φύσω, φῦσα
property χρῆμα, -ατος [n.]
prosperity ὄλβος, -ου [m.]
prosperous ὄλβιος, -η, -ον
protect (ἐ)ρύομαι, (ἐ)ρύσσομαι, (-ερ)ρυσάμην
prowess ἀλκή, -ῆς [f.] [dat. sg.: ἀλκί]
punish τίνομαι, τίσομαι, τῑσάμην
pursue διώκω, διώξω, δίωξα; ἐφ-έπω, ἐφ-έψω, ἐπί-σπον
push ὠθέω, ὤσω, ὦσα
put ἵστημι, στήσω, στῆσα; τίθημι, θήσω, θῆκα; put down κατα-τίθημι, etc.; put in position, put on ἐπι-τίθημι, etc.
put on δύω, δύσομαι, δῡσάμην or δῦν; ἔννῡμι, ἔσ(σ)ω, ἔσ(σ)α
put to sleep κοιμάω, κοιμήσω, κοίμησα

quarrel with νεικέω, νεικέσω, νείκεσ(σ)α
queen πότν(ι)α, -ης [f.]
quick καρπάλιμος, -ον
quickly αἶψα; τάχα; καρπαλίμως; ὦκα
quite [with adj. and adv.] μάλα

raft σχεδίη, -ης [f.]
rage μενεαίνω, —, μενέηνα
rain ὄμβρος, -ου [m.]
raise ἀείρω, —, ἄειρα; ὄρνῡμι, ὄρσω, ὄρσα [aor. mid. also: ὀρ(ό)μην]
ram [full-grown] ἀρνειός, -οῦ
ransom ἄποινα, -ων [n. pl.]
ray αὐγή, -ῆς [f.]
reach (by chance) κιχάνω, κιχήσομαι, κίχον
ready, make τεύχω, τεύξω, τεῦξα
realm δῆμος, -ου [m.]
rear τρέφω, θρέξω, θρέψα
reason λόγος, -ου [m.]
rebuke νεικέω, νεικέσω, νείκεσ(σ)α
receive δέχομαι, δέξομαι, δεξάμην
reckless σχέτλιος, -η, -ον
recompense ἄποινα, -ων [n. pl.]
refrain from ἀπ-έχω, etc.
region χῶρος, -ου [m.]
reign ἀνάσσω, ἀνάξω, ἄναξα
reins ἡνία, -ων [n. pl.]
rejoice χαίρω, χαιρήσω, χάρην [aor. pass. w. act. force]; rejoice (at) γηθέω, γηθήσω, γήθησα
relate κατα-λέγω, etc.; μῡθέομαι, etc.
release λύω, λύσω, λῦσα, λέλυκα, λέλυμαι, λύθην
remain μένω, μενέω, μεῖνα; μίμνω

remember μέμνημαι
remind μιμνήσκω, μνήσω, μνῆσα
renown κλέος, κλέ(ε)ος [n.]
reply ἀμείβομαι, ἀμείψομαι, ἀμειψάμην
reply, in reply ἀντίος, -η, -ον
rescue (ἐ)ρύομαι, (ἐ)ρύσσομαι, (ἐρ)ρυσάμην
resound ἰάχω
resourceful πολυμήχανος, -ον
respect αἰδέομαι, αἰδέσ(σ)ομαι, αἰδεσσάμην; ἅζομαι [pres. system only]
rest ἐρείδω, ἐρείσω, ἔρεισα; at rest ἔκηλος, -ον
restrain: see check
return (home) νόστος, -ου [m.]; I return νέομαι [pres. system only]; I return (home) νοστέω, νοστήσω, νόστησα
reveal φαίνω, φανέω, φῆνα
revere ἅζομαι [pres. system only]
revered αἰδοῖος, -η, -ον; πότν(ι)α, -ης [as adj.]
reverence αἰδέομαι, αἰδέσ(σ)ομαι, αἰδεσσάμην
rich πίων, -ονος
right ὀρθός, -ή, -όν; a right θέμις, -ιστος [f.]; it is right θέμις ἐστί
right here αὐτόθι [adv.]
right there αὐτόθι [adv.]
rise ὄρνυμαι, ὄρσομαι, ὀρ(ό)μην, ὄρωρα
rivalry ἔρις, -ιδος [f.]
river ποταμός, -οῦ [m.]
road ὁδός, -οῦ [f.]; κέλευθος, -ου [f., but often n. in pl.]
roam (back and forth) φοιτάω, φοιτήσω, φοίτησα
roar βοάω, βοήσω, βόησα
rock πέτρη, -ης [f.]
roll κυλίνδω
room δόμος, -ου [m.]
rope ὅπλον, -ου [n.]
rosy-fingered ῥοδοδάκτυλος, -ον
round about περί [adv.]
rouse ἐγείρω, ἐγερέω, ἔγειρα [aor. mid.: ἐγρόμην]
rowing-benches, with fine rowing-benches ἐΰσσελμος, -ον
ruin ἄτη, -ης [f.]
ruler κρείων, -οντος [m.]
run θέω
rush ὀρούω, ὀρούσω, ὄρουσα; σεύομαι, —, (σ)σευάμην or (σ)σύμην; rush (forward) ὁρμάομαι, ὁρμήσομαι, ὁρμησάμην
rush away, rush back (from) ἀπο-σεύω, —, ἀποσσύμην [non-thematic 2 aor.]; rush out of ἐκ-σεύω, —, ἐκ-σσύμην
rush forward ἐφ-ορμάομαι, ἐφ-ορμήσομαι, ἐφ-ορμησάμην
ruthless νηλ(ε)ής, -ές

sacred ἱερός, -ή, -όν
sacrifice ἱερεύω, ἱερεύσω, ἱέρευσα

sacrificial-fire πυρή, -ῆς [f.]

safe ἀπήμων, -ον

sagacious δαΐφρων, -ον

said (he, she) ἔφη [irreg. 3 sg.]; I said εἶπον [2 aor. system]

sail (over) πλέω, πλεύσομαι, πλεῦσα; sail ἱστίον, -ου [n.] [pl. often used for sg.]

salty ἁλμυρός, -ή, -όν

same αὐτός, -ή, -όν; at the same time ἅμα [adv., prep. w. dat.]

savage ἄγριος, (-η), -ον

save σώζω, σώσω, σῶσα; (ἐ)ρύομαι, (ἐ)ρύσσομαι, (ἐρ)ρυσάμην

savor κνίση, -ης [f.]

say λέγω, λέξω, λέξα; ἐννέπω, ἐνίψω, ἔνισπον; εἶπον [2 aor. system only]; φημί, φήσω, φῆσα; εἴρω, ἐρέω; μυθέομαι, μυθήσομαι, μυθησάμην

saying μῦθος, -ου [m.]

scowl, with a scowl ὑπόδρα [adv.]

Scylla Σκύλλη, -ης [f.]

sea θάλασσα, -ης [f.]; πόντος, -ου [m.] [= the deep]; ἅλς, ἁλός [f.]

search after ζητέω, ζητήσω, ζήτησα

seat θρόνος, -ου [m.]; δίφρος, -ου [m.]

seat myself καθ-ίζω, —, κάθ-ισα

seated ἥμενος, -η, -ον

second δεύτερος, -η, -ον; a second time δίς

see ὁράω, ὄψομαι, ἴδον, ἑώρακα, ἑώραμαι, ὤφθην; εἰσ-οράω, etc. [= watch, look at]; λεύσσω

seek ζητέω, ζητήσω, ζήτησα; ἐπι-μαίομαι, ἐπι-μάσσομαι, ἐπι-μασσάμην [= try to get my hands on]

seem δοκέω, δοκήσω, δόκησα; ἔοικα, ἐώκεα [pf. and plpf. w. pres. and impf. sense]; seem (like to) (ἐ)είδομαι, —, (ἐ)εισάμην

seer μάντις, -ιος [m.]

seize αἱρέω, αἱρήσω, ἕλον; μάρπτω, μάρψω, μάρψα; seize upon αἴνυμαι

select αἴνυμαι

self αὐτός, -ή, -ό

send πέμπω, πέμψω, πέμψα; ἵημι, ἥσω, ἧκα; send forth ἵημι; προ-ίημι; send with (someone) ὀπάζω, ὀπάσσω, ὄπασ(σ)α; send ὀτρύνω, ὀτρυνέω, ὄτρυνα

send away ἀπο-πέμπω, etc.

send off safely ἀπο-πέμπω, etc.

sending-off, safe sending-off πομπή, -ῆς [f.]

separate κρίνω, κρινέω, κρῖνα

servant δμώς, -ωός [m.]; servant-woman δμωή, -ῆς [f.]

set (of the sun) δύομαι, δύσομαι, δυσάμην or δῦν

set in motion σεύω, —, (σ)σεῦα or (σ)σύμην

seven ἑπτά

shadowy σκιόεις, -εσσα, -εν

shake πάλλω, —, πῆλα

shameful αἰσχρός, -ή, -όν

sharp ὀξύς, -εῖα, -ύ

shatter κεάζω, κεάσω, κέασ(σ)α

she [see appendix p. 239]

sheep μῆλον, -ου [n.]; ὄϊς, ὄϊος [m., f.] [dat. pl. also: ὄεσσι; acc. pl. always: ὄϊς]

sheet [a rope attached to the foot of the sail] πούς, ποδός [m.]

shelter σκέπας, -αος [n.]

shepherd ποιμήν, -ένος [m.]

shield σάκος, -εος [n.]

shining φαεινός, -ή, -όν; φαίδιμος, -ον [never f.]; σιγαλόεις, -εσσα, -εν

ship νηῦς, νηός or νεός [f.] [dat. pl. also: νηυσί; f.]

shooter of arrows ἰοχέαιρα, -ης

should (a) [= future possibility:] expressed by verb in opt., sometimes w. κε(ν) or ἄν;
  (b) [= ought:] χρή w. inf., and subj. in acc.

shout βοάω, βοήσω, βόησα; ἰάχω; γεγωνέω, γεγωνήσω, γεγώνησα, γέγωνα [pf. with pres. meaning]; ἀύω, ἀύσω, ἄυσα; ἀϋτή, -ῆς [f.]; βοή, -ῆς [f.]

show φαίνω, φανέω, φῆνα; I show myself φαίνομαι, φανέομαι, φάνην; I show δείκνυμι, δείξω, δεῖξα

shrewd πυκ(ι)νός, -ή, -όν

shriek κλάζω, κλάγξω, κλάγξα

shrink before ἀλέομαι, —, ἀλεάμην or ἀλευάμην

shun ἀλεείνω; ἀλύσκω, ἀλύξω, ἄλυξα

shut up (ἐ)έργω, ἔρξω, ἔρξα

sign σῆμα, -ατος [n.]

silence σιωπή, -ῆς [f.]

silent(ly) ἀκέων, -ουσα, —

silver ἄργυρος, -ου [m.]; of silver ἀργύρεος, -η, -ον

similar to ὁμοῖος, -η, -ον

simple νήπιος, -η, -ον

since ἐπεί

sinew ἴς, ἰνός [f.]

sink δύομαι, δύσομαι, δυσάμην or δῦν

Siren Σειρήν, -ῆνος [f.]

sit (down) ἕζομαι, —, ἕσα; ἵζω

sitting ἥμενος, -η, -ον

situated, I am ναιετάω

six ἕξ

skin χρώς, χροός [m.]

sky οὐρανός, -οῦ [m.]

slaughter φόνος, -ου [m.]; I slaughter σφάζω, σφάξω, σφάξα; ἱερεύω, ἱερεύσω, ἱέρευσα

slay κατά-πέφνον; πέφνον; κατα-κτείνω, etc.

sleek λιπαρός, -ή, -όν

sleep ὕπνος, -ου [m.]; εὕδω, εὑδήσω, εὕδησα; I put to sleep κοιμάω, κοιμήσω, κοίμησα

small ὀλίγος, -η, -ον

smash ῥήγνυμι, ῥήξω, ῥῆξα

smite πλήσσω, πλήξω, πλῆξα

snatch (up or away) ἁρπάζω, ἁρπάξω, ἅρπαξα or ἅρπασα

so   οὕτως; ὧδε; ὥς, ὡς
so long   τόφρα
soft   μαλακός, -ή, -όν; ἀπαλός, -ή, -όν
soil   ἄρουρα, -ης [f.]
some (one), something   τις, τι
somehow   πως
sometime(s)   ποτέ
son   υἱός, -οῦ or -έος [m.] [dat. pl.: υἱάσι]
song   ἀοιδή, -ῆς [f.]
soon   τάχα
sooner   πρότερος, -η, -ον; πρίν [adv.]
sorrow   πένθος, -εος [n.]   ; ὀϊζύς, -ύος [f.]
sort, what sort of   οἷος, -η, -ον [w. noun in same case]; sorts, of all sorts   παντοῖος, -η, -ον
soul   ψῡχή, -ῆς [f.]
sound   φωνή, ῆς [f.]
sparkling   αἴθοψ, -οπος
speak   φημί, φήσω, φῆσα; speak (to)   προσ-εῖπον [w. acc.]; εἴρω, ἐρέω; speak (in an assembly)   ἀγορεύω, ἀγορεύσω, ἀγόρευσα
speak among   μεταυδάω
spear   δόρυ, δούρατος or δουρός [n.]; ἔγχος, -εος [n.]
spear-point   αἰχμή, -ῆς [f.]
speech   λόγος, -ου [m.]; μῦθος, -ου [m.]
spirit   θῡμός, -οῦ [m.]; φρήν, φρενός [f.]
spit   ὀβελός, -οῦ [m.]
splendid   ἀγλαός, -ή, -όν
spoke, thus he spoke   ἦ
spread out   πετάννῡμι, —, πέτασ(σ)α
sprung from Zeus   δῑογενής, -έος
staff [usually a symbol of office]   σκῆπτρον, -ου [n.]
stake   μοχλός, -οῦ [m.]
stand   ἵσταμαι, στήσομαι, στῆν; stand by   παρ-ίσταμαι, etc.
stand up   ἀν-ίστημι, etc.
star   ἀστήρ, -έρος [m.] [dat. pl.: ἀστράσι]
starry   ἀστερόεις, -εσσα, -εν
start   ὁρμάω, ὁρμήσω, ὅρμησα; ὁρμάομαι, ὁρμήσομαι, ὁρμησάμην
stay   μένω, μενέω, μεῖνα
steep   αἰπύς, -εῖα, -ύ
steersman   κυβερνήτης, -ᾱο [m.]
stick   πείρω, —, πεῖρα
still   ἔτι
stir (up)   ἐπ-οτρύνω, -οτρῡνέω, -ότρῡνα; κυκάω, κυκήσω, κύκησα
stone   λίθος, -ου [m.]; λᾶας, λᾶος [acc.: λᾶαν; m.]
stood   στῆν [3 aor. system]
stop   παύω, παύσω, παῦσα
store-room   θάλαμος, -ου [m.]
storm   ὄμβρος, -ου [m.]; θύελλα, -ης [f.]
stout   παχύς, -εῖα, -ύ; στιβαρός, -ή, -όν
straight   ὀρθός, -ή, -όν; straight (towards)   ἰθύς [adv., w. gen.]
straight on, against   ἄντικρυ [adv., w. gen.]

straightway   ἄφαρ [adv.]
strange (one) [whose actions are unaccountable, wonderful, or superhuman]   δαιμόνιος, -η
stranger   ξεῖνος, -ου [m.]
stream   ῥόος, -ου [m.]
street   ἀγυιά, -ῆς [f.]
strength   κράτος, -εος [n.]; ἴς, ἰνός [f.]
stretch   τείνω, τενέω, τεῖνα, τέτακα, τέταμαι
strife   ἔρις, -ιδος [f.]; δηιοτής, -ῆτος [f.]
strike   βάλλω, βαλέω, βάλον; τύπτω, τύψω, τύψα
strip (off)   ἐξ-εναρίζω, -εναρίξω, -ενάριξα
strive to win   ἄρνυμαι, ἀρέομαι, ἀρόμην
strong   κρατερός, -ή, -όν; ἴφιος, -η, -ον; στιβαρός, -ή, -όν
such [w. adj. or adv.:]   οὕτως; such as   οἷος, -η, -ον; such (as this or that)   τοιόσδε, -ήδε, -όνδε; such   τοιοῦτος, τοιαύτη, τοιοῦτον; τοῖος, -η, -ον
suddenly   αἶψα
suffer   πάσχω, πείσομαι, πάθον; μογέω, —, μόγησα
suffering   πῆμα, -ατος [n.]
suitor   μνηστήρ, -ῆρος [m.]
summit   λόφος, -ου [m.]; summits   κάρηνα, -ων [n. pl.]
sun   ἠέλιος, -ου [m.]
superhuman power [a divinity]   δαίμων, -ονος [m., f.]
supper   δόρπον, -ου [n.]
suppliants   ἱκέται, -άων [m. pl.]
supplicate   γουνόομαι
supply   παρ-έχω, etc.
suppose   ὀίω or ὀίομαι, ὀίσομαι, ὀισάμην; ἔλπω or ἔλπομαι; I suppose [adv.]   που
surely   περ; τοι [never first word]
surpass   καίνυμαι, [pf. w. pres. sense:]   κέκασμαι
swear   ὄμνῡμι, ὀμέομαι, ὄμοσ(σ)α
sweet   ἡδύς, -εῖα, -ύ; γλυκύς, -εῖα, -ύ; γλυκερός, -ή, -όν
swift   ταχύς, -εῖα, -ύ [comp.: θάσσων, -ον; supl.: τάχιστος, -η, -ον]; ὠκύς, -εῖα, -ύ; καρπάλιμος, -ον; θοός, -ή, -όν
swift-footed   ποδάρκης, -ες
swiftly   ῥίμφα; ὦκα
swim   νήχω, νήξομαι, νηξάμην
swine   σῦς, συός [m., f.]
sword   ξίφος, -εος [n.]   φάσγανον, -ου [n.]

table   τράπεζα, -ης [f.]
take   λαμβάνω, λήψομαι, λάβον; take away   ἀφ-αιρέομαι, ἀφ-αιρήσομαι, ἀφ-ελόμην; take hold of   αἴνυμαι [w. acc.]; take vengeance upon   τίνομαι, τίσομαι, τῑσάμην
take away   ἀπο-αίνυμαι
take my fill of   τέρπομαι, τέρψομαι, τερψάμην or (τε)ταρπόμην
tame   δαμάζω, δαμάω, δάμασσα
teach   διδάσκω, διδάξω, δίδαξα

309

tear δάκρυον, -ου [n.] or δάκρυ, -υος [n.]

tearful δακρυόεις, -εσσα, -εν

tell λέγω, λέξω, λέξα; ἐννέπω, ἐνίψω, ἔνισπον; εἶπον [2 aor. system]; φημί, φήσω, φῆσα

tell in order κατα-λέγω, etc.

tempest λαῖλαψ, -απος [f.]

temple νηός, -οῦ [m.]

tend κομίζω, κομιέω, κόμισσα

tender ἁπαλός, -ή, -όν

tenth δέκατος, -η, -ον

terrible σμερδαλέος, -η, -ον; αἰνός, -ή, -όν

terror δέος, δέεος [n.]

than ἤ (or use comparative gen.)

that (a) [demonstr. adj. and pron.:] ὁ, ἡ, τό; κεῖνος, -η, -ο;

    (b) that, in order that [in purpose constr.:] ἵνα, ὡς, ὅπως, ὄφρα [neg. μή];

    (c) that [after verbs of saying, thinking, etc.:] ὅτι, or expressed by acc. and inf. constr.

Theban Θηβαῖος, -η, -ον

Thebes Θήβη, -ης [f.] [also pl.]

their(s) σφέτερος, -η, -ον

themselves αὐτοί, -αί, -ά

then [of time:] ἔνθα; ἔνθεν; τότε; ἔπειτα [not of time = therefore:] οὖν; ἄρα

there [adv.] τῇ; αὐτοῦ; ἔνθα; αὖθι

therefore οὖν; ἄρα [never first word]; τῷ

thereupon ἔπειτα

they [see appendix p. 239]

thick παχύς, -εῖα, -ύ; πυκ(ι)νός, -ή, -όν

thick-thronging ἀδινός, -ή, -όν

thigh μηρός, -οῦ [m.]

think δίω or δίομαι, δίσομαι, δισάμην; νοέω, νοήσω, νόησα

this [demonstr. pron. and adj.:] ὅδε, ἥδε, τόδε; οὗτος, αὕτη, τοῦτο

thither κεῖσε [adv.]

though περ [w. ptc.]; even though, although καί περ

three τρεῖς, τρῖα

three times τρίς

threshing-floor ἀλωή, -ῆς [f.]

threshold οὐδός, -οῦ [m.]

thrice τρίς

throng ὅμιλος, -ου [m.]; I throng εἰλ(έ)ομαι

through διά [prep. w. gen., acc.]

throughout κατά [prep. w. acc.]

throw βάλλω, βαλέω, βάλον

thunderbolt κεραυνός, -οῦ [m.]

thus οὕτως; ὧδε; ὥς, ὡς; thus he spoke ἦ

tie δέω, δήσω, δῆσα

time χρόνος, -ου [m.]

tip ἄκρον, -ου [n.]

Tiresias Τειρεσίας, -αο [m.]

to (a) [prep. w. acc.:] ἐπί [= upon, e.g., 'it fell to earth']; εἰς, [= into, toward]; πρός [= up to]; παρά [= up alongside];

    (b) [conj., = in order that:] ἵνα, ὡς, ὅπως, ὄφρα, or expressed by fut. ptc. or fut. inf.

together ὁμοῦ, ἄμυδις

together with ἅμα [adv., prep. w. dat.]

toil πόνος, -ου [m.]; I toil at πονέομαι, πονήσομαι, πονησάμην; κάματος, -ου [m.]; I toil μογέω, —, μόγησα; κάμνω, καμέομαι, κάμον

told εἶπον [2 aor. system]

tool ὅπλον, -ου [n.]

topmost ἄκρος, -η, -ον

touch ἐπι-μαίομαι, ἐπι-μάσσομαι, ἐπι-μασσάμην

towards ἐπί, πρός [preps. w. acc.]; ἀντίος, -η, -ον

tower πύργος, -ου [m.]

town ἄστυ, -εος [n.]

treasure θησαυρός, -οῦ [m.]

tree δένδρεον, -ου [n.]

trial, make trial of πειράω, πειρήσω, πείρησα

trickery δόλος, -ου [m.]

trim ἴσος, (ἐ)ίση, ἴσον

Trojans Τρῶες, -ων [m. pl.]

trouble πόνος, -ου [m.]; πράγματα, -ων [n. pl.]

Troy Τροίη, -ης [f.]; Ἴλιος, -ου [f.]

true ὀρθός, -ή, -όν; ἀληθής, -ές; νημερτής, -ές

truly ἦ; καὶ λίην; ἀτρεκέως; μήν

trusty ἐρίηρος, -ον [pl. 3 decl.: ἐρίηρες]

truth ἀληθείη, -ης [f.]

try πειράω, πειρήσω, πείρησα

tumult ὅμιλος, -ου [m.]

tunic χιτών, -ῶνος [m.]

turn τρέπω, τρέψω, τρέψα; ἑλίσσω, —, (ἐλ)έλιξα

twelve δώδεκα

twice δίς

two δύω or δύο [indecl.]

unchanged ἔμπεδος, -ον

under (a) [= at rest under:] ὑπό w. dat.;

    (b) [= motion up under:] ὑπό w. acc.;

    (c) [= from under:[ὑπό w. gen.;

    (d) under the influence of [= by] ὑπό w. gen.

understanding, I have φρονέω, προνήσω, πρόνησα

undisturbed ἔκηλος, -ον

unfailing νημερτής, -ές

unfortunate δύστηνος, -ον

unless εἰ μή

unseemly ἀεικής, -ές

until ὄφρα, ἧος [w. ind. if purely factual, w. purpose constr. if anticipatory]; πρίν [conj. w. inf. or anticipatory subj.]

unwilling ἀέκων, -ουσα

up ἀνά or ἄμ [adv.]

upon ἀνά; ἐπί [preps. w. gen.]

upwards ὑπόσε

urge ἀνώγω, ἀνώξω, ἄνωξα, ἄνωγα [pf. has pres. sense; plpf. has impf. sense]

urge on ὀτρύνω, ὀτρῠνέω, ὄτρῡνα; ἐφ-ορμάω, ἐφ-ορμήσω, ἐφ-όρμησα

utter αἰπύς, -εῖα, -ύ; I utter φωνέω, φωνήσω, φώνησα

uselessly αὕτως [adv.]

use violence against βιάζω

utensils ἔντεα, -ων [n. pl.]

valiant ἄλκιμος, -ον

vapor ἀϋτμή, -ῆς [f.]

vast ἄσπετος, -ον

vehement ἀδινός, -ή, -όν

veil κρήδεμνον, -ου [n.]

vengeance, I take vengeance upon τίνομαι, τίσομαι, τῑσάμην

very αὐτός, -ή, -όν [adj.]; μάλα [adv.]

vigorous θαλερός, -ή, -όν

violence, I use violence against βιάζω

virtue ἀρετή, -ῆς [f.]

voice φωνή, -ῆς [f.]; φθόγγος, -ου [m.]; ὄψ, ὀπός [f.]; I lift my voice φωνέω, φωνήσω, φώνησα

wage war π(τ)ολεμίζω, π(τ)ολεμίξω

wagon ἄμαξα, -ης [f.]; ἀπήνη, -ης [f.]

wail κλαίω, κλαύσω, κλαῦσα

wake ἐγείρω, ἐγερέω, ἔγειρα [aor. mid.: ἐγρόμην]

wall τεῖχος, -εος [n.]

wander ἀλάομαι, —, ἀλήθην, ἀλάλημαι [pf. has pres. sense]; πλάζομαι, πλάγξομαι, πλάγχθην

war πόλεμος, -ου [m.]

ward off ἀμύνω, ἀμῠνέω, ἄμῡνα

warm ἰαίνω, —, ἴηνα

warrior [often honorary title] ἥρως, ἥρωος [m.]; contracted gen.: ἥρως]

wash λοέω, λοέσσω, λόεσ(σ)α [frequently contracts to λούω, etc.]

waste away φθί(ν)ω, φθίσω, φθῖσα

water ὕδωρ, ὕδατος [n.]

watery ὑγρός, -ή, -όν

wave κῦμα, -ατος [n.]

wax κηρός, -οῦ [m.]

way ὁδός, -οῦ [f.]; κέλευθος, -ου [f., but frequently n. in pl.]; ἀγυιά, -ῆς [f.]

we [see appendix p. 239]

wealth χρήματα, -ων [n. pl.]

wealthy [sometimes w. dat. or gen.] ἀφνειός, (-ή), -όν

wear out [tr.] τείρω

weariness κάματος, -ου [m.]

weary, grow weary κάμνω, καμέομαι, κάμον

weave ὑφαίνω, ὑφανέω, ὕφηνα

wedded κουρίδιος, -η, -ον

weep (for) γοάω, γοήσομαι, γόησα; κλαίω, κλαύσω κλαῦσα [obj. in acc.]

well εὖ

well-balanced εὐήρης, -ες

well-built εὐκτίμενος, -η, -ον

well-greaved εὐκνήμις, -ῑδος

well-made εὐ-εργής, -ές

well-polished εὔξεστος, (-η), -ον

well-tilled εὐκτίμενος, -η, -ον

west wind Ζέφυρος, -ου [m.]

what [see "who"]; in what direction ὅπ(π)η; what sort (of) οἷος, -η, -ον [w. noun in same case]; what? τίπτε

whatever ὅ τι or ὅττι

when(ever) ἐπεί; ὅτε; ἦμος; ὁπ(π)ότε

whence? πόθεν

where [not in questions:] τῇ; ὅπ(π)η; ὅθι; ἵνα; from where? πόθεν; where? ποῦ

whether [in indirect questions:] εἰ; whether . . . or ἤ . . . ἦε

which [see "who"]

while ὄφρα, ἧος [w. ind. if purely factual, w. purpose constr. if anticipatory]

whirl ἑλίσσω, —, (ἐλ)έλιξα

white πολιός, (-ή), -όν; λευκός, -ή, -όν

white-armed λευκώλενος, -ον

who, which, what (a) [interrog. pron. and adj.:] τίς, τί
(b) [rel. pron. w. def. antecedent:] ὁ, ἡ, το
(c) [rel. pron.:] ὅς, ἥ, ὅ

whoever, whatever ὅς τις, ἥ τις, ὅ τι or ὅττι

whole ἅπᾱς, ἅπᾱσα, ἅπαν; οὖλος, -η, -ον

why? τί; τίπτε

wicked πονηρός, -ή, -όν

wide εὐρύς, -εῖα, -ύ

wife γυνή, γυναικός [f.]; ἄλοχος, -ου [f.]; ἄκοιτις, -ιος [f.]

wild ἄγριος, (-η), -ον

will βουλή, -ῆς [f.]; against the will ἀέκητι [adv.]

win ἄρνυμαι, ἀρέομαι, ἀρόμην

win over πείθω, πείσω, πεῖσα or πέπιθον

wind ἄνεμος, -ου [m.]; (fair) οὖρος, -ου [m.]

wine οἶνος, -ου [m.]

wine-dark οἶνοψ, -οπος

winged πτερόεις, -εσσα, -εν

wise σοφός, -ή, -όν

wish ἐθέλω, ἐθελήσω, ἐθέλησα

with μετά [prep. w. gen., dat.]; σύν [prep. w. dat.]

with a scowl ὑπόδρα [adv.]

with fine rowing-benches ἐΰσσελμος, -ον

with glancing helm κορυθαίολος, -ον

within ἔντοσθεν; ἔνδον; ε(ἴ)σω [advs.]

without change αὕτως [adv.]

woe ἄλγος, -εος [n.]; κῆδος, -εος [n.]; πῆμα,
 -ατος [n.]
woman γυνή, γυναικός [f.]
wonder (at) θαμβέω, —, θάμβησα
wood ὕλη, -ης [f.]
word λόγος, -ου [m.]; ἔπος, -εος [n.]; μῦθος, -ου
 [m.]
work ἔργον, -ου [n.]; I work (at) ἐπ-οίχομαι
world κόσμος, -ου [m.]
worthless πονηρός, -ή, -όν
worthy χρηστός, -ή, -όν
would (a) [vague future supposition or potential construction:] expressed by verb in opt., usually
 w. κε(ν) or ἄν;
 (b) would have [= contrary to fact in past:] expressed by impf. or aor. indic. w. κε(ν) or
 ἄν;
 (c) would that [= impossible wish:] εἰ, εἴθε
 or εἰ γάρ w. opt.
wound οὐτάω, οὐτήσω, οὔτησα or οὖτα
wrath μένος, -εος [n.]; χόλος, -ου [m.]
wretched λυγρός, -ή, -όν; δύστηνος, -η, -ον
wrought, cunningly wrought δαιδάλεος, -η, -ον

yearn (after) ποθέω, ποθήσω, πόθεσα
yearning ἵμερος, -ου [m.]
yet ἔτι [of time]; αὐτάρ [= nevertheless]; δέ [after
 μέν, in contrasts]
yield εἴκω, εἴξω, (ἔ)ειξα
yoke ζεύγνῦμι, ζεύξω, ζεῦξα
you [see appendix p. 239]
young νέος, -η, -ον
young one [of animals] ἔμβρυον, -ου [n.]
your [sg.:] σός, -ή, -όν; τεός, -ή, -όν; σεῖο, σευ;
 [pl.:] ὑμέτερος, -η, -ον; ὑμέων
yourself 2 pers. pron. w. the same case of αὐτός, -ή, -ό

Zeus Ζεύς, Διός or Ζηνός [m.]
Zeus-cherished διοτρεφής, -ές